Table of Contents

RESEARCH IN MARITIME HISTORY
NO. 36

POLICING THE SEAS: ANGLO-AMERICAN RELATIONS AND THE EQUATORIAL ATLANTIC, 1819-1865

MARK C. HUNTER

International Maritime Economic History Association

St. John's, Newfoundland
2008

ISSN 1188-3928
ISBN 978-0-9738934-6-5

Research in Maritime History is available free of charge to members of the International Maritime Economic History Association. The price to others is US $25 per copy, plus US $5 postage and handling.

Back issues of *Research in Maritime History* are available:

Research in Maritime History would like to thank Memorial University of Newfoundland for its generous financial assistance in support of this volume.

List of Tables

List of Illustrations

About the Author

MARK C. HUNTER < mhunter@munalum.ca > received his PhD in history in 2004 from the University of Hull, where he studied under Dr. David J. Starkey. Dr. Hunter completed his postdoctoral studies through a fellowship from the Institute of Social and Economic Research at Memorial University of Newfoundland. His research interests centre on the Atlantic world, especially on the issues of piracy, the slave trade and naval and maritime history. He has published essays in the *Journal of Military History*, *Mariner's Mirror* and the *International Journal of Maritime History*, among other journals. Dr. Hunter is currently working on a book on the Newfoundland branch of the Royal Naval Reserve.

Acknowledgements

I would like to thank the Social Sciences and Humanities Research Council of Canada and the Rothermere Trust, London, for funding for this project. I must also thank the Registrar's Office, University College London, who managed the administrative work for my funding from the Rothermere Trust. My thanks as well to Sarah Beighton, Picture Librarian, National Maritime Museum, Greenwich, for assistance with some of the images in this book. Finally, I would like to thank Dr. Andrew Lambert, Dr. Eric Grove, Dr. David J. Starkey and the anonymous reviewers for their input and advice.

Elements of chapters three and four also appeared as "Anglo-American Political and Naval Response to West Indian Piracy," *International Journal of Maritime History*, XIII, No. 1 (2001), 63-93; I acknowledge permission to reprint this from the International Maritime Economic History Association. Parts of chapters two and six appear in "The Hero Packs a Punch: Sir Charles Hotham, Liberalism, and West Africa, 1846-50," *Mariner's Mirror*, XCII, No. 3 (2006), 282-299 and are included here by the kind permission of the Society for Nautical Research.

Chapter 1
Introduction

Introduction

In the early nineteenth century, Britain and the United States were part of an Atlantic economic matrix. Both had interests in the equatorial Atlantic, a region that embraces the coastal zones of the Gulf of Mexico, Central America, northern Brazil and, across the Atlantic, the African coast from the Cape Verde Islands to south of the Congo River. This investigation focuses on the efforts of Britain and the US to suppress piracy and the slave trade in this region between 1819 and 1865. It shows that the two nations used sea power to attain their objectives, although the degree to which they applied it and the nature of its application varied according to wider political, diplomatic and strategic considerations. In essence, Anglo-American naval relations in this theatre not only served as a barometer of the vacillating relationship between the countries but also acted as a safety valve to alleviate tension when conflicting policies threatened to upset the sometimes precarious peace.

Figure 1.1:   Equatorial Atlantic

Note: Distances not to scale.

Source: Courtesy of the author.

This study defines Anglo-American naval relations during this era of relative peace as the level of cooperation (or friction) between the two. As chapter two shows, Britain and the US often deployed their navies in the same regions. The Americans divided their navy into several squadrons – Mediterranean, Pacific, Home, South America and Africa – as well as others when required, such as the West Indies.[1] But US naval policy fluctuated with the interests and power of supporters and opponents.[2] On the ocean, it encountered the larger Royal Navy (RN). British policymakers intended the RN not only to be able to counter the next two largest fleets, the French and Russian, but also to support colonies and trade.[3] In the Atlantic, the RN deployed to its North American and West Indies, Southeast Coast of America, Mediterranean and African stations.[4] The compatibility and conflicts between each in such regions comprise Anglo-American naval relations.

Andrew Lambert opined that naval relations was "the mechanism whereby Britain and France clarified their relationship; France challenged British maritime supremacy, and Britain responded."[5] This study will test this hypothesis, which has it that naval relations were an important cog in the broader wheel of Anglo-American diplomacy. The examination will elucidate the extent to which the interests, diplomacy and naval relations of the two states interacted. In this period, the extent of the unity of the interests of government and business in each nation dictated naval policy. Consequently, economic interests shaped not only political decisions but also naval relations. In Britain, government and the business class were united in their goal to protect and promote trade. They agreed to avoid conflict with other nations but accepted that sea power could be used against those who threatened legitimate commerce. To this end, the political elite determined that commercial growth in the equatorial Atlantic would only occur if naval force was used to push factors of production – land, labour and capital – away from the slave trade and into legitimate commerce. But the power of domestic slave interests permitted the US only to reach a consensus on commerce protection, conflict avoidance and the peaceful development of trade. The connection between slave-trade suppression and commercial growth was a forbidden topic.

---

[1]United States, *Annual Reports of the Secretary of the Navy* (Washington, DC, 1820-1860).

[2]John H. Schroeder, *Shaping a Maritime Empire: The Commercial and Diplomatic Role of the American Navy, 1829-1861* (Westport, CT, 1985), 3-18 and 37-41; and Craig L. Symonds, *Navalists and Antinavalists: The Naval Policy Debate in the United States, 1785-1827* (Newark, DE, 1980), 11-19.

[3]C.J. Bartlett, *Great Britain and Sea Power* (Oxford, 1963), 1-2, 34 and 125-128.

[4]Great Britain, National Archives (TNA/PRO), Navy List, 1820-1861.

[5]Andrew D. Lambert, "Politics, Technology and Policy-Making, 1859-1865: Palmerston, Gladstone and the Management of the Ironclad Naval Race," *The Northern Mariner/Le Marin du nord*, VIII, No. 3 (1998), 13.

The differences between the political economies of British and American naval deployment caused tensions in the equatorial Atlantic, but the similarities – the desire to maintain peace while advancing economic objectives – created a common peacetime concept of sea power that allowed naval relations to be a way to avoid conflict. As Robert Jervis suggested, "navies may be especially prone to be [a] destabilizing" influence on foreign relations. But Jervis also noted that a wider geographic and temporal analysis might help to assess whether naval requirements or culture influenced the relationship between navies and societies.[6] Accordingly, this study uses the equatorial Atlantic, Anglo-American relations and the wars against piracy and the slave trade as the primary avenues through which to test this argument. During the wars against the pirates, both nations sought commerce protection, although Britain was wary that forceful action against pirates and Spanish privateers would embroil other European powers in the conflicts before the UK achieved its commercial objectives. The British were suspicious that American deployment was a prelude to the seizure of Cuba, but the RN avoided overt espionage on American activity, knowing that it might harm relations. London adjusted naval actions to prevent conflicts with other nations or to become entangled in the Spanish-American rebellions. Once the piracy crisis ended, the Americans retrenched and left the RN as the dominant force in the Atlantic.

At the same time, Britain wanted the US to help to police the slave trade. As part of its anti-piracy patrol, Washington dispatched vessels to the West African coast to protect trade and render assistance to American colonies. But with the post-crisis retrenchment, Britain wondered when American efforts might resume. In the interim, the UK adhered to a liberal philosophy, lobbied for the suppression of the slave trade but avoided war. Still, the RN stopped US-flagged vessels it suspected of being slavers, a policy which increased tensions. Yet because both nations believed that sea power could foster the peaceful attainment of long-term goals, each concluded that it could advance its interests without conflict.

In the equatorial Atlantic, however, only Britain combined slave-trade suppression with commerce protection, expansion and strategic concerns. In contrast, the US believed that these were separate issues, and the contradiction generated bilateral tensions. Regardless, both nations reined in their officers when they caused offence; navies policed the peace but left serious disputes to the diplomats. While navies could be destabilizing factors in Anglo-American relations because of the "individual autonomy" of vessels at sea, governments were able to exercise a degree of control by deciding beforehand whom they

---

[6]Robert Jervis, "Navies, Politics, and Political Science," in John B. Hattendorf (ed.), *Doing Naval History: Essays toward Improvement* (Newport, RI, 1995), 44.

trusted with sensitive objectives during peacetime.[7] Therefore, Anglo-American naval relations became a conduit through which they could reduce conflict. This reveals that within the Anglo-American relationship the two were neither friends nor enemies; they worked to reconcile their differences so they could further their separate objectives.

Anglo-American Relations Studies

This book deals with international relations and the use of sea power in support of national interests. Consequently, I will place the use of sea power within the broader context of Anglo-American relations, a field that studies how interests converge and clash. To bridge the gap between naval history and Anglo-American relations, I will use an "interest theory" of naval analysis. Influenced by the so-called "New Naval History," this study will show how national interests, moulded by domestic and international commercial goals and political decisions, shaped naval relations. I will accomplish this by using a comparative methodology applied to policy, diplomatic and naval documents in the context of those interests in the equatorial Atlantic.

The objectives of this study derive from the historiography of Anglo-American relations in the wake of the War of 1812. The conflict focused on American commercial and maritime rights, its relationship with Britain and its territorial goals. Nations which believed in mercantilism governed the world, although this practice excluded the US from trade with the British colonies in the West Indies with which New England had a lucrative trade before the Revolution. Under the "Rule of 1756," the British declared that mercantilist doctrines also applied in war. If France, for instance, permitted only French vessels to trade between a colony and the mother country in peacetime, the same had to apply during wars.[8] Consequently, an underlying tension strained Anglo-American relations, and this increased during the Anglo-French wars.

Under the "Rule of 1756," Britain stopped American vessels from trading with France. Moreover, the British engaged in impressment, searching any vessel for "British subjects" to press into the service of the RN.[9] Ameri-

---

[7]*Ibid.*

[8]Howard Jones, *Crucible of Power: A History of American Foreign Relations to 1913* (Wilmington, DE, 2002), 70-71; and Julius W. Pratt, *A History of United States Foreign Policy* (2nd ed., Englewood Cliffs, NJ, 1965), 40 and 57-58.

[9]Scott Thomas Jackson, "Impressment and Anglo-American Discord, 1787-1818" (Unpublished PhD thesis, University of Michigan, 1976), 17-55 and 56-90, contains a discussion of British manning problems, impressment, American commerce and the degeneration of Anglo-American relations that led to the War of 1812. See also

cans were divided on the best approach to take with Britain. The Federalists increased national defence but "pursued a pro-British foreign policy abroad" to preserve peace and promote trade. Federalists, with support largely from the North, believed that war was too risky, while Republicans took a harder line to promote American rights. Thus, when talks to resolve the disputes with Britain failed, James Madison's Republican administration declared war in 1812.[10]

During the peace talks, Washington wanted the British to abandon impressment and the "Rule of 1756," as well as to define rules for blockade. Yet when Britain defeated Napoleon, the Americans lost an advantage. Nevertheless, the Duke of Wellington advised peace rather a long war that would further harm British finances. But rather than resolve the outstanding issues, both nations accepted a *status quo ante bellum* codified in the Treaty of Ghent. They restored seized territory and established joint commissions to settle boundary disputes.[11] They also agreed to discuss the future of slave-trade suppression.[12] Howard Jones concluded that the "treaty was ultimately an armi-

---

Kevin A. Payne, "Naval Impressment in Hull, 1793-1815" (Unpublished MA thesis, University of Hull, 1998).

[10]Julius W. Pratt, *Expansionists of 1812* (New York, 1925; reprint, Gloucester, MA, 1957), 10-11, asked if British maritime policy precipitated the war, did those in the American Northeast oppose it and those with few maritime interests, like the South and Northwest, support it. He concluded that blame for the war rested squarely on those who espoused a nascent "Manifest Destiny," although no one had yet coined the term. Many in the South wanted the US to expand into Spanish-controlled areas like Florida, while many in the Northwest wanted unencumbered expansion and the pacification of aboriginals who were nominally allied with the British. Consequently, Pratt believed that the expansionists of 1812 caused the war: "[t]he link between the designs of the Southwest and those of the Northwest was the existence of the alliance between Great Britain and Spain. It was widely assumed that war with Great Britain would mean war with Spain, and thus that expansion at the north and at the south would proceed *pari passu*." More recently, others have sought to link American domestic and international affairs with the cause of the war. For example, Donald R. Hickey, *The War of 1812: A Forgotten Conflict* (Urbana, IL, 1989), 5-8, 26-28, 46-47, 102 and 162-164, argued that US foreign and domestic policies were linked, and that Madison and the Republicans hoped to confirm American independence and unite their party. Therefore, he concluded that "many Republicans had come to believe that the rewards of war outweighed its risks."

[11]Harry C. Allen, *Great Britain and the United States: A History of Anglo-American Relations (1783-1952)* (London, 1954), 336-345; Pratt, *United States Foreign Policy*, 66-67; and Hickey, *War of 1812*, 281-299.

[12]W.E. Burghardt Du Bois, *The Suppression of the African Slave-Trade to the United States of America, 1683-1870* (New York, 1896; reprint, New York, 1970), 133-135.

stice by two countries that finally realized [that] their best interests lay in peace."[13] Moreover, the US Navy (USN) had held its own against the RN, and "[a]fter 1812 the British took America seriously as a naval power[.]"[14]

Historians of Anglo-American relations have therefore sought to understand the nature of the *status quo ante bellum*, although they differ on when the "special relationship" developed between the two. Most scholars have published their studies in the wake of important events, such as World War II, the Cold War or the 200th anniversary of American independence. The arguments function along a continuum where, at one pole, after the Revolutionary War Britain and America were friendly, and disputes were aberrations that had to be resolved. At the other limit, the two were enemies which only recently became friends when common enemies, like Germany and Soviet Russia, threatened both.

Several significant works are illustrative of trends in the field. Harry Allen wrote in 1954 that Britain and America only became friends during World War II. Prior relations were tense and almost led to war on occasions such as the Venezuela boundary dispute in 1895. He blamed the US for problems in the relationship. Most disputes were territorial and within North America, pressing more on American than British sensitivities. Others involved maritime rights, ranging from access to Atlantic fishing zones to the Navigation Acts. The British, however, had the necessary maturity, Allen believed, to be aware of its prior faults and to avoid "future dangers[.]" Nevertheless, Allen emphasized the growing Anglo-American economic connection in the relationship. Early on, as a debtor nation the US was dependent upon British finance. The economic dynamic created tensions, but during the nineteenth century it also maintained a strong connection "no matter how much she [America] disliked to admit it."[15] Writing a few years later, Charles S. Campbell concluded that Anglo-American relations were hostile until Britain wanted America's help with China and Germany in the late nineteenth and early twentieth centuries.[16] In the 1960s Kenneth Bourne concurred that Anglo-American friendship came late. After the War of 1812, some people promoted the bene-

---

[13]Jones, *Crucible of Power*, 84.

[14]Andrew D. Lambert, *War at Sea in the Age of Sail 1650-1850* (London, 2000), 202. See also 190-202 for details of the major naval battles of the War of 1812.

[15]Allen, *Great Britain and the United States*, 2, 17, 54 and 92-94.

[16]Charles S. Campbell, *Anglo-American Understanding, 1898-1903* (Baltimore, 1957), 1-24 and 346-347.

fits of trade, but others, like John Quincy Adams, believed that the two nations engaged in a "warfare of the mind."[17]

At the other end of the spectrum, Frank Thistlethwaite thought that the economic relationship made the countries closer "than any two other sovereign states." Labour and capital flowed from Britain to America, providing the US with the resources it needed to grow. While these elements linked the nations, Britain grew closer to the people of the American Northeast as its power grew over the South. British banking houses provided credit for American canals and railways, such as the Baltimore and Ohio and the Camden and Amboy lines. As Americans opened their interior, British bankers provided the necessary finance. Thistlethwaite concluded that this economic relationship "supported a structure of social relations" that "bound together important elements in Britain and the United States," such as Quakers, Utilitarian MPs, trade unions, Christian and peace groups, abolitionists and suffragettes. The connection thus was with reformers and the rising Northern industrial class. As a result, Britain was unable either to exert influence over all Americans or to overcome severe diplomatic crises, such as the one that resulted in the War of 1812.[18]

Meanwhile, H.G. Nicholas believed that although the Anglo-American relationship changed with the evolving "power ratio," war became less likely because of their civilian connections.[19] In 1974 Campbell conceded that while diplomacy kept the nations from going to war after 1815, economic and cultural connections fertilized their friendship.[20] Similarly, D. Cameron Watt argued that the perceptions of interest groups which controlled and managed each nation's foreign policy shaped the nature of the relationship. But Watt's analysis, which stretched from 1900 to 1975, emphasized American perceptions as the main factor. Each American intervention in Europe –

---

[17]Kenneth Bourne, *Britain and the Balance of Power in North America, 1815-1908* (London, 1967), 3-10.

[18]Frank Thistlethwaite, *The Anglo-American Connection in the Early Nineteenth Century* (Philadelphia, 1959), 3-4, 9-18, 39-70, 85-133 and 172-175.

[19]H.G. Nicholas, *Britain and the United States* (London, 1963), 11-31 and 166-180. Nicholas refined his argument that trade promoted friendly relations in *The United States and Britain* (Chicago, 1975), chapters 1-3.

[20]Charles S. Campbell, *From Revolution to Rapprochement: The United States and Great Britain, 1783-1900* (New York, 1974), 1-8 and 191-204. Marshall Bertram, *The Birth of Anglo-American Friendship: The Prime Facet of the Venezuelan Boundary Dispute – A Study of the Inter-reaction of Diplomacy and Public Opinion* (Lanham, MD, 1992), supported Campbell's conclusions but believed that newspapers and public opinion unified the relationship.

whether the First or Second world wars or the Cold War – only occurred because Washington perceived that its vital interests were threatened.[21]

Watt also argued that the commonalities and connections between elites in the two countries helped to mould Anglo-American co-operation. He concluded that "British policy towards the rôle of the United States in world politics has been governed by the search for and the failure to find a 'possible America' which would support or fulfil British ends." For Watt, the sociopolitical similarities made any failures in their relationship more acute and "regrettable."[22] Martin Crawford countered that common ties helped the nations settle disputes with diplomacy, while newspapers like *The Times* were conduits that kept open the lines of communication.[23]

Writing at about the time of the Second World War, Lionel M. Gelber contended that the nations came together if this suited their individual interests rather than for altruistic reasons. He concluded that after the Spanish-American War stability was important, and "Britain could begin to consider the United States an associated part of her defensive system" as the German threat increased. Later, he claimed that Britain needed American protection during the Cold War. While their goals sometimes clashed, Gelber claimed that a "dialectical process" led them to seek reconciliation for the "common" interest.[24] The present study reveals a similar dynamic at work in the equatorial Atlantic through each nation's use of sea power.

Historians of Anglo-American relations have thus reflected a broad spectrum of views. But there is general agreement that the "special relationship" was virtually non-existent from 1819 to 1865. There were unresolved disputes, such as the right of search, that led to clashes on the high seas, in particular over slave-trade suppression. An examination of Anglo-American naval relations in the equatorial Atlantic therefore can provide new insights into the dynamic of this relationship. This shows that while Britain and the US were neither friends nor enemies, the smallest dispute held the potential for an

---

[21]D. Cameron Watt, *Succeeding John Bull: America in Britain's Place* (Cambridge, 1984), 11-12.

[22]*Ibid.*, 161-163.

[23]Martin Crawford, *The Anglo-American Crisis of the Mid-Nineteenth Century: The Times and America, 1850-1862* (Athens, GA, 1987), ix and 1-14.

[24]Lionel M. Gelber, *The Rise of Anglo-American Friendship: A Study in World Politics, 1898-1906* (London, 1938), 1-17, 31-36 and 274-275; and Gelber, *America in Britain's Place: The Leadership of the West and Anglo-American Unity* (New York, 1961), 1-16. David H. Burton, *British-American Diplomacy 1895-1917: Early Years of the Special Relationship* (Malabar, FL, 1999), 6, observed similarly that World War One showed that "national self-interest need not be divisive."

unwanted war. This analysis shows that while tensions remained, the two sides worked to keep them under control. Each modified its maritime policy to accommodate the other while fighting piracy and the slave trade and pursuing its broader domestic and international objectives.

Naval History

Naval historians have often dealt with sea power in the context of national interests. Many consider Alfred Thayer Mahan the father of modern naval history, but the field has older roots. We can in fact trace it to John Knox Laughton, a Cambridge-trained mathematician who entered the RN in 1853 as an instructor. At Cambridge he imbibed a rigorous scientific ethic that, according to Andrew Lambert, he retained "for the rest of his life." Laughton applied scientific methods to both oceanic meteorology and naval history. While urging others to adopt a similar approach, Laughton understood that naval history was part of both international and domestic history, and he contributed to an "understanding of those wider pictures."[25]

Laughton hoped to develop a "new doctrine for the ironclad era" and conceived of some important concepts. For example, in a study of naval tactics in the period 1794-1805, he concluded that an nation could meet its objectives "by avoiding decisive action" and creating "strategic defeats" for its foes. Consequently, strategic plans "had to be developed that would *force* [emphasis in original] a reluctant enemy to fight[.]"[26] Laughton's concepts and methodology influenced future naval historians such as Sir Julian Corbett, Admiral Sir Herbert Richmond and Mahan.

In fact, Laughton recruited Corbett into the Navy Records Society and suggested that he study the Spanish War of 1585-1587. Using an archive-based approach, Corbett moved into strategic studies and found in Clausewitz's work "a theoretical structure that could contain, develop and elucidate the strong strategic and doctrinal framework provided by Laughton." Laughton also influenced Richmond who, like Laughton, used "academic study as the foundation for national strategy" and stressed "that naval operations merely formed a part of strategy[.]"[27] In the US, Mahan concluded that great naval battles often "decided" history. He looked to the past for the elements of sea power that made a nation great and concluded that they included geography, natural re-

---

[25]Andrew D. Lambert, *The Foundations of Naval History: John Knox Laughton, the Royal Navy and the Historical Profession* (London, 1998), 11-17, 25 and 47.

[26]*Ibid.*, 44-47.

[27]*Ibid.*, 157, 195-197, 221 and 224-225.

sources, population and the character of the people and their government.[28]
Mahan acknowledged Laughton's influence, and the latter in turn endorsed
Mahan's technique of teaching history "by examples." Lambert concluded that
the two learned from each other and shared a belief in "the importance of history in demonstrating the central role of naval power in national policy."[29]

Laughton's lasting influence, however, was methodological. On Corbett's death, Richmond wrote that "history is the raw material out of which a
knowledge of the principles of strategy and tactics is built[.]"[30] Several authorities on British and American naval history are relevant to this study because they have focused on the use of sea power in the national interest using
historical methods.[31] In a polemical strain, for example, Harold and Margaret
Sprout intended their study of American sea power as a warning to the US to
prepare for war. Similarly, historians like Craig L. Symonds have focused on
the "character of the people and government" and the battle in America between oceanic and landward interests – the "navalists" and "anti-navalists."[32]

Other historians have adopted a broader approach to assess how states
used sea power to support national interests and to discover what this revealed
about international relations. Richmond believed that armed force was "a
weapon which defends some vital interest" and that nations with overseas interests developed fleets that were "a flexible instrument, apt to the needs of the

---

[28]Alfred Thayer Mahan, *The Influence of Sea Power upon History, 1660-1805*
(Englewood Cliffs, NJ, 1980), 30-33. This work is a one-volume edition of *The Influence of Sea Power upon History, 1660-1783* (Boston, 1890; reprint, New York, 2004);
and *The Influence of Sea Power upon the French Revolution and Empire, 1793-1812* (2
vols., Boston, 1892; reprint, New York, 1980). Mahan also wrote other works, such as
The Life of Nelson: The Embodiment of Sea Power of Great Britain (2 vols., Boston,
1897; reprint, Annapolis, 2001). He expressed his theory of history skilfully in "Subordination in Historical Treatment," *Annual Report of the American Historical Association for the Year 1902* (Washington, DC, 1903), 49-63. For more on the influences on
Mahan's theories, see Thomas R. Pollock, "The Historical Elements of Mahanian Doctrine," *Naval War College Review*, XXXV, No. 4 (1982), 44-49.

[29]Lambert, *Foundations*, 126-130.

[30]*Ibid.*, 220.

[31]Mahan cautioned that there were factors other than the role of sea power in
establishing a great nation, a warning that most naval historians have ignored. See Paul
Kennedy, "The Influence and the Limitations of Sea Power," *International History
Review*, X, No. 1 (1988), 2-17.

[32]Harold Sprout and Margaret Sprout, *The Rise of American Naval Power
1776-1918* (Princeton, 1939; reprint, Annapolis, 1970), 7-12; and Symonds, *Navalists
and Antinavalists*, 11-12.

country[.]" Sea power, he argued, developed because of "spontaneous economic or social movements" and overseas development. Other nations, less dependent on the sea, also strove for sea power to acquire territory or trade "for the added wealth and strength and influence which it would confer[.]" As nations grew economically, rivalries spawned a desire for greater sea power. Richmond believed that the "need for security of an interest upon which the life and fortunes of the peoples depended brought it [sea power] into existence[.]" The English, for instance, developed sea power when their interests became "more widely diffused, [and] contact, and consequently the possibility of friction, with states far removed from the Channel" became more likely.[33]

Gerald S. Graham sought a deeper understanding of the dynamics of British sea power. He argued that while a society's economic base directed its use, Britain also had to consider the impact of politics and economics in devising naval strategy. Nonetheless, Graham was hard pressed to explain British naval policy in the early nineteenth century. Judging it to be largely passive and defensive, he thought that it revealed the nonchalant attitude of global hegemony. He concluded that British foreign policy was "partly paralysed by the mixture of [Lord] Palmerston's mailed-fisted diplomacy and the pacifist doctrines of the free trade school[.]" Therefore, Graham surmised, "British governments seemed to forget that command of the sea was the key not only to home defence but to the safety of overseas commerce and empire."[34] But as this study will show, this was far from the case.

C.J. Bartlett believed that strong individuals, like Lord Palmerston, were vital in moulding naval policy. Yet Bartlett also postulated that economics and the "triangular struggle" of naval, foreign and domestic affairs played a role.[35] Andrew Lambert showed that British naval development was timed to meet threats from rivals such as France. Leaders like Aberdeen used the navy as an instrument of diplomacy: "[i]n the Mediterranean he called for two less battleships than the French, to salve their wounded pride[.]" The RN was therefore an instrument that London used in peacetime to meet political needs. But where does an historian turn to understand the basis of those needs when much traditional naval history has focused solely on wars?[36]

---

[33]Herbert Richmond, *Sea Power in the Modern World* (London, 1934), 5-6 and 16-35.

[34]Gerald S. Graham, *Empire of the North Atlantic: The Maritime Struggle for North America* (London, 1958), viii, ix and 276-279.

[35]Bartlett, *Great Britain and Sea Power*, 101-102 and 104.

[36]Andrew D. Lambert, *Battleships in Transition: The Creation of the Steam Battlefleet 1815-1860* (Oxford, 1984), 13-19, 83-85 and 117-118; and Lambert, *The Last Sailing Battlefleet: Maintaining Naval Mastery, 1815-1850* (London, 1991), 39.

Interest-Based Naval Analysis

Although Mahan has certainly influenced the writing of naval history, others have also contributed. Laughton, Mahan, Richmond and others have given naval history not only continuity but also the historical rigour to understand the influence of broad factors on naval affairs. Recent maritime and naval historians have advocated a systematic approach that takes into account more than just battles, tactics and the roles of great commanders. One characteristic of the "New Naval History" is a desire to link naval affairs with wider historical concerns. John B. Hattendorf has written that naval power was one way that countries implemented national policies. He therefore contended that naval historians must acknowledge the interconnectedness of naval topics and broader national contexts.[37] In turn, the relationship between navies can reveal much about the relationship between the nations that own them.

An interest-based approach to naval history – looking at the motives for maintaining navies – allows for a broader analysis than a focus solely on battles and tactics. This approach reveals the dynamics of policy formulation and the relationship between sea power and international relations. Like Bartlett, Paul Kennedy believed that scholars must use broader variables to understand the development of British naval policy. He thought that historians could only understand concepts like "naval mastery" and "sea power" by analyzing "national, international, economic, political and strategical considerations[.]"[38] But how did nations use navies to support national interests short of war? Corbett recognized that national policies influenced naval deployment and that countries could use even small navies to implement national policies in localized areas without achieving complete command of the sea.[39] Lambert, for instance, showed in his study of the Crimean War that the RN could influence Russian strategy without drawing the Russian Navy into battle.[40]

---

[37]Hattendorf (ed.), *Doing Naval History*, 1-4.

[38]Paul Kennedy, *The Rise and Fall of British Naval Mastery* (London, 1976), xv-xvii, 24-27 and 98-110.

[39]Julian S. Corbett, *Some Principles of Maritime Strategy* (London, 1911; reprint, Mineola, NY, 2004), 1-9, 14-27, 87 and 100-101. For more on Corbett and Richmond, see James Goldrick and John B. Hattendorf (eds.), *Mahan Is Not Enough: The Proceedings of a Conference on the Works of Sir Julian Corbett and Admiral Sir Herbert Richmond* (Newport, RI, 1993), especially Hattendorf, "Mahan Is Not Enough: Conference Themes and Issues," 7-12; Daniel A. Baugh, "Admiral Sir Herbert Richmond and the Objects of Sea Power," 13-38; and Donald M. Schurman, "Julian Corbett's Influence on the Royal Navy's Perception of Its Maritime Function," 51-63.

[40]Andrew D. Lambert, *The Crimean War: British Grand Strategy, 1853-56* (Manchester, 1990), 169 and 293. But Basil Greenhill and Ann Giffard, *The British*

The nature of various interests shapes the level of naval involvement in implementing national policy, especially in wartime. But as I will show, this is equally true in an era of relative peace. Therefore, an "interest theory" approach to naval relations is important, and late twentieth-century naval strategists have articulated such a theory. A speaker at the Adderbury Maritime Strategic Dialogue, for example, concluded that "[m]aritime forces are particularly useful for interest-based strategies" and that the interests of two sides might "only clash at certain points."[41] Meanwhile, Jan Glete has theorized that navies acted "as instruments for a state in accordance with the demands of the interest base behind that state[.]" Glete postulated an "interest aggregation" of those willing to "cede their right of using violence[.]" Consequently, while the state acted "as an economic coordinator of resources brought or extracted from the society," nineteenth-century "Euro-American cruiser forces" became the "chief instrument of violence control."[42]

Piracy and the slave trade involved American and British domestic and international interests in the same region. This study will reveal that the two nations, in support of "interest aggregation," exerted regional influence to further their national interests while avoiding war through their actions against piracy and slave traders. A comparative analysis of British and American efforts to suppress piracy and the slave trade provides a significant indication of the role of sea power to support national interests and what it reveals about Anglo-American relations. Sea power allowed them to relate to one another and to mitigate potential conflicts.

I will argue that Britain and the US reacted differently to piracy and the slave trade, depending on their national interest aggregation, as each sought to protect and promote commerce and further larger objectives. Consequently, their different reactions and national interests shaped their naval deployment and relations. Divergent goals and strategies often clashed to generate tension. Regardless, their underlying policies shaped their use of sea power for "peaceful" purposes by avoiding conflict while furthering other goals. Rather than go to war, the two pursued a conciliatory approach in their conflicting naval policies. This analysis adds to our understanding of Anglo-American relations by showing how Britain and the US accommodated each other in the equatorial Atlantic.

Assault on Finland, 1854-1855: A Forgotten Naval War (Annapolis, 1988), 289-291, cautioned that British officers, like Keppel, were looking for a battle with the Russian fleet, unaware that the RN had defeated the Russian Baltic squadron "simply [by] being there."

[41]Eric Grove, *Maritime Strategy and European Security* (London, 1990), 140.

[42]Jan Glete, *Navies and Nations: Warships, Navies and State Building in Europe and America, 1500-1860* (2 vols., Stockholm, 1993), 400, 477-482 and 486.

Comparative Methodology and Sources

This study will offer a deeper understanding of the role of sea power, international and naval relations and the suppression of piracy and the slave trade
largely by using a comparative methodology. Dennis E. Showalter concluded
that naval history must address "systematically and comparatively the problem
of choice in state policy, strategic planning, and force structures" to create "a
'new naval history.'"[43] In 1995, Paul G. Halpern wrote that comparative naval
history could examine the operations of two or more navies or geographic regions using first-person accounts, official records and documents from different sides that cover the same event. These techniques will be used to satisfy
William R. Thompson's plea that naval historians ask explicit questions and
make explicit comparisons.[44]

By comparing Anglo-American interests and policies to examine how
these shaped naval deployment and cooperation, this study will generate important insights into the circumstances under which Britain and the US used
sea power. To link elements of naval history, sources such as newspapers,
policy, diplomatic and naval documents, and economic and naval statistics will
be used to assess how piracy and slave-trade suppression reflected national
interests and affected Anglo-American relations. While British and American
sources are often complementary, each has both advantages and limitations.
People, for example, often have agendas, while reporters can embellish stories
in the process of telling horrific tales of piracy. Nevertheless, newspaper accounts are important because they reveal what the public was likely to know
about an issue. The historian can use documents about policy formulation,
diplomacy and naval deployment to fill in the details. But these often contain
personal or national biases, while governments for the most part only published certain kinds of records. Moreover, all sources contain gaps, and the
historian can only use the evidence that survives. Still, a comparative methodology, using similar sources for two countries, can increase the accuracy and

---

[43]Dennis E. Showalter, "Toward a 'New' Naval History," in Hattendorf,
(ed.), *Doing Naval History*, 138.

[44]Paul G. Halpern, "Comparative Naval History;" and William R. Thompson, "Some Mild and Radical Observations on Desiderata in Comparative Naval History," in Hattendorf (ed.), *Doing Naval History*, 75-114. Several other authors have
written works of comparative naval history. For example, Clark G. Reynolds, *Command of the Sea: The History and Strategy of Maritime Empires* (London, 1976), xv-
xvi, sought to "discover the strategic alternatives and constants governing navies and
empires throughout the continuum of history by raising hypotheses to be tested by historical examination." Meanwhile, George Modelski and William R. Thompson,
Seapower in Global Politics, 1494-1993 (Seattle, 1988), 27-97, used aggregate ship
numbers to track "fluctuations in the concentration of global reach."

reliability of the analysis. Halpern advocated a "mirror technique." Researchers can fill gaps and reduce biases by looking in the archives of opposing governments, departments and navies.[45]

Used comparatively, British and American sources allow an analysis of the dynamics of the Anglo-American relationship at various levels. For example, newspapers like the *American Commercial and Daily Advertiser* and *The New York Times* provide "real-time" details of events and the opinions of various interest groups. The *Annals of Congress* and the *Congressional Globe* present congressional opinions, including petitions requesting support for African endeavours. Additionally, documents in the National Archives (NA), Record Group (RG) 45 (Naval Records Collection of the Office of Naval Records and Library, Records of the Secretary of the Navy) contain correspondence from American merchants and other parties interested in matters relating to piracy, slave-trade suppression, African colonization and commerce.

I have also used several American sources to analyze American decision making. Among them, the memoirs of John Quincy Adams reveal White House policy debates, in particular during President James Monroe's tenure. Adams' memoirs also provide his personal reflections, especially on the contentious issue of dispatching American naval forces to West Africa. The papers of Secretary of State Daniel Webster are important in analyzing decisions during the early 1840s when the US established a permanent West African force. The American sources reveal the ease with which leaders made decisions to police piracy but how, at the same time, they found it hard to make decisions about the slave trade. The sources reveal the political, economic and geographic constraints on those decisions.

I will also examine the ramifications of the American political process on international relations and naval deployment. Dispatches from US envoys in Britain, contained in the General Records of the Department of State (RG 59), reveal the interface between the American and British positions, as do British Foreign Office and Admiralty documents. The *US Serial Set* and Navy Department records divulge the opinions of naval officers and show how political considerations shaped naval policy. I have also examined American naval deployment through the *Annual Reports of the Secretary of the Navy* and sources contained in the Naval Records Collection of the Office of Naval Records and Library. For example, RG 45 contains Commodore Matthew Perry's letter books, the copious volumes of correspondence received by the Secretary of the Navy from squadron commanders and the Secretary's "confidential" letters.

In this work I compare and contrast American naval deployment, constraints and freedoms with those of their British counterparts. From the British perspective, one source for gathering information on diplomatic and naval relations and naval deployment is the published *British Parliamentary Papers*, in

---

[45]Halpern, "Comparative Naval History," 81-91.

particular the series on the slave trade. Charles Webster warned that these "Blue Books" might be misleading, and Lord Palmerston admitted that he could easily withhold materials from Parliament. Still, he also realized that since he depended upon public opinion for support, such deceptions could backfire. Thus, he demanded that "[a]ll important negotiations had to be fully recorded in the public despatches[.]" Webster also concluded that diplomatic correspondence was a special case. If the government published "false" records, the other government would know because it too had a copy of the correspondence. Metternich, for example, was so concerned about the authenticity of "Blue Book" diplomatic correspondence that he often "withheld communications" because "they might be produced to Parliament."[46] Consequently, *Parliamentary Papers* are yet another conduit into diplomatic relations, albeit ones that suffered from a lag during the printing process.

To balance biases in parliamentary records, this study also uses American diplomatic material, such as the dispatches from American envoys in London, to develop a clearer picture of the diplomatic process. Because Palmerston was Foreign Secretary and later Prime Minister for most of the period covered by this study, I have also used relevant material from his papers, as well as the papers of Lord John Russell and Lord Granville. For key periods, such as during the piracy crisis and the later era of tension with the US over the suppression of the slave trade and the fate of Central America, Admiralty (ADM) records were consulted, including correspondence between the government and naval officers. For the critical 1840s, I also consulted the papers of Sir Charles Hotham, British commodore along the West African coast, in the University of Hull Archives. Containing letters from the government, personal correspondence and his general and secret dispatches, this source helped to paint a more complete picture of British West African policy and how it fit with larger concerns.

I investigated the policies that shaped British naval deployment and gave them a wider perspective using various sources. In addition to the Hotham Papers, during the earlier piracy crisis ADM 2, Out-letters, showed British decisions. The logbooks of admirals like Sir Charles Rowley (ADM 50/136) and Jamaica station correspondence (ADM 1/273-275 and 128/34) revealed policy ramifications in-theatre. Critical Foreign Office (FO) comments on West African policy are contained in FO 2/4, Africa, and FO 84/775, Slave Trade Department. Correspondence from African commodores during the 1840s, and policy directives issued during a period of Anglo-American tension in the Gulf of Mexico in 1858, are in ADM 1, In-Letters. Important for comparing general Anglo-American naval relations was ADM

---

[46]Charles K. Webster, *The Foreign Policy of Palmerston 1830-1841: Britain, The Liberal Movement and the Eastern Question* (2 vols., London, 1951), I, 61-63.

7/712, an Admiralty file on the USN. Finally, I examined RN deployment in West Africa using station correspondence in ADM 123.

These sources revealed the impact of policy on British naval deployment against pirates, its freedom against slavers off West Africa and the problems the RN faced when Anglo-American interests clashed. Admiralty and US Navy Department sources, specific naval operations and the observations of one navy about the other also helped to assess the tension between having good Anglo-American relations and the use of sea power during this period. Finally, the influence of national interests on naval deployment in the Atlantic was followed statistically for the RN and USN with time series developed from *Annual Reports of the Secretary of the Navy* and Britain's *Navy List*. In addition, the analysis tested the accuracy of official observations on the slave trade against a database on slaving voyages compiled by David Eltis, Stephen D. Behrendt, David Richardson and Herbert S. Klein.[47]

This work explains how naval policy was used to define the Anglo-American relationship. Using the sources and methodology described, this study comprises eight chapters and a conclusion. In chapter two I place British and American goals and navies in the context of economic development, growing interests and relations in the equatorial Atlantic. Chapters three and four reveal that both nations worked toward a common policy during the Spanish-American rebellions but used sea power to protect commercial interests from pirate attacks. The chapters show the ease with which the US deployed force to protect against pirates, while Britain was restrained by commitments to the Concert of Europe. But Britain faced fewer constraints on the other side of the Atlantic against the slave trade. In that war, however, London was unable to convince the US to cooperate against the slave traders. Instead, Washington deployed a minimal naval force to West Africa only to placate the British.

Chapter five shows that by the 1840s the American use of sea power included furthering strategic objectives overseas. It formed a nexus with British policy and allowed both nations to avoid war. Their strategic views about the peaceful use of sea power allowed them to develop a common strategy for West Africa to try to mitigate disputes. The US deployed a permanent West African squadron to protect and promote commercial development and eliminate the need for Britain to stop US-flagged ships. Meanwhile, London believed that the RN could suppress the slave trade and encourage legitimate commerce under the banner of free trade. To emphasize differences in Anglo-American policy, chapters six and seven analyze British and American naval policies off West Africa after 1842. This reveals that by the late 1850s the dif-

---

[47]David Eltis, *et al.*, *The Trans-Atlantic Slave Trade: A Database on CD-ROM* (Cambridge, 1999). Readers should note that because this is a CD-ROM, citations will not contain page numbers. Results are generated through structured query language (SQL) calls to the database.

fering goals generated tension in Anglo-American relations. Finally, chapter eight explains that the two countries modified their use of sea power to reduce tensions and safely promote individual interests. Britain and the US were neither friends nor enemies, but their ideas about how to use sea power during peacetime was a mechanism through which they co-existed.

Chapter 2
The Atlantic

The French Revolutionary and Napoleonic wars left the US and Britain as the major players in the Atlantic. Postwar economic conditions are significant because their policies and growth shaped their naval deployment and relations. Their often divergent goals created conditions that might increase Anglo-American tensions in regions like the equatorial Atlantic where the two met on the "great common" in the West Indies and West Africa, two important areas for their emerging policies. While both nations eyed the other with suspicion, their "interest aggregation" preferred the peaceful pursuit of objectives.

While Britain and the US were wary of each other during crises, their adherence to the peaceful use of sea power provided a way to co-exist. Since British capitalists wanted growth and the protection of overseas trade, political leaders avoided provoking rivals like France and the US into combining to threaten these interests. Instead, London hoped to achieve its economic goals through an emerging free-trade policy, conflict avoidance and the "peaceful" use of sea power. While the US also felt that sea power could be used peacefully, its policies wavered as the nation went through growing pains.

The Atlantic Theatre

During the early nineteenth century, Western Europe was the most developed region on the Atlantic littoral, with London as the world's financial centre. Europe's share of manufacturing output and levels of industrialization grew, with Britain at the forefront (see tables 2.1 and 2.2). While manufacturing output in the US lagged until the early twentieth century, it was growing. As British and American industrial might and the hunger for more markets and resources grew, they backed up their aspirations with mechanized firepower. Nonetheless, a balance-of-power strategy governed geopolitical relations in the Atlantic. European powers worked to prevent France's aggressive rebirth, and its relative share of power fell. Meanwhile, conservative attitudes, like those of Prince Metternich, played a role in British strategic thinking. The continuance of the "rule of law" philosophy helped govern its foreign policy. As Albert H. Imlah has observed, the system maintained order in Europe and "helped to prevent [the] balance of power from degenerating into mere competition for power."[1] Yet as Barry Gough has noted, the "general linkage of navy to Empire continues to escape historians."[2]

Table 2.1
Percent of World Manufacturing Output, 1750-1900

Region	1750	1800	1830	1860	1880	1900
Europe	23.2	28.1	34.2	53.2	61.3	62.0
(UK)	(1.9)	(4.3)	(9.5)	(19.9)	(22.9)	(18.5)
US	0.1	0.8	2.4	7.2	14.7	23.6
Third World	73.0	67.7	60.5	36.6	20.9	11.0
Other	3.7	3.4	2.9	3	3.1	3.4
Total	100.0	100.0	100.0	100.0	100.0	100.0

Source: Paul Kennedy, *The Rise and Fall of the Great Powers: Economic Change and Military Conflict from 1500 to 2000* (London, 1988), table 6.

Table 2.2
Levels of Industrialization, 1750-1900

Country	1750	1800	1830	1860	1880	1900
Europe	8	8	11	16	24	35
UK	10	16	25	64	87	100
US	4	9	14	21	38	69

Note: UK = 100 in 1900.

Source: Kennedy, *Rise and Fall of the Great Powers*, table 7.

Gentlemanly Capitalists and British Strategy

In this context, Britain developed a free-trade policy, and political leaders adopted a liberal view of foreign relations that accepted interference with other powers only if British interests were threatened. As the former evolved, Lon-

---

[1]Paul Kennedy, *The Rise and Fall of the Great Powers: Economic Change and Military Conflict from 1500 to 2000* (London, 1988), 183-193 and 204-218; George Modelski and William R. Thompson, *Seapower in Global Politics, 1494-1993* (Seattle, 1988), 249-250 and 305; Clark G. Reynolds, *Command of the Sea: The History and Strategy of Maritime Empires* (London, 1976), 332; and Albert H. Imlah, *Economic Elements in the Pax Britannica: Studies in British Foreign Trade in the Nineteenth Century* (Cambridge, MA, 1958), 2-4.

[2]Barry M. Gough, "The Royal Navy and the British Empire," in Robin W. Winks (ed.), *The Oxford History of the British Empire* (Oxford, 1999), V, 340.

don felt it could work with other powers to achieve its economic goals while maintaining Britain's strategic commitments. Consequently, Gough concluded that "the term *Pax Britannica*...encompasses the maintenance of order and stability in various regions of the world" for the peaceful development of British interests.[3] This economic and diplomatic policy moulded Britain's use of sea power and its relations with the US.

The political elite and London's financial leaders in the City dominated British attempts to further commercial development "peacefully." They formed a cohesive group with similar backgrounds, while other interests lacked corresponding political power. The City, with its government connections, wanted to increase commerce within the framework of freer trade. In the western Atlantic, the British wanted access to Spanish markets while checking the moves of other powers. Along the coast of West Africa, while radical free traders sought to disband the African squadron, the political elite dominated and would not let other political groups stall its policy or drag the country into war. It sought to further its interests with sea power and modified its use when it threatened relations with other nations, like the US.

The connections between the financial and government sectors influenced the dynamics of British foreign policy. Leaders like Lord Palmerston warned investors which countries to avoid, while governments saw the advantage of British financial penetration into regions in which it had a political interest. D.C.M. Platt commented that "[b]usinessmen, politicians, and officials shared their beliefs, social status, and general interests to such an extent that they acted together." He reminded us that "Lenin wrote of the 'interlocking' of bankers, ministers, big industrialists and rentiers[.]"[4] But in the most succinct study of the phenomena, P.J. Cain and A.G. Hopkins concluded that the connection between the London financial sector and British policymakers pro-

---

[3]Barry M. Gough, "Profit and Power: Informal Empire, the Navy and Latin America," in Raymond E. Dumett (ed.), *Gentlemanly Capitalism and British Imperialism: The New Debate on Empire* (London, 1999), 73.

[4]D.C.M. Platt, *Finance, Trade, and Politics in British Foreign Policy 1815-1914* (Oxford, 1968), 3-5, 12, 18, 23 and 25. Indeed, the gentlemanly-capitalist thesis follows closely the Hobson-Leninist paradigm of financiers directing imperial expansion. See J.A. Hobson, *Imperialism: A Study* (London, 1902; reprint, London, 1988), chapters 4 and 6. Moreover, D. Cameron Watt, *Succeeding John Bull: America in Britain's Place* (Cambridge, 1984), 9-11, noted that the common backgrounds of each nation's elites and their perceptions of each other influenced their global outlooks in the twentieth century. In America, for example, Southerners, New Englanders and graduates of Ivy League schools such as Princeton and Harvard dominated the State Department. In Britain the financial elite, through membership in the Bank of England, Treasury and "the great merchant banks and major investment centres" have had more influence "in the formation of British policy" than "that of their industrialist equivalents."

vided the City with considerable influence in the Treasury and Colonial and Foreign offices.[5]

Gentlemanly capitalists, such as the Barings, moved in government circles, held considerable sway and provided financial and political connections across the Atlantic, within and between governments. Sir Francis Thornhill Baring, for example, was Chancellor of the Exchequer from 1839 to 1841 and later First Lord of the Admiralty. Meanwhile, in the early 1840s Robert Peel dispatched Sir Francis' uncle, Alexander Baring, Lord Ashburton, to settle the Maine-New Brunswick border dispute.[6] This mission also developed a way to allay US fears over the activities of the Royal Navy (RN) in West Africa.[7] As Barry Gough surmised, for gentlemanly capitalists "[a]mphibious diplomacy required a deft hand."[8]

Rooted in the landed aristocracy, the English gentlemanly class held money made from physical labour "in low repute." Instead, banking and finance, based in the City of London, appealed to them. From thence came the famous banking families, including the Barings, Rothschilds and Grenfells.

---

[5]P.J. Cain and A.G. Hopkins, *British Imperialism, 1688-2000* (2nd ed., London, 2001), 120-121. This is a one-volume edition of Cain and Hopkins' original *British Imperialism*. For more details on the gentlemanly-capitalist thesis, see Dumett (ed.), *Gentlemanly Capitalism*. For a review of the historiography of the British commercial elite and their activities in the nineteenth century, see Martin J. Daunton, "'Gentlemanly Capitalism' and British Industry, 1820-1914," *Past and Present*, No. 122 (1989), 119-158. Daunton concluded that the line between the gentlemanly capitalists and industry was less distinct than some advocates of the thesis suggest. But the merchant capitalists who dominated at any given point were tied to the emerging "new" world trade, and over time a small number of companies controlled the sector. Although the leaders in the City did not comprise a truly coherent group, its diversity gave it the flexibility to meet the changes that occurred during the nineteenth century.

[6]Philip Ziegler, *The Sixth Great Power: A History of One of the Greatest of All Banking Families, the House of Barings, 1762-1929* (New York, 1988), 118-119 and 158; and Ralph W. Hidy, *The House of Baring in American Trade and Finance: English Merchant Bankers at Work, 1763-1861* (New York, 1949), 45-48. For a general discussion of the Anglo-American merchant-banking houses and their interlocking nature, see Hidy, "The Organization and Functions of Anglo-American Merchant Bankers, 1815-1860," *Journal of Economic History*, I, supplement (1941), 53-66.

[7]Kenneth Bourne, *The Foreign Policy of Victorian England, 1830-1902* (Oxford, 1970), 50; Howard Jones, *To the Webster-Ashburton Treaty: A Study in Anglo-American Relations, 1783-1843* (Chapel Hill, NC, 1977), 95-102 and 132-137; and D.C.M. Platt, *Foreign Finance in Continental Europe and the United States, 1815-1870: Quantities, Origins, Functions and Distribution* (London, 1984), 144, 150 and 163. See also chapter 5 below.

[8]Gough, "Profit and Power," 79.

People in the City made money in "acceptable" ways, remained loyal to the traditional, governing class and connected the gentlemanly capitalists and government officials. Both groups were educated at universities such as Oxford and Cambridge and held similar world views because of their "gentlemanly ethic[.]" They celebrated "Britain's status as an international service centre" rather than its "position as the world's workshop." And abroad, the gentlemen nurtured similar groups with whom they could deal.[9]

Cain and Hopkins concluded that the gentlemanly class linked economics and official policy. The ability of the government to carry large post-war debts worsened during the depression of the late 1830s and early 1840s, but expansion, coordinated by the City, promised to increase trade and provide the government with increased revenues to meet those obligations. Decreased tariffs would increase foreign supplies of food for the growing British population while providing manufacturers with new markets. The City was the world's creditor and financed the development of Europe and the US, while increased world trade would be "handled, transported and insured by British firms." The gentlemanly capitalists saw empire as a "means of generating income" in acceptable ways, protected and promoted by the government.[10]

Tory and Whig ministries dominated early nineteenth-century governments. While both were concerned with stability and aristocratic ideals, the Whigs also believed in gradual reform and had the support of the City and the rising manufacturing classes. Largely from the same class, British governmental leaders supported the gentlemanly perspective. Tories Lord Castlereagh and George Canning, for example, believed in developing trade links to Latin America. This connection, Cain and Hopkins concluded, also explains Lord Palmerston's "aggressive imperialism during the severe depression of the 1830s and 1840s[.]" It was meant to expand British markets and to keep the "lower" classes content and "at arm's length." This led Palmerston, a Whig, to argue for free trade, which he was willing to impose on "reluctant rulers, to evict recalcitrant ones, and to advance 'legitimate commerce' by putting down the slave trade." His philosophy was logical because "he inherited beliefs espoused by the gentlemanly elite[.]"[11] The RN was a natural instrument to aid such "gentlemanly" interests, but at all levels London adhered to a liberal policy of minimal interference overseas.

With only brief exceptions, such as during the Conservative administrations of Sir Robert Peel, George Canning and Palmerston dominated British foreign policy in this period. Canning was Foreign Secretary from 1822 to 1827, when he briefly became Prime Minister before his death. Thereafter,

---

[9]Cain and Hopkins, *British Imperialism*, 38-43, 47-51 and 122.

[10]*Ibid.*, 55-57 and 82-85.

[11]*Ibid.*, 46-48, 52, 99 and 246.

with brief interruptions from 1830, Palmerston was Foreign Secretary and then Prime Minister until his death in 1865. Both men placed Britain's interests first. Canning wanted to placate other nations, but he was willing to act at the proper moment to secure British commercial interests.[12] Palmerston followed in Canning's tradition but subscribed to a philosophy in foreign policy that was an "amalgam of progress and stability[.]"[13]

E.D. Steele concluded that Palmerston's use of force depended on circumstances. He was willing to use it, for example, against Brazil, Japan and China, but it was "not evident in his handling of relations with France and America[.]" This was because the commercial and public sectors wanted peace and stability. They wanted Britain to play a role in Europe but "expected to enjoy [this] without a war...[that] might jeopardize prosperity[.]"Consequently, Palmerston sought to use other states to counter larger powers. He used Turkey, for example, to counter Russia and supported the Greek independence movement. He realized that France "was the rival of Britain overseas and the greatest danger to British security." But rather than war, he believed that French power was better "checked by cooperation[.]"[14] Britain adhered to a liberal philosophy, protected its merchants from physical harm and promoted economic growth, but it also maintained a *laissez-faire* posture unless other countries threatened British interests.

The Empire of Free Trade and the Equatorial Atlantic

The Foreign Office was keen to create a supportive overseas environment for British merchants. Still, when speculative ventures went wrong, such as loan defaults in Latin America, London refused to intervene. Palmerston was sensitive to their plight but maintained his liberal policy. In 1848, for example, he told British representatives abroad that they were to be "earnest and friendly" in promoting the interests of British investors. Only under extreme circumstances, such as dramatic losses, would he bring such private matters into the

---

[12]Muriel E. Chamberlain, "Reading History: New Light on British Foreign Policy," *History Today*, XXXV (July 1985), 45-48; and Harold Temperley, *The Foreign Policy of Canning, 1822-1827: England, the Neo-Holy Alliance, and the New World* (London, 1925; 2nd ed., London, 1966), 42-45 and 447-475.

[13]Bourne, *Foreign Policy of Victorian England*, 29-32.

[14]E.D. Steele, *Palmerston and Liberalism, 1855-1865* (Cambridge, 1991), 5 and 8; and Charles K. Webster, *The Foreign Policy of Palmerston 1830-1841: Britain, the Liberal Movement and the Eastern Question* (2 vols., London, 1951), II, 784-786 and 792.

diplomatic realm.[15] Instead, Britain shifted to a free-trade mentality to further commercial development, moving away from securing exclusive access to markets. In the early 1820s, William Huskisson, the new Board of Trade President, renewed calls for tariff reductions to promote trade. Meanwhile, reciprocity treaties reduced the scope of the Navigation Acts, and in 1825 London extended the policy to specific British colonial "free" ports as long as other nations reciprocated.[16]

With Britain at the forefront of the Industrial Revolution, the capitalists wanted trade barriers lowered so they could buy cheap primary resources and "undersell continental rivals." Parliament enfranchised the "middle class" in 1832 through the first Reform Bill, and they too began to support the free-trade movement. By the 1840s the government lowered duties on wool and cotton imports and coal exports. By the early 1840s, one supporter of free trade was Sir Robert Peel, the Prime Minister. The 1848 continental revolutions made the government wary of innovation, but Peel obtained vague commitments from other powers, like Prussia and the US, to lower trade barriers if Britain repealed the Navigation Acts. This occurred on 13 June 1849, but the British coasting trade remained protected, and government retained the power to retaliate if any country failed to grant British shipping similar concessions.[17]

Economically and strategically, Britain founded a new empire "to obtain a commercial end[.]"[18] Figure 2.1 shows the increase in total British commerce during the early nineteenth century; exports, for example, reached

---

[15]Bourne, *Foreign Policy of Victorian England*, 3-4; and Great Britain, National Archives (TNA/PRO), Foreign Office (FO) 83/110, Palmerston's Circular to British Representatives Abroad, 15 January 1848.

[16]Bernard Semmel, *The Rise of Free Trade Imperialism: Classical Political Economy, the Empire of Free Trade, and Imperialism, 1750-1850* (Cambridge, 1970), 218; and Imlah, *Economic Elements*, 17 and 3-14. The Navigation Laws applied to cargo imported into Britain and covered the European, colonial, African, Asian, American and coastal trades, as well as the fisheries. Traders had to bring goods directly to Britain in "British" (including colonial) ships; the vessels also had to be British-built and owned, and the master and three-quarters of the crew had to be British. See Sarah Palmer, *Politics, Shipping and the Repeal of the Navigation Laws* (Manchester, 1990), 41-42, 50-53 and 74-80.

[17]Ralph Davis, *The Industrial Revolution and British Overseas Trade* (Leicester, 1979), 62; Semmel, *Free Trade Imperialism*, 139-141; Reynolds, *Command of the Sea*, 329-330; Imlah, *Economic Elements*, 15; and Palmer, *Politics*, 98-113 and 154-163. For a broader discussion of the economic issues, see Peter Mathias, *The First Industrial Nation: An Economic History of Britain, 1700-1914* (London, 1969; 2nd ed., London, 1983).

[18]Semmel, *Free Trade Imperialism*, 150 and 157.

£125.1 million by 1861. As tables 2.3 and 2.4 show, trade between Britain and the US became the most valuable. Commerce with Africa and Latin America also expanded, although the latter stagnated after the 1820s. Still, British trade with all regions grew in the decade following Peel's reforms. The US, the West Indies, Latin America and Africa, on opposite sides of the Atlantic, were important regions in Britain's economic web where London hoped to balance economic interests with the need for peace and stability.

Figure 2.1: British Exports, Imports and Re-exports 1815-1861 (£ millions)

Note: Computed or declared values.

Source: Based upon data from B.R. Mitchell (ed.), *British Historical Statistics* (Cambridge, 1988), 451, External Trade, tables 2 and 3.

The British had important colonial interests in the Caribbean. Until emancipation in 1833, slave-produced crops fuelled Britain, but trade with the West Indies was generally in decline. Nonetheless, in the 1820s London wanted to secure access to other parts of Latin America. A deeper analysis of the motives behind these statistics reveals that, despite its stagnation, gentlemanly capitalists hoped for commercial expansion in the region. Often ignoring the lower classes, they believed that the demands of their gentlemanly counterparts represented the entire population and that Central and South Americans would buy large quantities of British goods. Upper-class Britons created an image of opportunity, although the region's population was too poor to purchase many British commodities. In 1829, Reverend Robert Walsh, for example, visited shops in Villa Rica, Minas Geraes, and reported them "filled with cotton goods from Manchester, broadcloths from Yorkshire, stockings from Nottingham, hats from London [and] cutlery from Sheffield[.]" But Platt concluded that "[m]any travellers, consuls or commercial men were by class and temperament disinclined to visit local markets and examine the goods on display." Instead, they visited gentlemanly shops along the main plazas that serviced local elites who demanded the same luxury goods as did the visitors.[19]

Table 2.3
Select British Export Destinations, 1814-1856 (£ '000)

Years	Africa	US	West Indies	Latin America
1814-1816	353	7348	6906	2476
1824-1826	372	5695	4123	5009
1834-1836	967	9438	4117	5047
1844-1846	1368	7162	3866	5634
1854-1856	2623	20,078	3947	8974

Source: Ralph Davis, *The Industrial Revolution and British Overseas Trade* (Leicester, 1979), 89.

Table 2.4
Select British Import Sources, 1814-1856 (£ '000)

Years	Africa	US	West Indies	Latin America
1814-1816	703	3976	16656	6227
1824-1826	681	6061	8577	3109
1834-1836	2017	13223	7946	3380
1844-1846	2898	14058	5937	4905
1854-1856	5218	30282	8709	9698

Source: Davis, *Industrial Revolution*, 93.

---

[19]D.C.M. Platt, *Latin America and British Trade 1806-1914* (London, 1972), 3-9 and 18; and Cain and Hopkins, *British Imperialism*, 18.

Latin America looked like an avenue for gentlemanly expansion, but in reality supply outpaced demand. British merchants flooded the region with a variety of commodities. John Luccock, a Rio merchant, received wallets, but exclaimed that such items were useless as there was no paper money. Large quantities of clothing were found through South America. One merchant company shipped 40,000 dresses to Lima on consignment, hoping for a profit. The British Committee of Merchants exemplified the elite's narrow analysis. The Committee opined in 1824 that Argentina lived on British imports. Still, Platt calculated that British merchants based their assessment on only a narrow sampling of places with which they dealt. By ignoring the non-elites, they overestimated the true demand.[20] But hopes and dreams encouraged interest in these regions and shaped diplomatic and naval relations. In Latin America, however, Anglo-American interests were likely to clash because of the proximity of US and British concerns and the collapsing Spanish-American Empire, with its last strongholds in strategically important Cuba and Puerto Rico.

With the homeland in chaos during the Napoleonic wars, the Spanish colonies in America declared their independence and launched privateers, while pirates took advantage of the turmoil to plunder trade. As David J. Starkey noted, the end of major Atlantic-wide conflict in 1815 exacerbated piracy as unemployed seafarers searched for work.[21] Consequently, throughout the period regional piracy matched John L. Anderson's types: it was part of the local economic system (intrinsic); connected with the degree of trade (parasitic); and linked with trade disruption (episodic).[22] As the South American wars of independence unfolded, pirates attacked local shipping in an organized manner and sold their plundered wares in the regional marketplace.[23] Robert Ritchie remarked that as the Atlantic economy expanded, and goods became more readily available, pirates conflicted with national goals.[24] Meanwhile,

---

[20]Platt, *Latin America and British Trade*, 21-25.

[21]David J. Starkey, "Pirates and Markets," in Lewis R. Fischer (ed.), *The Market for Seamen in the Age of Sail* (St. John's, 1994), 59-61.

[22]John L. Anderson, "Piracy and World History: An Economic Perspective on Maritime Predation," *Journal of World History*, VI, No. 2 (1995), 180-194.

[23]Mark C. Hunter, "Piraten im Golf von Mexiko im frühen 19. Jahrhundert," in Hartmut Roder (ed.), *Piraten – Abenteuer oder Bedrohung?* (Bremen, 2002), 52-65.

[24]Robert C. Ritchie, *Captain Kidd and the War against the Pirates* (Cambridge, MA, 1986), 12. See also Ritchie, "Government Measures against Pirates and Privateering in the Atlantic Area, 1750-1850," in David J. Starkey, E.S. van Eyck van Heslinga and J.A. de Moor (eds.), *Pirates and Privateers: New Perspectives on the War on Trade in the Eighteenth and Nineteenth Centuries* (Exeter, 1997), 10-28. But

Marcus Rediker, although also studying earlier pirate life, concluded that authorities wanted pirates policed because they had established themselves in opposition to the interests of the ascending capitalist society.[25] But Spain was too weak to prevent its American colonies from rebelling, continued the wars and refused to recognize them. Guatemala declared its independence in 1821; Mexico and the Central American states in 1823; followed by Argentina, Chile, Venezuela, Bolivia, Peru and Paraguay. The disputes drew in both the US and Britain because Cuba and Puerto Rico were strategically important, and the Spanish upheavals threatened yet another revolution that would draw in conservative Europeans.[26] Still, a positive image enticed Britain to exploit regional problems to secure access to markets and keep rivals at bay. Latent British mercantilism conditioned diplomacy and naval policy, and London wanted to limit the options of the other powers.

Kenneth Bourne has surmised that Canning feared the rise of the US, which was rapidly becoming a competitor in the region. Cuba was of particular concern because its strategic location gave any nation controlling it the power to threaten trade passing through the region. Canning also feared France and the US combining their naval power against Britain. Consequently, Bourne concluded that London wanted to defend its interests in the West Indies against American expansion by seeking to lock Washington into diplomatic commitments and circumventing any reason for the other European powers to flex their muscles as shipping came under pirate and privateer attacks. Therefore, Britain avoided too much pressure, such as occupying Cuba to stop piracy or being too forceful with local Spanish authorities over privateers. The same was true of British policy toward the Cuban slave trade. Too much force might drive the island from weaker Spain into US hands, posing a greater threat to British interests.[27] Samuel Flagg Bemis believed that London wished to main-

---

Ritchie dealt almost exclusively with the eighteenth century and concluded with the end of privateering after the Crimean War.

[25]Marcus Rediker, *Between the Devil and the Deep Blue Sea: Merchant Seamen, Pirates, and the Anglo-American Maritime World, 1700-1750* (Cambridge, 1987), 261-262.

[26]Modelski and Thompson, *Seapower*, 273; Jay Kinsbruner, *Independence in Spanish America: Civil Wars, Revolutions, and Underdevelopment* (Albuquerque, NM, 1994), 5-37, 46-69 and 81-100; Richard Pennell, "State Power in a Chronically Weak State: Spanish Coastguards as Pirates, 1814-50," *European History Quarterly*, XXV, No. 3 (1995), 353-355; and Jennifer Marx, *Pirates and Privateers of the Caribbean* (Malabar, FL, 1992), 267-268.

[27]Bourne, *Britain and the Balance of Power in North America*, 64-66; and Andrew D. Lambert, *Trincomalee: The Last of Nelson's Frigates* (London, 2002), 56-59.

tain a balance-of-power strategy in the region to keep other powers at bay while Britain solidified its hold over regions gained during the last war, its merchants accessed markets and its ships cornered maritime trades.[28]

West Africa was another region in the equatorial Atlantic which concerned the "free traders." African supplies to Britain would only increase if force was used to shift factors of production from the profitable slave trade to legitimate commodities. Indeed, there were alternatives to the slave trade within the African economy. The lubricant industry, for example, could use palm oil, which would transform the African palm oil trade. To this end, the strategy was to "draw Africa into Britain's sphere of influence by the creation of economic linkages and the development of dependent African economies" – in other words, by creating an informal empire.[29]

British trade with West Africa grew along with the Industrial Revolution. Industrialization in Britain demanded "legitimate" African goods. British participation in West African trade was limited initially to rich entrepreneurs who could afford to bear the risks involved. Exports from British West Africa to the UK rose from £252,814 in 1854 – largely composed of palm oil (40.2 percent) and timber (36.4 percent) – to £1,099,256 in 1884, mainly palm oil (53.9 percent) and nuts for oil (25.9 percent). At the same time, the establishment of regular steamship connections led to a marked change in British mercantile activities along the coast. Regular steam routes meant that merchants could arrange for a quicker turnover in merchandise and smaller inventories.

---

[28]Samuel Flagg Bemis, *A Diplomatic History of the United States* (New York, 1936; 5th ed., New York, 1965), 203.

[29]Ronald Robinson and John Gallagher, *Africa and the Victorians: The Official Mind of Imperialism* (London, 1961; 2nd ed., London, 1981), 1-8; Martin Lynn, "The 'Imperialism of Free Trade' and the Case of West Africa, c. 1830-c. 1870," *Journal of Imperial and Commonwealth History*, XV, No. 1 (1986), 24; and Hugh Thomas, *The Slave Trade: The Story of the Atlantic Slave Trade, 1440-1870* (New York, 1997), 564-565. For details of African political economy, see Joseph C. Miller, *Way of Death: Merchant Capitalism and the Angolan Slave Trade 1730-1830* (Madison, WI, 1988), 43-54 and 104-106. The Robinson and Gallagher thesis of an informal, free-trade empire in Africa has been controversial. Lynn believed that they were too prone to see early British activity in Africa in terms of the scramble that ensued later in the century and concluded that policy in London was different from what occurred in Africa. There was British "commercial penetration" but little control. British power was limited; the navy lacked the ability "to strike inland." The Ashanti people were the true power until the 1870s and defeated the British in 1806, 1823-1824, 1863 and 1869. For more on the Robinson and Gallagher debate, see William Roger Louis (ed.), *The Robinson and Gallagher Controversy* (New York, 1976).

Moreover, it freed them from the need to manage both the shipping and trading aspects of their businesses.[30]

Official Britain, however, had little desire for direct control over West Africa. Abolitionists convinced the government to establish colonies at Sierra Leone (1808), Gambia (1816) and the Gold Coast (1821), but only as centres from which legitimate commerce would replace the slave trade.[31] Elsewhere, the British signed free-trade and anti-slave trade treaties but policed the latter only with the permission of other countries. The goal was to protect British merchants, promote legitimate commerce and "achieve a virtual industrial monopoly for" Britain under the protection of the RN.[32] Such mercantile and shipping activities along the West African coast suited British foreign policy. Freely traded goods from the African coast fed British industry without the expense of formal colonies.

The RN thus held the "keys" to world trade routes for the gentlemanly capitalists. Gough opined that the power of the RN allowed London the special ability to protect trade, police any it deemed illegal and encourage the development of new avenues of growth that could be tapped by the British even if developed by others. Thus, Britain seized strategically important regions along important trade routes, locations like Lagos, Hong Kong, the Falkland Islands, Singapore and Aden.[33] The strategy employed would, Bourne asserted, keep the trade of non-Western nations open to outsiders, although the RN would ensure that Britain had preferential access over its rivals.[34] Nevertheless, it would take a concerted effort to rally international support to end the slave trade. If other countries, like the US, refused to let the RN stop their slave trade, it could only be suppressed if that nation then deployed a naval force to police its own citizens.

---

[30]Peter N. Davies, "Shipping and Imperialism: The Case of British West Africa," in Gordon Jackson and David M. Williams (eds.), *Shipping, Technology and Imperialism* (Aldershot, 1996), 48-61 and table 2.1.

[31]Philip D. Curtin, *The Image of Africa: British Ideas and Action, 1780-1850* (Madison, WI, 1964), 468-470; and Robinson and Gallagher, *Africa and the Victorians*, 27-30.

[32]Semmel, *Free Trade Imperialism*, 150 and 157.

[33]Gough, "Profit and Power," 71; Davis, *Industrial Revolution*, 10 and 65-69; and Kennedy, *Rise and Fall of the Great Powers*, 187-200.

[34]Bourne, *Foreign Policy of Victorian England*, 4-5.

British Naval Strategy and Deployment

Britain therefore used sea power during the early nineteenth century to meet its strategic and economic needs. Economic growth, policy and strategic interest conditioned naval deployment, and the "triangular struggle" between domestic, foreign and naval matters dictated naval policy in this period. British politicians agreed that the nation had to maintain a navy that could counter its two or three largest rivals. Although the RN was deployed around the world, the thrust of British strategy was directed toward India and providing safe passage through the Mediterranean and around the Cape.[35] Regardless, C.J. Bartlett concluded that the navy was also useful to Canning and Palmerston because it could be applied to the problems they encountered without exceeding the economic restraints or violating the wishes of Parliament.[36] Andrew Lambert has pointed out that when relations with Russia and France were good, "ships could then be sent to more distant stations."[37]

Cain and Hopkins concluded that Britain's "Blue Water" strategy flowed from this gentlemanly perspective. The role of the RN was defensive: to "prevent France from blockading her [Britain's] trade with the continent and to frustrate any attempt at invasion." But Britain also realized that it could never "control continental Europe" and used its naval power to compensate.[38] In the wake of peace, Britain abandoned few of its colonies and used the RN to exert influence over new regions. British "free traders" wanted access to places like Africa and Central America.[39] Paul Kennedy concluded that naval officers, diplomats, traders and financiers were key to advancing Britain's economic objectives. But the RN was the "stick" that enforced the benefits of commercial trade.[40]

---

[35]C.J. Bartlett, *Great Britain and Sea Power* (Oxford, 1963), 1-2 and 34; and Jan Glete, *Navies and Nations: Warships, Navies and State Building in Europe and America, 1500-1860* (2 vols., Stockholm, 1993), I, 426-432.

[36]Bartlett, *Great Britain and Sea Power*, 63-64, 101, 116-123, 136, 144 and 277.

[37]Andrew D. Lambert, *The Last Sailing Battlefleet: Maintaining Naval Mastery, 1815-1850* (London, 1991), 52.

[38]Cain and Hopkins, *British Imperialism*, 89-90.

[39]Glete, *Navies and Nations*, I, 426-432; and Richard Harding, *Seapower and Naval Warfare 1650-1830* (London, 1999), 36.

[40]Paul Kennedy, *The Rise and Fall of British Naval Mastery* (London, 1976), 150-154.

In periods when the elite came to believe in overseas expansion, those with influence over naval policy also favoured its protection. Lord Ellenborough, Peel's First Lord of the Admiralty, for example, believed in the RN's traditional peacetime role of commerce protection and, having been Governor-General of India, knew the importance of "distant stations" to England's well-being. In the face of the French threat, and the crisis with the US over Oregon, he advocated a show of strength. But Lord Aberdeen, the Foreign Secretary, wanted tensions reduced, and Peel believed that he could manage disputes with America. John Russell's appointee, Lord Auckland, and Palmerston in the Foreign Office continued British strategy.[41]

British liberals believed that trade would replace war, and the concept culminated during the *Pax Britannica*. While Britain was a powerful nation with a strong navy, imposing its will on other nations unilaterally invited military or economic retaliation that would harm trade. Because of Britain's distant colonial holdings and "commercial interests," it was in its interest to maintain peace. Albert Imlah has concluded that Britain's commercial interests dictated "moderate policies," and the nation's role "in the Concert of Powers was, therefore, essentially a mediating one."[42] "Grand Strategy" considerations went alongside those of commerce. For example, Britain's trade with the US was important but could be hurt, along with other markets, if Britain held steadfastly to old ideas. Therefore, by 1856 and the Declaration of Paris, the "New Rule" had replaced mercantilist naval practices. Most nations, except the US, rejected privateering, and shipping free of "contraband" was finally free from naval harassment. Palmerston told a gathering of Liverpool merchants that the "New Rule" meant that war would be limited to battles between professional government forces that left private commerce alone. The subtle influence of the navy was the preferred way to implement policy and maintain watch on other nations.[43]

The RN's Atlantic deployment pattern reveals the dynamics of British geopolitical and economic considerations (see figure 2.2). Immediately following the Napoleonic wars, RN vessels in the Atlantic were concentrated along the North American coast and in the West Indies. But the Mediterranean was fast becoming its focus. Deployment along the West African coast also grew and peaked in the 1840s and 1850s. Economic factors shaped the pattern of deployment in the Gulf of Mexico and along the African coast. Later analysis will reveal the nexus of British goals and how they affected Anglo-American

---

[41]Lambert, *Last Sailing Battlefleet*, 38-39, 47-48 and 50-54.

[42]Imlah, *Economic Elements*, 5-6.

[43]Kennedy, *British Naval Mastery*, 200-201; and Bernard Semmel, *Liberalism and Naval Strategy: Ideology, Interest, and Sea Power during the Pax Britannica* (Boston, 1986), 4, 8-10, 18-23 and 53-57.

relations in the equatorial Atlantic. Because of the overall strategy, Britain used sea power to expand its economic interests, but it modified its use when it threatened American sensitivities.

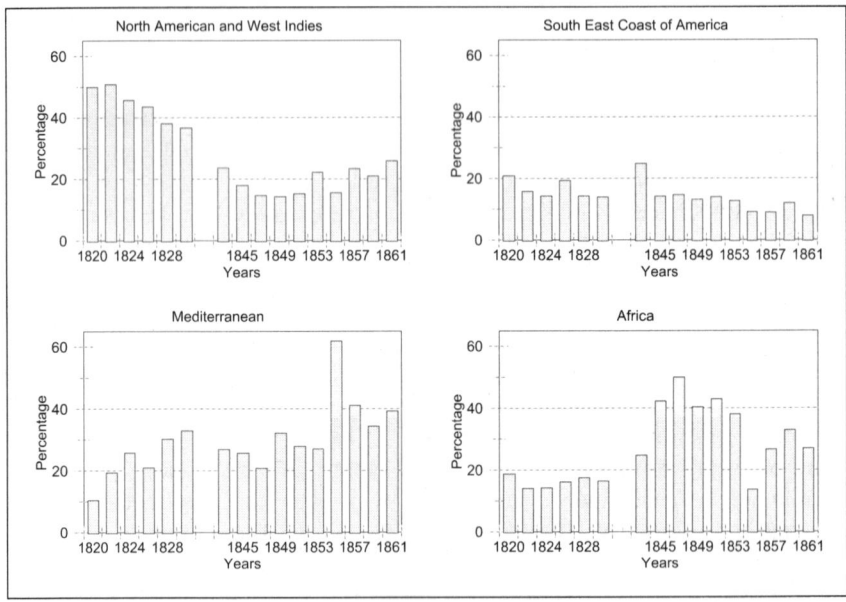

Figure 2.2:   Royal Navy Deployment, Atlantic, 1820-1830 and 1843-1861 (Percent of Ships)

Note: Vessel deployment in British home waters excluded.

Source: Calculated from TNA/PRO, Navy List, 1820-1861.

American Maritime Policy

Within the equatorial Atlantic, the West Indies, West Africa and the US were important to British economic power. While the British moved towards free trade, the Americans turned increasingly to coastal commerce, while its industrialists favoured protectionism. The foci of British and American maritime policy differed. This is significant because it helped to shape the American use of sea power. While American commerce also needed protection in these regions, it was the RN which protected the US from any European disturbances, freeing the Americans to invest instead in domestic economic development and to encourage foreign investment. In return, the British hoped that the US would work in concert on issues of common interest.[44]

While British gentlemanly capitalists believed in overseas development, Americans turned increasingly inward in the antebellum years. Unlike in Britain, there was little continuity of support for overseas American economic expansion. US deep-sea trade suffered from 1821 as Northern factories demanded greater volumes of cotton, thus feeding the coastal trade, which by 1831 had "supplanted foreign trade as the major activity of the merchant marine." Of the "distant trades," the most profitable was in the Pacific, especially with China. In the 1850s a vessel sailing from New York to California could make $80,000 in one voyage, and then earn another $50,000 by carrying tea to London from Hong Kong. In contrast, African commerce was a minuscule percentage of total American trade. While it almost doubled from 1840 to 1860, it still represented only about one percent by 1860.[45]

The North benefited from the growth in shipping before 1807 and developed insurance companies and business capital. When the re-export trade began to decline, Northern merchants shifted to cotton, and New York became the centre, dependent for its prosperity on the South. Meanwhile, New Orleans gained prominence for goods exported via the Mississippi, Missouri and Ohio rivers. The English textile industry demanded cotton, and from 1815 to the Civil War the Southern economy was largely based on this commodity.[46]

The US in 1817 enacted its own Navigation Act which required that imports be carried in American vessels or ships owned by the exporting country. Yet this policy could be lifted if another nation placed US shipping on an equal footing to its own. But the most significant aspect of the Navigation Act was the prohibition on the involvement of foreign vessels in the American coasting trade. As H. David Bess and Martin T. Farris concluded, "this formal

---

[44]Kennedy, *Rise and Fall of the Great Powers*, 229-230; and K. Jack Bauer, "The Golden Age," in Robert A. Kilmarx (ed.), *America's Maritime Legacy: A History of the U.S. Merchant Marine and Shipbuilding Industry since Colonial Times* (Boulder, CO, 1979), 27-36.

[45]Bauer, "Golden Age," 45 and 57-59; and Bauer, *A Maritime History of the United States: The Role of America's Seas and Waterways* (Columbia, SC, 1988), 84-92. On the China trade, see Paul E. Fontenoy, "Ginseng, Otter Skins, and Sandalwood: The Conundrum of the China Trade," *The Northern Mariner/Le Marin du Nord*, VII, No. 1 (1997), 1-16. Fontenoy concluded that "American attempts to penetrate this mythical market relied on massive exploitation of every opening, leading to market saturation and collapse, whereupon the cycle was repeated with a new commodity."

[46]Bauer, "Golden Age," 45 and 57-59; and Douglass C. North, *The Economic Growth of the United States, 1790 to 1860* (Englewood Cliffs, NJ, 1961), 62-71.

reservation of the coastal traffic known as cabotage provided the so-called first pillar of modern U.S. maritime policy."[47]

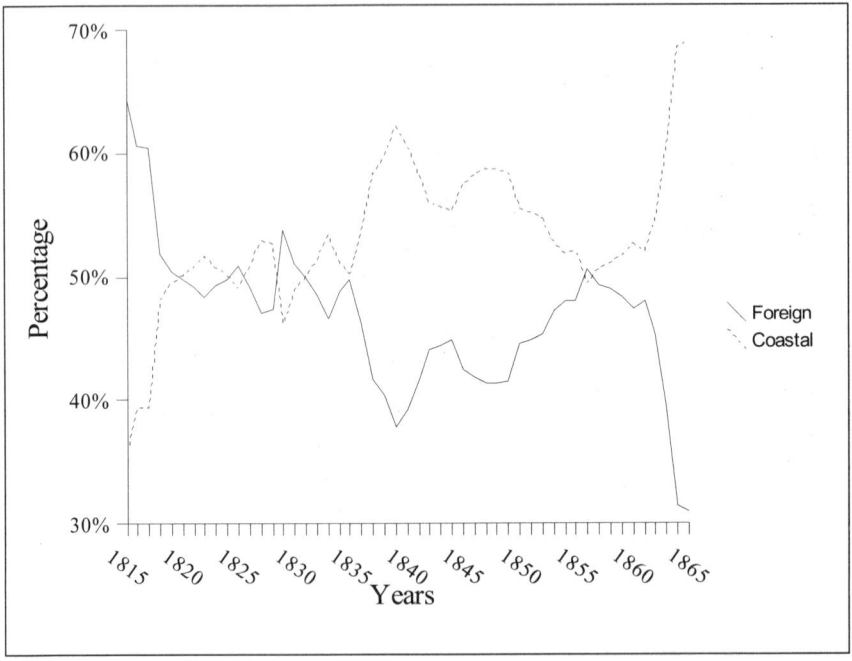

Figure 2.3:   American Maritime Trade, 1815-1865 (Percent of Registered Tonnage)

Note: Totals include vessels involved in whaling and the cod and mackerel trades. These trades composed less than ten percent of the trades (and often less than five percent) and were therefore omitted from this graph.

Source: Calculated from Ben J. Wattenberg (ed.), *Statistical History of the United States from Colonial Times to the Present* (New York, 1976), 750, series Q 417-432.

American shipping turned away from the cross-trades to focus on the import, export and coasting trades. While shipowners in general liked free trade, the rising manufacturing sector supported protectionism. Former "maritime" states, such as Connecticut, Massachusetts, New Jersey and New York, became industrial and increasingly protectionist. The result was that "by the outbreak of the Civil War the United States had forsaken her maritime orienta-

[47]H. David Bess and Martin T. Farris, *U.S. Maritime Policy: History and Prospects* (New York, 1981), 17; and Bauer, *Maritime History*, 104-107 and 117.

tion." Improvements in Great Lakes' transportation and railway construction also increased east-west trade and led to the development of urban centres, like Chicago and Cincinnati, along strategically important routes.[48] The result for American shipping and trade was dramatic. As figure 2.3 shows, US ships increasingly were involved in the coastal trade. The pattern suggests three distinct periods: from 1815 to 1835, foreign trade declined; from 1835 to 1855, coastal trade dominated, although there was a new growth in foreign trade; and after 1855 there was a steep decline in foreign trade and a renewed rise in coastal shipping. These trends are significant because they paralleled the deployment of US naval assets and helped to shape Anglo-American naval relations. During the earliest period American naval assets were based close to home to the detriment of West African deployment. American interests in using sea power to further long-term West African interests peaked in the middle period but declined again when the home waters took on a renewed importance thereafter. In periods of overseas decline, Americans who supported Atlantic expansion feared that the opportunity cost of neglect was British dominance.

America's Naval Policy

The pattern of American economic growth affected its use of sea power. US shipping during this period concentrated on the coastal trades, and foreign expansion was largely in non-British possessions. Consequently, the US was more concerned about its strategic and commercial interests close to home and in the Pacific. American naval policy focused on trade protection and reacted to any threats. The occasional calls for naval support for non-trading issues usually foundered on the American fear of a strong military, dislike of colonies and worries about becoming involved in European disputes. US naval policy was inconsistent, waxing and waning with temporary threats and the desires of individual leaders who supported its use for longer-term goals.

Figure 2.4 reveals that the general trend of US naval deployment from 1820 to 1860 was either close to home or in the Pacific. Sudden changes in deployment were to meet immediate threats, such as during the piracy crisis of the 1820s (chapters 3 and 4) and the Mexican War in the mid-1840s (chapter 7). There was a sudden decline in the Pacific in 1858 as Washington moved warships to home waters and South America to meet threats during diplomatic disputes with Paraguay and Britain (chapter 8). As Robert S. Wood has noted, in the absence of any clear threat, "U.S. naval developments will be determined by the resources allocated, the object of political-military engagements,

---

[48]North, *Economic Growth*, 77, 135-146 and 153; and Bauer, "Golden Age," 45 and 57-59. For more details on general economic developments in the US in this period see, for example, Stuart W. Bruchey, *Enterprise: The Dynamic Economy of a Free People* (Cambridge, MA, 1990).

and doctrines concerning the use of force – all of which are probably less determined by international anarchy and specific external challenges than by the
character of the regime."[49]

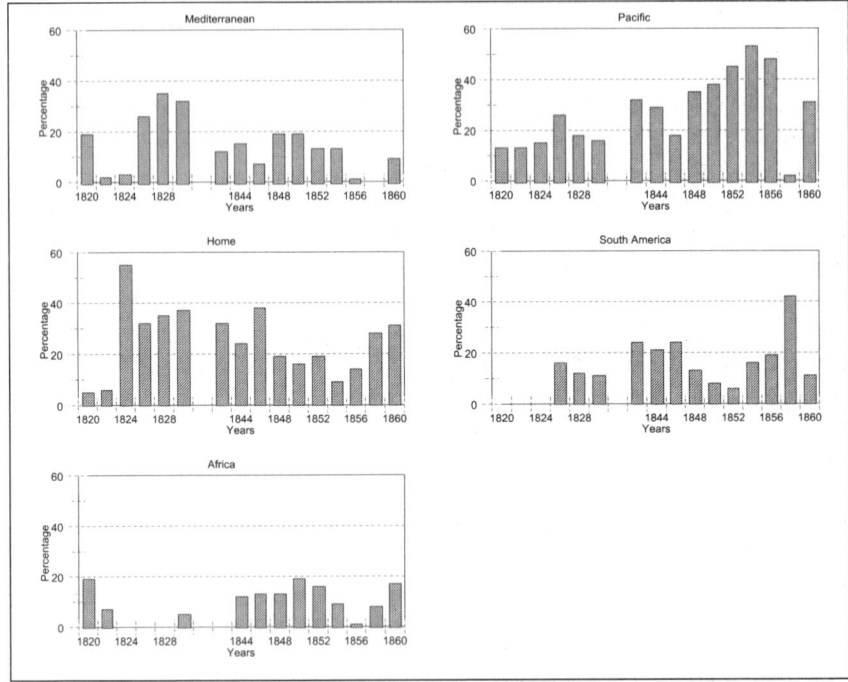

Figure 2.4: US Navy Deployment, 1820-1830 and 1842-1860 (Percentage of Ships)

Source: Calculated from United States, *Annual Reports of the Secretary of the
                Navy* (Washington, DC, 1820-1860).

US naval deployment during this era of relative peace reflected the
goal of using force to protect trade. During peacetime, warships sailed in the
Mediterranean, along Latin American coasts and in the Pacific in support of
American interests. The objective was to use battleships only to counter any
potential British blockade of its coast. Jan Glete has concluded that the "pre-
1812 navalist ambitions of using the battle fleet as a force to influence European power politics proved unrealistic in an age when Great Britain ruled the
oceans." Instead, the primary duty of the US Navy (USN) was "policing ac-

---

[49]Robert S. Wood, "Domestic Factors, Regime Characteristics, and Naval
Forces," in John B. Hattendorf (ed.), *Doing Naval History: Essays toward Improvement* (Newport, RI, 1995), 70.

tivities against much weaker nations or to fight trade warfare against the only nation that had a superior navy that mattered, Great Britain."[50]

Before the Civil War, the main role of the USN was to protect American lives and commerce. Over time the government began to use it to initiate trade contacts, collect scientific and commercial information and undertake diplomacy. But the Navy Department lacked consistent leadership to advocate expansion. While commerce and shipping grew, the US remained tied commercially to traditional markets in Europe and North America. Yet some Americans believed that their destiny lay in the Pacific and advocated a larger navy and commercial expansion.[51]

The "Navalists," largely from the North, wanted the navy to suppress piracy, "show the flag" and protect US economic and political interests overseas. But Thomas Jefferson's Republican party rejected a strong navy and promoted agrarian expansion. When Jefferson won the presidency in 1800, he focused only on coastal forts, floating batteries and gunboats. After the War of 1812 Americans began to promote commerce through diplomatic means. Leaders like John Quincy Adams worked to acquire new territory within North America, such as Florida, and to promote America's Pacific interests.[52] President Andrew Jackson, an "agrarian" Democrat, epitomized the naval philosophy of the period. He concluded that the "wide seas" that protected the US meant that only a small navy to patrol the home waters was required.[53]

The main goal of the USN was exploration and commerce protection. In this context, Secretary of the Navy Samuel L. Southard, for example, sent individual warships on survey cruises in the Pacific. In 1833 the Secretary reported that the navy had extended its "intercourse" with the Portuguese and African coasts. Furthermore, American warships had made cruises to the Indian Ocean, while the West Indies squadron became more of a "home squadron," with parts of it making annual visits to "Atlantic ports." Still, in March 1836 the Board of Navy Commissioners and the Secretary of the Navy pro-

---

[50]Glete, *Navies and Nations*, I, 439-440.

[51]John H. Schroeder, *Shaping a Maritime Empire: The Commercial and Diplomatic Role of the American Navy, 1829-1861* (Westport, CT, 1985), 3-5.

[52]Craig L. Symonds, *Navalists and Antinavalists: The Naval Policy Debate in the United States, 1785-1827* (Newark, DE, 1980), 11-19; and Harold Sprout and Margaret Sprout, *The Rise of American Naval Power, 1776-1918* (Princeton, 1939; reprint, Annapolis, 1970) 12, 54-55, 71 and 107-111. See also Spencer C. Tucker, *The Jefferson Gunboat Navy* (Columbia, SC, 1993), 10-35; and Schroeder, *Shaping a Maritime Empire*, 13-18.

[53]TNA/PRO, Admiralty (ADM) 7/712, "Extract from the President's Message, December 1830," 4 January 1831.

posed a focus on the defence of the Gulf of Mexico, the Mississippi Valley and other commercial routes close to home waters.[54] John H. Schroeder has argued that American naval policy adhered "to a traditional view that the navy was responsible for combating pirates, preserving neutral rights, and responding to the periodic outrages" rather than actively aiding in the expansion of US commerce.[55] By the late 1830s and early 1840s, however, the US began to use sea power to further its long-term economic goals.

Secretary of the Navy Abel P. Upshur became the strongest American advocate of the use of sea power not only to protect commerce but also to advance long-term US commercial interests. American outposts along the Chilean coast, on the Columbia River and in Upper California needed protection. He told Congress that countries like Britain and France had large navies to support their commercial endeavours. In 1842 he called for a stronger naval force in the Pacific "to prevent other nations, particularly Britain, from subjecting our trade to injurious restrictions and embarrassments." But even Upshur focused on home waters. He argued that the Gulf of Mexico, including states along the Mississippi and its tributaries, was important to national trade. In additional, he warned that most trade passed through the Gulf of Florida and that steam frigates could blockade it. Therefore, he concluded that "if we be without a naval force, that commerce may be annihilated at a cost which would not be felt by any tenth-rate maritime power!"[56]

On the eve of the Civil War, US naval strategy was little different from what it had been during the War of 1812. Opponents of a strong navy quelled calls for naval expansion. But a shift in US policy came with the election in 1857 of James Buchanan, a Democrat who supported his party's 1856 platform that called for freedom of the seas, free trade and rigid enforcement of the Monroe Doctrine. But Secretary of the Navy Isaac Toucey assured Congress that the executive was not pushing for a large peacetime navy to compete with "commercial powers." The resulting Buchanan policy was therefore reactive, responding to crises using the small USN. Moreover, Northern anti-

---

[54]*Ibid.*, "Extract of the Report" [of the Secretary of the Navy, 30 November 1833]; Schroeder, *Shaping a Maritime Empire*, 13-28 and 35-36; and Sprout and Sprout, *Rise of American Naval Power*, 12, 54-55 and 107-111.

[55]Schroeder, *Shaping a Maritime Empire*, 37-41. For examples of the exploring expeditions, see chapters 6-8; and Sprout and Sprout, *Rise of American Naval Power*, 123-150.

[56]Sprout and Sprout, *Rise of American Naval Power*, 118-120; United States, Congress, *Congressional Globe*, 27th Cong., 2nd sess., 1841-1842, appendix, 16-23, A.P. Upshur, "Report of the Secretary of the Navy, 4 December 1841;" and 27th Cong., 2nd sess., 1842-1843, appendix, 40-48, Upshur, "Report of the Secretary of the Navy, Navy Department, December 1842."

slavery advocates opposed an expanded shallow-draft navy solely for a slave South with expansionist goals.[57] With such divergent views, the USN only supported US commerce, particularly in the Pacific, and in regions where a minor crisis or short wars erupted. In contrast, the RN focused its attention on a variety of locations, but largely on the Mediterranean. Nevertheless, the problem for the British was to convince the Americans to dispatch warships to support British humanitarian and economic goals, such as the suppression of the slave trade, without precipitating war.

Anglo-American Economic Relations

The "dynamic" of the Atlantic economy involved the flows of trade, labour and capital, and on this there was broad agreement between the British and Americans. This probably kept the nations from going to war despite the fact that their diplomatic relations was more strained than their economic ties. Historians such as Allen and Thistlethwaite have concluded that a common culture, economy and political philosophy linked Britain and America. The British had obvious connections with the Northern intellectual and commercial class, while the South was linked with the old British Tory class that was "waning in force." A peaceful and stable US that encouraged foreign investment was thus important for the gentlemanly capitalists, who wanted to invest in America and reap the rewards of its development.[58]

Anglo-American economic ties connected the nations as trading partners and shaped their relations depending on circumstances. The cotton trade was important in the success of British ports such as Liverpool, and merchants on Merseyside developed close ties with merchant houses in New York and Philadelphia. British merchants settled in Philadelphia and New York, forming small British communities like Greenwich Village. By 1801, there was an American Chamber of Commerce in Liverpool. The US was also an exception to the British enforcement of the Navigation Laws. Under the Reciprocity Treaty of 1815, Britain allowed American ships to import US-produced goods into Britain without being subject to discriminatory duties.[59]

---

[57]Schroeder, *Shaping a Maritime Empire*, 63-65, 95-99, 117, 121-128, 130-132 and 188.

[58]Harry C. Allen, *Great Britain and the United States: A History of Anglo-American Relations (1783-1952)* (London, 1954; reprint, Hamden, CT, 1969), 101-121, 195 and 382-415; Frank Thistlethwaite, *The Anglo-American Connection in the Early Nineteenth Century* (Philadelphia, 1959), 172-175; and Platt, Foreign Finance, 140-171. See also the discussion in chapter 1 above.

[59]Thistlethwaite, *Anglo-American Connection*, 5-18 and 35-36; and Palmer, *Politics,* 41-45.

This treaty reflected the British reaction to growing US economic and shipping power after the War of 1812 and set the rules for trade and competition. Sarah Palmer has argued that reciprocity divided "Anglo-American business between the ships of the powers to the exclusion of other maritime nations" and allowed British shipowners to retain a "share of this business." Reciprocity was not free trade; Britain only allowed American ships to carry US exports to Britain, and British ships could only transport UK exports to America.[60] British access to the American coasting trade was prohibited, and talks to enable British vessels to deliver goods to California failed. While the British moved toward free trade, the US went in the opposite direction.[61] British and American economic philosophies would condition their relations at the diplomatic and naval levels, especially over piracy and slave-trade suppression.

The resulting trade flows reflected the focus of the US economy. Table 2.5 shows, among other things, that commerce with Africa was so insignificant that it failed to appear in the aggregate statistics. Meanwhile, exports to Cuba, Mexico, Canada and Asia grew. Nonetheless, Britain was the main destination; exports to the UK rose from US $123 million to US $694 million between 1821-1825 and 1856-1860. Table 2.6 reveals a similar pattern for imports into the US. Again, African imports were insignificant. Imports from Britain rose from US $152 million in the period 1821-1825 to US $602 million by 1856-1860. Cuba and Asia were the next most important sources.

Table 2.5
Select US Export Destinations, 1821-1860 (US $ millions)

Year	Canada	Cuba	Mexico	Britain	Asia	Africa
1821-1825	11	23	6	123	8	
1826-1830	11	28	20	117	7	
1831-1835	16	25	28	188	7	
1836-1840	18	30	18	274	6	
1841-1845	27	25	8	222	11	
1846-1850	40	28	11	349	13	
1851-1855	86	33	14	494	14	
1856-1860	128	51	19	694	26	

Note: Blanks indicate low value or no data. Wattenberg shows no exports to Africa before 1865.

Source: Wattenberg (ed.), *Statistical History of the United States*, 904, series U 317-334.

---

[60]Palmer, *Politics*, 53-54, 168-169 and 176-186.

[61]Allen, *Great Britain and the United States*, 75-77.

Table 2.6
Select US Import Sources, 1821-1860 ($ millions)

Year	Canada	Cuba	Mexico	Britain	Asia	Africa
1821-1825		33	1	152	41	
1826-1830		30	5	138	33	
1831-1835	5	44	5	220	45	
1836-1840	8	56	5	255	50	
1841-1845	4	38	5	178	40	
1846-1850	12	52	4	295	50	
1851-1855	41	89	5	564	88	
1856-1860	102	157	6	602	130	

Note: See table 2.5.

Source: Wattenberg (ed.), *Statistical History of the United States*, 907, series U 335-352.

The early nineteenth century also marked the beginning of a shift in Anglo-American economic relations. British shipments to the US fell from eighteen to ten percent of total British exports between 1825 and 1840, while US trade to Britain rose from thirteen to twenty-six percent of America's total exports. Allen believed that this marked a final shift in the Anglo-American balance of trade to American hands. Later, the proportion of total US exports that went to Britain fell by about twenty percent from 1880 to 1908. But this relative decline was in the context of rapid American economic growth and the penetration of new markets. For example, American exports to China increased by 126 percent between 1887 and 1897.[62]

The nineteenth century was a period of rapid economic growth in the US. European demand for American resources led to the increasing integration of the Atlantic economy. Cotton was the dominant American export, comprising over fifty percent before the Civil War. The need for virgin soil drove many in the South to call for the acquisition of Texas, Cuba and Mexico. It also fed the view that the Federal government had unnecessarily criminalized the slave trade. In such an atmosphere the White House, often sympathetic to the South, had little desire to pursue any substantial efforts to suppress the slave trade.[63] While there was an Anglo-American connection, it was tenuous, and their interests could clash easily. The US and Britain were trading part-

---

[62]*Ibid.*, 58-63.

[63]*Ibid.*, 54; and W.E. Burghardt Du Bois, *The Suppression of the African Slave-Trade to the United States of America, 1683-1870* (New York, 1896; reprint, New York, 1965), 151-158.

ners, but they also traded in common regions, like the Gulf of Mexico. Britain was overwhelmingly dominant elsewhere, especially in Africa. Meanwhile, some Americans wanted expansion into regions important to British interests.

After the War of 1812, Britain pursued a balance-of-power strategy in North America to keep the US from gaining Canadian resources and strategic points in the West Indies. On the American continent, this meant negotiating boundary settlements; in the West Indies, it implied limiting US influence. Meanwhile, the period was marked by the settlement of many Anglo-American territorial and trade issues. Relations improved on 29 September 1827 when the British made overtures to settle boundary problems. Meanwhile, Andrew Jackson's administration asked Britain if it would like to normalize US-West Indian trade. When the British agreed, on 29 May 1830 American ships were allowed back into West Indian ports. Talk rather than war also settled the Oregon boundary dispute, likely because the Americans wanted to devote their full attention to the conflict with Mexico rather than fight a two-front war. From 1849 to 1853, the Whigs governed the US, and relations with Britain were good. The Democrats, under Franklin Pierce and James Buchanan, were in power in the late 1850s, bringing some ripples to Anglo-American relations, but there was understanding on the British side.[64]

The British hoped to avoid conflict because, as Joshua Bates, a Barings' partner, noted during the Civil War, a long conflict would "be destructive of commerce and will materially reduce the profits of B.B. & Co."[65] British investment in the US during the early nineteenth century was small but concentrated in areas of potential growth. Backed by influential British banking houses like Baring Brothers, investment provided American banks with liquidity and railways with inexpensive capital. As one among many regions in the equatorial Atlantic for the gentlemanly capitalists, they desired stability to nurture their investments.[66] It was no coincidence, for example, that Peel dispatched Lord Ashburton, of the Baring family, to Washington in late 1841 to reduce Anglo-American tensions. To those ends, he concluded an agreement over naval cooperation in the equatorial Atlantic as a method to diffuse Anglo-American disputes over the application of sea power during peacetime.

---

[64]Allen, *Great Britain and the United States*, 101-121, 195, 336-340 and 382-415; Bourne, *Britain and the Balance of Power*, 53-69 and 85; Bourne, *Palmerston: The Early Years, 1784-1841* (New York, 1982), 577-580, 597 and 618-620; and Thistlethwaite, *Anglo-American Connection*, 172-175.

[65]Joshua Bates quoted in Platt, *Foreign Finance*, 147, fns. 35 and 48.

[66]Platt, *Foreign Finance*, 140-146 and appendix 3 show $300 million of British investment in 1852, peaking at between $400 and $500 million by 1857.

Anglo-American Naval Relations

In the decade after 1815 Britain was confident in its naval supremacy. While there was some concern about US naval intentions, most Britons believed that any threat could be managed. Yet some had been impressed by American ships in the War of 1812 and feared their potential if Washington undertook a major naval development. By the 1840s the Anglo-French naval rivalry had resumed and placed the nascent USN in a new perspective. But the French realized the benefit of allies and, wary of a repeat of the War of 1812, the Admiralty felt unease at the prospect of the French and Americans uniting once more against Britain. Consequently, it urged a "three-power standard" to match Russia, the US and France. Britain was concerned about other European powers and saw the USN as a threat during periods of tension. London dreaded facing all its enemies simultaneously, with the US and continental rivals aligned against it.[67]

While prepared to fight a war, London took special care to select squadron commanders, like Sir Charles Hotham (the main subject of chapter 6), with a reputation for cooperating with potential enemies and the tact to minimize conflict. I will show that sea power, while protecting commerce, provided a mechanism through which the nations could relate because they also used it to further long-term national objectives during peacetime. Britain and the US could use naval relations as forms of diplomacy that they could re-arrange or modify to defuse Anglo-American tension. American naval policy varied with the commitments of political leaders. Regardless, British leaders, united in their objectives, maintained watch on the US fleet.

From 1820 to 1842 a search of *The Times*, a newspaper with traditional connections to the elite, for general articles on the USN turned up about a dozen reports.[68] *The Times* reported on US naval construction and even manning problems. If anything, newspapers presented the British public with a picture of a small, infant force that was hardly a threat. *The Times* even concluded that Anglo-American naval relations were harmonious and probably would continue to be so in the future. A decade later it judged that the USN posed no threat to Britain.[69] Moreover, an article reprinted from the *Edinburgh Courant* remarked in early 1841 that Britain's steamships were superior and

---

[67]C.I. Hamilton, *Anglo-French Naval Rivalry 1840-1870* (Oxford, 1993), 1-13; and Bourne, *Foreign Policy of Victorian England*, 7-8 and 10.

[68]Martin Crawford, *The Anglo-American Crisis of the Mid-Nineteenth Century: The Times and America, 1850-1862* (Athens, GA, 1987), 17-19.

[69]*The Times* (London), 10 November 1820, 31 January 1823, 5 February 1827, 15 August 1828 and 7 July 1829.

"the Americans must plainly foresee, in a war with this country, the total destruction of their foreign trade."[70]

Official Admiralty assessments of the USN painted a similar picture.
In 1826 the Admiralty sent a naval officer to tour US naval facilities. He observed American naval construction but noted that some American officers
believed that naval expansion would founder due to a lack of sailors. Meanwhile, another RN officer observed in 1826 that the Americans thought that
their steamship, *Fulton*, was a failure. By 1838, the British had a low opinion
of the USN. The British ambassador at Washington concluded that "*I believe
that the United States are less prepared for War at this moment than they have
been at any previous period since the date of the Treaty of Ghent* [emphasis in
original]."[71]

With the USN largely believed to be impotent, Britain only became
wary of it during crises. For example, during a Canadian rebellion in the late
1830s the Admiralty received intelligence that the USN was preparing for war
and began to monitor the US fleet. Nevertheless, when the US did go to war,
for example with Mexico in the 1840s, London discovered that Washington
respected the rights of non-belligerents. Washington ordered its Gulf commander to continue the war with "vigour" but to "show every consideration to
neutral commerce." Although the Crimean War was a few years away, the
British saw the benefits of the emerging "New Rule" of the free-trade era and
peace with potential enemies.[72] Britain could manage the threat of the USN,
and this strategy fit well with British policy to interfere with other nations only
as a last resort to protect vital interests.

Conclusion

During the early nineteenth century, Britain and the US developed policies to
further and protect their commercial interests. The British elite hoped to promote overseas commerce peacefully in a more liberal trading environment.
The RN deployed to protect and further that objective. In contrast, American
commercial policy was largely directed inward; overseas commitments varied

---

[70]*Ibid.*, 6 October 1825. See also *Edinburgh Courant*, reprinted in *The Times*
(London), 10 April 1841.

[71]TNA/PRO, ADM 7/712, Admiral Sir Alexander Cochrane to Viscount Melville, 24 December 1826; Ambassador Fox, memo, 16 June 1838; William Gray,
memo, 12 July 1838; and "Extract from a Letter Received from Commander Crawford
Dulls...17 November 1838, on the State of the American Navy at New York."

[72]*Ibid.*, ADM 7/712, FO memo, 3 May 1839, "Extract of a Letter from the
Post Office Agent at Lisbon, dated 27 May 1839;" FO memo, 16 August 1841; and
Rear Admiral Sir George Seymour, 29 January 1848.

with the domestic climate and the views of individual leaders. But both countries had interests in the equatorial Atlantic, and their differing views about how best to pursue these created conditions in which tensions could rise. Americans were generally protectionists, and Britain feared that this different view of economic development could lead to trouble with the US, especially if it combined with another power during war. While bilateral relations were sometimes tense, it was in the best interests of both sides to maintain the peace and to resolve disputes in the equatorial Atlantic through methods short of war. The common view that sea power could be used to protect and develop their interests provided a mechanism through which both nations could relate and adjust their maritime polices peacefully.

Chapter 3
Anglo-American Policymaking, 1819-1834

British efforts to enlist American cooperation to suppress the slave trade originated in the war against piracy in the Gulf of Mexico in the 1820s. During that decade a consensus developed in the US to use sea power to protect trade from attack but left activities in West Africa largely to a private colonization society. Similarly, the British believed in diplomatic manoeuvres to achieve objectives in Latin America. Until Britain achieved its policy goals, London worked to protect commerce but softened its use of sea power for fear it would spark a conflict. Britain sought diplomatic cooperation with the US but remained suspicious that Washington wanted to seize Cuba. Nevertheless, London accepted American positions, such as the Monroe Doctrine, when they helped to further the larger British goal of warning off other European powers while securing access to Latin American markets. In the Gulf of Mexico, Britain and the US used their navies for commerce protection while leaving market access and expansion to diplomats. But they also began to use sea power to further long-term goals without resorting to war over their differences.

The Enlightenment ideas of free labour and support for the abolition of slavery were widespread in Britain. But the US clung to the slave system, and many Americans feared the consequences of African-American freedom. As a result, the status of the slave trade caused tension in Anglo-American relations as each pursued different policies. But Britain and America moved to reconcile their differences so that they could use sea power to further long-term goals in the equatorial Atlantic while reducing tension. The White House hoped to placate British demands to suppress US involvement in the slave trade but only took actions that were domestically acceptable, like dispatching single ships to the West African coast and providing limited support for colonization efforts to repatriate freed American slaves. In response, Britain decided to await the results rather than push for further action. The role of sea power in the equatorial Atlantic became a mechanism through which Britain and the US could resolve their disputes peacefully within the confines of their individual domestic and international interests.

British Policy and the Gulf of Mexico

In the wake of the European wars, the British believed that the use of sea power was a legitimate way to provide trade protection but left market access to merchants and diplomats. Consequently, while awaiting favourable conditions to recognize the rebel states, Britain moderated its policies to keep other European nations from intervening in Latin America. Although British interest in the region went back as far as the younger William Pitt, Britain was tied to its European commitments, and Spain refused to let Britain into colonial markets. Nonetheless, the British believed that friendship and trade with independent Latin American states was a way to circumvent Spain's mercantilist practices.[1] Although Britain played little part in the revolutions, Sir Home Popham attacked Buenos Aires in 1806 on his own initiative and precipitated an unwanted, if temporary, British occupation.

Popham was the son of the British consul in Tetuan, Joseph Popham. The Pophams returned to England where Joseph received a pension of £200 per year after being "made the scapegoat for the Government's inability to reach a reasonable relationship" with Emperor Ben Abdallah. Home moved in elite circles, attended Westminster School and was admitted to Trinity College, Cambridge, but it is unclear if he attended. Nevertheless, after the Buenos Aires affair, London merchants who hoped to penetrate South American markets when Napoleon blocked access to Europe supported him. Despite his court martial, the members of Lloyd's welcomed him as a hero.[2]

Meanwhile, when Napoleon threatened Portugal after invading Spain, Britain protected the Portuguese royal family as it sailed for Brazil; in return, it obtained a favourable trade agreement. Forcefully opening trade while at war was one thing, but during peacetime it was a delicate matter, although British merchants were supportive. Merchants replaced military leaders as Britain tried to develop trade with the Americas while hoping to prevent other powers, especially France, from gaining a foothold. But it was clear that foreign powers, even Spain, only entered Latin American waters with British permission. Even the revolutionary leader Simon Bolívar recognized in 1823 that Britain protected the rebel states from European interference.[3]

When liberal revolution rocked Spain in 1820, the US envoy to Britain, Richard Rush, was aware of the influence it might have on Spanish-American relations and dealings with Spain's South American colonies. Rush told Secretary of State John Quincy Adams that the Spanish revolution at-

---

[1]Charles K. Webster (ed.), *Britain and the Independence of Latin America, 1812-1830: Select Documents from the Foreign Office Archives* (2 vols., London, 1938; reprint, New York, 1970), I, 8-11.

[2]Hugh Popham, *A Damned Cunning Fellow: The Eventful Life of Rear-Admiral Sir Home Popham, KCB, KCH, KM, FRS, 1762-1820* (Tywardreath, 1991), 1-5 and 166-175.

[3]Webster (ed.), *Britain and the Independence of Latin America*, I, 8-11; and Samuel Flagg Bemis, *A Diplomatic History of the United States* (New York, 1936; 5th ed., New York, 1965), 203.

tracted great interest in England, in particular from merchants who urged the government to follow America's lead and recognize the rebel states. Rush concluded that despite British silence, the decision to open domestic ports to the new states spoke more loudly than words. But Britain, he concluded, had to consult with its Congress of Vienna allies before recognizing the new republics, and as things stood it seemed unlikely that it would grant formal recognition any time soon. When a Colombian representative asked Lord Londonderry to recognize the new state, he rejected the proposal, citing Britain's European commitments, and Echeverria told Rush that Londonderry surmised that the US was able to recognize the independence of the South American states because it was "freed from the incu[mbrance] of the Holy Alliance." But the British press, merchants and parliamentarians voiced increasingly loud concerns during the spring and summer of 1822 that Britain was not taking enough action against the pirates and privateers spawned by the turmoil. Rush concluded that it was unlikely that Britain could hold out much longer against this commercial interest aggregation.[4]

Britain did not want to provoke Spain and was reluctant to take aggressive action, especially against Spanish privateers. But the British still wanted to paint Spain as weak to heighten the stature of the rebels and increase the acceptability of recognition at home. Thus, London sat on the fence while British merchants and newspapers complained that the government's attitude hurt British trade and honour. But the growth of piracy began to harm the British trade that George Canning, the Foreign Secretary, wanted to expand. He told the Duke of Wellington that the conflict had "let loose a multitude of pirates and buccaneers, who lurk on the coasts and in the harbours of the Spanish Colonies." The pirates hid in Spanish-controlled territory, yet because of his overall strategy Canning was reluctant to take action. He told Wellington that Britain should accept Spain's weakness, press it no further and only take actions against pirates "where we experience the evil[.]"[5] Weak Spanish control over Cuba suited British goals best if Britain could not have the island itself.

Canning, once in the Foreign Offfice during the French Wars, later replaced Lord Castlereagh as Foreign Secretary. Canning opposed the Grand Alliance and the Concert of Europe. He espoused an "English" policy as op-

---

[4]United States, National Archives (NA), Record Group (RG) 59, General Records of the Department of State, Dispatches from United States Ministers to Great Britain, 1791-1906 (Dispatches, Britain), No. 116, Richard Rush to John Quincy Adams, 19 March 1820; No. 251, Rush to Adams, 10 June 1822; No. 254, Rush to Adams, 24 June 1822; and No. 257, Rush to Adams, 24 July 1822.

[5]Great Britain, National Archives (TNA/PRO), Foreign Office (FO) 92/48, reprinted in Webster (ed.), *Britain and the Independence of Latin America*, II, 73-75, George Canning to Duke of Wellington, 27 September and 15 October 1822.

posed to a "European" one and wanted to spur each nation to act independently and then use force at the right moment to secure British objectives. Canning wished to recognize the rebel Spanish-American states, gain access to their markets, use them to counter growing American military and economic power and bring them onto Britain's side if they were needed strategically. At the Congress of Verona in 1822, Canning instructed Wellington not to support any interference in Spain by the European powers. Canning wanted support from Cabinet, which included many members who were strongly anti-revolutionary, and as part of his plan he voiced annoyance at Spain for disrupting British trade in the Gulf of Mexico. By November, painting Spain as the guilty party, he told Cabinet that it had refused to cooperate and that a naval force was needed to protect British shipping from further attacks.[6] Canning felt that it was good to show that Spain was weak, allowing privateers and pirates to run free, so that Cabinet would be more likely to support the rebels.

US Policy against Pirates and Privateers

American policy toward the rebellious Spanish colonies was less complicated, but market expansion through diplomatic initiatives remained the goal. Politically, the primary aim was to convince Spain to recognize US possession of East Florida and Texas. John Quincy Adams, President Monroe's Secretary of State, was the primary negotiator in concluding the Adams-Onís Treaty of 1819 under which Spain recognized American control over Florida in exchange for $5.5 million in compensation, while the Americans abandoned claims to Texas. Henry Clay, the Speaker of the House of Representatives, continued to press for recognition. Adams held his ground, but when the Spanish wanted the US to rule out recognition, Adams replied that it would violate neutrality to take any position. By 1820 the liberal revolution enveloped Spain, and within a year it capitulated on the Florida treaty. On 4 July 1821, Adams recommended that Monroe recognize the new states. By May 1822 Congress had appropriated funds for diplomatic missions, and over the next four years Colombia, Mexico, the Central American Confederation, the United Provinces of La Plata, Chile and Peru received various levels of recognition. From 1826 to 1856, the US signed treaties with the new nations that provided for the appointment of consuls and granted most-favoured-nation status.[7]

---

[6]Harold Temperley, *The Foreign Policy of Canning, 1822-1827: England, the Neo-Holy Alliance and the New World* (London, 1925; 2nd ed., London, 1966), 42-45; and William W. Kaufmann, *British Policy and the Independence of Latin America, 1804-1828* (New Haven, 1951; reprint, New York, 1967), 136-144.

[7]Harry C. Allen, *Great Britain and the United States: A History of Anglo-American Relations (1783-1952)* (London, 1954; reprint, Hamden, CT, 1969), 364 and 372-374; Wesley P. Newton, "Origins of United States-Latin American Relations," in

When the Spanish-American territories revolted against their imperial overseer, American trade was caught in the crossfire. In response to the growing threat, on 3 March 1819 Congress enacted anti-piracy legislation which authorized the President to send warships to protect American shipping from pirates. It allowed US commanders to capture any armed ship and crew that had committed an act of piracy against an American or foreign vessel, deliver it into an American port for trial and free any US ship held by pirates. Finally, it permitted the courts to sell the pirate ships once condemned, while those convicted of piracy could face the death penalty.[8]

During the early stages of the revolutions, the US Navy (USN) only undertook limited policing efforts to counter piracy. But as attacks continued Congress, concerned about the US coasting trade, concluded that "the intercourse between the Northern and Southern sections of the Union, by sea, is almost cut off." In response, on 6 December 1822 Monroe wrote to the House of Representatives about the increased activities of Caribbean pirates. He believed that a strong force was needed that could operate in the shallow waters where the pirates hid. The House resolved into a committee of the whole to discuss legislation to authorize the President to fight the pirates.[9]

Representative Gideon Tomlinson, an "Anti-Jacksonite" from Connecticut, supported the proposal to improve the navy, claiming that growing American trade deserved a strong naval defence. His colleagues agreed and passed a new act authorizing the President to purchase and deploy those ships he deemed necessary to protect US shipping against pirates in "the Gulf of Mexico, and the Seas and territories adjacent." A sum of $160,000 was allocated. Congress, with little discussion, also made the temporary 1819 Act permanent on 30 January 1823.[10] While Americans traditionally abhorred a strong naval force, this fear gave way when US economic interests were directly threatened. With Congress firmly behind the President, the Navy De-

---

T. Ray Shurbutt (ed.), *United States-Latin American Relations, 1800-1850: The Formative Generations* (Tuscaloosa, AL, 1991), 20-23; and Bemis, *Diplomatic History*, 201.

[8]United States, Congress, *Register of Debates*, 18th Cong., 2nd sess., appendix, 31 January 1825, 49, "Report of the Committee of Foreign Relations of the House of Representatives, on Piracy and Outrages on American Commerce by Spanish Privateers;" and United States, Congress, *U.S. Statutes at Large*, III, 510-514 and 600.

[9]United States, Congress, *Annals of Congress* (*Annals*), 17th Cong., 1st sess., 1173-1175, House, 2 March 1822, and 17th Cong., 2nd sess., 349 and 371, House, 7 December 1822, James Monroe to House of Representatives, 6 December 1822; and *Advocate*, reprinted in *American Commercial and Daily Advertiser* (*ACDA*), 7 March and 4 April 1822.

[10]*Annals*, 17th Cong., 2nd sess., 371-381, House, 7 December 1822, and 33-35, Senate, 16 December 1822; and *Statutes at Large*, III, 720-721.

partment appointed one of the most famous American naval commanders, Commodore David Porter, to lead the fight to suppress pirates and privateers.

British Manoeuvres and Anglo-American Diplomacy

When the Americans "quickly" settled on a policy to deal with the pirates, Canning was under pressure to follow suit. *The Times* was often influenced by the political elite and is thus an important source to assess the views of those in government circles.[11] In early October 1822 it editorialized that Britain had failed to take sufficiently strong action against piracy. Significantly, it charged that the minister responsible had forfeited the people's trust, that merchants had suffered and that British trade in the West Indies had been damaged.[12]

Suitably warned, Canning soon took a firmer stand. He told Cabinet on 15 November that he feared that any power – like the US – that seized Cuba would have the ability to choke British trade to Jamaica, especially during a war. Canning concluded that the best way to protect British interests in the region was to settle the problems between Spain and the rebel colonies. He recommended that the government install civil agents in the various Spanish-American ports and continue efforts to protect British trade. Spain, he wrote, would force Britain to abandon its neutrality by seizing British ships simply for trading with the rebels. The revolution in Spain was no reason to be soft.[13] But insufficient support to go further forced him to declare British neutrality. He then virtually gave France permission to invade Spain, but warned against going into Portugal. On 6 April 1823 the French acted, swiftly overran Spain, and restored King Ferdinand to the throne.[14]

Behind the scenes, the British took a stronger diplomatic stand against Spain by threatening to use the Royal Navy (RN). In early 1823 Cabinet prepared to send a fresh squadron to the West Indies to seize Spanish ships in reprisal for continued operations against British shipping. Richard Rush asserted that when Spain became aware of British intentions, it acquiesced and released British ships. Rush concluded that Britain's handling of the affair was "considered as the first decided act of Mr. Canning's foreign administration[.]" He recommended that other powers should remember the British tactic

---

[11]Martin Crawford, *The Anglo-American Crisis of the Mid-Nineteenth Century: The Times and America, 1850-1862* (Athens, GA, 1987), 17-19.

[12]*The Times* (London), 5 and 8 October 1822.

[13]TNA/PRO, FO 72/266, reprinted in Webster (ed.), *Britain and the Independence of Latin America*, II, 2, 393-398, "Canning's Memorandum for the Cabinet," 15 November 1822.

[14]Kaufmann, *British Policy*, 144-148.

if they ever came to blows with the great power.[15] Rather than oppose American designs, Canning endeavoured to make the US an ally against a French incursion into Latin America.

During the summer and autumn of 1823, Britain and the US discussed their respective Caribbean strategies. While they failed to agree on a joint approach, they did reach an understanding. The Americans were worried that France might seize the Spanish colonies, and Rush told Canning that he hoped that the British would prevent this. Canning replied that he believed that the French would refrain from such an action, but he hoped that the British and Americans could formulate a common policy to counter any threat. Although the British agreed that they would do nothing to stop the colonial rebellions, talks stalled when Rush was unable to get Canning to issue a stronger declaration. The White House would only agree to a joint position if the British first recognized the colonies' independence, something Canning was unwilling to do for fear of tipping his hand too early to the Concert of Europe. Nevertheless, Rush assured Britain that the US had no desire to seize the colonies.[16]

Balancing his loyalties, Canning then decided to give France another chance. To this end he met with the French representative, Prince de Polignac, from 3-12 October 1823 and secured France's commitment to stay out of Spanish-American affairs. Canning wanted to conceal that he was actually plotting against the Europeans, but Rush was his Achilles' heel.[17] Rush believed that Britain was more worried about containing France than about what was happening in Spanish America and that it was using the US for its own strategic purposes. Moreover, he thought that the British Cabinet wanted the Spanish constitutional system to collapse, but only if this did not harm "British interests and British ambition." As for the naval situation in the West Indies, Canning informed Rush that the government was about to order the squadron to protect British trade by retaliating if Spain failed to refrain from attacking British shipping. Canning added that Britain was taking a similar stand with Colombia and wanted reparations for attacks on British shipping. If there were

---

[15]NA, RG 59, Dispatches, Britain, No. 289, Rush to Adams, 17 January 1823.

[16]TNA/PRO, FO 5/176, reprinted in Webster (ed.), *Britain and the Independence of Latin America*, II, 45-46, Stratford Canning to George Canning, date unclear; NA, RG 59, Dispatches, Britain, No. 323, Rush to Adams, 19 August 1823; No. 325, Rush to George Canning, 23 August 1823; No. 330, Rush to Adams, 8 September 1823; and No. 331, Rush to Adams, 19 September 1823.

[17]Kaufmann, *British Policy*, 156-158; and NA, RG 59, Dispatches, Britain, No. 336, Rush to Adams, 10 October 1823.

no results, the RN would blockade a Colombian port in response. Britain wanted America to communicate this threat.[18]

The Monroe Doctrine

The Americans went their own way by the end of 1823. Having already established a trading outpost near San Francisco in 1816, Russia declared ownership of the entire Pacific coast of North America in 1821 and announced that it would bar anyone from fishing or trading anywhere down the coast to 51° N. The US, probably as a warning, told the Russians that it would not stand by idly if a European power other than Spain tried to interfere with any Spanish territories in the Americas. This is the context in which Monroe made his famous speech on 2 December 1823 that later became known as the Monroe Doctrine. The warning to European powers to stay out of the Americas was directed not only as a caution to Russia but also to other Europeans against interfering in South America. The Europeans did not react, although by 1824 the Russians and Americans agreed to set the Alaska boundary at 54° 40' N.[19] But the Doctrine was significant because it declared the Americas to be within the economic and strategic sphere of the US.

Canning tolerated Monroe's declaration because it embodied his goal to keep European powers out of the region. Still, he was upset at Monroe's declaration of American hegemony. Canning asked how America could declare this when "America's geographic limits were actually unknown[.]" Nevertheless, rather than focusing on the semantics, by early February 1824 Britain was preparing to recognize Spanish-American independence once Spain had agreed. This led Rush to conclude that Britain would eventually take the "more direct and consistent course of the United States" towards the rebel states.[20]

Meanwhile, Canning tried to make the best use of Monroe's Doctrine. In Europe he tried to put forward the Polignac Memorandum as a prelude to the declaration. But the other powers by and large ignored Monroe's statement. The French proposed the establishment of Bourbon monarchies in Spanish America and after 1823 thought that the US should be excluded from any discussions on the issue. Dexter Perkins has concluded that Monroe's state-

[18]NA, RG 59, Dispatches, Britain, No. 336, Rush to Adams, 10 October 1823.

[19]Allen, *Great Britain and the United States*, 375; Bemis, *Diplomatic History*, 205-208; and Dexter Perkins, *The Monroe Doctrine, 1823-1826* (Cambridge, MA, 1932; reprint, Gloucester, MA, 1965), 3-17.

[20]NA, RG 59, Dispatches, Britain, No. 354, Rush to Adams, 27 December 1823; No. 361, Rush to Adams, 9 February 1824; Allen, *Great Britain and the United States*, 376-379; and Perkins, *Monroe Doctrine*, 17-32.

ment spurred the British to a more active policy but that its real significance lay in the future. While Canning publicly denied that Britain and the US were secretly cooperating over Latin American affairs, he stopped trying to quell rumours about his talks with Rush. By portraying the UK as the influence behind the Doctrine, he managed to swing South American opinion to Britain's side. Canning's next plan was to disrupt the European Alliance. In the end, the European powers were split on the status of Latin America, so Canning decided to act alone. But first he wanted to be sure that recognition of the rebel states would not come back to haunt Britain and that these territories were sufficiently pro-British to make recognition profitable.[21]

After a British commission to Mexico, Colombia and Buenos Aires confirmed that they were sympathetic to British interests, Lord Liverpool proposed the recognition of Mexico and Colombia in November 1824. In establishing formal diplomatic relations, Britain renounced a desire for special commercial treatment. This pleased the Latin Americans, and Mexico, Colombia and Buenos Aires soon entered into trade pacts with Britain, although these were only signed in 1827. The result was a temporary boom in investment in Latin America. Canning was proved correct in waiting until public opinion was favourable, and diplomatic conditions were right.[22] His wider objective secured, in late 1825 he tried to initiate a tripartite agreement with France and the US on piracy suppression and Cuba. He wanted to maintain the *status quo* with regard to the latter and to assure Spain that no one would take advantage of the situation to occupy Cuba or any of Spain's remaining colonies. But neither France nor the US was interested; in their view, the crisis was over.[23]

By 1825, as reports of piracy against US shipping declined, so did American interest in cooperating with Britain over a common naval policy. Early in the year President Monroe contended that the US should deploy greater force against the pirates but that it should also secure the cooperation of Spain and Cuba. He concluded that the options available were to pursue the pirates onto foreign territory; make reprisals against property where the pirates

---

[21]Perkins, *Monroe Doctrine*, 142-143, 248 and 260; and Kaufmann, *British Policy*, 165-175.

[22]NA, RG 59, Dispatches, Britain, No. 412, Rush to Adams, 30 December 1824; and Kaufmann, *British Policy*, 175-181. For the nuances of Canning's foreign policy, see Temperley, *Foreign Policy of Canning*, 447-475.

[23]TNA/PRO, FO 27/328, reprinted in Webster (ed.), *Britain and the Independence of Latin America*, 194-195, George Canning to Viscount Granville, 23 August 1825, "Projêt of an Engagement either Tripartite or Between (1) France and England, (2) England and the United States, and (3) The United States and France;" and NA, RG 59, Dispatches, Britain, No. 3, Rufus King to Canning, 24 August 1825, enclosed in King to Henry Clay, 24 August 1825.

hid; or blockade Cuban ports known to contain pirates.[24] But when debate resumed in Congress in 1825 about appropriations for anti-piracy measures, the lawmakers quickly asked whether the US even needed a navy. In the end, Congress agreed to continued American naval efforts in the Gulf, but at a price.

In the final analysis, "the present was a bill for the suppression of piracy, and not for the increase of the Navy." In rebuttal, Representative Daniel Webster, an Anti-Jacksonian from Massachusetts, told the House that if the British were able to deploy eighty to 100 large ships around the world, surely the US could build at least ten new vessels. But as the crisis waned, the final version of the bill was a compromise between those who still supported a strong navy and those who believed its time had passed. Section two stipulated that the President "is hereby authorized to cause to be sold...as he shall judge best for the public interest, the whole, or a part, of the vessels which were purchased under the authority of the act."[25]

Britain Achieves Dominance

Canning's Latin American policy was to use trade and influence to secure regional support. He avoided direct alliances or the use of naval power to advance British trade and sought to keep rivals from gaining a strategic foothold. The British finally checked the Americans in 1826 at the Panama Congress, which was called to discuss an American confederation, maritime rights, the Monroe Doctrine, Puerto Rico and Cuba. As the Americans became bogged down in domestic squabbles over Latin American policy, the British used their influence to shape events and left the Americans virtually impotent. The British representative, Edward J. Dawkins, was instructed to urge that the conference accept British maritime law, a position that was anathema to the US. In the end, Dawkins' suggestions "came to nought [sic], but thereafter such was the moral pre-eminence of Great Britain that the United States fell into a dark and chilling shade." Even Daniel Webster asserted that "Canning had completely established British influence in Hispanic-America[.]" Britain had more capital, a global trade network and a "navy [that] was far more important and much more in evidence."[26]

---

[24]*Register of Debates*, 18th Cong., 2nd sess., 198-199, 13 January 1825, Monroe to Senate.

[25]*Ibid.*, 18th Cong., 2nd sess., 729-732, House, 1 March 1825; and *Statutes at Large*, IV, 131, "An Act to Authorize the Building of Ten Sloops of War, and for Other Purposes."

[26]Kaufmann, *British Policy*, 202-217; and Webster (ed.), *Britain and the Independence of Latin America*, 52.

The result was that the US accepted that Britain had succeeded in consolidating its commercial interests and had the power to enforce its will. Albert Gallatin observed in 1827, for example, that the British intended to continue naval operations from Kingston, Jamaica, and to make Bermuda an important naval base.[27] By the early 1830s, the importance of British commercial and maritime interests became clear when tension increased between the US and Mexico. Louis McLane, the American envoy to the UK, believed that British commercial and mining interests in Mexico, and "a disposition to limit our control in the Gulf of Mexico," made it important for the government to ensure that "European policy [was] predominant in the New American states, and more especially in Mexico[.]" He also opined that "the supposed dependence of the Mexican government upon the interference and protection of Great Britain against Spanish aggression, gives to the People and government of this country [Britain] an influence which, if there be the disposition, may be exerted most prejudicially to our future relations."[28] British influence was clearly both commercial and naval, and Washington lacked the power to counter it short of all-out war.

British and American Slave-Trade Policy

While Britain and the US had similar goals in the equatorial Atlantic, an undercurrent of economic and diplomatic tension remained. This increased further over the issue of slave-trade suppression. While the British wavered for strategic reasons on policing piracy in the Gulf, their policy on the slave trade was clearer. When Britain began to use sea power to further its long-term objective of suppressing the slave trade, Washington feared that this was a device to restrict American freedom of the seas. From a British perspective, however, it was really a way to try to convince the US to help suppress the slave trade. When the latter became impossible because of American domestic concerns, Washington used its commitment to piracy suppression to try to placate the British. Rather than fighting over slave-trade suppression, both sides sought to mitigate their dispute so they could further their separate economic agendas.

While the British campaign against the slave trade began as a humanitarian enterprise, it quickly acquired economic and strategic overtones as Britain sought to develop an "informal" empire to feed its industrial growth. London mounted a solitary campaign to end slavery and the slave trade in a period when Africa took on an importance to British trade that rivalled British North America. Although trade in products produced by slaves was interrupted dur-

---

[27]NA, RG 59, Dispatches, Britain, No. 57, Albert Gallatin to Clay, 13 February 1827.

[28]*Ibid.*, No. 18, Louis McLane to Martin Van Buren, 21 May 1830.

ing the American Revolutionary War, slavery was still a vital part of the British colonial economy when Parliament suddenly decided to abolish the slave trade. Goods, such as coffee and sugar, which were produced by slave labour, had been competitive with those from colonies like Cuba and Brazil until the British abolished slavery. David Eltis has argued that the merchants and landed gentry should have campaigned for the continuance of slavery and the slave trade for economic reasons but instead committed "econocide."[29]

Ideas were important in this age, and the slow shift in British political opinion resulted from the spread of ideas borrowed from the Enlightenment. Seymour Drescher has concluded that a change in mentality spawned the abolition movement. He showed that support for abolition came largely from the newly industrialized parts of northern England. Northern workers were predisposed to be sympathetic to those, like African slaves, who had been separated from their families and exploited for economic reasons. The citizens of Manchester, for example, submitted 101 petitions to Parliament on the topic, while Liverpool, which had long been involved in the slave trade at many levels, failed to act. Manchester's support for abolition came in the face of the fact that the city's exports went largely to regions where the economy depended on money generated by slave-supported industries.[30]

Crusaders like William Wilberforce, the Hull MP, took up the cause in Parliament. Abolitionists believed that ending the slave trade would encourage the creation of "a self-sustaining labour force" in the colonies which would buy British goods and expand the home economy. To attain this objective, supporters proposed the creation of a colony for freed slaves in Sierra Leone in 1787; under the plan the British government would pay £12 per black. Over the next twenty years the movement grew, and on 1 May 1807 Parliament outlawed the slave trade. The last legal slaver, James de Wolf, then turned his attention to textiles. British economic involvement in West Africa had begun and so too had the intertwining of humanitarian and economic motives.[31]

The demise of the slave trade coincided with a realignment of the capital-labour relationship in Britain. The British applied *laissez-faire* market principles to the labour market, linking productivity, wages and consumption in a modern fashion. The ideology of the utilitarians and British Evangelicals

---

[29]David Eltis, *Economic Growth and the Ending of the Transatlantic Slave Trade* (New York, 1987), 4-6.

[30]Seymour Drescher, *Capitalism and Antislavery: British Mobilization in Comparative Perspective* (New York, 1987), 67-87. See also Drescher, "Whose Abolition? Popular Pressure and the Ending of the British Slave Trade," *Past and Present*, No. 143 (1994), 136-166.

[31]Hugh Thomas, *The Slave Trade: The Story of the Atlantic Slave Trade, 1440-1870* (New York, 1997), 494-498 and 539-556.

formed a nexus that conceptualized Africa and the slave trade as threats to free markets and free labour. By the 1830s, at about the time of the first Reform Bill, support for abolition shifted to the emerging middle class which began to argue that free labour was simply better.[32]

With slavery and the slave trade banned at home and in the colonies by 1833, the problem for Britain was to stop the slave trade conducted by other powers. In this era of peace and war-weariness, liberal Britain could hardly go to war to suppress the slave trade. Instead, the British crafted a diplomatic campaign to persuade others either to suppress their slave trade or give Britain the authority to do so. To this end, London attempted to secure treaties with other nations to stop and inspect vessels they suspected of being slavers. Suspected slavers were to be tried in Mixed Commission courts, and if they were found guilty, their vessels were to be condemned. The British preferred this mutual right-of-search approach because it gave them the most flexibility. Britain signed such treaties with the Netherlands (1822), Sweden (1824), Brazil (1826), Norway and Spain (1835) and Portugal (1842).[33] The latter sent as many as six warships to the West African coast, meaning that the slavers faced a combined naval force of up to sixty vessels.

Not all nations, however, succumbed to British pressure. Rather than sign a similar treaty, the French agreed to station warships off West Africa to intercept slavers sailing under their flag.[34] This system might have been effective except that slavers switched flags to avoid capture. But the main problem was with the US. Since the American South was primarily a slave economy, the Federal government was wary about entering into an overseas commitment to suppress the slave trade.[35] Furthermore, it feared British interference with its growing maritime trade if it granted the British the right to police the slave trade. These differing economic goals increased Anglo-American tension.

Slavery had existed in the US since the early seventeenth century, but so too had anti-slavery sentiment. In the early years of the Revolution, the Continental Congress restricted the importation of slaves. When Thomas Jefferson, himself a Virginia slave owner, wrote the first draft of the Declaration of Independence in 1776, he condemned the "peculiar institution," but under pressure from Georgia and South Carolina the final draft said nothing about slavery. The Articles of Confederation also were silent on slavery and the

---

[32]Eltis, *Economic Growth*, 18-21; and Drescher, *Capitalism and Antislavery*, 153.

[33]Eltis, *Economic Growth*, 85-86.

[34]*Ibid.*, 86-88.

[35]This was not an endorsement of the continuation of the trade, for the US had banned the importation of slaves in 1808.

slave trade. As a compromise the Constitution barred Congress from ending the slave trade until 1807 but allowed it to impose duties of no more than $10 on each slave imported. Further, it left it to individual states to decide upon the slave trade under its jurisdiction.[36] Thereafter, issues involving slavery were controversial matters involving "states rights" that the Federal government had to consider when making policy.

The process of outlawing the slave trade in the US was therefore gradual and conservative rather than a radical program that might threaten the Union.[37] On 22 March 1794, for example, Congress passed a law that forbade any American citizen or resident from equipping ships to buy or import slaves; if they disobeyed, they could lose their vessel and receive a fine. On 3 April 1798 Congress extended the law to include the Mississippi territory, banned the import of slaves under the threat of large fines and gave freedom to any newly imported slave. This law also banned Americans from serving on any vessel engaged in the transport of slaves and authorized the nascent USN to "seize vessels and crews employed contrary to the act." When President Jefferson reminded Congress in 1806 that the 1807 deadline for a decision on the slave trade was approaching, the lawmakers acted, and the President signed legislation to abolish it effective 1 January 1808. Significantly, however, the legislation contained no enforcement provisions.[38]

Despite the ban on the trade, entrepreneurs still landed slaves in independent Texas for import into the US. Smuggling of slaves occurred in Florida, Alabama and Georgia. Meanwhile, Baltimore shipbuilders, such as Stewart and Plunkett, continued to supply ships for the trade, and American firms insured slave ventures. In Washington, support for active measures to suppress the trade languished. One Secretary of the Navy, Paul Hamilton, was a slave owner; when he wrote to Charleston's senior naval officer, he seemed little concerned about the trade. President Madison, for his part, asked Congress to consider greater means to enforce the anti-slave trade laws, but in the end the 1807 Act only banned the international slave trade, did nothing about the domestic traffic and was virtually impossible to enforce. Indeed, once a slave trader got his human cargo into the US, there was no mechanism to prevent him from selling it. Traders often shipped slaves to Charleston or New Orleans and sold them publicly. The Virginia *Times*, for example, estimated that dealers sold 40,000 slaves in 1835 alone. Moreover, Americans continued their

---

[36]Thomas, *Slave Trade*, 478-482 and 499-501.

[37]David Brion Davis, "The Uncertain Antislavery Commitment of Thomas Jefferson," in Lawrence B. Goodheart, Richard D. Brown and Stephen G. Rabe (eds.), *Slavery in American Society* (3rd ed., Lexington, MA, 1976), 83-95.

[38]Great Britain, Parliament, *British Parliamentary Papers* (*BPP*), 1822, XXII, 44-441; and Thomas, *Slave Trade*, 544-552.

involvement in the Brazilian and Cuban slave trades. W.E.B. Du Bois found that the enforcement of US anti-slave trade laws in the Gulf of Mexico shortly after the War of 1812 was extremely poor. Despite reports from government officials in the region, Washington only dispatched a few revenue cutters in the late 1810s to suppress piracy from Amelia Island. When authorities captured slavers, it was largely by accident.[39]

Early Anglo-American Slave-Trade Diplomacy

Early Anglo-American efforts against the slave trade foundered because they were incompatible with American domestic interests. While Washington wanted to meet some of Britain's concerns, there were domestic constraints. Moreover, Americans feared that agreeing to British demands would interfere with US objectives in the realm of trade protection. Such concerns dominated the American focus at the political and naval levels. Although the White House tried to reconcile differences by meeting the British halfway on a mutual right-of-search treaty, the US was wary of a formal naval commitment for West Africa, a region far removed from American commercial interests. Instead, it committed to a minimal West African naval deployment as part of the West Indies anti-piracy patrol, hoping that it would protect American interests and reduce British criticism. Meanwhile, Britain declared that it would use only diplomacy to persuade other powers to suppress the slave trade rather than upsetting national sensibilities with overt displays of naval force. Both the US and Britain sought to minimize rather than exacerbate potential disputes.

On 12 May 1816, John Quincy Adams, in his capacity as US envoy to Britain, met with Castlereagh to discuss the Barbary States. During the meeting, Castlereagh commented that he was unable to convince Portugal and Spain to suppress the slave trade, but he committed not to go to war over the matter. He also warned the Barbary States that Britain would leave them alone "so long as they never applied it [slavery] to her [Britain's] subjects[.]" By 21 August, the British demanded that all Christian slaves be released and informed the Barbary States that they were in a state of war with Britain. But Castlereagh told Adams that the British were apprehensive about deploying a major naval force to the region. They were willing, however, to cooperate with other powers over issues of mutual concern.[40]

---

[39]W.E. Burghardt Du Bois, *The Suppression of the African Slave-Trade to the United States of America, 1683-1870* (New York, 1896; reprint, New York, 1965), 116; and Thomas, *Slave Trade*, 569-572.

[40]Charles Francis Adams (ed.), *Memoirs of John Quincy Adams: Comprising Portions of his Diary from 1795 to 1848* (12 vols., Philadelphia, 1874; reprint, Freeport, NY, 1969), III, 358-359 and 427-428.

But cooperation with the Americans over slave-trade suppression stagnated. During a meeting with Adams on 23 December, Castlereagh observed that slavers still operated out of southern US ports under the Spanish and Portuguese flags. He suggested that nations that had abolished the slave trade, like the US and Britain, use their naval forces cooperatively to arrest slavers flying the flags of any nation that had banned the trade; this was the mutual right of search. Castlereagh admitted that it was not his "intention to propose that the United States should take part in this system," and so Adams, wary of such proposals, refrained from responding. Adams revealed his true feeling after he met William Wilberforce in 1817. He acknowledged Wilberforce's influence in Parliament but concluded that Britain's right-of-search proposals were attempts to obtain in peacetime powers that it abused during the last war.[41] Initial hopes for joint Anglo-American policing operations against the slave trade thus languished, and the Americans voiced renewed objections to British claims of right of search, still a sore point after the War of 1812.

The US continued to reject British calls for a bilateral anti-slave trade treaty mainly because it believed in the total freedom of the seas, while Britain thought this only applied to legal trade and that it could stop those suspected of illegal activities or flying suspicious flags. In contrast, the US felt that other nations were obliged leave its vessels alone no matter what they were doing, although it agreed that piracy and slaving were wrong. Christopher Lloyd has argued that the US had in essence "extended the Monroe doctrine to cover their trading vessels at sea."[42] Adams warned, for example, that any interference with a US vessel in peacetime would be greeted by the American public with "universal repugnance." Moreover, the US felt that Britain wanted to restrict American freedoms. To allay this fear, the British countered that any treaty would be reciprocal, revocable and limited to "specified coasts and a definite number of ships." If either party objected, it could simply renounce the pact.[43]

Still, the Americans were confident that the High Court of Admiralty's ruling in the case of a French slave ship, *Le Louis*, restricted Britain's peacetime use of sea power. *Queen Charlotte*, a Sierra Leone colonial warship, captured *Le Louis* on 30 January 1816 near Cape Mesurado. Judge Sir William Scott believed that the condemnation of the ship rested on the legality of the visitation because the captain of the warship had no way of knowing if

---

[41]*Ibid.*, III, 454-455 and 556-558.

[42]Christopher Lloyd, *The Navy and the Slave Trade: The Suppression of the African Slave Trade in the Nineteenth Century* (London, 1949; reprint, London, 1968), 51.

[43]Hugh Graham Soulsby, *The Right of Search and the Slave Trade in Anglo-American Relations, 1814-1862* (Baltimore, 1933), 7-9 and 15-19.

there were slaves on board unless he stopped and searched *Le Louis*. The judge ruled that there was no provision in the law of nations for the search and seizure of a vessel in peacetime. The simple statement by France that it had abolished the slave trade was insufficient legal authority for another nation's warship to seize *Le Louis*. Meanwhile, the only law that banned the importation of slaves into French colonies dated from January 1817 and was therefore inapplicable to a vessel seized in 1816.[44] This ruling meant that the British had to seek agreements with other countries to search their ships for slaves or risk war. As a result, the US believed that Britain could do little against American ships without Washington's acquiescence.

America's Minimalist African policy and the 1819 Anti-Slave Trade Act

While Anglo-American treaty talks continued to fail, the White House moved forward unilaterally to protect and promote American interests. As in the discussions over a Gulf of Mexico policy, negotiations over the slave trade languished under the burden of divergent policies. The divisive slavery issue prevented the US administration from taking decisive action against the slave trade for fear of domestic turmoil. Instead, Washington only went as far as it judged domestic opinion would allow. Consequently, it decided on minimal naval deployment off the West African coast to support "private" American colonies that repatriated freed Africans.

In the early 1800s, slave revolts fomented fear among slaveholders that movements for abolition would undermine their society. They felt they needed a way to rid their territory of free blacks who, many in the South believed, were the source of agitation.[45] Pressure from organizations like the American Colonization Society (ACS), which wanted manumitted slaves repatriated to Africa, helped carry forward a minimal American commitment. The USN acted to support this effort by detaching an occasional ship from the West Indies piracy patrol.[46] American legislative action in 1819 is significant because naval efforts along the West African coast began as an indirect method of providing government support to private American colonization societies

---

[44]*BPP*, 1822, XXII, 447-449. A good introduction to prize law is Donald A. Petrie, *The Prize Game: Lawful Looting on the High Seas in the Days of Fighting Sail* (Annapolis, 1999).

[45]David M. Streifford, "The American Colonization Society: An Application of Republican Ideology to Early Antebellum Reform," *Journal of Southern History*, XLV, No. 2 (1979), 202-207; and Amos J. Beyan, *The American Colonization Society and the Creation of the Liberian State: A Historical Perspective, 1822-1900* (Lanham, MD, 1991), 2-6.

[46]Du Bois, *Suppression of the African Slave-Trade*, 98.

using the 1819 Anti-Slave Trade Act. But after other nations suppressed piracy, the USN retrenched, and Americans in West Africa noticed that Britain was the sole arbiter.

The ACS was formed in 1816 to promote the repatriation of freed Africans. It devised a scheme to resettle them in a colony similar to the one the British had established at Sierra Leone. Its leader, Reverend Robert Finley, hoped that wealthy Americans and the government would finance, promote and protect the settlement. He believed that the US could become the standard-bearer of Christianity in Africa. But the ACS's First Annual Report also revealed the more sinister goal of ridding America of an idle, "vicious and mischievous" race of freed blacks. Meanwhile, it gained many high-profile supporters, like Henry Clay, Speaker of the House; Daniel Webster, a Congressman from New Hampshire and naval advocate; and James Monroe.[47] In January 1817 the ACS asked Congress to support its colonization efforts but shied away from any mention of slavery. Congress wavered because it feared that a free black settlement in Africa would lead to conflict with other powers.[48]

Nevertheless, the ACS asked a supporter in Congress, Representative Charles Mercer, to introduce a new anti-slave trade bill in March 1819 which specified that the Federal government would police the slave trade. Surprisingly, Congress passed it with relatively little debate, especially compared to the anti-piracy legislation that was introduced and passed at the same time.[49] The Act gave the President the power to send American warships wherever he judged necessary to fight the slave trade, in particular along the African coast. The law ordered commanders to capture any vessel that had slaves on board, or that was outfitted for the slave trade in violation of the 1808 anti-slave trade law, and bring it to an American port. Finally, it also gave the President the power to deport freed slaves and to appoint agents to oversee operations. To accomplish these goals, Congress allotted $100,000.[50]

---

[47]P.J. Staudenraus, *The African Colonization Movement 1816-1865* (New York, 1961), 12-34; Beyan, *American Colonization Society*, 2-6; and Streifford, "American Colonization Society," 201-209.

[48]*Annals*, 14th Cong., 2nd sess., 481-483, House, 14 January 1817, B. Washington, President, ACS, to Senate and House of Representatives; and 14th Cong., 2nd sess., 939-940, House, 11 February 1817.

[49]*Ibid.*, 15th Cong., 1st sess., 1771-1774, House, 18 April 1818; 15th Cong., 2nd sess., 1430-1431, House, 1 March 1819; and Staudenraus, *African Colonization Movement*, 48-51.

[50]*Statutes at Large*, III, 532-533.

Monroe's Compromise

President Monroe used the provisions of the 1819 Act to support the ACS with the USN and to provide an American presence along the West African coast. Before the War of 1812 Monroe, along with William Pinkney, had negotiated an agreement with Britain that would have resolved wartime trade and blockade issues. But an uncompromising President Jefferson summarily rejected the Monroe-Pinkney Treaty. During the war, when Monroe served as Secretary of State and Acting Secretary of War, he remained wary of British motives concerning trade issues and maritime rights.[51] Consequently, when Anglo-American talks over the slave trade failed, President Monroe's minimal support became American policy until 1842. Under the Act the White House largely delegated responsibility for freed slaves to the ACS, while Washington provided the Society with a minimal level of naval support. This policy fit the mood of the nation and the President's style of leadership. In the era of the "Missouri Compromise" and increasing tension between North and South, such a policy was all that the White House could accomplish. Monroe, while listening to other people's opinions, was the final arbiter, especially in the realm of foreign affairs. When matters like the Missouri Compromise divided Cabinet, Monroe charted his own course and worked with Congress.[52]

The Missouri Compromise reveals the pressures that Monroe's government faced. Northerners saw slavery as a national problem, while Southerners believed that it was an issue for the states. A national debate followed that threatened to destroy the Union. In correspondence on 10 January 1820 the President privately expressed his desire that the US admit no new states unless they prohibited slavery, but he needed a compromise to save the nation. Senator Jesse B. Thomas proposed that the government ban slavery in regions of the Louisiana Purchase above 36° 30' but permit Missouri to enter the Union as a slave state.[53]

Congress approved the compromise, and Missouri and Maine – which prohibited slavery – entered the Union. The issue was, like everything connected with slavery, difficult for the government. Monroe convened Cabinet to discuss the issue, but only after Congress passed the legislation. He wanted to know if Congress had the right to legislate slavery; Cabinet agreed that it did. The President also wanted to know if the Compromise was only in force as

---

[51]Donald R. Hickey, *The War of 1812: A Forgotten Conflict* (Urbana, IL, 1989), 14-16 and 233; and Howard Jones, *Crucible of Power: A History of American Foreign Relations to 1913* (Wilmington, DE, 2002), 71.

[52]Noble E. Cunningham, Jr., *The Presidency of James Monroe* (Lawrence, KS, 1996), 21, 118, 125 and 187-188.

[53]*Ibid.*, 87-98.

long as a region was a territory. When he was unable to obtain a consensus, he rephrased the question to ask if the provision was constitutional; Cabinet agreed it was.[54] It is no wonder that Monroe's administration was reluctant to tackle anything related to slavery.

At the same time as the Missouri controversy, the ACS hoped that the USN would support its plans for African colonization. With both the colony and the navy on the West African coast, the nation could repatriate freed Africans and curtail the slave trade. Monroe met with his Cabinet in December 1819 to discuss American efforts against the slave trade. Among the Cabinet members was William H. Crawford, the Secretary of the Treasury, who was also the ACS's Vice-President. Crawford argued that the government should turn over its appropriation for the suppression of the slave trade under the 1819 Act to the ACS, but other Cabinet members objected. Secretary of the Navy Smith Thompson was wary about the endeavour, as was Adams, who not only feared spiralling costs but also the ramifications to the US if it led to the establishment of formal African colonies. Moreover, he felt that the government had no authorization to spend the appropriation to sustain freed Africans. Judd Harmon has concluded that Monroe "disregarded the opinions of Adams" when he provided funding to transport freed slaves back to Africa. Monroe also gave the Navy Department the authority to spend the $100,000 budget.[55]

The President had no qualms, however, about asking for the appointment of a US agent to handle the freed Africans and the provision of limited support for its efforts, such as the dispatch of a warship.[56] But Monroe had to face steady opposition, in particular from Adams, who remained wary of overseas colonies and suspicious of the motives of the ACS. Indeed, Adams confided to his diary that he felt that some slaveholders probably hoped to use the colonial system to rid themselves of freed blacks at the government's expense. Still, the President, echoing the sentiments of the ACS, believed that freed slaves were troublesome and that repatriation would rid the country of an element "who lived by pilfering, and corrupted the slaves[.]"[57]

Adams wrote in his diary that the ACS had "got the ear of the President, and Crawford" and had "already got their fingers into the purse[.]" The government was committed to paying for half the cost of the chartered vessel that was being readied to transport the colonists to the planned settlement at Sherbro Island. The President authorized funds for the voyage and decided to

---

[54]*Ibid.*, 102-104.

[55]Judd Scott Harmon, "Marriage of Convenience: The United States Navy in Africa, 1820-1843," *American Neptune*, XXXII, No. 4 (1972), 255-256.

[56]Staudenraus, *African Colonization Movement*, 51-56.

[57]Adams (ed.), *Memoirs*, IV, 292-293; and VI, 103-104.

send Congress a letter detailing the expenses, but only after the fact.[58] Du Bois has argued that these US anti-slave trade actions "may be regarded as the last of the Missouri Compromise measures."[59] Adams meanwhile distanced himself from the colonization effort and gladly handed it over to the Secretary of the Navy, writing that "[t]here is so much management in this affair, that I have no doubt much money will be expended to no useful purpose."[60] Nevertheless, the atmosphere growing from the Compromise created support for the ACS and its goal to rid the US of "troublesome" freed slaves.

The Compromise is also significant because it permitted the US to placate British concerns, to claim that it had modified its use of sea power and to establish a naval presence along the West African coast. On 23 December 1820 Monroe's Cabinet met to discuss the British proposals for the suppression of the slave trade submitted on 20 December and to work out the American response. Secretary Thompson believed that "by declining it [the right of search] we shall expose ourselves to the imputation of insincerity as to our purpose of suppressing the trade[.]" The British government would then use it with the Europeans and against the Americans in its global strategic moves. But Secretary of War John C. Calhoun disagreed and argued that it was more likely that Britain would use slave-trade suppression to buttress its power.[61]

Calhoun was a South Carolina slaveholder and conservative, and he was under pressure to protect Southern interests. In the 1810 Congressional elections he had been returned as one of the "War Hawks" who advocated taking a strong stand against Britain in the prelude to the War of 1812.[62] During the Missouri Compromise debate he refrained from making public statements, but he was in fact "strongly with the compromisers[.]" Irving H. Bartlett has shown that Calhoun feared the reaction if Southerners believed "that property in slaves was" threatened.[63] On 24 April 1820, for example, Thomas B. Robertson, a former Congressman from Louisiana, wrote Calhoun about the strategic issues the region faced. He feared that abolitionists were skewing the nation's priorities. Robertson despised the fact that Washington was spend-

---

[58]*Ibid.*, IV, 473-477.

[59]Du Bois, *Suppression of the Slave-Trade*, 98 and 121-122. Du Bois also undertakes an intricate discussion of US lawmaking.

[60]Adams (ed.), *Memoirs*, IV, 496.

[61]*Ibid.*, V, 216-217.

[62]Jones, *Crucible of Power*, 74.

[63]Irving H. Bartlett, *John C. Calhoun: A Biography* (New York, 1993), 19-42 and 109.

ing "hundreds and Thousands of dollars" to employ US warships "in protecting the Slaves of Africa and escorting them back" while "our Coast and the adjoining seas are exposed to the most daring depredations that the world has witnessed[.]" The people of New Orleans suffered at the hands of pirates who descended on the coast and stole property, including slaves.[64]

It is within this context that Calhoun told Cabinet that Britain had banned the slave trade and now wanted other nations to follow suit because British trade was under pressure from cheaper sources that employed slave labour. In this new era, Calhoun professed that Britain "could not bear to see a profitable trade enjoyed by rivals[;]" the suppression of the slave trade was the only way for Britain to increase its economic growth. America should refuse to agree to British proposals on nationalistic grounds, for if the US acquiesced it would simply become a British satellite. Thompson was finally outnumbered when Adams came down on Calhoun's side, although he reminded Cabinet that abolitionists pressured London and that the latter had to "conciliate them." Monroe listened to all sides before agreeing that the government should hold firm. If anything, the President believed that the American position would strengthen its stand against searching ships in wartime to impress sailors.[65]

Still, to allay British concerns Cabinet discussed several options, among them a permanent and separate US naval force for the African coast. Cabinet thought that this would be "inconvenient" and wanted to keep its options open to meet other national needs, such as those that Robertson demanded. Thompson, while disagreeing with Calhoun, admitted that a formal treaty would "deprive us of the power of adapting the disposal of all our naval force to the exigencies of circumstances from time to time." Instead, Cabinet agreed to remind London that the US had "a vessel constantly cruising on that coast, and that it was intended to keep such force there[.]" Cabinet felt that, in combination with its other African policy, it could modify the use of sea power as a compromise. It agreed that the US could order its naval commanders on the African coast to cooperate with the British. They could cruise together, if "useful or convenient," and exchange intelligence "for the furtherance of the common object" to allay Britain's concerns.[66]

Anglo-American discussions languished for several years, and an attempt in 1823 to conclude a compromise treaty that would have placed the suppression of the slave trade on the same level as the campaign against piracy failed. The treaty would have allowed naval ships to capture pirate-slavers of each nation but would have sent them to their home country for trial. The Brit-

---

[64]W. Edwin Hemphill (ed.), *The Papers of John C. Calhoun* (24 vols., Columbia, SC, 1971), V, 74-75, Thomas B[olling] Robertson to Calhoun, 24 April 1820.

[65]Adams (ed.), *Memoirs*, V, 217-218.

[66]*Ibid.*, V, 218-219 and 222-223.

ish agreed to the treaty, and Cabinet agreed to submit it to the Senate for ratification, over the objections of Adams. One of the biggest failures of Monroe's administration was the treaty's final rejection by Congress, which amended it to limit the right of search to the African coast, a position that London rejected at the time. As a result, Adams still had to deal with the British and their repeated requests for joint Anglo-American cooperation against the slave trade, but British leaders realized the domestic constraints that Washington faced.[67]

During the early 1830s Sir Charles Vaughan, the British Ambassador to Washington, told Lord Palmerston that the administration was wary of upsetting the South at a time when "Anti-Slavery Societies have roused the jealousy of all the Slave-holders[.]"[68] The British sought to bring the Americans into a treaty with the French, but Washington again rejected the proposal. Palmerston respected the American objections to the British extension of the right of search to their coastline. He concluded that it was "sufficient reason for not further pressing the adoption of such an article,"[69] since it would go against liberal ideals to push too hard.

Conclusion

During the 1820s, Britain and the US used diplomatic manoeuvres to secure their long-term objectives in the equatorial Atlantic. Britain, fearful of sparking European intervention in Latin America, carefully avoided provoking other nations, while Canning balanced his strategy and sought diplomatic cooperation with the US. While Britain was freer to act against slavers, domestic American unease over slave-trade issues and British motives hampered efforts to formulate a common policy to suppress the slave trade. Divergent economic and political interests meant that the two nations went their separate ways in the development of equatorial Atlantic policy. Both deployed navies to fight piracy, but only the RN worked to suppress the slave trade. Meanwhile, the USN deployed to West Africa to provide minimal support for private colonization in conjunction with its anti-piracy duties. When the immediate need to protect commerce ended, Washington reduced patrols, and West African deployment languished. But the US did offer to cooperate with the British to curtail the slave trade, if it proved convenient to do so. There were signs, however, that both nations might use peacetime sea power to further long-term

---

[67]Soulsby, *Right of Search*, 26-37; Cunningham, *James Monroe*, 170; and Adams (ed.), *Memoirs*, VI, 148-151 and 321-322.

[68]*BPP*, 1835, LI, 260-261, Charles R. Vaughan to Viscount Palmerston, 12 December 1833.

[69]*Ibid.*, 261-264, Vaughan to McLane, 25 December 1833; McLane to Vaughan, 24 March 1834; and Palmerston to Vaughan, 7 July 1834.

objectives and as common ground to calm disputes that affected their relationship.

Figure 3.1: The Head of Vincent Benevides, Executed South American Pirate

Source: National Maritime Museum, Negative No. D7531_9. © National Maritime
                Museum, London.

Chapter 4
Naval Relations and the Suppression of Piracy and Slaving, 1820-1830

Britain and the US believed in the use of sea power to meet immediate threats to commerce, but their respective political and economic considerations shaped their naval response to pirates and privateers during the 1820s. The US Navy (USN) protected American shipping, arranged convoys and hunted pirates in their lairs. The squadron protected the Gulf of Mexico and provided West African colonial support, but the former was the priority, and the government left West African issues to the American Colonization Society (ACS). The reality was that USN deployment was sporadic rather than the "constant cruising" Washington promised to placate the British. For its part, the Royal Navy (RN) policed the seas for pirates and privateers and monitored American naval activity. London dispatched naval reinforcements to the Gulf of Mexico, but they spent little time in the region. British naval deployment was more complicated and laboured under domestic political constraints.

Britain was suspicious of the American presence; nevertheless, the RN refrained from provoking the USN, or the vessels of other nations, in the Gulf of Mexico. London and Washington were wary of each other but kept the peace. In the Gulf, the only plan for cooperation depended upon circumstances and the discretion of local commanders. While the White House hoped that the British would cooperate with the naval force that the US was able to dispatch to West Africa, when piracy declined in the Gulf the Americans reduced their naval commitment. Consequently, there were even fewer USN cruises to the West African coast. When American vessels left the coast, Britons wondered when the US might return.

In contrast, in West Africa the RN was free to act as it chose against privateers, pirates and slavers. While the British wanted to suppress the slave trade for humanitarian reasons, officers also reported on the region's economic potential, in particular places like Fernando Po that could rival the West Indies. Still, divergent American and British policies, and accompanying domestic and global restraints, affected Anglo-American naval deployment and Britain's goal of achieving greater American activity along the West African coast. Again, cooperation was limited to that undertaken as the opportunity arose. But while their relations were tense, Britain and America co-existed in the equatorial Atlantic. Both sought to control their use of sea power rather than ignite a conflict, while furthering their growing objectives.

73

American Naval Response

American naval deployments in the equatorial Atlantic were largely responses to the threat of piracy. When the Spanish-American colonies rebelled, they threw the region into chaos. Furthermore, after 1815 surplus maritime resources poured into Central and South American waters. David Starkey has concluded that this "flow of Baltimore schooners and American seafarers, together with the picaroons of former Spanish and French privateersmen, contributed significantly to the *course independante* and the wars of liberation."[1] Privateers from both sides fought each other and interfered with British and American shipping. Moreover, they took advantage of Spanish weakness to launch raids from Cuba and the Yucatan Peninsula on the shipping of all nations.[2] Although this market returned to equilibrium, piracy was considered a threat to commerce, and governments dispatched navies "to eradicate, reduce or at least police it."[3] But before 1819 the US conducted few forceful naval operations to protect its trade against pirates or privateers. The situation worsened when a constitutional government was restored in Spain in March 1820. Most Spanish forces withdrew from Spanish America, but General Morales, the Spanish commander, declared that the 1200 miles of Spanish-American coastline in dispute was under blockade.[4]

The USN had to protect American shipping from pirates and privateers from Spain and its rebellious colonies. The extended US Anti-Piracy Act of 1820 covered actions against, or committed by, all ships and citizens, not just those of or against the US. Operations against pirates were simple because freebooters were the enemy of all nations, and American operations were free

---

[1]David J. Starkey, "Pirates and Markets," in Lewis R. Fischer (ed.), *The Market for Seamen in the Age of Sail* (St. John's, 1994), 76-77.

[2]Using the terminology employed in John L. Anderson, "Piracy and World History: An Economic Perspective on Maritime Predation," *Journal of World History*, VI, No. 2 (1995), 175-199, reprinted in C.R. Pennell (ed.), *Bandits at Sea: A Pirates Reader* (New York, 2001), 82-106, this piracy was not only episodic and tied to the disruption of trade but also an intrinsic part of the local economic system. For more on piracy in the region during this period, see Mark C. Hunter, "Piraten im Golf von Mexiko im frühen 19. Jahrhundert," in Hartmut Roder (ed.), *Piraten – Abenteuer oder Bedrohung?* (Bremen, 2002), 52-65.

[3]Starkey, "Pirates and Markets," 65-66.

[4]United States, Congress, *Register of Debates*, 18th Cong., 2nd sess., appendix, "Report of the Committee of Foreign Relations of the House of Representatives, on Piracy and Outrages on American Commerce by Spanish Privateers," 31 January 1825; and United States, Congress, *Statutes at Large*, III, 510-514 and 600.

from European complications. Still, by 1824 Washington was wary that Europeans would test the Monroe Doctrine, and US naval deployment in the early 1820s was primarily for trade protection. Meanwhile, American forces supported US commercial interests rather than altruistic activities like the suppression of the slave trade. The House of Representatives Committee on Naval Affairs in a discussion of piracy reported on 2 March 1822 on the distribution of USN vessels. At that time, *Franklin*, *Constellation* and *Dolphin* were in the Pacific on a mission to protect American commerce in general and US whalers in particular. *Constitution*, *Ontario* and the schooner *Nonsuch* were in the Mediterranean, tasked with commerce protection and as insurance against the Barbary States. The USN also had ships deployed in the Gulf to protect against pirates: *Hornet*, *Spark* and *Enterprise*, as well as the schooners *Alligator*, *Shark*, *Grampus* and *Porpoise* and gunboat numbers 158 and 168 patrolled the Florida and Georgia coasts, while *Macedonian* would soon sail from Boston for the Caribbean.[5]

For most of 1821 and 1822 the USN hunted pirates, tried to dislodge them from their dens and warned shipping about the activities of pirates and privateers. Sometimes, the navy captured and destroyed suspected pirates on the spot, but if conditions were favourable, commanders sent suspects to a US port for disposal. *Enterprise* captured four pirate schooners and a sloop off the notorious Cape San Antonio on 16 October 1821 while they were plundering *Lucies*, an American ship, and *Larch*, a British brig. Lieutenant Commander Lawrence Kearney ordered two of the schooners destroyed and sent the sloop and two other pirate schooners to Charleston, South Carolina. On 29 October, *Hornet* captured the pirate *Moscow* and sent it to Norfolk, while another unit destroyed a pirate boat at Cape San Antonio on 8 November, although the pirates escaped. The next US victory was again by *Enterprise*, which apprehended a thirty-three-ton pirate schooner on 21 December, but its crew of twenty-five escaped. A major triumph occurred on 7 January 1822 when the USN seized six pirate ships and destroyed five. *Spark*, under the command of Captain John H. Elton, also freed a Dutch sloop in January and sent the pirate culprit to Charleston. The navy destroyed or captured another ten pirates in March, including *Enterprise*'s assault on four pirate barges and three launches. The USN captured another five pirates in June, and on 28 and 30 June *Peacock* captured five pirate ships, destroying two and sending the rest to New Orleans; among the cargo recovered was eighty-nine bags of coffee.[6]

---

[5]*Statutes at Large*, III, 510-514 and 600; and United States, Congress, *Annals of Congress*, 17th Cong., 1st sess., 1173-1174, House, 2 March 1822.

[6]United States, Congress, *U.S. Serial Set*, LXXIII, 17th Cong., 2md sess., Senate, Document No. 1, 56, "Statement of Captures of Piratical Vessels and Boats Made by Vessels of the United States Navy in the West Indies," enclosure no. 1 in Smith Thompson to the President of the United States, 30 November 1822. Hereafter,

Figure 4.1:   Gulf of Mexico

Note: Locations approximate.

Source: Courtesy of the author.

Beyond offensive operations, an important task was to escort merchantmen through areas frequented by pirates. For example, *Hornet*, under Robert Henley, in February 1822 sailed from Havana to Pensacola with a convoy of twenty-two ships, mostly American. But US support for the rebel Spanish states hurt its fight against pirates around Cuba. The Charleston *Courier* reported on 17 April that the Cubans, still loyal to Spain, were annoyed at President Monroe's call for Spain to recognize the rebels and to suppress piracy. By May the USN had settled into a pattern of dispatching a warship to convoy vessels from Havana to the US every Sunday. Still, the actions of the privateers irritated the Americans, and in July Washington dispatched *Cyane*, under the command of Captain Robert T. Spence, "with extensive powers to put a stop to the outrages committed on our flag by Spanish Privateers."[7] Spence and other American officers warned Spanish authorities to leave US shipping alone. The protests were in vain, and Spanish privateering continued; the Spanish privateer *General Pereira*, for example, captured the US merchant

---

the *U.S. Serial Set* will be cited according to the recommended Library of Congress style, for example, *S. Doc.*, No. 1, 17th Cong., 2nd sess.

[7]*American Commercial and Daily Advertiser* (*ACDA*), 21 February, 24 April and 15 June 1822; and *Norfolk Beacon*, 22 February 1822, reprinted in *ACDA*, 26 February 1822.

brig *General Andrew Jackson* on 22 July. The Spanish representative, Don Francisco Gonzalez de Linarez, told Spence that the authorities on Puerto Rico were unaware of illegal actions by Spanish privateers and that the US would have to seek redress from "the treasury of Spain[.]"[8] Meanwhile, pirates continued to operate from Spanish territories, especially Cape San Antonio and Matanzas (see figure 4.1).

Increased US Action

Under continued pirate attacks and pressure from Congress, the White House appointed Commodore David Porter to command the expanded Gulf squadron on 21 December 1822; it sailed in February 1823.[9] The USN was most active in the Western Atlantic and the Gulf of Mexico during 1823, especially against pirates. Secretary of the Navy Samuel L. Southard reported that since the passage of the Act "authorizing an additional Naval Force for the suppression of Piracy," the department had sent more ships to that station. From the squadron's base on Thompson's Island, Key West, the Secretary ordered Porter to suppress piracy, protect US merchant ships, convoy specie from Mexico and cooperate with other nation's navies in the pursuit of pirates. Thompson stated vaguely that Porter had some leeway to pursue pirates into uninhabited regions where Spanish authority was ineffective, but he warned him to avoid chasing pirates into Spanish territory or provoking a confrontation with a foreign power.[10] In addition, under the auspicious of the anti-piracy patrol, Washington also dispatched ships to West Africa.

On station, Porter ordered *Shark*, under Matthew Perry, and three small schooners to patrol along the southern coast of Puerto Rico. Porter intended the entire squadron to sortie for San Juan to stop Spanish privateers from preying on US shipping. His interaction with the Spanish was tense and led to the death of one American from *Fox* when it entered San Juan harbour and nervous Spanish soldiers accidentally fired on it. After telling Miguel de la

---

[8]*Annals*, 17th Cong., 2nd sess., appendix, 1227-1229, "Statement of Arthur Edgarton, Mate of the Brig General Andrew Jackson," Autumn 1822; and Robert Trail Spence to Thompson, 3 September 1822. Spence and de Linarez carried on a lengthy correspondence over these issues; see *Annals*, 17th Cong., 2nd sess., appendix, 1230-1244.

[9]David F. Long, *Nothing Too Daring: A Biography of Commodore David Porter, 1780-1843* (Annapolis, 1970), 203-205.

[10]Great Britain, *British Foreign and State Papers* (*BFSP*), XI, 33, Samuel L. Southard, "Report of the Secretary of the Navy," 1 December 1823; Long, *Nothing Too Daring*, 207-208; and *S. Doc.*, No. 1, 18th Cong., 1st sess., 190, David Porter to Secretary of the Navy, 19 November 1823.

Torre, the governor of Puerto Rico, that the USN was there to protect American shipping, Porter returned to hunting pirates. While this was the primary goal, the squadron also convoyed merchant vessels. Porter reported that every Spaniard he encountered was well armed and could be a potential pirate, but he noted that if he stopped every Spanish ship, "their coasting trade would soon be entirely broken up." Since his arrival, the pirates had disbanded five of the ships that had watched his fleet, but he dispatched two schooners leeward of Matanzas to investigate more reports of piracy. Porter concluded that the squadron had two conflicting duties – convoying and search and destroy – and he decided to give greater attention to the former until more warships arrived. By mid-April the squadron had established its base at Thompson's Island, landed its supplies, equipped barges and deployed at various points around Cuba. Still, Porter was displeased that he was forced to use the small schooners for convoy duty rather than to hunt pirates.[11] Nevertheless, he felt that he had made progress against the pirates.

In March 1823 the USN captured *Pilot*, a schooner armed with a long twelve-lb. gun. Porter explained that he had dispatched *Wild Cat* and *Beagle* to find *Pilot*, which was "commanded by Domingo, the notorious head of this horde of desperadoes[,]" and another pirate ship, *Saragarina*. Meanwhile, he sailed in *Peacock* to Havana, but not finding *Pilot*, he decided to go to Thompson's Island to continue establishing the squadron's base. He then sent two barges, *Gallinipper* and *Mosquito*, and two schooners, *Fox* and *Jackall*, to sweep the seas for pirates between Havana, Cape San Antonio and Trinidad. After gathering intelligence about the possible whereabouts of the suspected pirates, *Wild Cat* and *Beagle* found *Pilot* near Matanzas and pursued it for most of a day, but it escaped to shore under the cloak of darkness. The naval captains sent the ships' boats ashore, where a fire fight ensued, and the Americans seized *Pilot*; Domingo and two other pirates escaped, but one "desperado" was killed.[12]

On 24 April 1823, after almost two months on station, Porter declared victory against the pirates. Convoying continued, and he had recently dispatched two barges to a bay near Point Yeacos to search for three pirate ships. Porter told Secretary Thompson that there were no longer any pirate vessels larger than an "open boat" operating along the Cuban coast. He also acknowl-

[11]Long, *Nothing Too Daring*, 210; *S. Doc.*, No. 1, 18th Cong., 1st sess., 186, Porter to Thompson, 3 March 1823; No. 1, 18th Cong., 1st sess., 136-139 and 147-148, Porter to Governor of Puerto Rico, 4 March 1823; Miguel de la Torre to Porter, 6 March 1823; Porter to Thompson, 28 March 1823; 18th Cong., 1st sess., 147-148 and 150-153, Porter to Thompson, 28 March 1823; and Porter to Secretary of the Navy, 16 April 1823.

[12]*S. Doc.*, No. 1, 18th Cong., 1st sess., 150-155, Porter to Secretary of the Navy, 16 April 1823; and C.K. Stribling to S. Cassin, 8 April 1823.

edged that it was not just the American squadron that forced the pirates to hide, for the larger pirate ship, *Saragarina*, had been captured "in her flight, from here [Matanzas], having been taken by two British sloops of war at the east end of the Island."[13] Meanwhile, the squadron's presence had a "moral effect" on both sides: Spain recalled some of its privateers, and the rebel states became more careful in issuing commissions. It was only the presence of a naval force and cooperation from local authorities that were effective in stopping piracy.

Despite an epidemic of sickness in the squadron, *Ferret* and *Beagle* sailed from Thompson's Island on 14 June 1823 for Trinidad and southern Cuba, but they separated on 16 June when *Ferret* sailed for Havana where *Ferret* discovered a pirate barge. An officer and five men launched a boat to investigate since the water was too shallow for *Ferret*. Within fifty feet of the barge, gunfire erupted, striking *Ferret*'s boat at the waterline and causing a small, but manageable, leak. As sea conditions worsened, *Ferret* withdrew, firing from a distance on the pirates. But the freebooters held their ground, and the seas prevented *Ferret* from maintaining a steady firing pattern. *Ferret* withdrew briefly, but when it returned the Americans came face to face with a Spanish warship. The situation might have led to an encounter, but the Governor of Matanzas received word that *Ferret* was in a pitched battle with the pirates and sent the warship *Matae* to render assistance. He also dispatched troops to the coast, and when the Americans returned to the bay the pirates abandoned their position and scuttled their ships. Porter suspected that these were the same pirates who had attacked the American ship *Mary Joan* near Matanzas Bay. He concluded that if piracy was reported quickly and punished, it would deter the pirates from launching renewed attacks.[14]

In July 1823 Lieutenant Commander W.H. Watson, commanding the barges *Gallinipper* and *Mosquito*, was on patrol from Cayo Francis to Cayo Blanco when he encountered a suspicious schooner, which turned out to be a former Spanish ship, *Catalina*, on its first cruise under the command of the pirate Diabolito. The schooner was sailing with a launch and approaching some merchant ships. *Gallinipper*, with Watson onboard, had the tactical advantage windward of the suspicious formation and quickly bore down on the ships. But the schooner was well armed, and when Watson raised *Gallinipper*'s flag, the schooner raised Spanish colours, opened fire and then lowered its flag. Watson ordered evasive action and signalled *Mosquito* to close in. Thus confronted, the pirates took defensive action and sailed downwind with

---

[13]*Ibid.*, 18th Cong., 1st sess., 150-156, Porter to Secretary of the Navy, 16 April 1823; Stribling to Cassin, 8 April 1823; and Porter to Thompson, 24 April 1823.

[14]*Ibid.*, 18th Cong., 1st sess., 164-166, Thomas M. Newell to Porter, 25 June 1823; Porter to Secretary of the Navy, 24 June 1823; and Newell to Porter, 25 June 1823.

the Americans in hot pursuit. But there was nowhere to hide, and after a brief fire fight, the Americans captured the schooner and launch, killing most of their crews. Some tried to escape on the launch or by swimming ashore, but the Americans opened fire with muskets, throwing the pirates into confusion and forcing those on the launch into the water, while the American boats blocked their retreat. The Americans took five prisoners; four others managed to escape but were arrested by the authorities in Matanzas.[15] With the USN on the scene, the Spanish took their international responsibilities more seriously.

The primary US mission had succeeded, and the Secretary of the Navy believed that piracy had been suppressed around Cuba. He therefore extended the squadron's range to include West Africa to assist the ACS and on the return voyage to watch for slavers. Porter replied that if his West Indian force was larger, a ship could sortie to Africa every six weeks. In the interim, because of the increased patrol area, Porter divided the squadron into two divisions and planned "by a constant routine, [in] giving equal protection to our colony on the coast of Africa and guarding against the slave trade[.]" The deployment sowed the seed for US naval expansion to West Africa, but Washington's use of sea power in home waters to staunch immediate threats to commerce weakened it. The US also realized that it had to be careful in using sea power close to the interests of other nations. Significantly, Washington removed Porter from command and replaced him with Commodore Lewis Warrington when the former's actions threatened relations with Spain. Stephen Cabot, an American merchant, reported that Spaniards who fled to Fajardo, Puerto Rico, had robbed him. When the Spanish arrested a US officer gathering intelligence on the island on 14 November 1824, Porter and 200 men went ashore to demand redress. Porter's landing occurred in a region under direct Spanish control, and Washington feared it would test the Monroe Doctrine. Porter, officials opined, showed poor diplomatic skills, and they found him guilty of conduct unbecoming on officer, insubordination and disobeying orders.[16] To prevent a wider dispute, Washington sacrificed Porter.

Decline of US Naval Operations

While the Americans were wary that the Monroe Doctrine might be tested, the US also found that pirate activity in the Gulf had changed. As piracy declined,

---

[15]*Ibid.*, 18th Cong., 1st sess., 170-171, W.H. Watson to Porter, 11 July 1823.

[16]*Ibid.*, 18th Cong., 1st sess., 189-192, Porter to Secretary of the Navy, 19 November 1823; 18th Cong., 2nd sess., 116-117 and 119-120, Porter to Southard, 20 January 1824; Porter to Southard, 8 April 1824; Long, *Nothing Too Daring*, 216-217, 219 and 227-229; and *BFSP*, XI, 33-35, Samuel L. Southard, "Report of the Secretary of the Navy," 1 December 1823.

so did American naval efforts. By late 1824 Secretary Southard concluded that the pirates now hid in creeks and bays, venturing forth only to attack unprotected ships. Warrington attributed the decline in piracy to US naval deployment on the Cuban coast. Convoys and patrols forced the pirates to change their tactics. They now attacked in small, open boats, but only if no warships were in the vicinity. Then they fled to places "far removed from the scene of their late exploit[.]"[17]

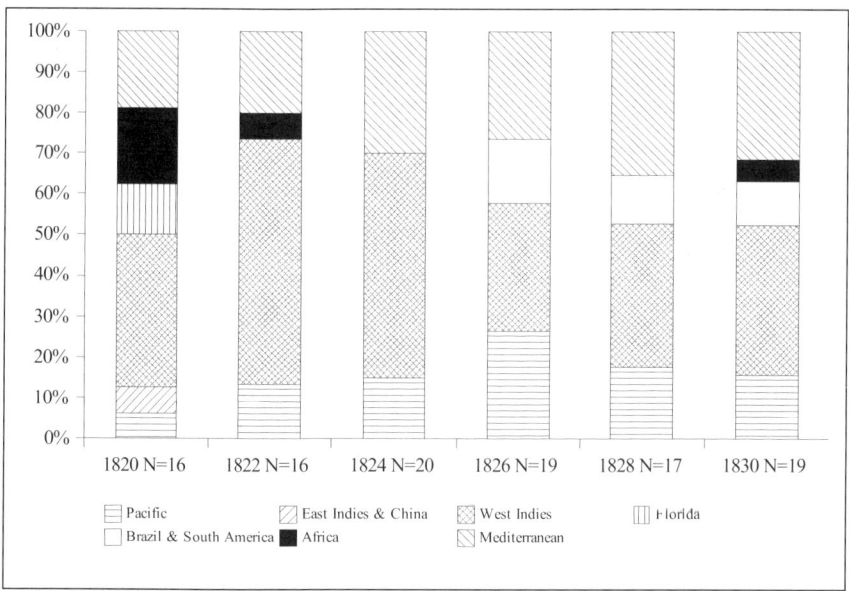

Figure 4.2: US Navy Deployment, 1820-1830

Note: N = Number of Warships.

Source: Calculated from United States, *Annual Reports of the Secretary of the Navy* (Washington, DC, 1820-1830).

Given the pirates' tactics and strategies, Warrington concluded that it was virtually impossible to stop the remaining piracy everywhere, since the only effective strategy would be to search every bay and creek where pirates

---

[17]*BFSP*, XII, 571-572, Southard to the President," 1 December 1824; *S. Doc. No.* 2, 19th Cong., 1st sess., 104-105, Lewis Warrington to Southard, 15 February 1825; Warrington to Southard, 10 March 1825; and 117-119 and 122-123, Warrington to Southard, 27 April 1825.

might hide and examine every ship deemed suspicious.[18] Regardless, by December 1825 Southard declared that the war against piracy was over. The West Indian squadron still had the barges, the sloop *Hornet*, brig *Spark*, frigate *Constellation* and corvette *John Adams*, but the schooner *Fox* was the only ship purchased under the anti-piracy naval appropriations that remained in service.[19] Although the threat from pirates and privateers had diminished, the American naval presence was still strong close to home waters. Consequently, the African naval commitment remained sporadic, with deployments in 1820, 1822 and 1830 when the need arose for commerce protection (see figure 4.2).

British Naval Deployment against Pirates and Privateers

The RN's North American and West Indies squadrons successfully suppressed piracy, but station commanders worried about how far this stretched their forces. Still, the RN had the strength to cast a wide net to catch those who harmed British interests. For example, on 19 September 1820, the privateer *Venganza*, from Margarita, attacked the British ship *Eliza* at 22° 56'N by 58° 45'W. The suspect, whose fate is unclear, was bound for the Mediterranean, and the Admiralty issued orders to the Mediterranean, Gibraltar, Tenerife, North American, Jamaica, Leeward Islands, South American and Coast of Africa stations to apprehend it.[20] But British geopolitical concerns reduced the strength of this net in the Western Atlantic. While the US expressed some concern over relations with other nations, the British had European allies to deal with until Canning settled on his policy. Therefore, while London monitored nations like the US, it also restricted its use of sea power rather than threaten relations with other nations over "minor" issues.

Britain dispatched naval reinforcements, but only in response to complaints from British merchants that the US was doing the RN's work. The British were suspicious of the US naval deployment and feared that it threatened its strategic interests in the Gulf. Nevertheless, when piracy ended and the troubles in Latin America subsided, Congressional support for naval expansion waned. This left the Americans knowing that the security and stability of the region depended upon the long-term presence of the RN.

---

[18]*S. Doc.*, No. 2, 19th Cong., 1st sess., 117-119 and 122-123, Warrington to Southard, 27 April 1825.

[19]*Ibid.*, 19th Cong., 1st sess., 104, Southard, "Report from the Navy Department," and appendix A, 2 December 1825.

[20]Great Britain, National Archives (TNA/PRO), Admiralty (ADM) 2/1585, J.W. Croker to Sir Graham Moore, *et al.*, 12 January 1821, Croker to Senior Officer of HM Ships at Gibraltar, 12 January 1821; and Croker to Captain Bartholomew, 12 January 1821.

Contrary to some newspaper reports, the RN acted against pirates and privateers in the West Indies. Naval officers reported that while they stopped some vessels suspected of piracy, they had insufficient proof to condemn them, and there had been no attacks on British shipping. The Admiralty believed that pirates had settled at Cape San Antonio to watch for warships. But on station, officers found that even pirates knew basic naval tactics. When a warship stationed off Cape San Antonio was blown offshore, the pirates emerged and attacked. Regardless, the Admiralty believed this was still the best strategy. Following the pirates into the dense jungles of western Cuba was not an option; what the British needed was for the Spanish government to send an adequate naval force to the region to suppress piracy.[21]

J.W. Croker of the Admiralty wrote to Admiral Sir Charles Rowley about piracy around Cuba and the government's futile efforts to convince Spain to address the problem. The Admiralty had received "representations" from British insurance underwriters and merchants about pirate attacks emanating from Cape San Antonio that cost money and hurt trade. But because of the geopolitical ramifications, London had to ask the Spanish government to act or allow the British onto its territory. Consequently, Croker told Rowley that "you [are to] send one of your cruizers off Cape [San] Antonio to protect the British commerce, and, if it be possible *without violating the Spanish Territory* [emphasis added]" stop the pirates. Rowley thus took few strong actions, although the warship *Tyne* sailed into Santiago de Cuba on 14 June, liberated *Swift* and obtained compensation for its illegal seizure by a Spanish privateer.[22]

Still, Rowley ordered his ships to act against pirates. On 16 May he ordered one of the warships stationed off Cape San Antonio to help protect British commerce until he received word that the local Spanish authorities intended to act. When Rowley obtained intelligence from customs officials that pirates infested the waters around Sambero and Dog Island, he ordered a ship "to examine those places frequently." By July 1822 Rowley seemed to have settled into a patrol pattern that tried to balance trade protection with the hunt for pirates. For example, on 5 July 1822 he ordered *Sybille* to convoy merchantmen bound for Savanilla, Santa Martha and Carthagena. *Tamar* would soon sail to escort trading vessels to the Gulf of Mexico and "look into the inlets in the neighbourhood of Cape [San] Antonio, and endeavour to get hold of the pirates[.]" Sir Charles, the youngest son of Sir Joshua Rowley, was

---

[21]*The Times* (London), 24 July 1822.

[22]TNA/PRO, ADM 2/1585, Croker to Sir Charles Rowley, 23 March 1822; and ADM 50/136, Rowley, Journal, entries for 22 March, 10 April, 1 and 5 May and 24 June 1822.

from a naval family; because he felt that the squadron was "fully occupied," he feared any more requests from merchants for help.[23]

The above examples show that Rowley's deployment was reactive to threats. But Britain's broader foreign policy moulded the naval effort. Part of Canning's stronger action in late 1822, for example, was to dispatch naval reinforcements in response to calls at home for greater trade protection. He hoped to allay the fears of other nations over this exercise of sea power. The French, for instance, were concerned, so Canning asked the British ambassador to France, Sir Charles Stuart, to calm their fears. Moreover, although Cuba was the focus of anti-pirate operations, London ordered its naval commander to consult with the local authorities before acting. Canning explained that only if the Spanish accepted the British offer was the RN to give its "active assistance for dislodging and punishing the offenders." If the local authorities refused, the RN was only "reluctantly" to seek out pirates.[24] Britain had to balance the needs of the gentlemanly capitalists with the use of sea power if either threatened Canning's diplomatic goals or relations with other nations.

As a result, the Admiralty sent *Seringapatam*, under Captain Samuel Warren, *Redwing* (Captain George Trefusis) and *Grecian* (Lieutenant Cawley) to Cuba to hunt for pirates. The small force arrived at Cape San Antonio on 21 November 1822 and found *Hyperion* sailing for Jamaica with thirty captive pirates. On 22 December another warship, *Scout*, sailed into Havana with nineteen prisoners, eight French and eleven English, captured in Honduras Bay. But the force quickly gave up and on Christmas Eve 1822 sailed for England. The Admiralty believed that Rowley's force was sufficient for convoying; when on 29 November J.W. Buckle, Chairman of the Ship Owners' Committee, requested convoys for the West Indies, the Admiralty replied that they had already been established.[25]

The US press noted the half-hearted British efforts to combat piracy in the West Indies during 1822. The Charleston *City Gazette* declared on 6 January that it was glad that British warships were "at last following the laudable example" set by the USN. The American press was surprised at the compla-

---

[23]*Ibid.*, ADM 50/136, Rowley, Journal, entries for 16 May, 25 June and 5 and 27 July 1822; and *Dictionary of National Biography*, s.v. "Rowley, Sir Charles" and "Rowley, Sir Joshua."

[24]*Ibid.*, Foreign Office (FO) 27/265, reprinted in Charles K. Webster (ed.), *Britain and the Independence of Latin America, 1812-1830: Select Documents from the Foreign Office Archives* (2 vols., London, 1938; reprint, New York, 1970, II, 109-110, Canning to Sir Charles Stuart, 1 December 1822.

[25]*Hampshire Telegraph*, reprinted in *The Times* (London), 3 February 1823; TNA/PRO, ADM 2/1586, Croker to Rowley, 11 November 1822; and Croker to J.W. Buckle, 30 November 1822, printed in *The Times* (London), 2 December 1822.

cency of the British government. The *American and Commercial Daily Advertiser* exclaimed that "[i]t is a matter of surprize, that the British Government does not keep a force, as the U. States do, in the neighbourhood of Cuba, for the protection of their commerce." American envoy Richard Rush was amazed that "in this year of 1822, we should have witnessed the [surprising] fact...of the commerce of England having been protected" by the USN. But in London, *The Times* editorialized that while the Americans deployed under Porter, Britain took "things with their usual apathy and indifference, and take no notice of these depredations."[26] No one seemed to understand British naval policy.

Considering London's wider geopolitical concerns, the Admiralty warned commanders not to become inadvertently involved in the ongoing regional wars. Gerald Graham and R.A. Humphreys concluded that on the South American station the RN acted as "consuls and diplomats; to protect British interests, at a time when British trade was establishing its first direct and legitimate contacts." This was a delicate operation, and the captains deployed were "usually men of considerable experience in action – [and] in general performed their duties with notable discretion and distinction."[27]

Farther north, Admiral Rowley's orders reflected the Admiralty's restraint regarding the piracy threat. On 30 January 1823 he ordered Captain James Lilliecrap to sail for Santiago de Cuba to seek restitution for Spanish privateer attacks. Nevertheless, if Havana refused to address the problem, Lilliecrap was to "immediately leave port" and inform the Cuban Captain-General that he would detain any Spanish privateer entering or leaving port. Rather than take stronger action against Spain, Rowley ordered Lilliecrap to look for pirates in the Bay of Honda, Colorados Reef and Cape San Antonio. While convoys were established to escort vessels past Florida, London also wanted to maintain strict neutrality. To this end, the Admiralty warned Captain Thomas J. Cochrane that British warships were forbidden to "convoy any Merchant Vessels avowedly loaded with Articles Contraband of War." When Vice Admiral Halsted in 1824 forwarded a request from the Secretary of State of Colombia for RN protection for specie transports from Jamaica to Colombia, the Admiralty responded that the RN could only convoy specie if "the goods were bound for England or belonged to British merchants."[28]

---

[26]*ACDA*, 14 January and 15 June 1822; United States, National Archives (NA), Record Group (RG) 59, Dispatches, Britain, No. 269, Richard Rush to John Quincy Adams, 28 September 1822; and *The Times* (London), 6 May 1823.

[27]Gerald S. Graham and R.A. Humphreys (eds.), *The Navy and South America 1807-1823: Correspondence of the Commanders-in-Chief on the South American Station* (London, 1962), xi.

[28]TNA/PRO, ADM 1/273, Rowley to James Lilliecrap, 30 January 1823; ADM 2/1586, Croker to Rowley, 24 April 1823; John Barrow to Captain Thomas J.

Table 4.1
RN Pirate Captures for which Head Money Awarded, 1821-1847

Year	Gulf of Mexico/ West Indies	African Coast	Medi-terra-nean	Grecian Archi-pelago	East Indies	Other	Total
1821			1				1
1822	3			1			4
1823	7	1					8
1824	4						4
1825				4			4
1826	1		1	6			8
1827			2	4			6
1828	1						1
1829							
1830							
1831							
1832							
1833					1		1
1834						1	1
1835							
1836					5		5
1837							
1838					1		1
1839							
1840					1		1
1841							
1842							
1843					2		2
1844					2	1	3
1845		1					1
1846					1		1
1847					1		1
Total	16	2	4	15	14	2	53

Note: For missing years there were no reports of pirate captures for which head money was awarded. "Other" indicates an unclear geographic location. Year refers to the date of payment.

Source: Calculated from Great Britain, Parliament, *Parliamentary Papers* (*BPP*), 1850, LV, 49-56, Return of Amount Paid as Head-Money for Capture of Pirates, 1826-1849, J.T. Briggs, Accountant-General of the Navy, 6 March 1850.

Cochrane, 19 July 1823; and ADM 2/1587, Barrow to Vice Admiral Halsted, 5 June 1824 and 4 June 1825.

RN operations continued against the pirates in 1824, but an analysis of head money awarded for captured pirates shows that thereafter piracy declined and anti-piracy operations moved on to other regions (see table 4.1). For example, the Admiralty issued a briefing on 22 September 1827 to the West Indies senior commander, Vice Admiral C.E. Fleming, and to Commodore Francis Augustus Collier, son of Vice Admiral Sir George Collier, on the Africa station, reporting that a British ship had been attacked by pirates *en route* from Africa to England. On 22 March 1828 the Admiralty issued similar orders to African and West Indies commanders when *New Prospect*, a London merchant ship, was attacked by a pirate at 22° 23'N by 36° 41'W. London wanted the RN to use all necessary means to stop the pirates, despite the locations of the attacks.[29] British actions reveal that working to protect gentlemanly interests was one thing, but action against privateers and local authorities was another because it went against the liberal ideal of British foreign policy.

Anglo-American Naval Relations and Piracy Suppression

Faced with a common threat, Britain and the US used sea power to provide immediate commerce protection. But suspicious of each other and constrained by their own objectives and diplomacy, the joint use of sea power occurred only as circumstances arose. While the USN was effective in limited, regional efforts when US interests were threatened, the RN, deployed all along the North American and West Indies station, was the only force capable of policing the wider seas. As US anti-piracy efforts ended in the late 1820s and naval policymakers again retreated, the American government realized that even the region close to shore depended on the RN for protection. When piracy flared periodically, the Americans and British cooperated, but with the pirates moving farther afield it was the RN that had the wide net necessary to protect economic interests in the equatorial Atlantic.

But when a piracy crisis erupted, the RN and USN found themselves operating in the same waters, and the former worried that American actions would upset the regional balance of power. In early 1823, for example, William Gray, British consul in Virginia, told Rowley that the American deployment to Key West was planned as "a more permanent footing in Cuba." Although British Ambassador Stratford Canning believed that the US would even use "intrigue" to prevent the island falling into the hands of another power, he tried to allay Rowley's fears. Nevertheless, Rowley concluded that it was pru-

---

[29]*Dictionary of National Biography*, s.v. "Collier, Francis Augustus;" TNA/PRO, ADM 2/1588, Barrow to C.E. Fleeming [also Flemming and Fleming in the records] and copy to [Francis Augustus] Collier, 22 September 1827; and ADM 2/1589, Barrow to Collier, with similar letter to Flemming and Senior Officers of HM Ships at Barbadoes [sic], 10 May 1828.

dent to dispatch HMS *Athol* to gather intelligence on American activities.[30] The RN took a consistently cautious approach.

An American officer, probably Lieutenant Lawrence Kearney, told Captain Bourchier of *Athol* that he was patrolling for pirates and that the Key West base had only minimal provisions and a guard of about 100 marines. Bourchier decided that it would raise suspicions if he sailed to Key West to gather more information, but he concluded that the Cubans wished to remain under Spanish sovereignty.[31] Although the British laid aside their suspicions of the US, cooperation was still limited. The British cooperated with the Americans against pirates, but joint suppression of privateering was never discussed. Yet Anglo-American naval relations in the Gulf were amicable, and the British avoided raising the suspicions of their American counterparts.

Porter made special mention of the RN's Jamaica station in his 1823 report. He thought that the US squadron was large enough to carry out its duties and was willing to leave Anglo-American cooperation to "circumstances." Although he did not provide any examples, one case of cooperation occurred in 1823. Two American naval schooners joined HMS *Bustard*, commanded by Captain R. Maclean, to hunt pirates. When Maclean joined Porter in *Sea Gull*, they cruised along the Keys, tested the accuracy of Admiralty charts and provided aid to some of Maclean's sick crew. The Admiralty was pleased "at the good understanding and cooperation which has taken place between the British & American Squadrons."[32] Working together helped calm relations.

Porter's successor, Lewis Warrington, seemed more inclined to cooperate with the British. On 21 March, for example, an American formation under Lieutenant Commander Isaac McKeever fell in with a British detachment from HMS *Dartmouth* to search for a pirate ship that had recently attacked shipping. While the British had no intelligence about its location, McKeever did and proposed a united operation. The British agreed that the schooners remain in Cadiz Bay, along with *Sea Gull*, while McKeever took a barge and two small cutters to sail with a British barge and two more cutters.[33]

---

[30]TNA/PRO, ADM 1/273, William Gray to Rowley, undated, enclosure in Rowley to Croker, Admiralty Office, 17 March 1823; [Stratford] Canning to Rowley, 7 February 1823; and Rowley to Captain Bourchier, undated [c. 27 March 1823].

[31]*Ibid.*, ADM 1/274, Bourchier to Rowley, 10 April 1823.

[32]*Ibid.*, ADM 1/275, R. Maclean to Porter, 23 July 1823; Maclean to Edward Owen, 20 and 26 September 1823; ADM 2/1586, Croker to Owen, 6 October 1823; and *S. Doc.*, No. 1, 18th Cong., 1st sess., 191, Porter to Secretary of the Navy, 19 November 1823.

[33]*S. Doc.*, No. 2, 19th Cong., 1st sess., 113, Warrington, 3 April 1825; and 19th Cong., 1st sess., 114-117, Isaac McKeever to Warrington, 1 April 1825.

At Jutia Gorda Key they discovered a suspicious vessel which raised the Spanish flag. The pirates attempted to fire, with little luck, as the formation's boats bore down. McKeever hailed the pirate ship and told its commander to go ashore and hold his fire. The force captured the pirate captain, but then gunfire erupted. When the British and Americans stormed the ship, some pirates scurried below deck, while others fled into the bushes. In the end, the force failed to find the pirates, so they took the prize and sailed to the pirate lair at Key la Cosinerra, set it ablaze and sailed back to Jutia Gorda, where they burned pirate shore facilities. Warrington applauded the British "for their efficient co-operation[.]" The Admiralty was also pleased with the outcome. Nevertheless, it remained cautious and warned commanders to be careful to stay clear of the region's disputes.[34]

London's geopolitical strategy moderated its use of sea power. While the RN could hunt for pirates at sea, it had to be careful about going ashore while Britain considered whether recognizing the rebel states would further its commercial objectives. British policy concerns also helped shape its responses to the US. The Americans wanted a common policy towards Latin America but first insisted that the British recognize the rebels. Britain wanted a common policy toward Cuba and piracy, but by this time piracy was checked, and the US saw a formal agreement as unnecessary. The only true commonalities were trade protection and conflict avoidance, but these provided a mechanism through which the nations could relate peacefully within the same region.

During the conflict in the Gulf of Mexico, the personal opinions of US commanders and British European and regional strategy influenced Anglo-American cooperation. The early war against the slavers reflected this reality. US domestic policy impaired Anglo-American cooperation, while the RN was free to act with few constraints against non-American-flag vessels. But US efforts along the West African coast were in support of its colonization schemes, and American naval deployment was limited to occasional vessels diverted from anti-piracy duties. When those tasks ended, and Washington reduced its anti-piracy force, US naval efforts in West Africa declined. Americans along the coast then found that the RN was their sole protector.

The ACS, Colonization and Limited US Support

The White House hoped that its limited West African response would placate the British and the ACS, but before the 1819 Anti-Slave Trade Act, the ACS had little experience on the West African coast. It started colonization efforts in November 1817 by dispatching the Reverend Samuel J. Mills and Ebenezer

---

[34]*Ibid.*, 19th Cong., 1st sess., 113 and 116-117, McKeever to Warrington, 1 April 1825; Warrington, 3 April 1825; and TNA/PRO, ADM 2/1587, Barrow to Halsted, 4 June 1824 and 15 April 1825.

Burgess to look for land suitable for a colony between Sherbro Island and Sierra Leone (see figure 4.3). Colonization efforts stagnated, however, as the ACS gathered funding and government support. Meanwhile, US African agent Samuel Bacon warned Navy Secretary Thompson as early as 1820 that the role of American colonization efforts should be clear and explained to prevent misunderstandings with other powers.[35] Washington agreed for domestic and international reasons and was wary of too forceful a presence on the coast.

The ACS's actions were most forceful under the tenure of its agent, Jehudi Ashmun, who told the Secretary of the Navy that the colony was in a state of war with the natives and that 800 had attacked the colony on 11 November 1822. Captain Laing of the British Light Infantry negotiated a settlement, but the colony still needed an American warship to maintain US interests along the coast. Its absence harmed relations with other powers, and Ashmun believed that relying on British aid put both the US government and the ACS in positions of obligation to the British. Consequently, by the spring of 1826 Ashmun began to wage war against the slavers by using a readily available naval force: Colombian privateers who had expanded their operations to the West African coast. An American, Captain John Chase, commanded the Colombian armed schooner *Jacinta*. Ashmun used this resource, took thirty troops to Trade Town and joined another Colombian cruiser, *El Vencedor*, to fire broadsides into the town, driving the natives into the woods. But the Secretary of the Navy and the President condemned these actions because the government had not "intended to authorize...a forcible and warlike attack upon the citizens or subjects of any nation[.]" The Navy Department warned the agent to keep the business of the ACS and the US separate.[36]

---

[35]Frankie Hutton, "Economic Considerations in the American Colonization Society's Early Efforts to Emigrate Free Blacks to Liberia, 1816-36," *Journal of Negro History*, LXVIII, No. 4 (1983), 376-277; Amos J. Beyan, *The American Colonization Society and the Creation of the Liberian State: A Historical Perspective, 1822-1900* (Lanham, MD, 1991), 51-53; NA, RG 45, Naval Records Collection of the Office of Naval Records and Library, Records of the Secretary of the Navy, Correspondence of the Secretary of the Navy Relating to African Colonization, 1819-1844, Letters Sent (Letters Sent Relating to African Colonization), Thompson to Samuel Bacon, 17 January 1820; and NA, RG 45, Correspondence of the Secretary of the Navy Relating to African Colonization, 1819-1844, Letters Received (Letters Received Relating to African Colonization), Bacon to Thompson, 12 March 1820.

[36]NA, RG 45, Letters Sent Relating to African Colonization, Southard to John Peaco, 2 April 1827; *S. Doc.*, No. 1, 18th Cong., 1st sess., paper f, 122-123 and paper g, 124, Jehudi Ashmun to Secretary of the Navy, 26 November and 7 December 1822; 19th Cong., 2nd sess., 99-101, Southard to Peaco, 10 August 1826; No. 1, 19th Cong., 2nd sess., 98-99, John Chase, 31 July 1826; and P.J. Staudenraus, *The African Colonization Movement 1816-1865* (New York, 1961), 89 and 161-168.

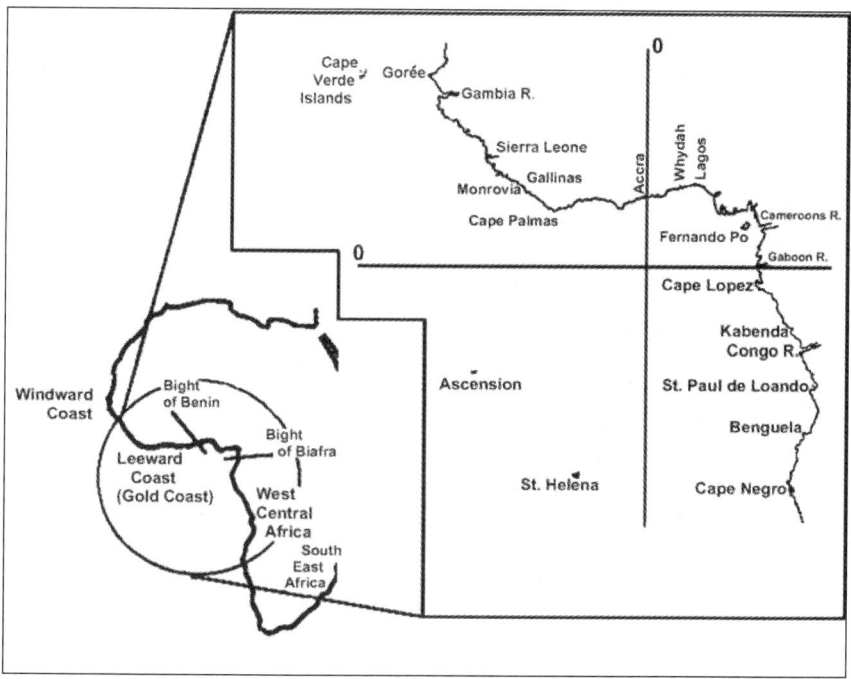

Figure 4.3:   West Africa

Note: Locations are approximations only.

Source: Courtesy of the author, with area zoom based on map contained in United
                   States, National Archives (NA), Record Group (RG) 45, Squadron Let-
                   ters, CVIII, African Squadron, Francis H. Gregory to William Ballard
                   Preston, 3 September 1850.

Washington wanted a discrete approach to West Africa that respected
the national mood and minimized potential conflict. Instead, Ashmun's actions
gave ammunition to those who opposed the President's Africa plan. Senator
Robert Young Hayne, a Jacksonian from South Carolina, declared that Ashmun's actions reflected poorly on the US and threatened the trade of other nations. Congressional support for US efforts fell so far that by 23 May 1828 the
House passed a Bill to close the US African agency, and the Senate began a
full, if short, debate on funding for slave-trade suppression. Many agreed that
the ACS's use of government funds was improper, and on 3 March 1831 they

asked the President to resume talks with other powers to suppress the slave trade rather than continue a potentially destabilizing policy in the region.[37]

The domestic imperatives were clear. On 28 March 1832, Senators opposed to colonization claimed that it threatened the Union and Southern sensibilities. They warned that any discussion of colonization would "undoubtedly tend to increase the excitement which now prevails in one quarter of the Union" over abolition.[38] Perhaps to avoid a full US overseas commitment, Congress placed the onus on the White House to open talks with the British on a more effective means to suppress the slave trade. When the talks failed, the White House abandoned the issue. In the long term, as tempers between North and South flared, little else could be accomplished as long as American interests in Africa and slave-trade suppression were linked. Nevertheless, the concept emerged that peacetime naval relations with other powers in distant lands could be a stabilizing influence for American interests.

Limited US Naval Support

The limited naval support for West African endeavours reflected the limited government backing for African colonization. The government only provided the USN with forces it could spare from the West Indian anti-piracy patrols. When Washington reduced the forces on that patrol, it had ramifications for US efforts in Africa. Judd Scott Harmon has concluded that the USN and the ACS had a "marriage" that complemented each other in the effort to suppress the slave trade. Harmon claimed that the navy made regular voyages to the coast but failed to state whether a November-December cruise, for instance, meant 30 November to 7 December or an entire two-month patrol. In reality, it was hardly a "naval force" on "constant patrol of the coast[;]" US ships were only there for brief periods at the end of piracy patrols.[39]

As the piracy crisis deepened, US warships first had to tackle the immediate threat before sailing to a region far removed from America's primary interests. For example, after relinquishing some pirate prizes, *Shark* (Matthew

---

[37]*Register of Debates*, 19th Cong., 2nd sess., 290-296 and 326-334, Senate, 7 and 9 February 1827; 20th Cong., 1st sess., 2753, House, 23 May 1828; 20th Cong., 1st sess., 808-809, Senate, 24 May 1828; and 21st Cong., 2nd sess., 850, House, 3 March 1831.

[38]*Ibid.*, 22nd Cong., 1st sess., 642-646, Senate, 28 March 1832.

[39]Judd Scott Harmon, "Marriage of Convenience: The United States Navy in Africa, 1820-1843," *American Neptune*, XXXII, No. 4 (1972), 264-276. See also Harmon, "Suppress and Protect: The United States Navy, The African Slave Trade, and Maritime Commerce, 1794-1862" (Unpublished PhD thesis, College of William and Mary, 1977).

Perry) arrived on the African coast on 23 August 1822 but left again nine days later. Perry reported that he heard of no American ships involved in the slave trade. The Cape colony was fine and relations good with the natives. The latter observation reveals how little time Perry must have spent on the coast, given the tensions that erupted into native attacks by November. *Shark* then returned to the West Indies, sailing past the pirate lair of Cape San Antonio and onward to Norfolk via the Gulf of Florida. Meanwhile, *Cyane* arrived off the West African coast in the spring of 1823 after a "long cruise in the West Indies" hunting pirates. Shortly thereafter, Captain Robert T. Spence filed his report from quarantine in New York after a year on patrol.[40]

By 1826 the USN had reduced its anti-piracy efforts as that crisis waned. On 4 August 1826 Ashmun noted the impact of what had transpired on the other side of the Atlantic and believed it had ramifications for the West African coast. The English, French and Colombian "navies" had put the pirates and slavers on the defensive. Nonetheless, on 20 July 1826 pirates had attacked an American brig and schooner and seized $5000 worth of cargo. Moreover, the American settlement owed a debt to the RN, then cruising in the Bight. Ashmun realized that the RN had the widest net in which to catch pirates and slavers but feared for the colony's fate without American aid.[41]

On 18 March 1827, Lieutenant Commander Otho Norris of USS *Shark* confirmed some of Ashmun's observations. Norris sailed from the Chesapeake for Mesurado on 30 November 1826, arriving at the Cape on 12 January and at Trade Town on 29 January where it chased a small French slaver manned by seventeen French sailors, flying the French flag and armed with a brass pivot gun. The colony was doing well, but in December 1826 a British warship captured a pirate brig that had attacked a US merchant ship at Mesurado Roads that August.[42] In the absence of consuls and diplomats, the US needed a naval presence in the region to relate to other powers.

As the 1830s ended, slavers continued to hide under the American flag, but the US naval response continued to be reactive. Because of reports on the activities of slavers, the Secretary of the Navy, James K. Paulding, sent a warship to the coast. Paulding wrote that it would protect commerce and pursue "these pirates [slavers] who thus make the American flag a cover to such

---

[40]*S. Doc.*, No. 1, 18th Cong., 1st sess., paper h, 125, Matthew C. Perry to Secretary of the Navy, 12 December 1822; No. 2, 18th Cong., 1st sess., paper j, 128 and paper l, 130-134, Spence to Ashmun, 1 April 1823; and Spence to Secretary of the Navy, 27 June 1823.

[41]NA, RG 45, Letters Received Relating to African Colonization, Ashmun to Southard, 4 August 1826.

[42]*S. Doc.*, No. 1, 20th Cong., 1st sess., 224-225, Otho Norris to Charles Ridgely, 18 March 1827.

disgraceful purposes."[43] In all, US naval actions along the West African coast
were confined to tacit support of colonization efforts. Due to this policy, the
USN took little significant action against the slave trade. With such a small
naval force and a reluctance to agree to British proposals to cooperate against
the slave trade, Anglo-American naval cooperation was limited and informal,
as in the Gulf of Mexico. But off West Africa, the less constrained RN used
sea power more fully in support of British policies.

The Royal Navy off West Africa

During the 1820s and early 1830s, the RN on the West African coast was responsible for suppressing the slave trade and hunting stray pirates. But it had
to contend with slavers who had at least the tacit approval of their governments. By the 1840s, other nations participated in anti-slaving operations, but
the RN realized that blockading ports was ineffectual.[44] Africa was also important to the British as a secondary trade route to India, and the RN's presence
would address the concern that other powers might block British access to India via the Cape of Good Hope.[45] During the 1820s, the RN also reported that
the African coast had a great potential to contribute to Britain's economic
growth. This too had to be protected from pirates, privateers and slave traders
who interfered with the expansion of legitimate British commerce.

After the passage of the 1807 act banning the slave trade, Britain created a squadron to patrol the 3000 miles of West African coast.[46] Christopher
Lloyd concluded that this force was not a priority for the Admiralty since on
average the station only had ten warships. David Eltis supported this view by
calculating that only about four percent of British naval manpower was devoted
to the coast in the 1820s and 1830s.[47] Nevertheless, British naval deployment

---

[43]NA, RG 45, Letters Sent Relating to African Colonization, J.K. Paulding to
Thomas Buchanan, 22 July 1839.

[44]W.E.F. Ward, *The Royal Navy and the Slavers: The Suppression of the Atlantic Slave Trade* (London, 1969), 38-39 and 196-199.

[45]Ronald Robinson and John Gallagher, *Africa and the Victorians: The Official Mind of Imperialism* (London, 1961; 2nd ed., London, 1981), 13-14; and Clark G.
Reynolds, *Command of the Sea: The History and Strategy of Maritime Empires* (London, 1976), 333-343.

[46]Hugh Thomas, *The Slave Trade: The Story of the Atlantic Slave Trade,
1440-1870* (New York, 1997), 574 and 576.

[47]Christopher Lloyd, *The Navy and the Slave Trade: The Suppression of the
African Slave Trade in the Nineteenth Century* (London, 1949; reprint, London, 1968),

matched the strategic philosophy of the period. An analysis of RN deployment patterns (figures 4.4 and 4.5) reveals that the West Indies peaked during the piracy crisis, while the Mediterranean became increasingly important, as indicated by the doubling of armament deployed from 576 to 1082 guns in 1828-1830 during the deepening crisis over Greek independence. Clearly, deployment fluctuated along with British strategic concerns. Meanwhile, the size of the West African squadron also varied with London's overall strategic and economic concerns. It was expected to combine slave-trade suppression, trade promotion and protection of this important route to India from potential French threats.

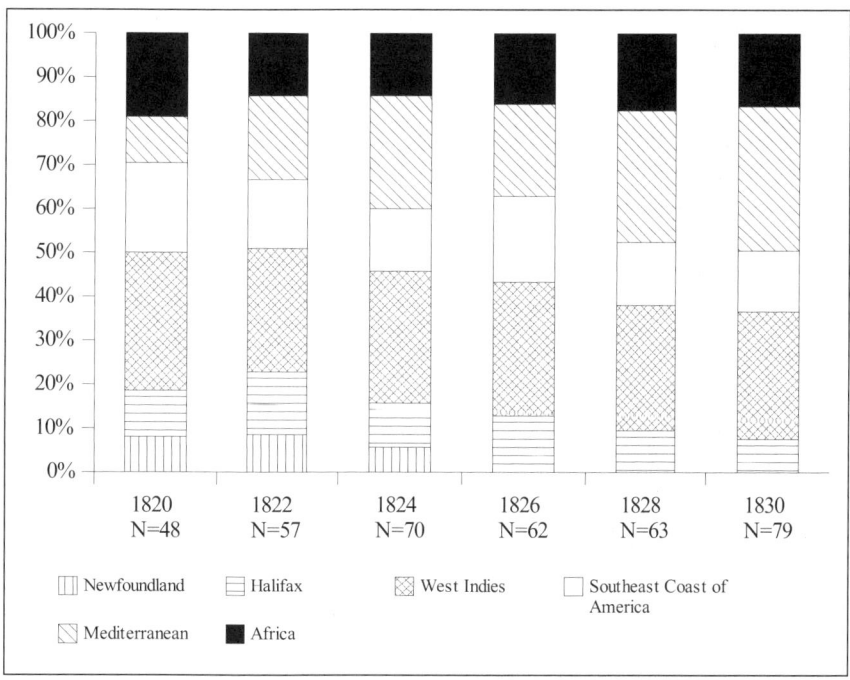

Figure 4.4: Royal Navy Vessel Deployment, Atlantic, 1820-1830

Note: Vessels such as supply depots, convict ships, vessels conducting surveys, etc., are not counted. N = Number of Warships.

Source: Calculated from TNA/PRO, Navy List, 1820-1830.

69-73; Ward, *Royal Navy and the Slavers*, 97 and 113; and David Eltis, *Economic Growth and the Ending of the Transatlantic Slave Trade* (New York, 1987), 92.

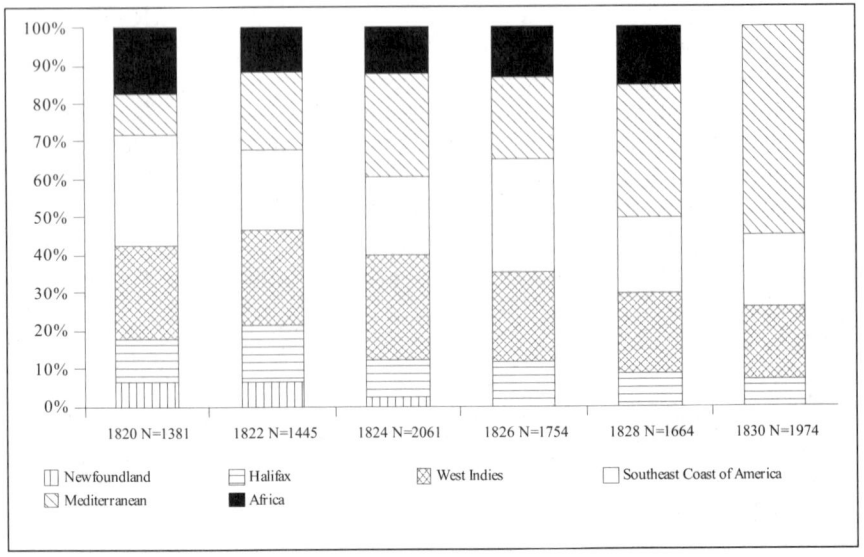

Figure 4.5: Royal Navy Armament Deployed, 1820-1830

Note: Armament information for the Africa station is missing from the Navy
             List for 1830. N = Number of guns deployed.

Source: See figure 4.4.

Africa represented between fourteen and nineteen percent of the RN's
Atlantic deployment between 1820 and 1830, or between nine and thirteen
ships carrying a total of 167 to 258 guns. The squadron usually consisted of up
to two sixth-rate, twenty-eight gun, light frigates and a fourth- or fifth-rate,
forty- or fifty-gun flagship. The sloop was the squadron's workhorse. Its draft
was small enough that it could traverse river bars, undertake coastal operations
and chase slavers. A blockade along the entire coast to suppress the slave trade
was "impossible;" instead, the RN cruised between "specific points." The
patrol areas comprised Senegal to Sierra Leone, Sierra Leone to Cape Coast
Castle and Cape Coast Castle to the Bights. From 1832 to 1839, the West African station was combined with the Cape station and was responsible for an
area from 10°S on the east coast to Cape Verde. Even when the Admiralty
again removed the West African squadron from Cape command, its jurisdiction was expanded to include the area from Cape Verde to Benguela.[48] While

---

[48]Lloyd, *Navy and the Slave Trade*, 69 and 78; and Ward, *Royal Navy and the
Slavers*, 25-37.

patrolling the coast, the squadron's officers also relayed important information back to London.

While the British were interested in suppressing the slave trade for humanitarian reasons, naval officers also reported on Africa's economic potential. In 1821 Commodore George R. Collier reported that the interior might soon be opened to British trade. In addition, the island of Fernando Po, with soil that rivalled that in the West Indies, was strategically located to block the slave trade. Collier believed that if the RN stationed warships there it could blockade the Camaroons, Del Rey, Calabar and Bonny River and sortie below the equator. Merchants from Glasgow and Liverpool were interested in Fernando Po, for wood, oysters and fish were plentiful, and Collier managed to trade with some natives who came down to the beach. The island intrigued his superiors, and an Admiralty memo at the beginning of the Fernando Po section of his report noted "[e]tract made for Lord Melville 19 Nov[ember] 1823."[49]

Figure 4.6: Fernando Po

Source: National Maritime Museum, Negative No. PU1916. © National Maritime
        Museum, London

---

[49]TNA/PRO, ADM 1/1675, "Commodore Sir G.R. Collier's Final Report on the Coast of Africa, 1821."

The region had potential, and perhaps English "gentlemen" could help develop it. First, though, someone had to suppress the slave trade to shift local production factors into "legitimate" commerce. British merchants, for example, complained about the duties that King Peppel forced them to pay on the Bonny River, where slave traders received preference. Peppel said that although the slave trade was his primary means of support, he would end it if Britain sent a seventy-four-gun ship, loaded with tribute, to his kingdom annually. Commodore Sir Robert Mends believed warships would help make the reluctant king an ally. But the Americans and French were more troublesome than the natives. After encounters with their merchant vessels, Mends concluded that the French and Americans "had determined to put every one of our people to death who fell into their hands[.]"[50] Station commanders believed that sea power was important to further British interests in the region.

Admiralty instructions to Commodore Mends and others provide indications of naval duties during the 1820s. The RN was to provide assistance to British African settlements and interdict the trade in slaves by British ships and those countries with which Britain had anti-slaving treaties. In contrast to the Gulf of Mexico, the Admiralty told Mends to hunt Spanish slavers because Spain's right to take slaves from below the equator had expired. In accordance with treaty stipulations, the Admiralty sent orders from 6 February 1821 to 21 March 1822 to vessels on the East Indies, Cape of Good Hope, South American, Leeward Islands and Jamaica stations to stop Spanish and Portuguese slavers. But despite these efforts, slaving continued. The navy found that slavers often loaded their human cargo upriver, hoping to stay clear of British warships. For example, on 10 August 1821 *Myrmidon* found six French slavers in the Bonny River. Meanwhile, the British tried in vain to seize some Spanish ships, but they became embroiled in a fire fight. Captain Henry Leeke decided to take *Myrmidon* upriver "to punish the renegadoes for their insolent conduct." The Spanish abandoned their two vessels when the warship approached, and Leeke's force freed 130 slaves from the schooner and 154 from the brig. Leeke preferred this course because the King of Bonny allegedly preferred slavers and refused to deal with legitimate British merchants. Only if they suppressed the slave trade, some officers believed, would legitimate commerce flourish.[51] The navy had to protect this growing endeavour.

---

[50]*Ibid.*, ADM 1/2188, "A Report on the State of the Slave Trade in the Western Coast of Africa by Commodore Sir Robert Mends," 26 June 1822, enclosure in Cap. M 262, Mends to Croker, 14 October 1822; and Cap. M 174, No. 6, Mends to Croker, 17 April 1822.

[51]Great Britain, Parliament, *Parliamentary Papers* (*BPP*), 1822, XXII, Communications from and Instructions to Naval Officers, Relative to Suppression of Slave Trade, 1821-22, No. 2, "Extract from the Instructions Issued by the Lords Commissioners of the Admiralty...to Commodore Sir Robert Mends," 31 October 1821; and

The RN also met threats to legitimate commerce from privateers operating along the coast. Commodore Collier concluded that Spanish slavers were the biggest threat in the early 1820s. He explained that despite the fact that Spain had signed an anti-slaving treaty with Britain, Spanish subjects carried on the trade. While Collier found no privateering papers, he encountered ships that had sailed from Havana and were outfitted for this task. For example, on 16 February 1821 *Myrmidon* stopped the Spanish privateer *Charlotta* before it bought slaves at Gallinas.[52] From his reports, "piracy" and the slave trade were linked, and the "piracy" that spread around the equatorial Atlantic world was a major contributor to the slave trade on the West African coast.

As late as September 1825 Commodore Charles Bullen reported that armed "Spanish" ships arrived daily along the coast and annoyed British traders. He concluded that these vessels obtained "their cargo for trade chiefly by plunder; by which means they are enabled to purchase their slaves at a much more reasonable rate than other vessels[.]" Bullen tried to chase one of the pirates, the Spanish brig *Alerta*, but it ran into Lagos Roads, loaded its slaves and quickly sailed for Havana before he could intercede. Moreover, ships in the slave trade took advantage of Spanish letters of marque to cloak their activities. For instance, in November 1825 William Pennell, British consul in Bahia, reported that *Carlota*, a Spanish privateer, had sailed with seven British sailors and was probably involved in the slave trade. On 25 February 1826 the Admiralty passed along the intelligence regarding *Carlota* to its vessels along the African coast.[53]

Early Anglo-American Naval Cooperation

Britain and America deployed their navies and used sea power in various parts of the equatorial Atlantic for divergent "short-term" objectives. The conduct of Anglo-American naval relations illuminates the state of their wider connec-

---

1823, XVIII, No. 1, Communications from and Instructions to Naval Officers Relative to the Suppression of the Slave Trade, 451-452, No. 1, Henry John Leeke to Mends, 12 September 1821.

[52]TNA/PRO, ADM 1/1675, Cap. C 84, Collier to Croker, 4 March 1821; and Leeke to Collier, 20 February 1821, enclosure in, Cap C 84, Collier to Croker, 4 March 1821.

[53]*Ibid.*, ADM 1/1572, Cap. B 215, No. 29, Charles Bullen to Croker, 12 September 1825; and *BPP*, 1826, XXVI, Communications from and Instructions to Naval Officers Relative to the Suppression of the Slave Trade, March 1825-January 1826, 529, No. 7 and enclosures 1 and 2, Barrow to Bullen, 25 February 1826; William Pennell to Consul Chamberlain, 23 November 1825; and Pennell to Viscount of Queluz, 21 November 1825.

tions. Since the two had different objectives, their cooperative uses of sea power were minimal and intended to stave off potential conflict rather than to resolve outstanding issues. Thus, the Americans hoped to placate the British by deploying US sea power to suppress the slave trade. But this sporadic effort failed to impress Britain, and the RN remained the only force willing to police the entire equatorial Atlantic. Yet to achieve its economic goals, London needed American cooperation to suppress the slave trade and encourage legitimate commerce because Whitehall was unwilling to wage all-out war to attain those objectives.

Soon after the restoration of peace, the British intensified their efforts against the slavers and pressured John Quincy Adams for US support. On 30 December 1820 Adams explained that the President wanted some form of cooperation with Britain to suppress the slave trade. Despite the clear evidence that the American naval presence on the West African coast was sporadic, Adams claimed that US warships had "for some time [been] kept stationed on the Coast which is the scene of this odious traffic" and that this would continue in the future. The British government accepted this bland assurance and instructed the Admiralty to pass it on to its African squadron. Meanwhile, Adams stalled and only told the Navy Department of the "agreement" on 15 September 1821. Nevertheless, in 1820 and 1821, *Hornet* and *John Adams* sailed with HMS *Snapper*, and the British and Americans exchanged intelligence.[54]

Although Britain accepted the American position, it quickly realized that it was more rhetoric than reality. Nonetheless, it used naval relations with the US to communicate its sincerity. In May 1821 the Foreign Office and the Admiralty ordered RN ships to give "general assistance" to any US warships as long as this was "consistent with the existing treaties and rights of both nations, and with the friendly relations and perfect amity subsisting between them." In addition, Stratford Canning attempted to foster a degree of commonality between the nations and forwarded to Adams details of the Admiralty's instructions. Canning hoped that this would provide guidance for the composition of orders to "any American vessels destined to cruise on the coast of Africa." But he told the Admiralty that "[i]t does not appear that the American government has, at this moment, more than one vessel, a schooner, expressly commissioned against the Slave Trade[.]"[55]

---

[54]Earl E. McNeilly, "The United States Navy and the Suppression of the West African Slave Trade, 1819-1862" (Unpublished PhD thesis, Case Western Reserve University, 1973), 51-52; and NA, RG 45, Letters Received Relating to African Colonization, "Extract of a Letter from the Secretary of State to Mr. Canning dated Washington 30 December 1820," in Adams to Thompson, 15 August 1821.

[55]*BPP*, 1822, XXII, Communications from and Instructions to Naval Officers Relative to the Suppression of the Slave Trade, 593, No. 1 and enclosure B, "Copy of a Letter from Mr. [John] Barrow to Commodore Sir George Ralph Collier," 24 May

Nevertheless, Canning told Adams that Britain would consider American proposals for some system of joint patrol, rather than fighting over their differences. His government was willing to consider a proposal for the "cruizers of the several maritime powers [merged] into one common force for the protection of the African coast[.]" The White House replied that it wanted Anglo-American forces to cooperate "by all suitable means," but only if it was convenient were American ships to cruise with the RN or provide the British with information related to the slave trade.[56] Despite American dithering, British representatives concluded that Anglo-American naval efforts had the potential to resolve their diplomatic differences.

In 1821 Collier reported that in response to the passage of strong American laws against slaving, US officers carried out their task with "the greatest zeal." Stratford Canning also had some praise for the limited American effort. The American schooners along the African coast in the early 1820s had some effect. Although the US ship *Alligator* had captured four slavers believed to be American vessels, he noted the weak American commitment. *Alligator* had left the coast, and Canning had no idea when a replacement might appear.[57] The two nations had hit upon a limited form of cooperation, but the US was present on the coast for other reasons. American policy goals resulted in limited numbers of ships on the West African coast. Thus, Anglo-American cooperation remained largely informal and unsuccessful. While relations were sometimes tense, the two opted for limited cooperative efforts while hoping for better solutions to points of contention.

The most successful operations resulted from intelligence sharing. For example, in late 1821 the RN stopped the slaver *Dolphin* whose captain was confident that the British would free it because it flew American colours. Meanwhile, the British had devised a plan for Anglo-American cooperation that might alleviate their differences. They offered to repair and man *Augusta* and put it under the command of an American officer, Midshipman Harry D.

1821; Correspondence with Foreign Powers on the Slave Trade, 502, No. 70, Stratford Canning to Marquess of Londonderry, 4 June 1821; and Joseph Planta, Foreign Office, 12 May 1821.

[56]*Ibid.*, 1822, XXII, Correspondence with Foreign Powers on the Slave Trade, 502-503, enclosure in No. 70, Canning to Marques of Londonderry, 4 June 1821; Canning to Adams, 1 June 1821; 506, third enclosure in No. 72, Canning to Londonderry, 4 September 1821, "Instructions to American Ships of War;" and NA, RG 45, Letters Received Relating to African Colonization, Adams to Thompson, 15 August 1821.

[57]TNA/PRO, ADM 1/1675, "Commodore Sir G.R. Collier's Final Report on the Coast of Africa, 1821;" and *BPP*, 1822, XII, Correspondence with Foreign Powers on Slave Trade, 1821-22, 503, No. 72, Canning to Londonderry, 4 September 1821.

Hunter. If the ship encountered an American slaver, Hunter would seize it; otherwise, the British would do so. On 5 February 1822 Captain Benedictus Kelly, commanding British West African forces, sent an officer to *Augusta* and handed over intelligence about *Dolphin*, then reportedly in the Rio Pongo. Hunter told Secretary Thompson that "[i]n pursuance of my duty as the only Naval Officer on the coast" he had sailed in *Augusta* to investigate. He located the vessel and concluded from its log that it also went by the name *Florida* until it sailed for the African coast from Charleston to buy slaves. Flushed with success, Hunter and the British then continued their patrol.[58]

Nevertheless, by the close of the decade the RN remained the only effective force across the equatorial Atlantic. After the coronation of King William IV, US envoy Louis McLane provided Washington with details on what was being done to fight the last vestiges of piracy on the West Indian-West African route. The brig *Manzanares*, accused of piracy, sailed from Havana on 31 August 1829 for the African coast and while *en route* attacked the Boston vessel *Candace*. The US government stationed warships off Havana and Matanzas and ordered *Manzanares* captured. On 14 July 1830 McLane received word from Lord Aberdeen that the RN brig *Black Joke* had captured *Manzanares* on 1 April off Gallinas and delivered it to the Mixed Commission court at Sierra Leone. It had violated the Anglo-Spanish treaty on the slave trade, and the British found more than 300 slaves on board.[59]

Conclusion

During the 1820s Anglo-American relations were often tense, but the two nations sought to use sea power to minimize disputes while furthering their separate objectives. When the disintegration of the Spanish-American Empire threatened British and American trade, they deployed navies to protect it. Traditional American policy abhorred a strong navy, but when US interests were threatened policymakers reached a compromise. Washington sent Commodore Porter to the Gulf of Mexico, and the USN patrolled for pirates, warned off privateers and instituted convoys. After the US achieved this goal, the navy had clear objectives and little political interference from Washington except for the warning to avoid provoking other nations. In contrast, the RN was subject to the policy restraints imposed by Canning, who wanted conditions to be ripe

---

[58]NA, RG 45, Letters Received Relating to African Colonization, R.F. Stockton to Harry D. Hunter, 16 December 1821; Hunter to Thompson, 19 February 1822; and E. Ayres to Thompson, 24 February 1823.

[59]*Ibid.*, Dispatches, Britain, No. 21, McLane to Martin Van Buren, 6 July 1830; W.F. Maclean to Aberdeen, 22 April 1830, in McLane to Van Buren, 6 July 1830; No. 22, Aberdeen to McLane, 10 July 1830; and William Smith to Aberdeen, 8 April 1830 in McLane to Van Buren, 14 July 1830.

before recognizing the rebel states. London was wary of forceful actions for fear of sparking European intervention before it secured its own objectives. Consequently, naval reinforcements were restrained.

While concerned with the US in the Gulf, London wanted a larger American force on the African coast and had few qualms about giving access to a potential rival. At this same time, Britain was becoming aware of the economic potential of West Africa. Strategic considerations along the West African coast mirrored those in the Gulf of Mexico. In the former region, the British had a clear objective – slave-trade suppression – and needed Washington's help to stop slavers that hid under the US flag. But although the Americans reached a consensus to deploy a large naval force to suppress piracy, slave-trade suppression was more complex due to domestic conditions. Still, the Americans diverted the occasional vessel from the Gulf piracy patrol to the West African coast to appease Britain. When the piracy threat ended, US naval retrenchment left the West African coast devoid of American warships, and the RN was unchallenged until it was in the American interest to establish a permanent African squadron.

Chapter 5
A Naval Compromise, 1830-1842

By 1842 Anglo-American interests had converged sufficiently to reach an agreement on naval cooperation along the West African coast. Although the tactical use of sea power to hunt slave traders and to provide commerce protection had the potential to generate Anglo-American conflict, the strategic decision to use it to further long-term objectives peacefully provided a conduit through which the nations could reduce tensions. In Britain, lobbyists like Fowell Buxton pressured the government to use the Royal Navy (RN) to suppress the slave trade to promote legitimate African commerce. But leaders like Lord Palmerston and Sir Robert Peel subscribed to the liberal philosophy of only pushing other powers so far over issues like slave-trade suppression. Cooperation was preferable to war. Britain connected the growth of African commerce with the suppression of the slave trade but refrained from using force to impose its views on "established" nation-states. The US government also came under increasing pressure from Northern merchants to protect and promote avenues to increase commerce in places like the West African coast.

By the early 1840s Secretary of State Daniel Webster and Secretary of the Navy Abel P. Upshur promoted the use of the US Navy (USN) to achieve peaceful, strategic goals. But the political climate in the US remained wary of slavery-related issues, and Anglo-American tensions remained high over the issue of the freedom of the seas. The *Amistad* and *Creole* cases, for example, raised the ire of many in the South who feared that the authorities might interfere with slavery. But a rebellion in Canada, and the Maine-New Brunswick border dispute, provided opportunities to settle outstanding bilateral issues. Peel sent Lord Ashburton to Washington for talks with Webster that led to a settlement of the border dispute and agreement on a plan for cooperation in West Africa. British liberalism and America's growing commercial ambitions meant that a compromise was possible over the use of sea power on the African coast. While American and British warships would cruise in pairs, to avoid conflict the USN would stop suspicious American-flag vessels, and the RN would only stop suspicious vessels belonging to other nations.

Palmerston's Foreign Policy, the Slave Trade and the United States

Liberals believed in "representative government" and "majority rule." The French revolution of 1830, for example, liberalized the constitution and established a constitutional monarchy; "order prevailed, the *bourgeois* [emphasis in original] were in control, the business of France and Europe could continue." Significantly, the revolution showed the British elite that gradual *evolution* was possible. Domestically, it enabled passage of the first Reform Bill (1832), which gave power to a broader constituency.[1] Henry John Temple, an Irish landowner and later Lord Palmerston, was a member of the elite, accepted liberalism and a *laissez-faire* philosophy but also wanted to protect British interests. Internationally, he supported free trade, despised the slave trade and pushed other powers, like the US, to suppress it. But keeping the peace was even more important. As Muriel Chamberlain concluded, Palmerston adhered to Castlereagh's doctrine of non-interference in the affairs of other nations as long British interests were protected. Palmerston therefore "pleaded for a right to 'interfere' in every way 'short of actual force.'"[2]

He first gained prominence in foreign affairs when Canning kept him in the War Office, and he grew in stature as Foreign Secretary (1830-1834; 1835-1841 and 1846-1851) and finally as Prime Minister (1855-1858 and 1859-1865). While he studied the works of Adam Smith as a young man in Edinburgh, he believed that there was a role for diplomacy.[3] Palmerston's approach was to use force only as a last resort to secure British objectives. Confident in this plan, he sought cooperation with other powers to further British goals. Because of his longevity and influence, he symbolized the remarkable continuity in British foreign policy during this period.

His philosophy matched his foreign policy outlook. In 1837, for example, he linked his foreign and trade policies when discussing the crisis over access to Chinese markets with Lord Minto at the Admiralty. Palmerston believed that unless Britain wanted to go to war with every maritime power to "maintain a monopoly" on trade, the nation must accept "American & French settlements in the Eastern seas." Besides, he concluded, bringing commerce and "civilization" to the "savage races" would help all "civilized & trading nations." Only when a power like France threatened to create a monopoly would he support intervention. Instead, his primary goal remained "the balance of power in Europe, as the essential prerequisite for the security of the United Kingdom."[4]

---

[1]Charles K. Webster, *The Foreign Policy of Palmerston 1830-1841: Britain, the Liberal Movement and the Eastern Question* (2 vols., London, 1951), I, 76-80.

[2]Muriel E. Chamberlain, *Lord Palmerston* (Cardiff, 1987), 33-40.

[3]Kenneth Bourne, *The Foreign Policy of Victorian England, 1830-1902* (Oxford, 1970), 84-86.

[4]Kenneth Bourne, *Palmerston: The Early Years, 1784-1841* (New York, 1982), 552 and 623-626.

The "Eastern Question" and its relationship to the Liberal movement illustrates Palmerston's style of foreign policy. The drive for Greek independence from the Ottoman Empire in the late 1820s was something that public opinion in Britain, France and Russia supported as "liberal." But Britain had to balance liberalism with its strategic concerns. The European powers supported Greek independence and joined at Navarino (1827) to destroy the Turkish and Egyptian fleets that sought to stifle it. But another danger was clear: "[f]rom Constantinople she [Russia] could challenge the whole British position in the Mediterranean[.]" Consequently, Britain had to strengthen Turkey to counter Russia and balance the strategic loss suffered by the political success of liberalism. The Turkish vassal in Egypt, Mohammed Ali, also caused problems. He vied for more power and threatened British trade routes through the Red Sea to India. It thus seemed that "wherever the British found their progress impeded by the Egyptians they found the French behind the Egyptians." Anglo-French relations grew tense when Thiers became the French Premier and openly supported Ali.[5] In the international realm, liberalism meant noninterference in the affairs of other nations but was also predicated upon ensuring that Britain's long-term interests remained secure.

By 1839 Palmerston was concerned that the Russians would take advantage of the situation, and the RN was deployed to the Dardanelles. He hoped that it might satisfy Ali if the Great Powers gave him "hereditary possession of Egypt" in exchange for an end to his occupation of Syria. But Ali refused, and the British bombarded Acre in response. France failed to support him and instead signed the Straits Convention on 13 July 1841 that forbade warships to use the Dardanelles in peacetime.[6]

While a liberal, Palmerston was keen to use the world as a chessboard to protect British interests. His primary goal was to show the French that Britain was the sole hegemonic master. He confided to Lord Auckland after the bombardment of Acre that "we have won Austria to us, to be our Bosom Friend; we have got Russia to be our Most devoted ally; & we have France humbled to the Dust, and gushing her Teeth in the Bitterness of impotent Resentment, and detected and exposed Frauds." Palmerston was aware of the link between strategic and economic concerns and believed that the RN would ensure that Britain remained on top. In constructing a balance sheet for the previous year and looking to the future, Palmerston explained to Auckland that:

> [t]he French Nation will have to pay some sixteen millions sterling for the false play they have been guilty of, & for the

---

[5]Webster, *Foreign Policy of Palmerston*, I, 76-87; and Bourne, *Foreign Policy of Victorian England*, 38-43.

[6]Bourne, *Palmerston*, 577-580 and 618-620; and Chamberlain, *Lord Palmerston*, 54-55.

Follies they have committed; while our excess of expenditure for the year just elapsing will be only £200,000; and from 800,000 to one million, will be for the next ensuing year, place us in a condition to disregard the French armaments by giving us a superior navy afloat.[7]

It was a great game for Palmerston, who relished in balancing one European power off against another. He was particularly pleased that French activities had driven "all Germany into a defensive Union...and have forced the Confederation to establish a system of practical organization which separate Interests and Mutual Jealousies." Palmerston believed that Britain had constrained Paris economically, militarily, diplomatically and politically. He concluded that "the enormous expenses the French have incurred for no Reason whatever, and without the slightest advantage will tend to cool down their warlike ardour." He was therefore satisfied that he had met his objective of maintaining the balance of power in Europe. He wrote that "the Events of the last Twelve months have very much tended to render the Continuance of Peace in Europe secure. Russia has been muzzled, and France humbled."[8]

Strategically secure, Palmerston believed that Britain could now focus on expanding its economic domain. He advised Auckland, for example, to consolidate the gains in Asia, particularly in Afghanistan and Persia. With the other European powers tied down, Palmerston felt that Britain could turn its hegemonic position to an advantage. The ultimate goal was clear: to open, expand and protect British trade. He explained to Auckland that since European competition "is fast excluding our Productions from the markets of Europe...we must unremittingly endeavour to find in other parts of the world new vents for the Produce of our Industry." But while he adhered to the tenets of free trade, he believed that it should be backed with force. He assumed that "the wants of the Human Race [are] ample enough to afford a Demand for all we can manufacture; but it is the Business of the Government to open and to secure the Roads for the merchant" but feared an alliance between France and Russia. He felt that British strategy was sound: "the naval Power of England...would make such a scheme hopeless."[9]

Given Palmerston's bellicose nature, others, such as Sir Francis Thornhill Baring, believed that he needed to be controlled. Some "Free Trad-

---

[7]University of Southampton (US), Hartley Library (HL), Archives and Special Collections (A&SC), Broadlands Archive (BA), MS 62, Palmerston Papers (PP), General Correspondence (GC)/Auckland (AU)/45-68, Palmerston to Auckland, 22 January 1841.

[8]*Ibid.*

[9]*Ibid.*

ers," the press and many of his colleagues feared that his forceful individuality would upset their objectives. While willing to let other powers have access to China, he also privately bellowed to Auckland his willingness to use force in the Pacific. In December 1840 Palmerston advocated a watchful and steadfast approach to Eastern policy. He confided to Auckland that if "our China operations succeed we shall stand well, in our Eastern Policy, China India & Syria will all have been witness to our vigour and success." In January 1841 he confided to Auckland that he was certain that Britain would have to use force to advance its objectives. He believed that

> We might storm the Boque [sic] Forts and take possession of
> Canton; or we might push up the Yantse [sic], or some of
> those other great Rivers, and take possession of some of the
> great Cities on their Banks; or we might push a force up the
> Peiko, and take possession of the Town ... either of these
> blows would I am convinced bring the Emperor to Terms.

Furthermore, he added, "I do not attach much importance to the argument that vigorous operations would Irritate the Chinese People; That argument is equally good against war with any nation."[10]

Indeed, if Palmerston went too far his peers might dismiss him because "it was dangerous for him to act without Cabinet support." Thus, by the late 1840s "there emerged something of an inner Cabinet on foreign affairs" comprising Landsdowne, Prime Minister John Russell and Palmerston. Russell in 1851 advised Palmerston to placate other powers rather than sour relations, and David Brown has shown that to "some extent Russell did succeed in keeping Palmerston in check." Perhaps such constraints convinced Palmerston to put such put personal views aside.[11] This is the light in which his slave-trade policy and relations with the US must be seen. While he believed in advancing and protecting British interests, as a liberal he realized that Britain had to avoid war with the major powers over minor issues.

Palmerston supported the idea to replace the slave trade at its origins with legitimate British commerce, but he was also conservative and initially

---

[10]David Brown, *Palmerston and the Politics of Foreign Policy, 1846-55* (Manchester, 2002), 74-76 and 89-90; and US, HL, A&SC, BA, PP, GC/AU/45-68, Palmerston to Auckland, 24 December 1840 and 22 January 1841. Although Britain's China and Pacific policies are beyond the scope of this study, see, for example, D.K. Fieldhouse, *Economics and Empire, 1830-1914* (London, 1973; reprint, Ithaca, NY, 1984), 159-223; and Gerald S. Graham, *The China Station: War and Diplomacy, 1830-1860* (New York, 1978).

[11]Brown, *Palmerston*, 74-77 and 88-93.

voted against abolition. Still, he recognized that public opinion was against the slave trade, thus making the issue good political capital. He had failed to appreciate this when he first ran for Parliament, and it eroded some of his support. For several political and economic reasons, Palmerston constantly pressured other powers, like the US, for treaties to suppress the slave trade. He thus rested recognition of Texas on its agreement to such a treaty, and when Portugal seemed reluctant to meet its treaty obligations, Parliament gave him the power to "treat their slavers also as if they were British criminals." Kenneth Bourne concluded that Palmerston's anti-slave trade zeal was part of his "personal mythology[.]"[12] Palmerston exclaimed in 1845, while briefly out of power, that Peel's government was apathetic to the plight of slaves. He opined that "Power is valuable only for its employment, and [I] cannot conceive any Pleasure greater than Employment of Power to put an End to [the] Slave Trade."[13] Ronald Robinson and John Gallagher have claimed that naval action in West Africa represented "Palmerstonian principles in action" to eliminate "barriers of artificial monopoly and restriction" in order to expand trade and propagate "liberal civilisation and British parmountcy [sic]."[14]

Although he came to support slave-trade suppression, Palmerston's liberalism also meant that he was "personally uninterested in adventurous schemes to contest American power." When it came to the US-Canada border disputes, for example, Bourne concluded that "his policy was merely to postpone the matter by arranging joint surveys and commissions...until American feelings were quietened [sic] down[.]" Russell feared an Anglo-American war over the issue but concluded that "Palmerston was definitely playing it down in order to concentrate on Egypt[,]" a more important concern. British liberals desired to relate to the US without going to war unless important interests were threatened. Palmerston grasped those opportunities that materialized, but while trying to obtain a slave-trade treaty with Texas he tempered his approach to secure greater influence there.[15]

By contrast, in the US petitions against slavery flooded Congress, and Southern members decided to end the debate. The political climate was cool toward anything connected with slavery, which shaped American diplomatic and naval relations with Britain. For example, during his Presidency John Quincy Adams avoided dealing with slavery. Southern opinion forbade any talk of ending the system. In 1836, in the face of opposition from Adams who

---

[12]Bourne, *Palmerston*, 622-624.

[13]US, HL, A&SC, BA, PP, Slave Trade (SLT)/26, Palmerston [c. 1845].

[14]Ronald Robinson and John Gallagher, *Africa and the Victorians: The Official Mind of Imperialism* (London, 1961; 2nd ed., London, 1981), 38.

[15]Bourne, *Palmerston*, 586-587 and 597.

exclaimed that debate was an issue of freedom of speech, Congress used the so-called "Gag Rule" to suspend debate. A climate of fear had settled on the nation, and President Martin Van Buren agreed to veto any bill that tried to suppress slavery. Samuel Flagg Bemis concluded that a "white terror backed up the heavy legal censorship with vigilance committees and lynch law."[16] Because of domestic American considerations, Britain's option was either war with the US or continued diplomatic pressure. It chose the latter.

Market Expansion and Anglo-American Diplomacy in the 1830s

During the piracy crisis of the 1820s the British feared that the RN would interfere with the government's desire to secure exclusive access to trade in the western equatorial Atlantic. But during the 1830s and early 1840s, London used sea power to further the growth of national wealth under the joint banner of slave-trade suppression and free trade. The combined pressure led Britain to abolish slavery in all its colonies. As a result, Britain increased its efforts to use sea power to end the slave trade. But many believed that the trade continued because of American participation, and Britain felt that the US had to be convinced to police American citizens involved in the traffic and slavers of other nations who hid under the protection of falsely flying the American flag.

During the late 1830s, British Quakers, Fowell Buxton's Society for the Extinction of the Slave Trade and others continued to pressure the government to act. People like Buxton hoped to encourage the development of legal African goods, like palm oil. He believed that if the government used the RN to "drive them [slave traders] out of a river and keep them out, then the African's hunger for trade goods might lead him to turn to oil." The two primary methods to implement the new strategy were to "Impede the Traffic" and "Establish Commerce." He thought that natives would welcome trade with Europeans if they received encouragement. Buxton urged the government to sign treaties with natives and to "settle factories and send out trading ships."[17]

In a private letter to Palmerston, Buxton explained the connection between extinguishing the slave trade and promoting British commerce. He volunteered to work with the government to stop the traffic. Advising Palmerston of an upcoming speech, Buxton warned that he would condemn Portugal for its lack of action and "urge you [Palmerston] to endure it no longer." Moreover,

---

[16]Samuel Flagg Bemis, *John Quincy Adams and the Union* (New York, 1956), 326-340 and 352-383.

[17]Hugh Thomas, *The Slave Trade: The Story of the Atlantic Slave Trade, 1440-1870* (New York, 1997), 650-658 and 701; J. Gallagher, "Fowell Buxton and the New African Policy, 1838-1842," *Cambridge Historical Journal*, X, No. 1 (1950), 38-39; and R.H. Mottram, *Buxton the Liberator* (London, 1946), 118-126. The direct quotes originate from Mottram and reprints from Buxton and his Society.

he would "show that all treaties must be nugatory till by a combination of the civilised nations it is declared Piracy. & I shall labour to convince you & the House that the accomplishment of such a measure is not hopeless." For Buxton, the ramifications for British interests were clear. He explained to Palmerston that "the Slave Trade cuts off the commercial nations of Europe & America from commerce with one quarter of the Globe." Further, he reminded the Colonial Office that Africa offered the potential of "millions of customers, who may be taught to grow the raw material which we require, and who require the manufactured commodities which we produce."[18] Buxton thus appealed directly to the gentlemanly capitalist ethic that might see Africa's investment potential, helped by the power of the RN.

Palmerston agreed with such a use for the navy and offered £50,000 for the island of Fernando Po, but Spain rejected the offer. Still, British steamers used the strategically located island to refuel, and by 1843 the Spanish appointed British merchant John Beechcroft governor. In 1841 Britain sent a naval expedition up the Niger in search of new avenues of trade. The expedition signed treaties with natives to abolish the slave trade and to export legitimate goods to the UK. But otherwise the expedition was a failure as the men succumbed to African disease and returned home in disgrace.[19] Regardless, British humanitarian aims for slave-trade suppression had created a nexus with the economic goal of developing Africa, and it established British strategy for the eastern equatorial Atlantic for the next twenty years. Nevertheless, because the US was a major market for slaves, American cooperation was needed to further British policy. But London was unwilling to go to war to force a change in American attitude.

Instead, London continued to apply diplomatic pressure on the Americans. As long as slavers hid under the US flag, British strategy was futile. American representatives in London were aware of the British position and the public pressure on the government. In 1833 the US envoy told Washington about the zealots and lobbyists who sent petitions to the government and about the public outcry against the slave trade that left London little room for manoeuvre. Still, the British tried to woo the Americans informally to let the RN stop US-flagged ships. Each time, the Americans reiterated their belief that

---

[18]US, HL, A&SC, BA, PP, SLT, Buxton to Palmerston, 29 May 1847; and Buxton, as quoted in Gallagher, "Fowell Buxton," 45.

[19]Thomas, *Slave Trade*, 650-658 and 701; and Gallagher, "Fowell Buxton," 47-58. Technological problems constrained European penetration into Africa. Until the advent of modern medicine, white Europeans succumbed to African diseases to which they had no natural immunity (Gallagher, "Fowell Buxton," 50-51 and 56). For details on the technological problems that faced European expansion, see Daniel R. Headrick, *The Tools of Empire: Technology and European Imperialism in the Nineteenth Century* (New York, 1981), esp. chapter 3.

this would violate the freedom of the seas.[20] Throughout the 1830s, Anglo-American disagreements over the slave trade accumulated. The British claimed that American ships were involved in the trade and pressed the US to act.

The 1830s was a bad decade for slaves. After the Haitian revolts in the early years of the century and British abolition of slavery, Cuba and Puerto Rico met the demand for cheap, slave-grown sugar and coffee.[21] Between 1831 and 1835, traders embarked 104,641 slaves along the African coast and delivered 88,493 to their destination. The next five-year period was even more horrific: the number of slaves embarked increased by three-fold to 328,540, of which 282,416 arrived safely at their destination. The majority of the slaves captured during the decade came from West Africa. West-Central Africa accounted for thirty-five percent of the slaves captured in 1831-1835, while the Bight of Biafra (27.7 percent), the Bight of Benin (23.8 percent), Sierra Leone (11.3 percent), Senegambia (1.52 percent), the Windward Coast (0.45 percent) and the Gold Coast (0.31 percent) also contributed. Data collected by scholars indicate that during 1836-1840 the slave trade focused particularly on West-Central Africa (50.50 percent). Other regions were less prominent: Southeast Africa (26.3 percent), the Bight of Biafra (8.82 percent), the Bight of Benin (8.56 percent), Sierra Leone (4.22 percent), Senegambia (0.72 percent), the Gold Coast (0.53 percent) and the Windward Coast (0.33 percent).[22]

This was the height of the slave trade in the mid-nineteenth century. During 1831-1835, there were 329 slave-trade voyages, a number which increased to 957 during 1836-1840. It is difficult to assess the origins of vessels involved in an illegal activity cloaked in secrecy, but there is no indication of any involvement in slaving voyages by people from the ports of New York, Baltimore or New Orleans. But the evidence does show that during 1831-1835 one slaving vessel was built in Maryland and that during 1836-1840 the number increased to three. It is likely that these statistics are an indication of a wider, better-concealed involvement by the port of Baltimore and its famous clipper ships. Indeed, historians have found that during 1831-1835 two vessels involved in the slave trade were registered in the US; by 1836-1840, the number had risen to thirty-four.[23]

---

[20]United States, National Archives (NA), Record Group (RG) 59, Dispatches, Britain, Nos. 67 and 68, Vail to Edward Livingston, 22 and 29 May 1833.

[21]Herbert S. Klein, *The Atlantic Slave Trade* (Cambridge, 1999), 39-40 and 184.

[22]David Eltis, *et al.*, *The Trans-Atlantic Slave Trade: A Database on CD-ROM* (Cambridge, 1999).

[23]*Ibid.*

The 1286 voyages – an average of 129 per year – during the 1830s brought slaves largely to New World destinations. Of the 329 voyages between 1831 and 1835, 241 (73.3 percent) were successful, while the British managed to stop 24.6 percent of the voyages. The remaining 2.1 percent met with other unsuccessful outcomes. The main destination was Cuba (64.7 percent). Other regions lagged considerably, led by Sierra Leone (14.6 percent), Rio de la Plata (8.10 percent), the Southeast Coast of Brazil (five percent) and Bahia (4.21 percent). Of the 957 voyages during 1836-1840, 670 (seventy percent) were recorded as successful, while the British stopped 267 (27.9 percent). But the destinations of the slaves were somewhat different. Demand shifted to the Southeast Coast of Brazil, which received 54.9 percent of the slaves. Cuba was the second most prominent destination (28.7 percent), followed by Sierra Leone (6.1 percent), Pernambuco (3.91 percent) and Bahia (2.52 percent).[24]

The battle was going poorly for the British. Although the slaver success rate fell by 3.3 percent, the number of voyages increased dramatically. Palmerston was convinced that the Americans were to blame but believed that if pressured they would act. During the 1830s he forwarded numerous reports on the involvement of specific US-flagged vessels, enclosing extracts from the British commissioners at Havana who believed that slavers were encouraged by the President's stand that he would not sign a slave-trade treaty.[25]

Despite the diplomatic pressure, the US continued to focus on commerce protection. The Americans only became interested in negotiations when their coastal trade in slaves was threatened. During late 1837 and 1838, Washington asked Britain to sign an agreement to govern slaving vessels involved in the "legitimate" internal US slave trade that were shipwrecked on nearby British islands. But in November 1838 US envoy Andrew Stevenson informed Washington that Britain refused to consider this treaty because it was inconsistent with policy. He concluded that if Britain signed such a pact, nations like Spain and Portugal would want similar agreements. Stevenson advised that further talks with the present British government would be futile.[26]

London believed that increased American investment in the Cuban sugar trade had sparked an increased demand for cheap slave labour on the island. In the 1830s slavers took advantage of the lack of Anglo-American cooperation in the suppression of the slave trade. Flying the US flag, for ex-

---

[24]*Ibid.*

[25]*Ibid.*; and NA, RG 59, Dispatches, Britain, No. 14, Palmerston to Andrew Stevenson, 17 December 1836, in Stevenson to John Forsyth, 22 December 1836; and "Extract from British Commissioners at Havana, 25 October 1836," in Palmerston to Stevenson, 17 December 1836, enclosed in Stevenson to Forsyth, 22 December 1836.

[26]*Ibid.*, No. 56, Palmerston to Stevenson, 10 September 1838; and Stevenson to Forsyth, 5 November 1838.

ample, protected them due to the likelihood of a diplomatic dispute if the RN stopped an American-flag vessel. If a trader encountered the rare US warship, it could show foreign papers and be no concern to the Americans. Britain concluded that "Spanish, Portuguese, and Brazilian Slave Traders, with out-laws and pirates of all nations, are now flocking under the cover of the American Flag." British representatives claimed that ships were built and equipped in American ports, sailed to the Cape Verde Islands or Havana under the American flag and were handed over to Portuguese or Spanish owners. When the RN encountered American ships such as *Washington*, *Joseph Hand* and *Cleopatra* on the West African coast in late 1837, it concluded that Baltimore was particularly involved.[27]

Statistics provide some support for this argument: slaver voyages from Havana increased from 173 voyages in 1831-1835 to 214 in 1836-1840.[28] In 1838 *Venus*, a Baltimore-built ship, sailed for Brazil under US colours, where it switched to the Portuguese flag and headed to the African coast. The British could find no legal papers legitimizing the transfer, and "in any case, her outward voyage, with equipment for the Slave Trade, was protected by her American character." In early 1839, Rear Admiral Elliot concluded that the slavers had become too sure of themselves. They failed even to have an American on board to take over as captain if they were stopped and simply kept one of the crew on hand with a certificate of naturalization as a US citizen. The main weapon was paperwork under which to hide.[29]

In response, Britain sent several slavers to the US to pressure Washington to act. In some cases this worked. For example, the District Court of New York condemned *Wyoming* on 15 October 1839 for violating US law. But the case against *Butterfly* rested solely on the fact that it had large boilers and other items that might be used in the slave trade. Despite the lack of solid evidence, the judge decided "that there is strong *prima facie* proof that this vessel

---

[27]*Ibid.*, General Records of the Department of State, Notes from the British Legation in the U.S. to the Department of State, 1791-1906, XIX, 14 March 1836-7 November 1839, H.S. Fox to Forsyth, 30 October 1839.

[28]Eltis, *et al.*, *Slave Trade: A Database*.

[29]NA, RG 59, Notes from the British Legation in the U.S. to the Department of State, 1791-1906, XIX, 14 March 1836-7 November 1839, Fox to Forsyth, 30 October 1839; enclosure No. 6 [appears to be also numbered No. 26], George Elliot to Charles Wood, Admiralty, 6 February 1839; Great Britain, Parliament, *Parliamentary Papers* (*BPP*), 1841, XXX, 844, Correspondence with Foreign Powers Not Parties to Conventions Giving Mutual Right of Search of Vessels Suspected of the Slave Trade, 1840 (Class D), second enclosure in No. 124, James Buchanan to Palmerston, "Copy of a Paper Found on the Person of the Captain in Command of the Schooner 'Catherine,' when Captured by the 'Dolphin,' and proved on the Trial," n.d.

was, when arrested, employed in the Slave Trade." He found *Butterfly's* US master guilty, fined him $2000 and imprisoned him for two years.[30]

Palmerston was pleased with the American reaction to the bold British actions. He reminded them that under US law ships had to meet several conditions to be legally American. They had to fly the US flag, have a crew that was two-thirds American and a captain, first, second and third mates who were US citizens. If the Americans agreed, the British could use that definition to enable the RN to seize slavers which raised the US flag only when challenged by a warship. But Washington rejected the proposal, and in December 1839 Palmerston received the discouraging opinion from the Queen's advocate that under US law a ship and its cargo brought into New York for participating in the slave trade could be condemned only for irregularities in its papers. Consequently, Palmerston ordered the British consul in New York, James Buchanan, "not to take charge of such vessels" in the future. Palmerston had made his point and refrained from pushing the Americans too far on the issue. Nevertheless, in response to British interference, Donald L. Canney has concluded that President Martin van Buren ordered *Grampus* and *Dolphin* to the West African coast.[31]

American Economic Interest in West Africa

While formal Anglo-American talks stalled, US Ambassador Stevenson continued informal discussions with Palmerston, who still wanted the Americans to suppress the slave trade. These discussions reveal Washington's desire to guarantee that US commerce was protected, but its unwillingness to do anything significant about the slave trade. Britain realized that its naval force interfered with legitimate American commerce, but London claimed that there was no choice unless the US dispatched a naval squadron to the West African

---

[30]*Ibid.*, 805-806, 836-840 and 844-845, enclosure in No. 121, Buchanan to Palmerston, 16 April 1840, "Judgement. The United States v. the Schooner 'Butterfly,' 13 April 1840;" No. 125, Buchanan to Palmerston, 17 August 1840; No. 85, Palmerston to Fox, 30 May 1840, first enclosure in Thomas Stillwell and Sons to Palmerston, 29 April 1840; and Warren S. Howard, *American Slavers and the Federal Law* (Berkeley, 1963), 38-40.

[31]*BPP*, 1840, XLVII, 369-270, 416, and 419-423, Correspondence with Foreign Powers Not Parties to Conventions Giving Mutual Right of Search of Vessels Suspected of the Slave Trade, 1839-1840 (Class D), No. 141, Palmerston to Fox, 3 August 1839; No. 162, Buchanan to Palmerston, 15 November 1839, third enclosure, Buchanan to B.F. Butler, 4 November 1839; No. 167, Buchanan to Palmerston, 30 November 1839, third enclosure, *New York Morning Herald*, 2 December 1839; No. 168, Palmerston to Buchanan, 31 December 1839; and Donald L. Canney, *Africa Squadron: The U.S. Navy and the Slave Trade, 1842-1861* (Washington, DC, 2006), 26-27.

coast. Palmerston added that the US could accomplish "great good" if it let British warships inspect suspicious American-flag vessels.[32] While the British no longer sent seized American ships to the US, the RN continued to harass US-flagged ships. It was a campaign of irritation that caught legitimate trade in the middle and increased Anglo-American tension.

As harassment continued, pressure increased on Washington to send US warships to Africa to protect growing American trade. One such case involved *Edwin*, owned by Farnham and Fry of Salem and used by P.J. Farnham and Co. of New York in the West African trade. The company traded cloth, beads and other items with the natives at Ambriz, north of Angola, in competition with English trading stations. *Edwin*'s captain told American officials that the ship had sailed from Ambriz with some cargo when on 22 July 1839 HM sloop *Columbine* fired on and boarded it. The captain reminded the British lieutenant "of his having received and hospitably entertained" him "at the factory of Messr. P.J. Farnham and Co. about a month before" and informed him that he was involved in a legal trade. But despite this assurance, the British refused to release *Edwin* until they finished their search. Palmerston told Stevenson that his government would investigate but that it would help if the US sent its own warships to West Africa to enforce the law.[33]

During the early nineteenth century Northern attention was focused on naval protection to promote long-term economic interests. Consequently, Britain and the US came to share a common belief that sea power could be used to further the growth of national wealth, although they disagreed over the role of slave-trade suppression in this equation. New Englanders and others with West African interests pressured Washington to protect and promote American endeavours with sea power. The economic opportunities also elicited sympathy from politicians who later held power over the nation's foreign policy. These men, especially Daniel Webster (Secretary of State, 1841-1843 and 1850-1852) and Abel P. Upshur (Secretary of the Navy, 1841-1843 and Secretary of State, 1843-1844), believed in using sea power to protect and further trade and compromised with Britain to further this goal. The evolution of the US position allowed for a much-anticipated resolution of Anglo-American maritime difficulties along the West African coast.

---

[32]NA, RG 59, Dispatches, Britain, No. 88, Stevenson to Forsyth, 29 February 1840.

[33]*BPP*, 1840, XLVII, 493, Correspondence with Foreign Powers Not Parties to Conventions Giving Mutual Right of Search of Vessels Suspected of the Slave Trade, 1840 (Class D) (Further Series), No. 72, Stevenson to Palmerston, 5 February 1840; George W. Slacum to Forsyth, 16 October 1839; George Elliot, 22 July 1839; depositions of James Dayley, Richard Darling and others, 12 October 1839; and No. 73, Palmerston to Stevenson, 15 February 1840.

During this period, the Mid-Atlantic and New England states industrialized and began to service broader markets. The wool and boot industry, largely based in Massachusetts, grew along with the iron industry, which supplied railway ties, iron stoves and other products. Douglass C. North has shown that the "surge of expansion that began in 1843 was an era in which the Northeast had ceased being a marginal manufacturing area and could successfully expand into a vast array of industrial goods."[34] With increased growth, particularly in the Northeast, trade with other regions, including West Africa, grew. Merchants in Liberia, like one Mr. Carey, shipped coffee to Richmond, while others sold rice, palm oil, dyewood and ivory. In turn, Liberian "elites" liked Western goods, such as bread, butter, ham and molasses, and frowned on local produce.[35] Nevertheless, Jonathan Goldstein has argued that rich, politically connected New England merchants lobbied the Jackson administration to protect their Pacific interests after a series of pirate attacks, such as against *Friendship* of Salem in 1831. USS *Potomac*, *Peacock* and *Boxer* were sent to the region, where the first laid waste to a Malay village. By 1841, the government had established a permanent US Pacific squadron.[36] But the African trade was the domain of smaller New England merchants.

From 1832 to 1864, there were 558 arrivals in Salem from Africa carrying wood, palm oil and other items traded predominately along the West African coast. Samuel Eliot Morison has argued that the West African trades "afforded a good living to many swapping Yankees, who had insufficient capital for the grand routes of commerce."[37] African products entering the US were generally charged a duty of ten percent or less. Given these opportunities, American merchants prospered; as George E. Brooks has written, "these were the golden years for the West African trade."[38]

---

[34]Douglass C. North, *The Economic Growth of the United States, 1790 to 1860* (Englewood Cliffs, NJ, 1961), 156-176.

[35]Amos J. Beyan, *The American Colonization Society and the Creation of the Liberian State: A Historical Perspective, 1822-1900* (Lanham, MD, 1991), 116-118.

[36]Jonathan Goldstein, "For Gold, Glory and Knowledge: The Andrew Jackson Administration and the Orient, 1829-1837," *International Journal of Maritime History*, XIII, No. 2 (2001), 137-155.

[37]Samuel Eliot Morison, *The Maritime History of Massachusetts, 1783-1860* (Boston, 1921; reprint, Boston, 1979), 33 and 221-222.

[38]George E. Brooks, *Yankee Traders, Olds Coasters and African Middlemen: A History of American Legitimate Trade with West Africa in the Nineteenth Century* (Boston, 1970), 95-97.

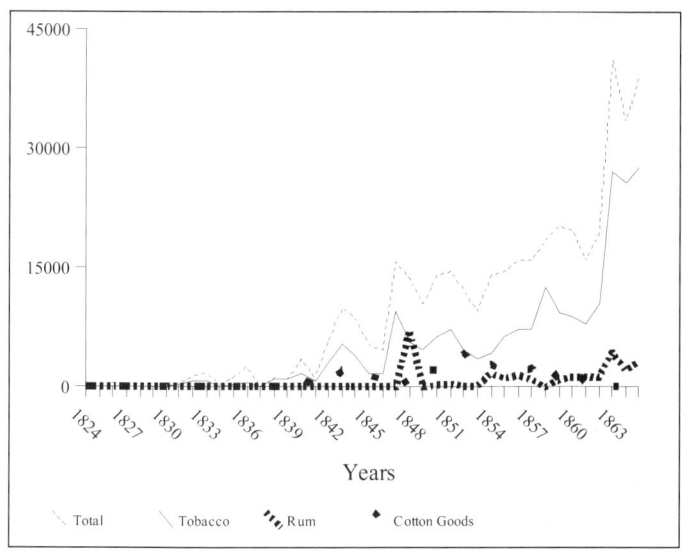

Figure 5.1:   US Exports to Sierra Leone, 1824-1865 (£)

Note: Small amounts of lumber/shingles and flour are excluded.

Source: Calculated from George E. Brooks, *Yankee Traders Old Coasters and African Middlemen: A History of American Legitimate Trade with West Africa in the Nineteenth Century* (Boston, MA, 1970), 305-306.

At its peak, American trade to Africa was primarily in rum and tobacco. In return, the US obtained palm oil, peanuts, ivory and hides; the latter were in particular demand in the expanding shoe industry. The trades were small and concentrated which helps explain their absence from aggregate statistics. Figure 5.1 shows that trade with Sierra Leone began to grow in the mid-1830s, but exports never exceeded £50,000. Imports to the US (figure 5.2), largely hides and palm oil, were similarly small. This trade declined after the 1870s due to increased competition from monopolistic European trading companies and cheaper goods shipped from Europe by steamers.[39] But Washington came under increasing pressure from the North to protect and promote overseas commerce by using the USN during the "take-off" phase.

---

[39]*Ibid.*, 6-7, 97 and 126-129.

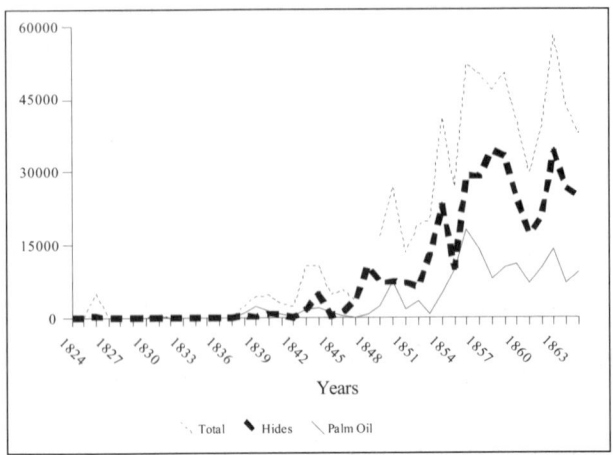

Figure 5.2: US Imports from Sierra Leone, 1824-1865 (£)

Note: Gaps in graph represent missing data from Brooks. Small amounts of pea-
            nuts and wood are excluded.

Source: Calculated from Brooks, *Yankee Traders*, 307-308.

While the trade was small, it was growing and important to those with
a financial stake in West Africa. Salem merchants, such as Robert Brook-
house, Jr., David and Thomas P. Pingree and Charles Hoffman, pleaded for
greater US naval involvement off West Africa. For example, in 1836 Secretary
of the Navy Mahlon Dickerson wrote Stephen C. Phillips, an associate of
Charles Hoffman, that the government supported US West African interests,
but Hoffman suggested that the navy dispatch a brig or schooner to the coast
along with a barge to sail from Sierra Leone to Cape Verde.[40] Trade with
Gambia was important to Hoffman, and George Rendell, the colony's governor, was "very friendly to free trade and commerce with Americans[.]"[41]

Yet this was an era of freer, not free, trade. The London firm of Foster and Smith, according to Hoffman, had "waged a war against the trade of
the United States" to Gambia and had succeeded in imposing a sixpence tariff

---

[40]Daniel F. Vickers to Mark C. Hunter, personal correspondence, 26 April
2002. Vickers notes that Hoffman, who is recorded in a database on Salem merchants
and shipowners, first sailed to Africa in 1833. He worked his way up in Salem society,
marrying Ruth Felt whose family was involved in "fisheries and coasting." After his
wife's death, he remarried in 1840 to Eliza King and was in the "top wealth decile on
Salem's tax lists from 1835...until 1850" when Vickers stopped tracking him.

[41]NA, RG 45, Letters Received Relating to African Colonization, Hoffman to
Mahlon Dickerson, 26 July 1836.

on American liquor, tea and other products "except tobacco and lumber." If British and American firms both had liquor, the natives preferred the former. Hoffman believed that the long-term benefits of sea power were clear. The chief cause of trade restrictions on the River Nunez was the presence of British factory owners who had established their facilities first. Hoffman concluded that these "monopolizing factors" fleeced American profits, while the RN convinced local monarchs to discriminate against the US.[42]

Nevertheless, the pleas of Americans like Hoffman languished in Washington. On 6 November 1839 a representative of the "Colonization Rooms" wrote Secretary of the Navy James K. Paulding about the slave trade and West African commerce. He claimed that the British had a monopoly on West African trade and was suspicious of Buxton's emerging plans for the African coast. The representative concluded that if the slave trade was suppressed, Britain would control all the commerce on the coast to the detriment of America. Moreover, the show of naval force had instilled native "respect" for Britain. Natives left British ships untouched if run ashore but often pillaged American craft. Consequently, the US had to send a naval force to the region and give the American Colonization Society (ACS) more power to purchase land, found colonies and establish shore factories for the benefit of American trade.[43] Americans feared the commercial motives of other powers, especially Britain, and worried that they would lose trade unless Washington made a political decision to nurture economic growth through sea power.

Incidents close to American waters threatened to bring the issue of freedom of the seas and slave-trade suppression to a violent climax. The *Amistad* case created special problems for American diplomats. Slaves being transported in the vessel along the Cuban coast revolted, but at night the crew secretly sailed toward the US. After it arrived in New York in August 1839, the US Supreme Court declared the slaves free after a stirring presentation by John Quincy Adams. This showed the futility of the American position under the 1819 US Anti-Slave Trade Act. If courts could free illegally captured slaves who found their way to the US, this could open the door for other nations to free those captured by illegal American slavers. Soon thereafter, slaves revolted on *Creole*, which was engaged in the legal coastal slave trade, and sailed the ship to Nassau, a British possession. The British hung those responsible for killing crewmembers but freed the others. Southerners protested that this was another example of British interference and demanded justice.[44]

---

[42]*Ibid.*

[43]*Ibid.*, [illegible], Colonization Rooms, Washington, DC, to James K. Paulding, 6 November 1839.

[44]Bemis, *John Quincy Adams and the Union*, 384-413.

By February 1840 Washington had time to digest Palmerston's suggestions but concluded that it was still politically impossible to shift its position. The US felt that the earlier 1824 attempt had failed and that the domestic political situation was still no better. The State Department wrote that:

> [t]he opposition then manifested, and which compelled great caution and reserve in future dealings, with the subject, has, it must be admitted, been strongly fortified by recent events [the *Caroline* incident and Northeast boundary dispute], and especially by the present state of the relations between the different powers who have entered into conventional arrangements upon the subject.[45]

Adams meanwhile concluded that Anglo-American relations had reached an impasse over the suppression of the slave trade, writing in his diary that the slave trade "is with us a forbidden topic."[46]

Crisis and Opportunity

Rebecca Berens Matzke has shown that during Anglo-American disputes between 1838 and 1846 Britain used naval power to pressure America. Although dismissing War Office "anxiety" about the US and the resulting war plans as simply the "duty of the military experts[,]" she believed that London, fresh from defeating Ali, was willing to deploy similar naval force against the US. She claimed that the Admiralty planned to bombard American coastal cities like New York if Britain failed to get its way. Rejecting the evidence that neither side had the political will for an apocalyptic confrontation, she was perplexed that the Maine-New Brunswick border dispute did not lead to war. Britain's failure to "park warships off the US coast, as it might have done against an underdeveloped nation," was also problematic. Matzke concluded that Palmerston hoped the US would "give way when in the wrong[,]" but she was unsure of how Britain dealt with the risk that domestic American opinion might accidentally push the US to war. She avoided entirely the component of

---

[45]*BPP*, 1840, XLVII, 508-511, Correspondence with Foreign Powers Not Parties to Conventions Giving Mutual Right of Search of Vessels Suspected of the Slave Trade, 1840 (Class D) (Further Series), No. 85, Fox to Palmerston, 1 March 1840; and Forsyth to Fox, 12 February 1840.

[46]Charles Francis Adams (ed.), *Memoirs of John Quincy Adams: Comprising Portions of his Diary from 1795 to 1848* (12 vols. Philadelphia, 1874; reprint, Freeport, NY, 1969), X, 450.

the Webster-Ashburton Treaty that provided a mechanism for controlling the very sea power that she believed was a deterrent against America.[47]

During 1837 and 1838 a rebellion erupted in Canada. This event, coupled with the *Caroline* crisis (see below) and the Northeast boundary dispute, offered an opportunity to resolve outstanding Anglo-American issues, including the suppression of the slave trade. The crisis is significant because it reveals how Anglo-American interests and connections could overcome disagreements. The US was under pressure to police the slave trade, but it also wanted to protect and promote legitimate American commerce on the West African coast. Rather than seeking confrontation, Britain's new Prime Minister, Sir Robert Peel, and his Foreign Secretary, Lord Aberdeen, sought conciliation with the US. The result was a compromise which both hoped would end the controversy over slave-trade suppression. Both believed that the compromise, which focused on the use of sea power in the equatorial Atlantic, would be a conduit for their relations and reduce tensions. Their navies would cruise together off West Africa to suppress the slave trade while not offending the national sensibilities of either nation.

During the rebellion, Canadian rebels chartered the American ship *Caroline* to transport "passengers" and "supplies" to an island stronghold. The British became aware of the plan and attacked *Caroline* on the American side of Niagara Falls, a serious violation of US sovereignty. While Washington worked to calm its citizens, the British sent Lord Durham to study the cause of the rebellion (he eventually recommended responsible government). Soon thereafter, a new dispute flared along the disputed Maine-New Brunswick border. Secretary of State Webster also worked to keep the peace, and after the death of President William Henry Harrison the British accepted liability for the *Caroline* affair. Governmental changes in London also helped.[48]

Sir Robert Peel, who was in power from 1841 to 1846, took the "tread softly and carry a big stick" approach with the US and wanted a negotiated settlement. The *New York Herald* urged the US to take the opportunity to settle outstanding issues. Peel forwarded the *Herald*'s view to Lord Aberdeen, his new Foreign Secretary, explaining that he understood how British actions in stopping and searching American-flag vessels during peacetime might lead to war. He believed that the RN should take steps to stop needless British visits to vessels on the African coast. To resolve the disputes, Peel and Aberdeen sent Lord Ashburton to the US. Ashburton owned land in Maine (although not

---

[47]Rebecca Berens Matzke, "Britain Gets Its Way: Power and Peace in Anglo-American Relations, 1838-1846," *War in History*, VIII, No. 1 (2001), 23, 25-27, 32, 37-40 and 43.

[48]Howard Jones, *To the Webster-Ashburton Treaty: A Study in Anglo-American Relations, 1783-1843* (Chapel Hill, NC, 1977), 19-60.

in the disputed region), knew Daniel Webster, had an American wife and possessed the power to negotiate treaties as a special ambassador.[49]

As early as 1797 Ashburton had promoted the benefits of investing in the US. While participating in informal peace talks to end the War of 1812, he confessed the rigidity of British maritime doctrine and admitted that London would never abandon impressment. As President of the Board of Trade in 1834-1835 when Peel was in power, many Americans had come to respect him as a long-time supporter of trade liberalization. Baring Brothers were bankers to the US government, provided capital for American expansion and had resources that exceeded those of American houses "at least until the 1850s and 1860s."[50] Consequently, Ashburton's mission sent a message not only that London was concerned about the financial implications of an Anglo-American dispute but also that the US should remember where funding for critical aspects of American economic development was raised.

D.C.M. Platt has shown that financing, like that provided by Baring Brothers, provided the US with "cheapened credit and it accelerated growth." Still, Bourne concluded that Ashburton "represented pacifying factors of Anglo-American trade which men like Aberdeen and Peel, though not Palmerston, believed was already so much more important than squabbles over frontiers or even national honour." It was in both British and American interests to settle the disputes that had festered. This would enable the US to maintain access to British credit and give investors the stability they craved. Aberdeen explained that he sent Ashburton with full powers to settle all issues including the right of search. But Aberdeen knew that the US would never submit to a mutual right-of-search treaty and did not resubmit the request.[51] In-

---

[49]Norman Gash, *Sir Robert Peel: The Life of Sir Robert Peel after 1830* (London, 1972; revised ed., London 1986), 498-499; and Ralph W. Hidy, "The Organization and Functions of Anglo-American Merchant Bankers, 1815-1860," *Journal of Economic History*, I, supplement (1941), 63.

[50]D.C.M. Platt, *Foreign Finance in Continental Europe and the United States, 1815-1870: Quantities, Origins, Functions and Distribution* (London, 1984), 144, 150 and 163; Donald R. Hickey, *The War of 1812: A Forgotten Conflict* (Urbana, IL, 1989), 284; Jones, *To the Webster-Ashburton Treaty*, 95-102; and William D. Grampp, "How Britain Turned to Free Trade," *Business History Review*, LXI, No. 1 (1987), 86-112. See also chapter 2 above.

[51]Platt, *Foreign Finance*, 163; Bourne, *Foreign Policy of Victorian England*, 50; NA, RG 59, Dispatches, Britain, No. 5, Edward Everett to Daniel Webster, 31 December 1841, with apparent postscripts dated 3 and 4 January 1842; and *BPP*, 1842, XLIV, 453-455, Correspondence with Foreign Powers Not Parties to Conventions Giving Mutual Right of Search of Vessels Suspected of the Slave Trade, 1841 (Class D), No. 273, Aberdeen to Stevenson, 13 October 1841.

stead, the nations reached a compromise over the use of sea power that they hoped would mitigate Anglo-American tensions.

Anglo-American Interests and the Webster-Ashburton Treaty

The change in Washington during 1841-1842 was significant because those in the executive branch were willing to use sea power overseas. They were sympathetic to merchants with West African interests and willing to compromise with the British to advance their respective commercial policies. Previous US administrations under James Monroe and John Quincy Adams preferred to deploy American sea power reactively against threats like piracy close to home waters. But the White House now had a Secretary of the Navy willing to protect and promote American trading interests over the long term. In December 1841 Secretary of the Navy Abel P. Upshur explained to Congress the USN's role. The nation needed a stronger navy to patrol the Brazilian and West African coasts to suppress the slave trade and protect American trading rights.[52] The early 1840s thus coincided with a period in Anglo-American relations that opened the door to the settlement of some outstanding issues between the countries and the establishment of a US West African squadron.

Upshur worried that because so many nations coveted West African trade, the USN needed to be present to protect American business interests in the long term. But the situation had grown worse in 1842. Due to a restricted budget, no US vessels patrolled the coast, and Upshur reported that American trade had suffered as a result. Natives had also attacked US vessels and murdered their crews. One such case involved the schooner *Mary Carver*. The USN sent a warship to demand reparations, with little success, and Upshur concluded that American commerce required more vessels to patrol the area. He believed that the recent agreement with the British gave the Americans an opportunity to protect American interests on the West African coast.[53]

Britain and America negotiated the agreement that settled the issue of slave-trade suppression until the Civil War within the context of both nations' political constraints and growing American concern for overseas trade. The focus of the talks was the boundary dispute between Maine and New Brunswick, but negotiators also formulated a plan for joint naval patrols along the West African coast which would allay American fears over the right of search and British concerns about the lack of US commitment to suppress the slave trade. The arrangement was based in part on the European Quintuple Treaty

---

[52]United States, Congress, *Congressional Globe*, 27th Cong., 2nd sess., appendix, 17-20, Upshur, "Report of the Secretary of the Navy, 4 December 1841."

[53]*Ibid.*; and 27th Cong., 2nd sess., appendix, 39, Upshur, "Annual Report of the Secretary of the Navy, December 1842."

and a cooperation agreement between the RN and USN that had been disavowed. The result was a compromise that initially met the goals of both sides.

The Quintuple Treaty

The talks that began in Washington in 1842 were a continuation of the Quintuple Treaty negotiations among the European powers. The latter treaty laid out rules of engagement for multinational naval forces patrolling the West African coast to prevent disputes. Initiated by the British, in late 1841 Aberdeen convinced Russia, Prussia and Austria to meet in London to discuss a mutual right-of-search agreement. When the Quintuple Treaty was finalized in December, Britain invited the US to become party. The new American envoy, Edward Everett, reported that the British seemed willing to abandon the right to impress seamen and to limit their anti-slavery activities to the African coast if the US came on side. Ashburton had discussed the Quintuple Treaty with him, and Everett asked Webster if an Anglo-American exchange of notes would be sufficient to seal the deal. The British abandonment of the right of impressment and the policy of stopping Americans ships involved in the "coasting" slave trade would relieve "the chief objections to our joining in the General Agreement[.]" Respected Massachusetts maritime jurist Judge Joseph Story also supported the Quintuple Treaty and suggested that the US participate in the plan.[54]

But President John Tyler, who was a slave owner, disagreed. He was wary about entangling the US in agreements with foreign powers, something that went against traditional American foreign policy. In the meantime, the US Ambassador to Paris and Presidential hopeful, Lewis Cass, spoke out against the Quintuple Treaty. Perhaps seeking political capital, he professed that the treaty violated America's freedom of the seas. Probably because of his influence, the French also rejected the treaty, although other powers signed it, but not the US.[55] Because the Americans rejected it, London next pursued a bilateral agreement that addressed specific American concerns. Britain was also concerned about the French naval presence on the West African coast and wanted to implement a balance-of-power strategy using sea power. But the British desire to watch its traditional rival would later strengthen American suspicions about London's true intentions.

---

[54]Jones, *To the Webster-Ashburton Treaty*, 74-75; and Charles M. Wiltse and Harold D. Moser (eds.), *The Papers of Daniel Webster* (14 vols., Hanover, NH, 1974-1989), I, 491-496, Everett to Webster, 21 January 1842, "Private; and I, 537-538, Joseph Story to Webster, 19 April 1842.

[55]Wiltse and Moser (eds.), *Papers of Daniel Webster*, I, 717-721, Lewis Cass to Webster, 3 October 1842; and Jones, *To the Webster-Ashburton Treaty*, 74-76.

Regardless, the Quintuple Treaty was a sound compromise that laid the groundwork for international cooperation to police the slave trade while respecting the differing opinions of the various parties over the application of "peacetime" sea power. It permitted warships to stop a vessel only on the "reasonable" belief that it was involved in the slave trade, was equipped for that trade or had been involved in the trade during its voyage. But the "high contracting parties" were also aware of the strategic implications of the use of sea power and its potential to cause conflict. Undoubtedly the French, British, Russians and other regional powers would have objected to such a right on any number of grounds. Therefore, they mitigated its ability to harm their diplomatic relations. The treaty stipulated that the "said mutual right of search shall not be exercised within the Mediterranean Sea[,]" a strategically sensitive region for all the nations. Finally, the agreement ordered naval officers to cooperate with other naval forces where practicable.[56]

It was in this atmosphere that the Webster-Ashburton talks addressed specific American concerns. Webster was from New Hampshire and was a Federalist until that party collapsed, when he joined the Republicans. Like many Americans, he had been wary of war with the British in 1812 and as Secretary of State adopted a conciliatory approach. But Webster also wanted to uphold American rights. On 29 January 1842, for example, he wrote Everett about the *Creole* case. Webster explained that the vessel, travelling from port-to-port along the American coast, carried slaves along with other goods. The British had no right to interfere with the vessel to free the slaves, as no British laws were, in Webster's opinion, broken. Webster asked Everett to bring the government's position to the attention of London. He also asked for compensation for the vessel based upon Lord Palmerston's opinion of 1837 in the cases of *Enterprise*, *Encomium* and *Comet* that people in legal possession of slaves but who were interfered with in British territories, were entitled to compensation. The Secretary noted that it was unreasonable to afford non-British entities a British character and give them "English privileges" or freedom in such cases.[57]

The ramifications were clear to Webster: "Would any one [sic] contend that the fact of their [slaves] having been carried into England by force, set them free" even though they might be slaves being legally transported on

---

[56]Great Britain, *Foreign and States Papers* (*BFSP*), XXX, 272-291, "Quintuple Treaty."

[57]William H. Rehnquist, "Foreword: Daniel Webster and the Oratorical Tradition," in Kenneth E. Shewmaker (ed.), *Daniel Webster: "The Completest Man"* (Hanover, NH, 1990), ix; Richard N. Current, "Daniel Webster: The Politician," in *ibid.*, 1-2; Howard Jones, "Daniel Webster: The Diplomatist," in *ibid.*, 203-224; and Wiltse and Moser (eds.), *Papers of Daniel Webster*, I, 177-185, Webster to Everett, 29 January 1842.

the American coast? Further, he was concerned that legitimate US coastal trade near British possessions was threatened. To mitigate Anglo-American tension, Webster proposed a modification to both nations' use of sea power. He held the liberal ideal that each country must uphold the "doctrine of non-interference" in each other's trade and "domestic regulations," or world peace "will be always in danger." He hoped that Ashburton's visit would settle the matter. As a compromise, Webster suggested that America and Britain keep separate naval forces on the West African coast. The forces would "act in concert...in order that no slave ship, under whatever flag she may sail, shall be free from *visitation* and *search* [emphasis in original]."[58] British and American warships would cruise in pairs. The USN would search American-flag ships, and the RN would inspect those of other nations. The compromise would allow Anglo-American relations to move forward, and reduce and prevent tensions, while each nation pursued its wider, and often divergent, objectives.

The Tucker-Paine Agreement

Webster and Ashburton based the joint-cruising proposal on an agreement between RN Commander William Tucker and USN Lieutenant John S. Paine. The agreement had been disavowed by the previous US administration, but Webster decided to use it as a basis for solving the impasse over the Quintuple Treaty so that the nations could "hunt in couples." Ashburton agreed that if the plan was put into the treaty, the issue of the right of search would "settle itself."[59] The Tucker-Paine Agreement is therefore significant as a barometer of how Anglo-American interests changed and shaped their diplomatic and naval relations. Interests moulded their use of sea power to avoid conflict while furthering economic goals. Where once divergent interests meant the disavowal of the agreement, now that their interests had converged sufficiently there was a basis for compromise.

The Tucker-Paine Agreement was reached in March 1840. Lieutenant Paine had sailed in the US warship *Grampus* to the West African coast to join the warship *Dolphin*, already there under the command of Lieutenant Charles H. Bell. *Grampus* was sent on two missions: to protect US "mercantile interests" and ostensibly to stop the abuse of the US flag by slavers. Consequently, West Africa's senior RN officer, Commander William Tucker, proposed to Paine that the two cooperate to suppress the slave trade, and they agreed to seize any vessel engaged in, or thought to be engaged in, the slave trade. If it

---

[58]Wiltse and Moser (eds.), *Papers of Daniel Webster*, I, 177-185, Webster to Everett, 29 January 1842; and I, 543-544, Webster to Everett, 26 April 1842.

[59]*BPP*, 1843, LIX, 550-551, Correspondence with Foreign Powers Not Parties to Conventions Giving Mutual Right of Search of Vessels Suspected of the Slave Trade, 1842 (Class D), No. 149, Ashburton to Aberdeen, 25 April 1842.

was an American vessel, the British would turn it over to *Grampus* or another US warship; otherwise, the British would send it for trial under the terms of its treaties with other powers.[60]

Lord Palmerston was pleased with the agreement and forwarded related documents to Washington. Meanwhile, it proved successful along the coast. For example, on 3 March 1840 the RN brig *Bonetta* under Lieutenant John L. Stoll seized a suspected slaver, *Sarah Anne* from New Orleans, after receiving information that it was operating in the Rio Pongo. Traders had outfitted the ship for slaving, constructed a deck to house the slave children, provided enough water and food for slaves, and loaded firewood. When the British tried to free the ship from shallow water, gunfire erupted. The RN returned fire and captured the ship. But since it was an American vessel, on 16 March Stoll asked Paine if he could turn *Sarah Anne* over to him; the latter agreed.[61]

The British made other seizures of US-flagged vessels and justified their actions under the terms of the Tucker-Paine Agreement, but once they sent the ships to the US the results were disturbing. The courts freed one vessel, *Tigris*, and compensated its owners. There was also outrage in Washington over Paine's actions. Navy Secretary Paulding, originally appointed Secretary of the Board of Navy Commissioners by President Madison in April 1815, told Paine that he had exceeded his powers. Under no circumstances were British warships allowed to stop and seize American-flag vessels, even if the RN was to hand the suspect to an American warship.[62] But the Tucker-Paine Agreement laid the groundwork for the slave-trade suppression provisions of the Webster-Ashburton Treaty under which nations agreed to use their naval relations as a safety valve for their diplomatic disagreements.

The new administration saw the benefits of using sea power to further the long-term goals of promoting commerce and mitigating diplomatic disputes over the suppression of the slave trade. During the negotiations, Webster consulted Bell and Paine about the West African coast. The officers believed that

---

[60]NA, RG 59, Notes from the British Legation in the U.S. to Department of State, 1791-1906, XX, 12 January 1840-14 February 14, 1842, Fox to Forsyth, 15 August 1840, with enclosures, William Tucker to George Elliot, 12 March 1840; Tucker to Lieutenant John S. Paine, 10 March 1840; Paine to Tucker, 10 March 1840; and Tucker and Paine, "Agreement," 11 March 1840.

[61]*Ibid.*, Fox to Forsyth, 18 August 1840, with enclosures, Palmerston to Fox, 29 June 1840; John L. Stoll to Paine, 16 March 1840; and Paine to Stoll, 16 March 1840.

[62]W. Patrick Strauss, "James Kirke Paulding," in Paolo E. Coletta (ed.), *American Secretaries of the Navy* (2 vols., Annapolis, 1980), I, 165; Jones, *To the Webster-Ashburton Treaty*, 73; and Earl E. McNeilly, "The United States Navy and the Suppression of the West African Slave Trade, 1819-1862" (Unpublished PhD thesis, Case Western Reserve University, 1973), 102-103.

American "fair traders" were "sometimes obstructed" by "armed British merchantmen, sustained by British cruisers." British merchants and naval officers
made trade agreements with natives which secured for Britain "the exclusive
trade with the tribe or district." Bell and Paine suggested that the Americans
make similar treaties, but that they "should not be made to the exclusion of
other mercantile powers trading on the coast, as has sometimes been done; and
all treaties should contain a prohibition of the slave trade." Finally, Bell and
Paine believed that the US and Britain should cooperate and cruise in pairs.[63]

With the Quintuple Treaty and the Tucker-Paine Agreement as terms
of reference, the British and Americans agreed to a joint-patrol provision and
placed it in the Webster-Ashburton Treaty. Word of the finalization of the
treaty reached London in September 1842. Everett reported that proclamations
in the American press against some provisions of the boundary settlement "will
not be without an influence in recommending them to the favour of the British
public." Moreover, Everett concluded that the ratification of the treaty would
also please the government and allow Britain to free troops from North America for the "Chinese and Afghan wars."[64]

President Tyler agreed with the basic plan but made some modifications. He amended the language to ensure that it applied only to the African
coast and only to enforce agreements with the American government. The US
Congress and the British Parliament approved the treaty, although it had de-
tractors. Senator Thomas Hart Benton, for example, thought that an African
squadron was too expensive. Meanwhile, Congressman James Buchanan believed that the treaty was not reciprocal and that the British could do as they
pleased. Southerners were more interested in expanding their cotton market in
Britain, although some voiced concerns that the treaty failed to protect slavery.
But the historian of the treaty, Howard Jones, concluded that many Senators
were tired of talking about the subject and offered few comments. When the
Senate approved the treaty by a vote of thirty-nine to nine, the public seemed
supportive. In Britain, Palmerston, temporarily out of office, was jealous that
someone else had negotiated the treaty, and Lewis Cass, still ambassador to
Paris, called it "maritime metaphysics" and questioned whether the British had
truly acquired a right of search.[65] Cass' opposition is important because when
the issue climaxed in the late 1850s he was Secretary of State under James

---

[63]Wiltse and Moser (eds.), *Papers of Daniel Webster*, I, 547-555, Webster to
Bell and Paine, 30 April 1842; and Bell and Paine to Webster, 10 May 1842.

[64]NA, RG 59, Dispatches, Britain, Nos. 21 and 24, Everett to Webster, 19
August and 1 September 1842.

[65]Jones, *To the Webster-Ashburton Treaty*, 143 and 161-176; and Hugh Graham Soulsby, *The Right of Search and the Slave Trade in Anglo-American Relations,
1814-1862* (Baltimore, 1933), 88-117.

Buchanan. Yet Britain and the US showed that they would rather modify their sea power policies than threaten Anglo-American relations.

Conclusion

During the 1830s and early 1840s, British and American leaders believed that they could use sea power to police maritime markets and encourage trade growth in the equatorial Atlantic. But they differed on the priority of the suppression of the slave trade as opposed to the right of the British to search American-flagged vessels. During this period the British maintained pressure on the US to police the slave trade yet avoided war. London presented the Americans with evidence that showed the abuse of the US flag. British pressure even went so far as to bring suspicious US vessels to New York. The Americans objected, although they prosecuted the cases, but the Queen's advocate told Palmerston to curtail his efforts to twist the American hand.

Informal Anglo-American talks resumed in this climate. Meanwhile, the British continued to stop ships that they felt flew the US flag illegally along the West African coast and interfered "accidentally" with legitimate US commerce, as in the case of *Edwin*. Yet because of internal American political considerations, the British concluded that putting pressure on the Americans was futile, and London was unwilling to push the issue into war. Instead, the Maine-New Brunswick border dispute, growing US industrialization and receptive administrations in London and Washington seized the opportunity to settle the dispute over the application of peacetime sea power. The Webster-Ashburton Treaty marked their commitment to fight the slave trade from the West African side while reducing tension and preventing conflict that might arise over the tactical use of navies.

With an American squadron present, the RN no longer needed to stop American-flagged ships. The treaty appeased both sides. By 1844, Aberdeen reported that Anglo-American cooperation helped suppression; Britain would reduce the number of RN cruisers along the Brazilian coast and devote more resources to West Africa. Upshur, now Secretary of State, told Everett that the British could no longer interfere with the US flag: the USN protected American commerce and suppressed the slave trade.[66] The presence of the USN might help British strategy, but legal problems in the US would curtail American activity against slavers, just as sympathetic US commanders hoped to act. In the end, the American priority was commerce protection and expansion, and the navies rarely cruised in pairs.

Anglo-American naval deployment reveals that the Americans focused on trade protection and "showing the flag" to further long-term economic

---

[66]NA, RG 59, Dispatches, Britain, Nos. 164 and 168, Everett to John C. Calhoun, 18 and 27 July 1844; and Soulsby, *Right of Search*, 104.

growth. In contrast, the RN combined slave-trade suppression with the introduction of free trade. The navies implemented their nations' policies using sea
power, but their strategies differed and affected their naval relations. The reality off West Africa was different than what many hoped for because the nations had different objectives. As differences grew, tensions rose. Yet their
decision to use sea power to further long-term goals peacefully also meant that
they were willing to solve their disputes by modifying the use of their navies in
a continual process of accommodation. Sea power provided a mechanism
through which the nations related to further their objectives without going to
war.

Chapter 6
The Royal Navy and West Africa, 1843-1857

By the 1840s the Royal Navy (RN) was deployed along the West African coast to further long-term British objectives to suppress the slave trade and, short of war, to relate to other powers. The RN was one of the main instruments of British trade policy and, unlike in the US, humanitarian efforts merged with trade and strategic goals. At home, the government had to overcome the demands of radical free traders to disband the squadron and allow unfettered commerce, even if slave produced. But the government supported those who felt that only slave-trade suppression would encourage legitimate commerce. A unified West African strategy suited the nation's economic and strategic needs. Consequently, RN activities were different than those of the US Navy (USN), although both shared the belief that sea power could further long-term goals peacefully. Their different strategies created the conditions under which Anglo-American tension might rise.

In Britain the elite secured its objective of using sea power to push African "factors of production" away from the slave trade and into legitimate commerce. The RN also eagerly signed trade treaties with natives to match similar French activities and counter its traditional rival. The British installed sympathetic native leaders, as at Lagos in 1851, and enforced agreements with recalcitrant chiefs. As a result, the British captured 634 slavers, dwarfing the American effort during the same period.[1] But London also wanted peace maintained with other nations and selected naval officers for the West African coast, like Sir Charles Hotham, with a reputation for diplomacy. Nevertheless, British actions reinforced American fears that it sought to dominate the coast, while Britain believed that US involvement in the slave trade was growing. Mutual suspicion increased Anglo-American tension and created the potential for an Atlantic-wide war, with France and America allied against Britain, a scenario the British wanted to avoid.

The Abolitionist North and Free Traders

In Britain, there were divergent views on the economics and morality of slavery that the government strove to overcome. It found support from the abolitionists for a West African policy that involved the suppression of the slave trade and the encouragement of legitimate commerce. In contrast, while the

---

[1]David Eltis, *et al.*, *The Trans-Atlantic Slave Trade: A Database on CD-ROM* (Cambridge, 1999).

free-trade movement opened the possibility of developing Africa, radicals believed in strict non-interference. Nevertheless, the early abolition movement
thrived on morality in areas with low unemployment and a growing economy
where support for slavery might have been expected to compensate for infla-
tionary pressures with cheap goods. It was a "geographic" phenomenon, centred on the industrial masses of northern England.[2]

After 1846 and the end of the duty on sugar, British opposition to the
RN's blockade of the African slave coast increased. Many believed that it was
uneconomical and blocked slaves from reaching the West Indies where they
could produce cheap sugar. The radical free traders saw it as a contradiction to
support free trade in sugar while at the same time limiting the supply of the
labour that produced it. The campaign to end the naval patrols began in 1845
in Parliament, where William Hutt wanted to encourage the development of
African trade. But like many other radical free traders, he also wanted a regu-
lated slave trade. Some, like Jose E. Cliffe, testified before Hutt's committee
studying the issue that Africans were "Natural Slaves" created by God, and for
the British to stop them went against His will.[3]

Bernard Semmel concluded that the radicals succeeded in repealing
the Navigation Acts and then set their eyes on British naval strategy. They and
other liberals believed that Britain's strategy to use force to stop another's
trade "was both immoral and opposed to her true interests." Instead, Hutt and
his supporters adhered to strict *laissez-faire*. Through the natural course of
events, slaves would rebel and overthrow their masters. But supporters of abolition, like the African Institute and Fowell Buxton, had a higher ideal and
countered that they needed the RN to suppress the slave trade and protect legitimate commerce. A free black population would till the soil and produce
goods for export rather than be transported to foreign lands.[4]

While Hutt worked to abolish the squadron, the Lords established
another committee in 1849 chaired by the Lord Bishop of Oxford to study the
slave trade.[5] Most witnesses were naval officers, including Commodore Sir

---

[2]Seymour Drescher, *Capitalism and Antislavery: British Mobilization in Comparative Perspective* (New York, 1987), 10-16.

[3]Philip D. Curtin, *The Image of Africa: British Ideas and Action, 1780-1850*
(Madison, WI, 1964), 443-447; and Christopher Lloyd, *The Navy and the Slave Trade:
The Suppression of the African Slave Trade in the Nineteenth Century* (London, 1949;
reprint, London, 1968), 101-114.

[4]Bernard Semmel, *Liberalism and Naval Strategy: Ideology, Interests and Sea
Power during the Pax Britannica* (Boston, 1986), 40-42 and 53-57.

[5]David R. Murray, *Odious Commerce: Britain, Spain and the Abolition of the
Cuban Slave Trade* (Cambridge, 1980), 210-214.

Charles Hotham, recently returned from Africa, who believed the squadron should remain. Indeed, the most significant witnesses testified about the need for force to suppress the slave trade on economic grounds. With high profits from slavery, the British had to force Africans to move factors of production into producing legitimate exports. Otherwise, trade might do the same thing, with British goods used to barter for slaves who would then be brought to places like Brazil and Cuba. Witnesses concluded that British industry and the tariff collectors would see little benefit because slave traders had little compunction about underselling legitimate merchants when bartering for slaves. The elite, symbolized by the Lords, concluded that the only way to further British economic goals was to use sea power to push Africans into legitimate commerce; the government agreed and shaped its naval policy accordingly.

The most important testimony came on 5 July 1849 from James Mac-Queen, the famous geographer. Jeffrey Pardue has shown that MacQueen advocated expanding the "British Empire at a time when it was of little interest to most people in his country." But MacQueen, a Glasgwegian, also moved in gentlemanly circles. The Scotsman's family had no connections, but "[o]ver the years, he did build up a network of influential friends, from powerful West India merchants" to "banking men, such as John Irving and Lord Ashburton[.]" Still, he accepted "his subordinate position in this hierarchy, which helped define his role as an 'agent' for powerful metropolitan interests[.]" In this role, he acted as the Colonial Bank's agent, founded the Royal Mail Steam Packet Company and was a geographic information broker. Pardue explained that the "ties with which MacQueen helped bind the periphery and the metropolis" also "helped centralize power in the metropolis."[6]

In the emancipation debate MacQueen, with ten plantations and 1000 slaves, defended West Indian slavery. In the end he accepted emancipation but disagreed on its timing. He also realized that the West Indian colonies were "on the decline" and looked toward "Africa for new imperial opportunities." In 1821 he advocated expansion to a number of regions, like Fernando Po and the Niger. Later, he forged uneasy alliances with former foes, like Buxton, to further development plans for Africa. As an Africa expert and a member of the elite, he was "solicited by the Colonial Office to be its agent for the Niger Expedition of 1841," although he did not take the position. Pardue asserted that "his constant promotion of Africa, in the hopes of 'selling' the public and the government on the continent's potential to Britain, was much like an agent's." He was an intermediary upon whom the elite called to support its case, even if MacQueen disagreed with policy decisions, such as slave-trade suppression. He believed that the African squadron was a waste of money but

---

[6]Jeffrey David Pardue, "Agent of Imperial Change: James MacQueen and the British Empire, 1778-1870" (Unpublished PhD thesis, University of Waterloo, 1996), 1-5 and 18.

conceded that if the government was intent on the task, half-hearted measures were insufficient to push African factors of production away from the slave trade to create a level field for legitimate commerce.[7]

MacQueen hoped to encourage African agricultural development and offered a strong explanation for the current dynamic of the African economy. British merchants benefited from increased commerce, the side effect of a growing slave trade, as their products entered the slave-trade circuit. If the squadron was withdrawn, British exporters might see their trade increase "tenfold." But MacQueen calculated that because slavers made profits in places like Brazil, they had no problem "undersell[ing] the legal trader" as long as slaves were obtained in return. Quantity sold might increase, but the value of products would stagnate. Moreover, if a legitimate British merchant went to the African coast for palm oil, he would encounter British produce that had already fallen into the slave-trade economy. This had a detrimental impact on the palm oil industry; ironically, MacQueen opined, palm oil production only increased if "domestic slaves increase."[8]

MacQueen explained that Africa was capable of producing legitimate products, especially cotton, "to an unbounded extent." The only thing that prevented such expansion was "the disturbance which the Slave Trade everywhere creates." It competed for factors of production that the market needed to generate a favourable balance of trade between Africa and Britain. If the goal of the gentlemanly capitalists and others was to increase commerce between the UK and Africa, it had to flow both ways to benefit Britain by increasing the value of trade and hence swelling the coffers of government and City financiers. Those involved in the African trades, MacQueen confirmed, had supporters in Parliament. A number were Liverpool firms, including Horsfall, Jackson and Tobin, plus Matthew Forster of London. When prompted by the committee, MacQueen noted that Jackson and Forster were MPs.[9]

Others also offered testimony that slave-trade suppression benefited commerce. On 18 June 1849 Robert Stokes, involved with African affairs since 1800, testified that imports from West Africa to Britain between 1783 and 1787 never exceeded £90,500 per year, and British exports to the region never topped £50,000. But after the ban on the slave trade, he reported that imports to Britain from Africa had risen to £535,577, and exports from Britain had reached £693,911 by 1810. The rise in palm oil exports was the most dra-

---

[7]*Ibid.*, 2-3, 61, 84, 96, 100-102, 106-108 and 222-224.

[8]Curtin, *Image of Africa*, 428-431; and Great Britain, Parliament, *Parliamentary Papers* (*BPP*), 1850, IX, Select Committee of the House of Lords to Consider the Best Means for the Final Extinction of the African Slave Trade, 262-263 and 265-268.

[9]*BPP*, 1850, IX, Select Committee of the House of Lords to Consider the Best Means for the Final Extinction of the African Slave Trade, 267-268 and 273.

dramatic component of the trade, increasing from 2599 cwts. in 1790 to 414,570 cwts. by 1846. This increasing commerce provided governments with additional revenue. The Customs House on the Gold Coast in 1839, 1840, and 1841 collected £32,687 l. 4s. 0d at a tariff rate of about three percent, "indicating the value of the importations in those three years to have been upwards of a million sterling[.]" Stokes found the same phenomenon at Gambia.[10]

Ralph Dawson was also involved in the Africa trades from 1827 to 1839 with the merchant house of Wilson and Clegg. He told the committee on 22 June 1849 that he used three ships that could load upward of 1000 tons of palm oil. But Liverpool houses dominated because of the port's history with the slave trade, grafting their new operations on top of prior connections; Africans looked upon vessels from London or Bristol with scepticism. He concluded that natives had no incentive to shift into legitimate commerce because these needed local production factors which were scarce due to the more profitable slave trade.[11] While the latter provided some profits to British merchants, these would expand dramatically, some testified, if government suppressed the slave trade. But in the end, the radicals who wanted to end slave-trade suppression lacked the power and influence to overcome the cohesive group of merchants, abolitionists and gentlemanly capitalists who wanted it to continue.

The Lords concluded that the slave trade prevented the growth of legitimate African commerce. They believed, for instance, that "[c]otton and almost all tropical productions might, it appears, be largely produced in Africa if this one master impediment [the slave trade] were removed[.]" The Lords recommended that "the cost of the Squadron should be set against the advantage of nourishing and maintaining a valuable and increasing lawful trade, which must be utterly extirpated if the Cruisers were withdrawn, and which might be developed to an unlimited extent if the Slave Trade were suppressed." The opportunity cost of withdrawing the squadron was clear to the elite. Rather than disband it, government should improve it.[12] Moreover, wider parliamentary opinion supported the Lords when the issue came to a vote.

Cain and Hopkins explained that the land-owning, military and financial classes dominated the economic interests of MPs at mid-century, especially among the Conservatives. These lawmakers, the authors established, had aristocratic roots; averse to making money with their hands, they preferred

---

[10]*Ibid.*, 191-192.

[11]*Ibid.*, 211-219.

[12]*Ibid.*, 590-592.

investments.[13] The economics of slave-trade suppression were clear to the elite; only the presence of the RN would encourage legitimate commerce and substantial economic growth. While Hutt rejected the Lords' report in Parliament on 19 March 1850, Whig Prime Minister Lord John Russell rose to the squadron's defence. When he made the issue a confidence vote, the House rejected Hutt's motion to disband the squadron by 232 to 154.[14] The "interest aggregation" believed that it needed the RN to further British economic and strategic objectives in the region.

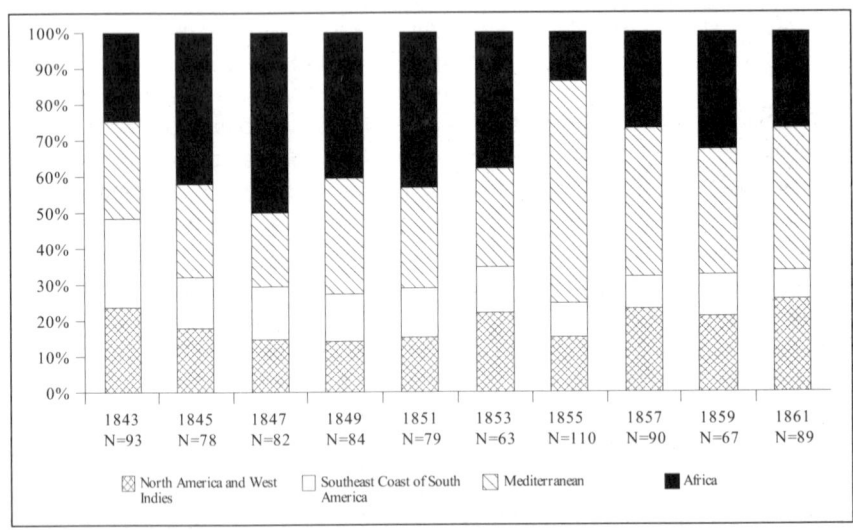

Figure 6.1: Royal Navy Vessel Deployment in the Atlantic, 1843-1861

Note: Steamships were also present, but only armed ships, or tugs attached to other vessels and thus able to contribute to force projection, were counted. N = Number of Warships.

Source: Calculated from Great Britain, National Archives (TNA/PRO), Navy List, 1843-1861.

---

[13]For example, in 1868 45.9 percent of Conservative MPs had landowning interests, but only 26.1 percent of the Liberals did. See P.J. Cain and A.G. Hopkins, *British Imperialism, 1688-2000* (2nd ed., London, 2001), 132.

[14]Lloyd, *Navy and the Slave Trade*, 112-113; and Murray, *Odious Commerce*, 214.

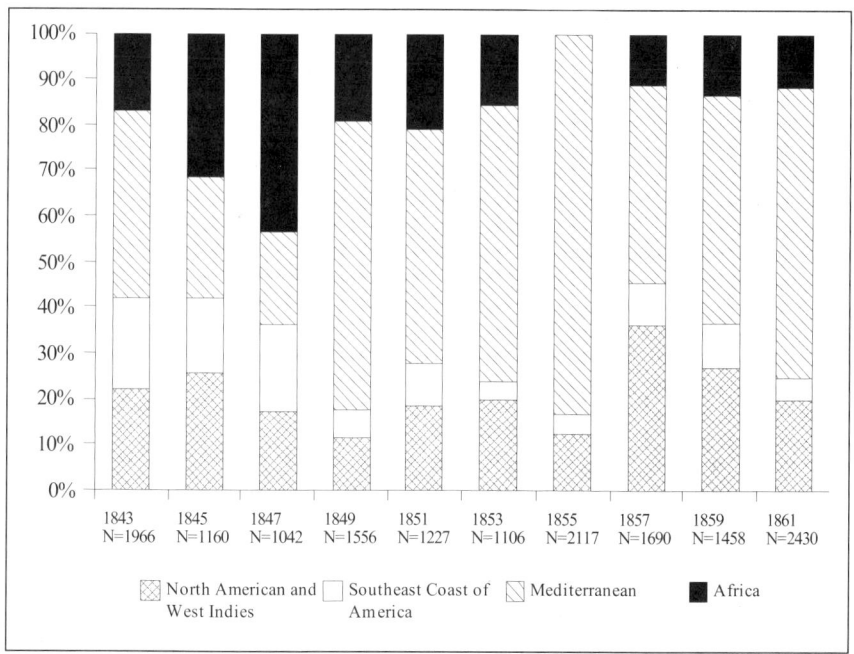

Figure 6.2: Royal Navy Armament Deployed, 1843-1861

Note: See figure 6.1. In 1855 there were six guns deployed to Africa, but the small number is obscured by the overwhelming number deployed to the Mediterranean. N = Number of Guns Deployed.

Source: See figure 6.1.

With support in London for the nexus of British goals, the station's strength grew during the 1840s and 1850s. Figure 6.1 reveals that British naval commitment to the coast rose from twenty-three vessels in 1843 to a peak of forty-one vessels in 1847; London maintained the squadron at about twenty-four vessels for the rest of the 1850s. Figure 6.2 shows a corresponding pattern for the total armaments deployed on British warships along the coast. Although the Mediterranean maintained its strategic importance, especially during the Crimean War, as indicated by its majority in guns deployed, in terms of number of warships Africa became the largest station in the Atlantic theatre. There the RN enforced free-trade agreements to further British commerce, suppressed the slave trade and kept watch on rivals, such as France. The elite also deployed the latest technology to the coast to accomplish the task. The number of steamships in the squadron increased from about twenty percent in 1845 to eighty percent by the end of the 1850s (see figure 6.3). As Basil Greenhill and Ann Giffard noted, because a British commander's commission during this era rested on his connections, "we have here a system in which the rating of steam paddle wheel vessels depended upon patronage rather" than just its technological prowess. It also indicated the government's intentions.[15]

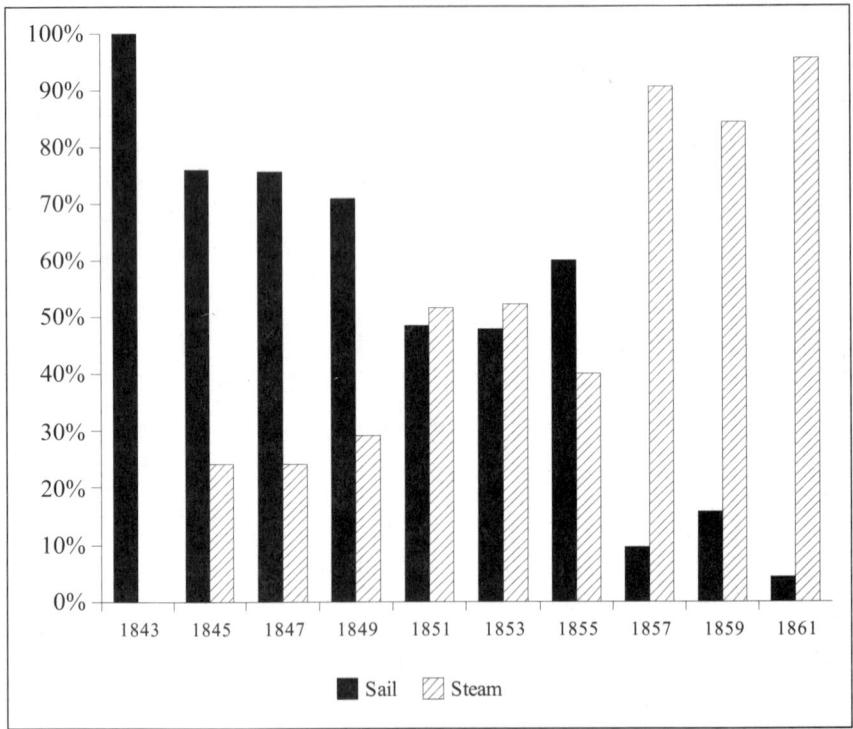

Figure 6.3: Royal Navy West African Squadron, 1843-1861 (Percentage Steamships)

Source: See figure 6.1.

   With a liberal mentality for foreign policy, the government also selected commodores, like Sir Charles Hotham, whom they hoped would maintain peace and alleviate disputes. As a result, the British used force only on rare occasions and against non-nation-states, like the installation of a new ruler for Lagos who was more sympathetic to British objectives. London avoided conflicts with other nations and hoped that the Webster-Ashburton Treaty would facilitate Anglo-American cooperation against the slave trade and go far

---

[15]Basil Greenhill and Ann Giffard, *Steam, Politics and Patronage: The Transformation of the Royal Navy, 1815-54* (London, 1994), 163 and 172. Deployment percentages were calculated from Great Britain, National Archives (TNA/PRO), Navy Lists, 1845-1859.

to furthering British objectives. Nevertheless, its strategy raised suspicion on the US side because the British seemed to be consolidating their dominance on the West African coast. Consequently, the conflicting goals of the RN and USN increased Anglo-American tensions and had to be relieved.

Royal Navy Operations, Slavers and Free Trade

Against the background of competing interests over West Africa and slave-trade suppression, the government maintained its commitment to the latter and to the nation's strategic needs. While Britain and America had settled differences over the suppression of the slave trade and borders, London still feared that France and the US would unite against Britain. Aberdeen held out the hope that he could sever Franco-American friendship by allying with France to guarantee Texan independence. But Anglo-French relations soured when the latter attacked Morocco in 1844, while their interactions in other regions also deteriorated. Again, Aberdeen turned to the US and settled the Oregon boundary dispute.[16] Still, the British remained wary of global French intentions. Along the West African coast, this meant that London used the RN to check French moves and to implement trade treaties with natives to counter similar French actions. But Britain also selected commodores it hoped would keep Anglo-French relations from spiralling out of control. Regardless, Britain's strategy reinforced US suspicions of its motives.

The British attitude varied with France's monarchical or republican leanings. London maintained a balance-of-power strategy, but it was a careful doctrine meant to contain France without sparking war or a Franco-American alliance. In West Africa the primary French settlements were Senegal and Gorée, but devising a policy in France against the slave trade was more difficult than in Britain. Paul Kielstra has shown that French abolitionists lacked the power and influence of their British counterparts. Thus, French abolitionist goals failed to form a nexus with wider political and economic concerns: "Colonists, merchants and manufacturers called it [the slave trade] a life-line; nationalists, a reaffirmation of French power." As a result, after the wars French "merchants, colonists and nationalists looked to" the rival of the slave trade to "restore fortunes devastated by a quarter-century of war." Co-operation with Britain was impossible, and after France rejected the Quintuple Treaty it dispatched its own naval force to the West African coast.[17]

---

[16]Kenneth Bourne, *The Foreign Policy of Victorian England, 1830-1902* (Oxford, 1970), 54-55.

[17]Paul Kielstra, *The Politics of Slave Trade Suppression in Britain and France, 1814-48: Diplomacy, Morality and Economics* (New York, 2000), 16-17 and 21; and W.E.F. Ward, *The Royal Navy and the Slavers: The Suppression of the Atlantic Slave Trade* (London, 1969), 120-121.

While tensions with other nations remained high, Britain hoped to contain rather than exacerbate them. By 1848, revolutions in Europe spread from Italy to France and Austria, removing Louis Philippe and Metternich in the process. The turmoil spared only Russia, Britain and Belgium. In response, Britain and Russia hoped to "preserve the Balance of Power, and especially to contain revolutionary France."[18] Palmerston was concerned about the new French Republic but believed that "the Powers should not stimulate republican aggression by taking too strong a line." He reiterated Britain's non-interference policy and announced that London would recognize newly established regimes. Regardless, Palmerston worked with varying degrees of success to prevent French interference in the revolutions in the other countries. But Bourne also concluded that "he was always careful in 1848-1849 to put Britain's interests and the preservation of the Balance of Power first."[19]

Palmerston confirmed his foreign policy philosophy before Parliament in March 1848. He declared that his goal was to maintain peace and friendly relations with other countries as long as this was in Britain's interests. The government had sought to extend and protect British commercial endeavours. While countries might work together, he concluded that "it is our duty to make allowance for the different manner in which they may" implement their policies, even if they differed from British goals. But he exclaimed that "I would adopt the expression of Canning, and say that with every British Minister the interests of England ought to be the shibboleth of his policy."[20]

Having been out of power several years during Peel's ministry, Palmerston privately remained concerned about the French. In October 1847 he wrote Lord Auckland, the First Lord of the Admiralty, to explain that while Louis Philippe was old and far from "immortal," he could still "trick us in every way." But if others came to power they might try to bully Britain, so London remained wary.[21] Yet Britain applied "pragmatic" liberalism to Anglo-American relations in the slave trade. British goals and strategy were clear and were reflected in how London and its naval and diplomatic representatives dealt with other nations on the West African coast. London would check the French presence along the coast but realized that open conflict with Western

---

[18]Bourne, *Foreign Policy of Victorian England*, 63.

[19]*Ibid.*, 63 and 68; and University of Southampton (US), Hartley Library (HL), Archives and Special Collections (A&SC), Broadlands Archive (BA), Mss. GC/WE, No. 189, Palmerston to Lord Westmorland, 29 February 1848.

[20]Great Britain, Parliament, *Hansard*, 3rd ser., XCVII, 121-123, Palmerston's Reply to His Critics, 1 March 1848.

[21]US, HL, A&SC, BA, Palmerston Papers (PP), GC/AU/45-68, Palmerston to Auckland, 9 October 1847.

nations, like France and the US, had to be avoided to keep them from coming together against Britain, as had occurred during the War of 1812.

Sir Charles Hotham and Deterrence in West Africa

British strategy to counter the French along the African coast had ramifications for the entire equatorial Atlantic. Anglo-French relations could drag the region into war, and the British worried that they could face a war on "two fronts" with France and the US as in 1812. London therefore implemented a sea power policy to maintain peace on the African coast and selected its commanders accordingly. Naval officers therefore became important tools for the governing elite as the RN linked the periphery to the metropolis economically and strategically. Station commanders "answered to the Lords of the Admiralty, who in turn took their cue from the Cabinet and invariably the Secretary of State for Foreign Affairs."[22]

Life and relations at sea reflected Victorian society ashore in the selection of officers for command positions. Officers were generally members of the upper class, and some, like the chaplains and naval instructors, were educated at Oxford and Cambridge, further linking classes ashore and afloat. Consequently, officers connected to the governing class faired better during the so-called post-war "slump" of high officer unemployment described by Michael Lewis. For example, Rear-Admiral Richard Dundas, the First Sea Lord's son, was "almost constantly employed during the slump years." Lewis concluded that the "post-war Navy, full and by, was considerably more class-bound" than during the wars.[23]

For the period 1814-1849 Lewis showed that about forty-six percent of naval officers were from what could be called "gentlemanly-capitalist families." Approximately eighteen percent were the sons of peers or baronets, and twenty-eight percent were the sons of landed gentry, an increase of 5.8 and 0.2 percent, respectively, from the 1793-1815 war period. Some respondents, when asked about their class origins, may have tried to pass for a higher class and thus distorted the figures. Indeed, Lewis believed that there were more officers from the business and commercial class than the statistics indicated (0.4 percent). He noted, for instance, that the growing power of the commercial classes, who were obtaining titles during the period, explained the increasing number of peers and baronets. Of 228 captains in 1849, for example, Lewis showed that while about twenty-nine percent were sons of naval offi-

---

[22]C.I. Hamilton, *Anglo-French Naval Rivalry 1840-1870* (Oxford, 1993), 13; and Barry M. Gough, "Profit and Power: Informal Empire, the Navy and Latin America," in Raymond E. Dumett (ed.), *Gentlemanly Capitalism and British Imperialism: The New Debate on Empire* (London, 1999), 75.

[23]Michael Lewis, *The Navy in Transition* (London, 1965), 21, 124 and 145.

cers, fifty-four percent were the sons of peers, ministers, barons and landed gentry.[24]

Because of class connections, First Lords of the Admiralty were keen to help certain naval officers. In 1846, for instance, Lord Auckland told Prime Minister Russell that "Captain James Ryder Burton...is very anxious to be knighted" and would accept retirement if he received this honour. Auckland explained that Burton was married to a Lord's daughter and that other Lords supported his knighthood. As a result, Auckland recommended that the "favour should be granted to him."[25] But a high unemployment rate among officers also enabled the Admiralty to choose whom to place in command, even if its ability to retire useless officers was limited. Therefore, London's elite selected as commanders others from their class whom they believed could be trusted. The command of Commodore Sir Charles Hotham, on the coast from October 1846 to March 1849 and connected to the gentlemanly elite, illustrates British West African strategy. London ordered Hotham to suppress the slave trade, advance British economic and strategic objectives and monitor French moves carefully.

His superiors told Hotham to counter French activities that might give them a foothold in Africa from which to harm British interests. For this purpose, Hotham signed treaties with natives for slave-trade suppression and the furtherance of free trade. Britain meant the treaties to match similar French activities without sparking war. With uncertainty in Europe, the British were fearful that a conflict might spread across the ocean and involve the US. Meanwhile, Hotham also sought to show that the squadron could effectively suppress the slave trade to counter opposition from radicals in Parliament. Overall British strategy, however, reinforced American suspicions that London sought to drive other nations from avenues of growing commerce, rekindling Anglo-American tension.

The Admiralty selected Hotham to deal with the French because of his successful experience in balancing strategic and diplomatic issues elsewhere. Moreover, he was a member of the gentlemanly elite, a son of a Yorkshire landholding family.[26] Charles' cousin was the Third Lord Hotham, his father

---

[24]*Ibid.*, 21-22, 24, 26 and 30.

[25]TNA/PRO 30/22/5D, Lord John Russell Papers, c. 1800-1913 (RP), Auckland to Russell, 26 October 1846.

[26]Lewis, *Navy in Transition*, 37-39 and 58-95. Lewis notes that while Yorkshire's share of naval officers increased from ninth to fifth place between 1793-1815 and 1814-1819, it was still far below its proportion of the English population. He concluded that "the general run of naval officers still remained so very aristocratical [sic] as to be largely unaffected by the masses of the labouring classes." In 1814-1849 Kent, Devonshire Hampshire and Cornwall were the top four geographic origins of officers.

was Reverend Frederick Hotham and his uncle was Vice-Admiral Sir Henry Hotham. On the maternal side, his grandmother's brother, John Cartwright, was connected to political philosophers like Edmund Burke and was involved in the anti-slavery movement.[27]

A member of the elite, Charles' youth was typical. He attended Westminster School, London, and at age twelve left to study for entrance to the Naval College at Portsmouth, where he spent two years and graduated in second place, doing well in geography and seamanship. Early in his career, he also gained experience in maritime and diplomatic relations. He battled pirates as a young officer on the fifth-rate *Cambrian* in the Mediterranean and was part of a diplomatic delegation to Ibraham Pasha, the Egyptian commander who suppressed the Greek resistance. Hotham's first command was *Cordelia*, a small brig deployed first to the North Sea and then to the Mediterranean, where his uncle Admiral Sir Henry Hotham commanded the station. But when Sir Henry died in 1833, Charles lost an important connection needed for his next commission, and he suffered during the next eight years of Whig rule.[28]

Charles remained ashore at Suffolk during this period and tried to maintain a gentleman's profile in London until his next command. When the political winds shifted to Sir Robert Peel in 1841, the Admiralty placed Hotham in command of the six-gun, paddle-wheel steamer *Gorgon* in November 1842 and dispatched him to South America. By December, he sortied to the Plata region, which was unstable after the wars of independence. After a war with Brazil over the Banda Oriental, Britain worked to maintain peace in the region and helped Plata and Brazil reach an agreement for Uruguayan independence, although "the sovereignty of Uruguay remained in dispute for another forty years."[29]

When Hotham arrived, the ports of Montevideo and Buenos Aires were in such a rivalry that the latter's navy had blockaded the former. Meanwhile, the army of Manuel Oribe, the deposed President of Uruguay, laid siege to Montevideo and threatened American, French and British citizens. Shirley Roberts concluded that the RN had to balance protecting British subjects, furthering the nation's commercial interests and avoiding becoming embroiled in

---

[27]Shirley Roberts, *Charles Hotham: A Biography* (Carlton, Vic, 1985), 1-11.

[28]*Ibid.*, 20-28; J.J. Colledge, *Ships of the Royal Navy* (2 vols., New York, 1969-1970), I, 70; and Norman Gash, *Aristocracy and the People: Britain 1815-1865* (London, 1979), 156-186. While Whig administrations dominated, Peel had a 100-day ministry after the 1835 general election.

[29]Roberts, *Charles Hotham*, 11-17 and 35-39.

local disputes. Hotham took the position that he should remain neutral while trying to reconcile the "conflicting interests" of various parties.[30]

Figure 6.4:   Sixteen-Gun HM Brig *Acorn* in Chase of the Slaver *Gabriel*, 1841

Source: National Maritime Museum (NMM), Negative No. PX9195
                        © National Maritime Museum, London.

But a dictator, Juan Manuel Rosas, was in power in the Republic, and as he waged almost constant war on the surrounding nations the turmoil threatened to drag in foreign countries to protect their citizens. The French and British decided to wait Oribe out, but Montevideo looked about to collapse, and Oribe's threat to attack thousands of French and British citizens might be realized. Rosas also blockaded the Parana River, an important "communication and trade route for inland centres in Argentina, Uruguay and Paraguay." If Rosas succeeded, it would have terminated all trade in the region. The British and French decided to act to end the threat. Hotham was in charge of the British forces and worked well with his French counterpart, thus proving his ability to balance strategic needs and international relations in a highly contested

---

[30]*Ibid.*, 39-41.

region. The two sides secured the Parana and broke the blockade at Obligado which British traders met with applause. But diplomats were more pleased that it marked a renewed friendship between Britain and France.[31]

Hotham's sister, Anne Barlow, wrote that "the Admiralty were extremely anxious *he* [Hotham; emphasis in original] should take it [the African command], as it was at that moment of great consequence to have peace with France, and they thought him most acceptable to the French on account" of their successful cooperation along the South American coast. Roberts noted that Captain Joseph Denman already had experience along the African coast, "was dedicated to the anti-slavery cause" and had a strategy to stop slave trading by blockading suspected ports. But London's support for him dissolved when "the Government was obliged to provide his legal defence and to accept responsibility for his actions" for destroying Portuguese trading facilities and freed slaves at Gallinas in 1841. When the Admiralty sought to replace Commodore L.T. Jones, they looked to Hotham, who had the "discretion and diplomatic ability, to avoid international and legal wrangles[.]" In March 1846 Lord Ellenborough believed that "the Royal Navy must be capable of crushing the US Navy within six months of the start of hostilities to prevent France from declaring war."[32] But while prepared for the worst, Ellenborough and other British policymakers hoped to prevent relations in the Atlantic from spiralling into conflict.

On reports of Commodore Denman's zealous actions along the West African coast, at Gallinas, New Cestos and Sea Bar, Lord Aberdeen, the Foreign Secretary, wrote in 1842 to the Law Officers of the Crown to ask whether his actions were justifiable and legal. The Law Officers concluded that Denman's actions in coming to the aid of a woman and child, "free British subjects detained at Gallinas," were commendable but illegal. They opined that "however desirable it may be to put an End to the Slave Trade, an eminent good should not be obtained otherwise than by lawful means." Consequently, when Hotham received his appointment on 20 May 1846, Ellenborough wrote that no other officer "could be entrusted who would carry out the very delicate and

---

[31]*Ibid.*, 50-61.

[32]University of Hull (UH), Brynmor Jones Library (BJL), Archives and Special Collections (A&SC), Hotham Family Papers (HFP), DDHO 10/47, Sir Charles Hotham, biographical notebook by Mrs. Anne Barlow; Roberts, *Charles Hotham*, 64-76; Lloyd, *Navy and the Slave Trade*, 92-100; and Rebecca Berens Matzke, "Britain Gets Its Way: Power and Peace in Anglo-American Relations, 1838-1846," *War in History*, VIII, No. 1 (2001), 36.

difficult duties...with judgement and discretion, or with more cordial cooperation in the part of our allies the French" than Hotham.[33]

The tenure of Lord Auckland, First Lord of the Admiralty during
most of Hotham's command, reveals how British policy worked on the African
coast. Auckland, was educated at Christ Church, Oxford, and served in several
Whig ministries: for example, as President of the Board of Trade in Lord
Grey's 1830 government. He later replaced Ellenborough as First Lord of the
Admiralty when Russell came to power in 1846 and Palmerston returned as
Foreign Secretary. As David Brown notes, Russell's new government was a
"factional" ministry. He preferred men like Auckland, Lansdowne, Minto and
Sir John Hobhouse, but was cool toward Palmerston, Grey and Clarendon.
The gentlemanly capitalists feared in particular that Palmerston's bellicose
tendencies might threaten their interests.[34]

Nonetheless, correspondence between Auckland and Palmerston was
cordial, and the two often dined together. But in tone, Palmerston's side of the
correspondence revealed a man more willing to be forceful than Auckland. To
allay Palmerston's fears, Auckland wanted not only to deter the French in the
Mediterranean and English Channel but also "to keep the ships of the two nations apart, if only to avoid accidents."[35] He therefore selected diplomatic naval officers for sensitive foreign stations and beseeched Palmerston to instruct
them to avoid gunboat diplomacy. Furthermore, the Law Officer's opinion of
Denman's actions was copied to Palmerston – perhaps as a warning – although
it is unclear by whom.

Auckland acted as a conduit between the factions in Russell's Cabinet
and the strategic needs and economic constraints of the nation and its navy. In
October 1846, for example, he informed Russell that he had received correspondence from Palmerston about Spain, reiterating his criticism of Peel's
government for letting France advance its influence there, but Auckland now
advised caution. Although problems in Spain might threaten British citizens
and property, he believed that the Mediterranean admiral should "be careful to
act within the strictest bounds of moderation and neutrality...so long as those

---

[33]US, HL, A&SC, BA, PP, SLT, J. Dobson to Earl of Aberdeen, 8 April
1842; and UH, BJL, ASC, HFP, DDHO 10/1, Hotham, General Correspondence,
Lord Ellenborough to Hotham, 20 May 1846.

[34]*Dictionary of National Biography*, s.v. "Eden, George, Earl of Auckland;"
and David Brown, *Palmerston and the Politics of Foreign Policy, 1846-55* (Manchester, 2002), 55.

[35]Andrew D. Lambert, *The Last Sailing Battlefleet: Maintaining Naval Mastery, 1815-1850* (London, 1991), 50-54.

differences are confined to the affairs of the Country and do not directly affect British interests."[36]

Auckland also had to consider the RN's wider finances in his decisions. He believed that it was necessary to meet the French threat, but he also had to respond to demands for economy from the Prime Minister. Liberals believed that it was imperative to avoid war and keep expenses low. While Auckland therefore demanded that Britain maintain its strength against potential threats like France and the US – in particular in the Pacific – he ordered his station commanders to be cautious to avoid an unwanted war. In 1846, for instance, Russell suggested that the navy dispatch seven ships-of-the-line to the Mediterranean and deploy fourteen ships to the Channel. Auckland replied that the navy had the ships but lacked sufficient men to accomplish the goal. He explained that the RN had to cover a vast area and had broad duties to perform. He told Russell that:

> we have a large surveying establishment to maintain – we have nearly thirty sloops and brigs on the coast of Africa, each of them ought properly to be relieved every eighteen months, and we have not reliefs [sic] for the purpose, and, again, on such large stations as that which comprehend China, Australia, and the East Indies.[37]

By 1848, Russell believed that Britain's naval forces could in fact be reduced. But Auckland again advised caution. To suggestions that the RN reduce its Pacific forces, Auckland countered that "in 1833 the French had not Tahiti, nor the Americans California and Oregon, and that neither of them had, as now, strong squadrons in that sea." Furthermore, he noted that Britain had disputes with France over Syria, Tahiti and Spain. Consequently, he advised that "[w]e might make great reductions on our side if financial embarrassment or domestic divisions should appear permanently to divert the resources and exertions of France from the maintenance and increase of her navy, but let us at least wait a few months and see what is done." Even as the 1848 revolutions rocked France, Auckland noted "that we are showing ourselves ready to depart from a senseless competition in the exhibition of strength, at a time when there is no pretence for using it, or money to pay for it."[38]

---

[36]TNA/PRO, RP 30/22/5D, Palmerston to Russell, 6 October 1846; and Auckland to Russell, 5 October 1846.

[37]*Ibid.*, RP 30/22/5C, Auckland to Russell, 8 September 1846.

[38]*Ibid.*, RP 30/22/7C, Auckland to Russell, 30 August 1848; and 30/22/7/D, Auckland to Russell, 17 December 1848.

Auckland therefore had to balance economics with strategy. As a result, he agreed with Palmerston that it was important to monitor French activities. On 27 August 1848, for example, he told the Foreign Secretary that he planned to send Captain Caffin to visit "the principal seaports of France, and to make such observations as may occur to him." But Auckland realized that British naval officers should be aware of the broad consequences of their actions, in particular with France. In November 1847, for example, as he prepared to send a new admiral to the Pacific, Auckland told Palmerston that "it may not be enough to say to him that he is not to be quick in quarrel." Therefore, he thought that Palmerston should also tell the admiral to protect British citizens and property "and maintain the honour and rights of his country with moderation." Earlier, on 7 June 1848 Auckland had told Palmerston that he had sent a "private letter" to the commander on the Mediterranean station warning him that "he should no where parade his fleet against the French fleet."[39] The British meant the RN to counter French designs that might threaten the route to India rather than start a war.

Over the intervening period, Auckland reviewed overall strategic concerns regarding the French in a variety of regions. For West Africa, he told the Prime Minister that

> we have at this moment for the prevention of the Slave Trade, twenty sailing vessels carrying 213 guns – The French have twenty three vessels carrying 184 guns – we have four steamers of 1450 horse power – They have five steamers of 840 horse power – Many of their vessels are small and we are altogether stronger than they are.

Still, Auckland's primary concern was that in "Europe the French have mainly accumulated their strength in the Mediterranean...and they have wished by an exhibition of great naval strength to extend their political influence upon the nations bordering on that sea." But he concluded that "[w]e have [the] wherewithal to press hardly and immediately upon Tahiti, and the Island of Bourbon, and the African settlements and the West Indian possessions of the French."[40] Nevertheless, London adhered to a pragmatic liberalism, to further its slave-trade objectives while containing potential conflicts.

Auckland took this approach toward West Africa, on the one hand wanting to maintain British interests but on the other wishing to avoid added expense and stress on the RN if peace prevailed. He preferred a passive, lib-

---

[39]US, HL, A&SC, BA, PP, GC/AU/45-68, Auckland to Palmerston, 2 November 1847 and 7 June and 27 August 1848.

[40]TNA/PRO, RP 30/22/6H, Auckland to Russell, December 1847.

eral approach and communicated this to Hotham, telling him to remain vigilant, to exercise "very sound discretion[,]" and to keep him informed about the French squadron. Auckland warned that "the keenness of appetite for gain is too great to give you any certainty of mercy." Furthermore, Liverpool merchants pressed Auckland to increase naval protection along the coast because with the French navy there, French "traders have advantages in consequence[.]" But Auckland doubted the reports and reminded Hotham that collecting "debts" for the merchants was beyond the squadron's mandate.[41]

When the revolutions began to engulf Europe in 1848 and threatened the integrity of the British realm, it put the spotlight on the West African squadron because London feared a general war in the Atlantic. In February 1848, Auckland told Hotham to honour the integrity of the British flag but to be cautious with the French. Lord Dundas at the Admiralty was more explicit. He feared that Revolutionary France might be involved in intrigues, in particular in Ireland, which might "plunge us into war." Therefore, the African squadron must also guard against the French in West Africa. Consequently, Dundas believed that the calls in Parliament to abolish or reduce the African squadron were unwise.[42] We must interpret British naval policy for the West African coast in this light. The squadron's activities reflected London's hope to counter French moves while furthering British objectives without sparking a general war.

D.K. Fieldhouse believed that early in the century there was "relative harmony in West Africa between Britain and France" because "commercial competition was for long limited in scope and intensity."[43] But Hotham's command shows otherwise. He told the Admiralty in 1847 that "[n]o one can entertain a moment's doubt of the burning desire of the French to increase their Trade and form Colonial establishments on this coast. In plain English – to turn their Treaty which obliges them to keep up a large force in Africa to a good account." Hotham was also aware of the strategic importance of the African coast, especially during crises. In a secret dispatch to Auckland in March 1848 he remarked that the possession of St. Helena, for example, "would give them [the French] the command of our Indian Trade and be a capital coal depot for their steamers[.]" Given their proclivity for the *guerre de course*, Hotham concluded that the French made "no secret of their intention to avoid

---

[41]UH, BJL, A&SC, HFP, DDHO 10/2, Auckland to Hotham, 9 and 10 August 1846 and 23 August and 24 September 1847.

[42]*Ibid.*, DDHO 10/2, Auckland to Hotham, 24 February 1848; DDHO 10/3, Dundas to Hotham, 30 July 1848; and *Dictionary of National Biography*, s.v. "Dundas, Sir James Whitley."

[43]D.K. Fieldhouse, *Economics and Empire, 1830-1914* (London, 1973; reprint, Ithaca, NY, 1984), 134.

[direct] combat, & destroy in every possible way our trade[.]" Nevertheless, he felt that the British West African squadron had little to fear "unless by an accident a shot is exchange[d.]" Hotham believed that French officers were "too much occupied with the late events" to be concerned with the British.[44]

The situation was tense, and Hotham and London were wary, but they hoped to match French moves while keeping relations from degenerating. The African squadron provided deterrence, but the British were keen to prevent the spread of any conflict across the entire Atlantic. As early as December 1847, London asked Hotham if he had considered plans for war with France. Auckland believed that the African squadron was adequate and that "you would [be] able to clear the African seas of the French flag[.]" But as the 1848 crisis deepened, Hotham increasingly took the French fleet seriously and feared the ramifications if war erupted. He noted that "the subject of greatest anxiety...will probably be the attitude assumed by the United States." If Britain adhered to the right of search during war, it would undoubtedly draw the Americans into the conflict. Therefore, he believed that Britain should be prepared to strike and defeat the US first to "leave us comparatively disengaged and able to cope with more formidable enemies" rather than fight a two-front war.[45]

Free Trade Treaties and Deterrence

The RN's treaty-making efforts were the most significant aspect of its work. They reveal how in this era the navy was an instrument of foreign policy and provided a mechanism through which Britain could relate to other nations and avoid war. In the beginning, the British signed treaties with East African states like Zanzibar and Muscat. By 1838, the Foreign Office suggested that the practice be extended to West Africa via the RN. At first the treaties called for the end of the slave trade, respect for British property, permission to trade with anyone along the African coast and most-favoured-nation status for Britain. But David Eltis concluded that "[t]hese were sweeping provisions that reflected the broader cultural goals of British policy." Still, Africans were reluctant to agree to the British terms, and London had to settle only for most-favoured-nation status and anti-slave trade provisions. The experience in West Africa marked a shift in the philosophy of British naval deployment: in the

---

[44]TNA/PRO, Admiralty (ADM) 1/5574, No. 122, Hotham to Secretary of the Admiralty, 3 May 1847; UH, BJL, A&SC, HFP, DDHO 10/11, Hotham to Auckland, 21 March 1848; Hotham to Dundas, c. June/July 1848; Hotham to Hamilton, August 1848; and Hotham to Auckland, c. September 1848.

[45]UH, BJL, A&SC, HFP, DDHO 10/2, Auckland to Hotham, 20 December 1847; and DDHO 10/11, Charles Hotham, "Memorandum Drawn up by Order of the 1st Lord of the Admiralty," 24 November 1848.

Gulf of Mexico Britain had been concerned solely with securing exclusive economic advantages, and the RN played only a policing role. Yet the historians of slave-trade suppression have shown that the treaties Britain signed with African rulers were to further economic or slave-trade policy.[46]

In reality, London also meant the treaties with West Africans to be a subtle way to neutralize France without sparking war. In November 1846 Hotham reported to Captain Brisbane that the Admiralty had warned that the French were active in "obtaining Commercial Treaties on different parts of the coast[.]" Hotham concluded that the RN had neglected to undertake a similar task because officers "considered themselves tied by the tenor of the slave instructions[.]" But consistent with Auckland's wishes, Hotham ordered Brisbane to investigate French activities. If they had signed commercial treaties with natives, he was to "collect an imposing force and use all your endeavours" to do the same. Nevertheless, Hotham warned that "I need hardly add that transactions of this character require the strictest secrecy combined with prudence and caution[.]"[47]

Hotham further explained the strategic importance of the treaties to Alexander Murray, captain of *Favourite*, who became the primary treaty-maker. The French were obligated to keep a force along the coast for slave-trade suppression but were "eager to turn the powerful force...to advantage[.]" British treaties with natives would help contain France. The French, Hotham explained, had signed nine treaties with natives which sowed "the seeds for future commercial advantages[.]" Even so, in this era of peace the British could not stop the French moves militarily. Instead, Hotham suggested that "we can neutralize their schemes by a similar course of action, and it is here that I require your services[.]" He ordered Murray to cruise the coast, collect intelligence about the French and then gather an "imposing force" to convince the natives to sign treaties with the British as well. Ideally, Hotham wrote, these treaties should include provisions to suppress the slave trade, but at minimum they should be the same as those signed with the French. Hotham believed that the French would be jealous once they discovered the British countermoves. Consequently, in February 1847 he told Auckland of the cautious way in which intended to proceed: "I shall be careful to insert the clause reserving equal power to both countries – I shall avoid making a mystery

---

[46]David Eltis, *Economic Growth and the Ending of the Transatlantic Slave Trade* (New York, 1987), 88-89.

[47]UH, BJL, A&SC, HFP, DDHO 10/8, Hotham to Captain Brisbane, 16 November 1846.

where no real occasion exists[.]"[48] The treaties were designed to use free trade to maintain a balance of power.

Treaties signed between the RN and the natives in the spring of 1847 provided a significant indication of how British goals fit together. The treaties adhered to a format orchestrated in London to shift African factors of production into legitimate commerce while also meeting Britain's strategic needs. Although they were designed to end the slave trade, where the natives lacked the power to do this Britain obtained permission to do so on their behalf. For example, in the winter of 1847 the British signed a treaty with the chiefs of Manna in the Gallinas region. Hotham was pleased that the chiefs had approached him about a treaty to "alter the character of the trade of their country, and substitute palm-oil for slaves." As planned, they agreed "to show no favour and give no privilege to ships and traders of other countries which they do not show to those of England."[49] In August, Hotham told the Admiralty how the French had responded to Murray's treaty-making efforts:

> it has reached my ears that he [Murray] received this answer,
> – "If power had not been reserved to the King of the French
> to become a party, the Treaty would have been ille-
> gal"...Under these circumstances, I trust their Lordships will
> approve of my exercising some caution in the matter. Our re-
> lations with our allies are even now difficult to maintain, and
> I am loath to take any step which may create a breach.[50]

By 1848, Hotham reported that his squadron was doing all it could to help British merchants along the coast. While the government had adopted a free and peaceful trade policy, he discovered that the merchants had a cutthroat philosophy and "expect a man-of-war to come in and fight their battles." Nevertheless, while Murray cruised and signed treaties, Hotham believed that the presence of the RN, like that of the USN, helped maintain peace and "friendly

---

[48]*Ibid.*, Hotham to Alexander Murray, 25 November 1846; and Hotham to Auckland, 13 February 1847.

[49]*BPP*, 1847-1848, LXIV, 446-451, Correspondence with British Commissioners and Representatives from British Vice-Admiralty Courts and Naval Officers on the Slave Trade, 1847-March 1848 (Class A), No. 266, Hotham to Secretary of the Admiralty, 3 May 1847, with treaty enclosures; and TNA/PRO, ADM 1/5574, No. 12, Hotham to Secretary of the Admiralty, 11 February 1847, with treaty enclosures.

[50]TNA/PRO, ADM 1/5574, Hotham to Secretary of the Admiralty, 10 August 1847.

relations" with the natives. He concluded that Britain should continue operating in a quiet and peaceful manner to promote legitimate trade.[51]

Figure 6.5: Anchorage off Bonny River, Sixteen Miles from the Entrance

Source: NMM, Negative No. PU1929 © National Maritime Museum, London.

The British had met some of their goals, and Hotham told the Admiralty that he was pleased that Commander Murray "has shown great discretion and judgement in the delicate duties entrusted to him." He contended that "[a]s far as can be prevented by Treaty no other nation will obtain an advantage over the trade of Great Britain, we have Treaties on almost every part of the Coast." By May 1848, the British had signed twelve more treaties with African chiefs, including some that Murray admitted never had domestic slavery. Instead, it is clear that the treaty-making efforts were part of a larger British plan to promote trade. For example, the treaty with Sherbro was significant because Sierra Leone carried on a timber trade, and the Sherbro chief was "about to open the forests on the River Kazamanca."[52]

---

[51]*BPP*, 1849, LV, 259-260, Correspondence with British Commissioners and Representatives from British Vice-Admiralty Courts and Naval Officers on the Slave Trade, 1848-1849 (Class A), No. 182, Hotham to Secretary of the Admiralty, 14 March 1848.

[52]TNA/PRO, ADM 1/5574, No. 122, Hotham to Secretary of the Admiralty, 3 May 1847; and *BPP*, 1849, LV, 263-277, Correspondence with British Commissioners and Representatives from British Vice-Admiralty Courts and Naval Officers on the Slave Trade, 1848-1849 (Class A), No. 187, Hotham to Secretary of the Admiralty, 3 May 1848, with treaty enclosures and observations from Murray; and 308-310, No.

By 1857 there were forty-five treaties that provided the RN with the justification to go ashore and destroy slave establishments. On 16 March 1847, for example, when Murray met with the chiefs at Cape Mount and presented them with evidence that the slave trade was still being pursued from the property of Theodore Canot, they agreed to destroy the facilities. The British also sometimes used shows of force to persuade Africans to sign treaties. For instance, in July 1849 Commander Hugh Dunlop and eighty-six men of the Second West India Regiment met with natives to restore peace in the region around Sherbro. But Dunlop told Commodore Arthur Fanshawe that "care has been taken to secure the commercial interests of the colony [Sierra Leone] by clauses inserted [in the peace agreements] for the protection of British subjects and trade." Fanshawe was pleased; when he forwarded copies of the treaty to London, he noted that "their Lordships will perceive my Lord Palmerston's wishes on this head have been anticipated...I shall now direct Commander Dunlop to take every advantage of it, as the means of further effecting the close and efficient Blockade of the Gallinas."[53]

Countering the Radical Free Traders

Kenneth Bourne has concluded that the drive for treaties might have started as a way to reduce naval commitments on the African coast. But while finances affected Auckland's naval planning, the purpose of the West African squadron was to protect British interests from French intrigue while being cautious to prevent any dispute that might draw France and the US together. Fearing overt confrontation with the French, the government justified its presence to parliamentary committees in terms of slave-trade suppression and commercial advancement. In 1847 Auckland told Hotham that people at home were starting to question the point of the squadron, given the cost in money and lives. But he thought that they were mistaken in their objections, telling Hotham that "the

---

227, Hotham to Secretary of the Admiralty, 10 January 1849, and enclosure 2, "Engagement with the King and Chiefs of the Bonny."

[53]Eltis, *Economic Growth*, 89; *BPP*, 1847-1848, LXIV, 454, Correspondence with British Commissioners and Representatives from British Vice-Admiralty Courts and Naval Officers on the Slave Trade, 1847-March 1848 (Class A), No. 268, Hotham to Secretary of the Admiralty, 3 May 1847, enclosure 2, Murray to King of Cape Mount, 15 March 1847, and enclosure 3, "Minute of a Meeting with the Chiefs of Cape Mount," 16 March 1847; TNA/PRO, ADM 1/5596, Hugh Dunlop to Arthur Fanshawe, 16 July 1849, enclosure in No. 321, Fanshawe to Secretary of the Admiralty, 31 August 1849; and No. 299, Fanshawe to Secretary of the Admiralty, 31 August 1849.

withdrawal of your squadron would throw back all those seeds of civilisation and of legitimate commerce which may yet thrive under your protection[.]"[54]

Auckland opined that discussions in Parliament were fraught with "partisanship and exaggeration[.]" The goal of British sea power had to be clear in the wake of the criticisms. Auckland wrote that "if not for the suppression of the slave trade, [then] at least for the protection of British commercial interests & the maintenance of [the] treaties with the African chiefs," the squadron must remain in force. He concluded that British commerce with the region was increasing, and "[t]he merchants, some of whom are now crying out and ready to censure whatever is done by our cruisers, would be the first and loudest to complain if they were withdrawn[.]" Hotham agreed, opposed any legalization of the slave trade and believed that only total suppression would further British goals. Otherwise, slavers would undersell Britons in either legitimate trade or the slave trade. Besides, Hotham countered, "we are not such losers as he [Hutt and others] would imagine...every article sold on the coast is manufactured in England[.]"[55]

To counter criticisms, on 19 July 1848 Hotham filed a specific report on RN activities over a four-year period. For a twenty-one-month period, from 1 April 1844 to 31 December 1845, under Commodore Jones' command, the squadron captured ninety-six slavers and freed 5965 slaves. But from 14 October 1845 to 13 July 1848, under Hotham, it captured 131 slavers and freed 11,214 slaves. Later, Hotham testified in support of the maintenance of the squadron. He too believed that it was impossible to suppress the slave trade along the entire length of the coast. But he thought that if the squadron was withdrawn, the slave trade would increase. Furthermore, he concluded that piracy would also grow and drive legitimate merchants from the coast.[56] Only the presence of the RN would advance British goals.

With strategic and economic factors combined, the British plan of action was clear: the West African squadron must remain. Upon returning to Britain, Hotham testified on 16 and 17 May 1849 to the Lords' Committee studying the slave trade. Near the end of his testimony, when asked whether the African squadron should be modified, Hotham replied that the "question

---

[54]Kenneth Bourne, *Palmerston: The Early Years, 1784-1841* (New York, 1982), 622; Ward, *Royal Navy and the Slavers*, 202; and UH, BJL, A&SC, HFP, DDHO 10/2, Auckland to Hotham, 13 March and 30 December 1847.

[55]UH, BJL, A&SC, HFP, DDHO 10/2, Auckland to Hotham, 12 June and 6 October 1848; and DDHO, 10/8, Hotham to Auckland, 5 December 1847.

[56]*BPP*, 1849, LV, 287, Correspondence with British Commissioners and Representatives from British Vice-Admiralty Courts and Naval Officers on the Slave Trade, 1848-49 (Class A), No. 200, Hotham to Secretary of the Admiralty, 19 July 1848 and enclosure in No. 200; and Roberts, *Charles Hotham*, 80-82.

now put is entirely a purely commercial one." He argued that the RN was Britain's only true authority on the coast for "British subjects resident and trading there, [thus] I do not think that we could do with less than 10 or 12 ships; even supposing we relinquished the attempted blockade of the West Coast of Africa." He contended that "without a small squadron, I do no think our own commerce could exist."[57] British commercial and naval allies, slave-trade suppression and economic and strategic goals formed a unified policy.

Enforcing British Goals

Historians have worked from the "whiggish" assumption that British African activity was a prelude to the scramble for Africa later in the century. Christopher Lloyd wrote, for example, that the "story of the annexation of Lagos shows how slowly, and almost accidentally, the British began to embark on a policy" which ultimately gained for her those possessions in Africa[.]"[58] But British actions were part of an overall strategy for the coast. Only Britain enforced free trade and slave trade treaties with West Africans to advance wider objectives. Furthermore, London also appointed consuls like John Beecroft to the African coast to show Africans the benefits of increased trade. As well, the RN launched military strikes with the cooperation of sympathetic native allies to enforce British policies, as with the attack on Lagos in 1851. Where in the Gulf of Mexico Downing Street feared that naval action would harm its trade policies, in West Africa Britain enforced its new informal free trade empire with sea power, installing new rulers with whom the gentlemanly English capitalists could deal. But the significance of the enforcement activities is that Britain only undertook them against weak native powers where forceful encounters could further British objectives without widening the conflict. To those ends, when Britain blockaded or attacked native powers it notified its nominal allies, such as the US, and rivals like France.

Britain's consuls on the West African coast were representatives of the elite and, with the navy, used the threat of force to further British objectives by installing sympathetic allies. For example, on 30 June 1849 Palmerston appointed Beecroft as the British consular agent for the Bights of Benin and Biafra. Palmerston instructed him to prevent any disputes between natives and British vessels that called in regional ports. Palmerston hoped that this would encourage the growth of legitimate trade to displace the slave trade. Yet in the spirit of freer trade he told Beecroft to "impress upon the minds" of native leaders the benefits of trading with Americans and Europeans. Mean-

---

[57]*Ibid.*, 1850, IX, Select Committee of the House of Lords to Consider the Best Means for the Final Extinction of the African Slave Trade, 147.

[58]Lloyd, *Navy and the Slave Trade*, 149.

while, to further gentlemanly objectives Beecroft was to gather intelligence about coastal and interior commerce and note what "European commodities" were most desired.[59] The policies were linked: the freer trade mentality, promotion of legitimate British commerce and the suppression of the slave trade with naval support to maintain influence to counter the French. It neutralized other powers and advanced British interests without fomenting conflict.

Downing Street firmly articulated this policy in a 15 November 1850 memo. In marked contrast to its earlier policy toward Central America, Britain assured other European powers that it wanted all nations placed on an equal footing in West Africa. Palmerston believed that commerce was the best method to bring "civilization" to Africa. The nexus with the freer trade philosophy was clear: "there is room enough in the West & populous countries of Africa for the commerce of all civilized nations[.]"[60] Consequently, the British attempted to enforce treaties but rarely used force. The exception was in 1851 at Lagos, where British goals met continual resistance.

Since April 1850, Palmerston, through his African representatives, had tried to "induce" the Chief of Lagos to sign a treaty. The RN had blockaded the Whydah region west of Lagos, the major slave port. The slave trade then moved to the next best location, the region of creeks and lagoons that stretched about 150 miles around Lagos. Palmerston told Beecroft that a treaty with Lagos would help to end the slave trade along the entire African coast north of the equator. He ordered him, in concert with Commodore Fanshawe, to undertake the necessary steps to convince the Chief of Lagos to sign the treaty to suppress the slave trade and make laws forbidding anyone within his territory, including Europeans, from conducting the trade. The treaty also gave the RN policing powers over Lagos and the right to free into British colonies any slaves ready for sale. The last two articles of the treaty governed free trade and included an offer to the French to be party to the agreement. Palmerston told Beecroft to tell the natives that legitimate commerce was more important than the slave trade and to warn them that if "the Chief should show a disposition to refuse compliance, you should beg him to remember that Lagos is near to the sea, and that on the sea are the ships and the cannon of England[.]"[61]

---

[59]TNA/PRO, Foreign Office (FO) 84/775, Africa (West Coast): Consular, Palmerston to John Beecroft, 30 June 1849.

[60]Lloyd, *Navy and the Slave Trade*, 112-113; Ward, *Royal Navy and the Slavers*, 193-201; TNA/PRO, FO 2/4, Africa: (West Coast), Consular, January to December 1850, Herman Merivale to Addington, 15 November 1850; and Palmerston, memo, 20 December 1850.

[61]Ward, *Royal Navy and the Slavers*, 205; *BPP*, 1852, LIV, 309, Papers Relative to Reduction of Lagos by H.M. Forces on West Coast of Africa, No. 23,

Still, talks with Lagos languished, and by September 1851 Palmerston had lost his patience. The government ordered a blockade of the Dahomey coast until that chief signed an agreement, but Palmerston had other plans for Lagos. The British would reinstall the previous chief, Akitoye, whom slavers had removed for planning to sign a treaty with the British. Palmerston concluded that if the slave trade was expunged from Lagos, it and the nearby river would become a haven for legitimate trade: "instead of being a den of barbarism, [it] would be a diffusing centre of civilization." Consequently, on 14 October the Admiralty ordered Commodore Henry Bruce to blockade the coast and attack Lagos in a manner of "your discretion and judgement."[62]

A British force, along with Beecroft, assembled and tried again to negotiate with the Chief of Lagos, but when talks failed, the British attacked, opening fire with "shrapnel shell and round-shot." HMS *Niger* fired shells as the boats stayed out of range of the shore. Lord Granville, Palmerston's replacement, told Beecroft that he had acted inappropriately by failing to warn the Chief about the consequences if he refused to capitulate. But events had overtaken the slow communications along the coast and with London. On 30 November boats from HMS *Harlequin* and HMS *Volcano* destroyed slaving stations and some vessels. On 17 December Bruce told Beecroft that he had orders from London to attack Lagos and install Akitoye on the throne.[63]

The attack began on 26 December, under heavy opposing gunfire, and ended on Sunday, 28 December. A chief from a nearby village told the British that the natives had evacuated Lagos and that the British were victorious. By 1 January 1852, the newly installed King Akitoye met with Bruce on HMS *Penelope* to sign the treaty. It is unclear if the British attacks on Lagos had any impact on the opinions of the King of Dahomey, but the blockade of that region probably induced him to a friendlier disposition. By late December 1851, British representatives reported his change of heart and arranged treaty-signing ceremonies. Granville was pleased with the satisfactory outcome. In the end, the rulers of Lagos proved weak, and by 1861 the British formally annexed it,

---

Palmerston to Beecroft, 20 February 1851, with treaty enclosure; and 311-312, No. 25, Palmerston to Beecroft, 21 February 1851.

[62]*BPP*, 1852, LIV, 361-362, Papers Relative to Reduction of Lagos by H.M. Forces on West Coast of Africa, No. 43, Palmerston to Admiralty, 27 September 1851; and 364, No. 45, Admiralty to Henry Bruce, 14 October 1851.

[63]*Ibid.*, 375-376, No. 56, Hamilton to Stanley, 7 January 1852, enclosure 1, L.G. Heath to Secretary of the Admiralty, 17 December 1851; 393, No. 64, Granville to Beecroft, 24 January 1852; and 413-416, No. 69, Beecroft to Palmerston, 3 January 1852.

although parliamentary debate over keeping the limited British possessions continued.[64]

Nevertheless, Martin Lynn has suggested that Britain had little power along the West African coast; the attack on Lagos was the power of the "Man on the Spot," Beecroft. Lynn speculated that "questions of policy played a very minor role in the actual seizure of Lagos itself[,]" although he agreed that Palmerston had linked slave-trade suppression and British economic expansion. But it is unreasonable to assume that London's West African policy was solely the work of Beecroft. Lynn admits that the consul was a poorly educated and arrogant negotiator who was "clearly ill at ease in his relations with his superiors in Whitehall." Instead, it is logical to surmise that Beecroft, like the naval officers, anticipated Palmerston's wishes. Beecroft was part of the system of gentlemanly "'decision-makers' who ran the imperial government from Whitehall and the 'men on the spot' who administered the possessions overseas – both the mandarins and the guardians of empire."[65] With the help of the RN, Beecroft helped install rulers sympathetic to British goals.

While the British undertook forceful actions against natives, the RN was careful to advise Western nations, like France and the US, of impending actions in order to prevent misunderstandings. Under pressure at home to show results, and with an increase in the slave trade from the Gallinas region, Hotham authorized an attack on 3 and 4 February 1849. During the attack, the British destroyed slave factories at Solyman and Gallinas. Still, Hotham explicitly told vessels under his command to refrain from interfering with other nations' warships and to inform merchant vessels of the blockade. Unlike the American position, Hotham declared that as "the trade of Gallinas has been proved to be connected with slave exportations, and the goods imported used for that sole purpose, you will make no difference between vessels of any nation loaded with any description of cargo." Furthermore, he duly informed the French commodore of the blockade and asked him to "give public notice of

---

[64]*Ibid.*, 413-418, Beecroft to Palmerston, 3 January 1852, and enclosure in No. 69, "Engagement with the King and Chiefs of Lagos;" 434-436, No. 73, J. Parker to Addington, 17 February 1852, with enclosures; 436, No. 75, Granville to Beecroft, 23 February 1852; and Ward, *Royal Navy and the Slavers*, 219.

[65]Martin Lynn, "Consul and Kings: British Policy, 'the Man on the Spot,' and the Seizure of Lagos, 1851," *Journal of Imperial and Commonwealth History*, X, No. 2 (1982), 150-167; and Raymond E. Dumett, "Exploring the Cain/Hopkins Paradigm: Issues for Debate, Critique and Topics for New Research," in Dumett (ed.), *Gentlemanly Capitalism and British Imperialism*, 9.

this Blockade to the French authorities on the West Coast of Africa, and to the Masters of French Vessels calling at Gorée."[66]

The right of blockade had been an important factor in Anglo-American tension since before the War of 1812. The US believed that neutrals had to be given proper notice of a blockade and that the blockading nation had to have sufficient power to enforce it. Donald R. Hickey wrote that "[t]hese were the principles that the British recognized in theory but did not always follow in practice." Nevertheless, off West Africa Hotham took steps to notify the Americans of the blockade. He asked his US counterpart to alert all "American Citizens trading on the West Coast of Africa." Meanwhile, Commander Alexander Murray from HMS *Favourite* noted that Hotham had instituted a blockade with "sufficient and effective force on the territory of Gallinas" and told the Americans that the blockade extended from 11° 35' West to 11° 45' West. Consequently, US Commodore Benjamin Cooper recognized the blockade and told Washington that he had directed his vessels to respect it "agreeable to the laws of nations."[67] The British used sea power to further their goals while assuring that other powers were aware of their "peaceful" intentions, a courtesy that was respected.

Increase in the Slave Trade

Whether from naval actions and treaties or the laws of supply and demand, the British concluded at first that their policy had been successful. In the wake of the reform of the sugar duties, the slave trade increased because Cuban plantations needed more slaves. Still, scholars have shown that the slave trade from West Africa declined after 1850, corresponding with the renewed British commitment to suppression. But after 1853-1854 the slave trade again increased after the death of 16,000 slaves in Cuba from cholera and a renewed demand for slaves on sugar plantations (see figure 6.6).[68] Consequently, by

---

[66]Lloyd, *Navy and the Slave Trade*, 100-101 and 120; TNA/PRO, ADM 1/5596, Hotham to W.B. Monypenny, 8 February 1849, enclosure 1 in x 77, Hotham to Secretary of the Admiralty, 10 February 1849; and Hotham to French Commodore, 4 February 1849, enclosure 2 in x 77, Hotham to Secretary of the Admiralty, 10 February 1849.

[67]Donald R. Hickey, *The War of 1812: A Forgotten Conflict* (Urbana, IL, 1989), 12; United States, National Archives (NA), Record Group (RG) 45, Letters Received by the Secretary of the Navy from Commanding Officers of Squadrons, CVII, African Squadron, Hotham to Commodore Bolton, 4 February 1849; Murray to Benjamin Cooper, 7 February 1849; and Cooper to John Young Mason, 7 February 1849.

[68]Murray, *Odious Commerce*, 208; and Hugh Graham Soulsby, *The Right of Search and the Slave Trade in Anglo-American Relations, 1814-1862* (Baltimore, 1933), 138.

late 1856 and early 1857, the British concluded that the only major demand for slaves must be in the US and Cuba. The Americans, London believed, must be the only ones standing in the way of the successful implementation of British policy. Britain and the US had different objectives that once more caused Anglo-American tension to rise despite the Webster-Ashburton Treaty and the care that Britain took in implementing naval policy in West Africa.

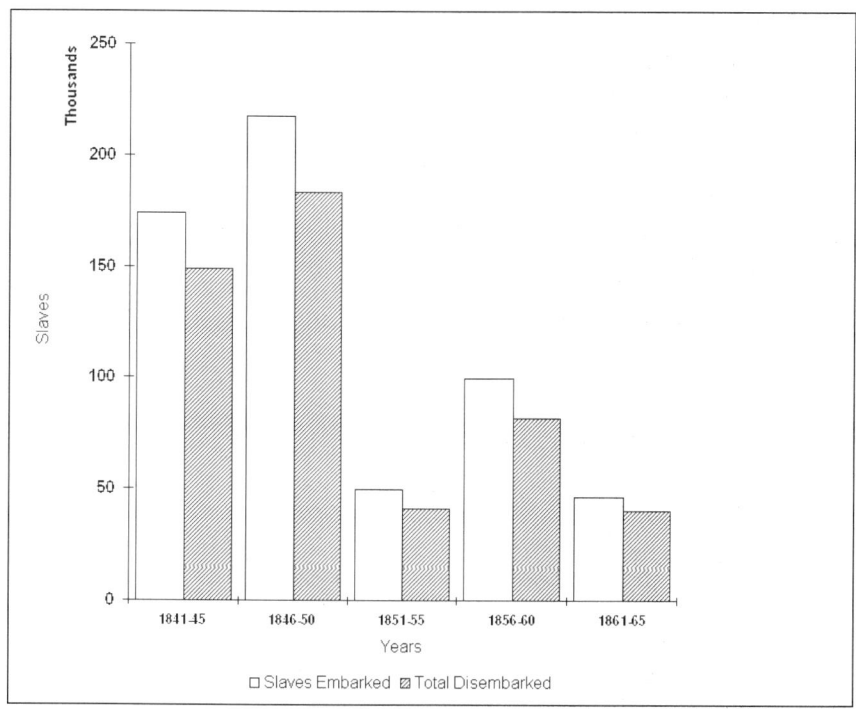

Figure 6.6:   Slaves Embarked and Disembarked, 1841-1865

Note: The period 1866-1870 was not plotted because the slaves embarked totalled only 858, while those disembarked totalled 700.

Source: David Eltis, *et al.*, *The Trans-Atlantic Slave Trade: A Database on CD-ROM* (Cambridge, 1999).

Legal and political conditions in the US in the mid-1850s contributed to the increased use of the American flag in the slave trade. US courts had placed limits on who could be held responsible for the voyage and on the types of incriminating evidence that would be admissible. In the American political climate, no political party was willing to introduce legislation to tighten the law and "[o]nly with the end of the slave trade did the decisions of the Southern New York district cease to harass law enforcement officers." By 1855 those with a vested economic interest in slavery in the South called for the repeal of anti-slave-trade laws and international commitments to slave trade suppression. Each year there was a Southern Commercial Convention that passed resolutions against slave-trade suppression and the Webster-Ashburton Treaty. There was building momentum against the continued suppression of the slave trade. Meanwhile, a similar backlash against slave-trade suppression gripped Congress.[69]

Under these conditions, Britain concluded that three American ports dominated the traffic and were responsible for the difficulties. Vessels from New York and Baltimore often sailed directly to the African coast, while those from New Orleans sailed first to the Canary Islands with flour and there gathered information about slave markets. In New York, Spanish and Portuguese slavers, like J.A. Machado, became naturalized American citizens to gain protection under US law. Machado had engaged in legitimate activities in Gambia and Sierra Leone, while in Whydah and surrounding ports he was involved in the slave trade as well. J.V. Crawford, acting British Consul at Havana, also believed that the Americans were to blame. Over 1857 and 1858 he tabulated that one Norwegian, one Peruvian, seven Spanish and fifty American-flagged vessels had sailed from Cuba for the trade.[70]

Vessel sales and slaver operations hid easily in New York among legitimate vessels. For example, Figaniere, Reis and Co. of 81 Front Street was a front company for slavers, and in Havana suspicion arose whenever someone sold a US vessel. Slaver operations from New York by 1857 also coincided with an increase in slave demand caused by increased agriculture in the US and Cuba. Furthermore, a depression in 1857 increased the incentives for slaving voyages and for American shipbuilders to sell vessels for the trade. Slavers outfitted in New Orleans in the spring of 1857, but they moved their operations to Havana after authorities seized one vessel.[71] Consequently, by the spring of 1857 increased slaver activities echoed along the West African coast and harmed Anglo-American relations.

A variety of British sources connected to gentlemanly capitalists blamed the Americans for the continued slave trade. The warship *Alecto*, at the Congo on 14 December 1856, for example, encountered the American vessel

---

[69]Warren S. Howard, *American Slavers and the Federal Law* (Berkeley, 1963), 155-159 and 167-169; and W.E. Burghardt Du Bois, *The Suppression of the African Slave-Trade to the United States of America, 1683-1870* (New York, 1896; reprint, New York, 1965), 169-175.

[70]TNA/PRO, ADM 123/164, B. Campbell to Commodore Wise, 16 November 1857; and ADM 123/177, J.V. Crawford to Lord Malmesbury, 3 September 1858.

[71]Howard, *American Slavers and the Federal Law*, 50-59.

Ellen. The British boarded the ship, inspected its papers and discovered that it was from New York. But when the master refused to open his hatches – and having no evidence to detain the ship – the British released it. Meanwhile, in April 1857 Commodore John Adams told London that one of his officers visited Palma and found the "great and increasing trade in palm oil" had replaced its slave trade. He thought that the only remaining problem was the Americans, blamed the lack of US warships on parts of the coast and hoped that London would convince Washington to do more.[72]

Table 6.1
Slaver Port of Origins, 1841-1870

Year	New York	New Orleans	Baltimore	Havana	Other	Total
1841-1845	0	2	0	41	598	641
1846-1850	1	0	0	3	714	718
1851-1855	11	1	0	10	105	127
1856-1860	30	18	1	42	145	236
1861-1865	10	1	0	15	88	114
1866-1870	0	0	0	0	3	3

Source: See figure 6.1

Evidence in *The Trans-Atlantic Slave Trade: A Database on CD-ROM* generally confirms the pattern. Table 6.1 shows that the number of slavers from New York and New Orleans had increased in 1856-1860 compared to the previous five-year period. Statistics also reveal that the trade was becoming extinct in some areas while it remained vibrant in others. Figure 6.7 shows that the Bight of Biafra and southeast Africa (including the Cape of Good Hope) declined as relative sources of slaves from 1851-1855 compared with later periods. From 1856 onwards, slave traders primarily focused their activity on West-Central Africa and the Bight of Benin, at the limit of the American patrol from its base on the Cape Verde Islands.[73]

---

[72]*BPP*, 1857-1858, LXI, 117, Correspondence with British Commissioners and Representatives from British Naval Forces on the Slave Trade, April 1857-March 1858 (Class A), No. 151, John Adams to Secretary of the Admiralty, 18 April 1857; No. 152, Adams to Secretary of the Admiralty, 1 May 1857; and 188, enclosures 1, 2 and 3 and No. 152, Commander Hunt to Commander Hickley, 15 January 1857; and Hickley to Adams, 17 February 1857.

[73]Eltis, *et al.*, *Slave Trade: A Database*. Eltis, *Economic Growth*, 164-165, 182-184 and 253-254, concluded that many shifts were the result of supply and demand and that "legitimate" commerce did not replace the slave trade. While the former became profitable, the combined revenues from both were so small that they did not com-

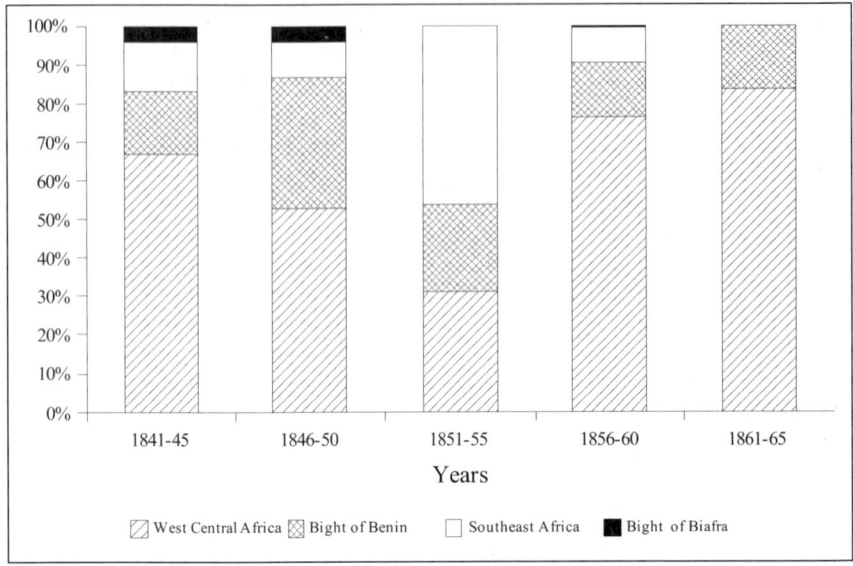

Figure 6.7: Relative Origin of Slaves, 1841-1865

Note: Percentage calculated less unspecified regions. Total percentage also in-
               cludes other regions that were of such small percentages that they failed to
               appear on the graph and were thus omitted.

Source: See figure 6.6.

  Moreover, the destination of American slavers from suspect ports was
concentrated in similar African locales. For the period 1856-1860, for example, the thirty vessels whose port of origin was originally New York obtained
82.5 percent of their 9878 slaves from West-Central Africa; 10.1 percent from
the Bight of Benin; and 7.44 percent from other unspecified African regions.
Similarly, the eighteen slavers originally from New Orleans obtained 80.3 percent of their 6202 slaves from West-Central Africa; 6.88 percent from the
Bight of Benin; and 12.9 percent from other unspecified African regions. New
York vessels sent about seventy percent of their slaves to Cuba, and New Orleans ships landed about sixty percent of their slaves there.[74]

---

pete for African "factors of production." But his own statistics show that slaving from
Lagos dropped from eighty-two vessels in 1841-1850 to five vessels in 1851-1860,
values too dramatic for the influence of naval activity to be excluded fully.

  [74]The remaining percentages were distributed over a variety of other destinations; Eltis, *et al. Slave Trade: A Database.*

On both sides of the Atlantic, British representatives blamed the Americans for the continuance of the slave trade. A British judge on the Mixed Commission Court at Havana reported on 12 April 1857 that the Cuban slave trade was extensive. At least fifteen ships involved had sailed from New Orleans within the previous two months. Vessels from other American ports had also sailed, while "several vessels have also gone from this Port [Havana] and Matanzas." In addition, Consul Benjamin Campbell at Lagos believed that there was an American conspiracy to continue the slave trade to populate Cuba with slave labour as a prelude to annexation. Palmerston, now Prime Minister but still with an eye on foreign affairs, noted that Campbell's dispatch explained "some of the reasons why the US govt severely encourage the slave trade to Cuba[.]" But Palmerston remained convinced that an attack on the African side of the slave trade was best. If any chiefs had broken their treaties with the British, London should punish them as it had done in Lagos.[75]

Conclusion

Britain had to balance its strategic needs with domestic political demands. But with the elite behind the squadron, the RN maintained its commitment to suppressing the slave trade, implementing free trade policies and countering the French threat. Equally important, British strategy was to maintain good relations with other powers along the coast, including the US. British strategy was more than a "haphazard array of local treaties and a scattering of British consuls."[76] Instead, the RN carefully pursued treaties with natives and gave other powers the option to participate. Furthermore, the RN was forceful against those natives who refused to capitulate but careful to inform other Western powers, like the US, of impending actions, such as blockades. One goal of the Webster-Ashburton Treaty was to govern the use of sea power along the West African coast in order to reduce Anglo-American tension through the presence of both the RN and USN. With the latter on the coast, British warships could avoid the need to stop US-flagged ships; Britain hoped that America would suppress its involvement in the slave trade.

But British and American objectives were different. While the RN combined most aspects of British strategic policy for the West African coast, for the Americans slave-trade suppression was a distant second to furthering

---

[75]TNA/PRO, ADM 123/177, Shelburne to Admiralty, 8 May 1857; and Crawford to Earl of Clarendon, 13 April 1857; and FO 84/1031, Bight of Benin (Lagos): Campbell to Clarendon, 1 August 1857, and Palmerston's attached minute on the letter, 6 October 1857.

[76]Andrew Porter, "Introduction: Britain and the Empire in the Nineteenth Century," in Andrew Porter (ed.), *Oxford History of the British Empire, Vol. 3* (Oxford, 1999), 15.

US commerce and protecting it from British interference. As the differences between British and American strategies accumulated, tensions again rose. Consequently, despite British care the different strategies of the two nations conflicted. Britain remained irritated as American involvement in the slave trade continued. Moreover, British power on the coast grew and exacerbated American suspicions. But modifications to both nations' use of sea power provided a mechanism through which Britain and America could relate, reduce tensions and avoid war.

Chapter 7
The US Navy and West Africa, 1843-1857

The deployment of the US West African squadron is significant because its duties reflected the government's goals. Its main duty was to protect and promote American commerce and prevent British interference with US-flagged ships. Slave-trade suppression was too contentious domestically for the US Navy (USN) to focus on it off West Africa. While the USN captured some slavers and sent them to the US, because of the squadron's small size, legal constraints and its primary goal, Americans failed to patrol the entire coast in search of slavers. Instead, the American attack on Berriby in 1843 epitomized the squadron's purpose. This conflict instilled in natives "respect" for Westerners and their traders to the pleasure of both British and American observers. American and British goals differed, but the presence of the two navies furthered their objectives. To these ends, the small US force periodically cruised along the coast, collected commercial intelligence, "showed the flag" and occasionally used force to show that it was serious.

Nevertheless, the home waters remained important, as during the Mexican War (1846-1848) when West African deployment was further curtailed, and those warships that remained also had to protect US shipping in the eastern Atlantic from potential attack by Mexican privateers. With commerce protection and promotion the primary objective, individual views on slavery rarely rose beyond occasional operational comments. Washington, unsympathetic to slave-trade suppression, wanted commerce protected, and naval officers were charged with the task. Only officers like Andrew Hull Foote, sympathetic to the cause of the American Colonization Society (ACS) and slave-trade suppression, exhibited any enthusiasm for the secondary objective.

With slave-trade suppression and commerce protection separate issues, the British were sceptical of American sincerity. In turn, the US feared British commercial advances, in particular the growth of steamship lines that provided regular communications between the African coast and London. US commodores, such as Isaac Mayo, believed that unless the government acted, American merchants would be driven from the African coast by their more efficient British counterparts who were aided by regular steam lines and protection by the Royal Navy (RN). Despite the Webster-Ashburton Treaty and some mutually beneficial effects of sea power, the separate objectives and strategies of the RN and USN generated tension between the countries.

The New American Squadron

In addition to its tactical use, the "role [of navies] began to change in other significant and unforeseen ways[.]" The American economy and foreign trade were growing, and "[p]oliticians, public officials, and newspaper editors all predicted a future bonanza for Americans in the vast reaches of the Pacific." The ideals of commerce protection and promotion unified American political leaders, who used the USN overseas to "show the flag" and carry out diplomatic duties. Where in war an "impulsive and heroic" officer like Oliver Hazard Perry was effective, in peacetime the "deliberate, careful, and thoughtful" behaviour of his brother, Matthew, was more appropriate to further American interests along a coast overflowing with diplomatic sensitivities. At this time, many Americans believed that naval officers needed to be diplomats. Some, like Abel Upshur, advocated the creation of a Naval Academy, in part to provide officers with an education suited to a variety of roles as the nation's needs evolved. Matthew Perry, like Hotham, symbolized the use of sea power in this era. He was sent to West Africa, advised Navy Secretary George Bancroft on the establishment of the Naval Academy and "opened" Japan to US trade.[1]

Commodore Matthew Perry, the first commander of the US African squadron, was familiar with the West African coast, having sortied there during the piracy crisis. Perry underestimated the extent of the slave trade in the 1820s, but his ship rarely cruised off West Africa. Desensitized to the horrors of the slave trade from his youth, and with little government support for slave-trade suppression, Perry's concern was to protect American commerce and settlements. Perry was from Newport, Rhode Island, a maritime community that delved into "speculative ventures" like the legal slave trade. John Schroeder concluded that Perry's youth "taught him that both [slavery and the slave trade] were acceptable and tolerable[.]" His brother, Raymond, married into the D'Wolf family, who had slaves on its Cuban plantation. Senator James D'Wolf, his father-in-law, had voted against the earlier plan to give the British the right to search American-flagged vessels. Although Matthew supported the goals of the ACS, his objections to slavery remained muted. He believed that it was a Southern problem.[2]

In contrast to its strong support for commerce protection and promotion, Washington's commitment to slave-trade suppression was less enthusiastic. Upshur supported naval expansion, but he and President Tyler were Vir-

---

[1]John H. Schroeder, *Matthew Calbraith Perry: Antebellum Sailor and Diplomat* (Annapolis, 2001), 22-25, 97, 125-126 and 164-183; and Mark C. Hunter, "'...With the Propriety and Decorum which Characterize the Society of Gentlemen: The United States Naval Academy and Its Youth, 1845-1861" (Unpublished MA thesis, Memorial University of Newfoundland, 1999), 39-47.

[2]Schroeder, *Matthew Calbraith Perry*, 3-9, 15-21 and 40-41.

ginians who owned slaves. Soon after Perry's deployment, James K. Polk, a Democrat from Tennessee, entered the White House; he too was a slave owner. Moreover, the domestic slave trade continued, even in the nation's capital. During Perry's command, the position of Secretary of the Navy changed five times, but three of the new Secretaries were Southerners. Schroeder surmised that John Quincy Adams reflected the national mood when he asserted that if the administration was insincere about the slave trade, the British were equally mischievous because of their continued disregard for the freedom of the seas. He thus supported Upshur's instructions to Perry to be wary of the British.[3]

Given the national sentiment, it is understandable that Upshur reminded Perry that American commerce on the African coast was "becoming every day more and more valuable" and needed protection. But Upshur also warned Perry to respect the rights of other nations. Foreign warships, like those of Britain, acted at their peril if they boarded a US-flagged vessel to ascertain its true nationality. If the vessel proved to be American, the foreign country was liable for damages if the masters and owners sought redress, but otherwise Upshur barred Perry from action. While he hoped that Perry would cooperate with the British, he granted him wide discretion.[4]

Washington wanted American rights protected while preserving relations with nations like Britain. Significantly, Washington renewed the instructions given to Perry with little variation for each subsequent commodore, but there was little further strategic or tactical communication. The Secretary ordered Perry to cruise from Madeira and the Canary Islands to the Bight of Biafra, then along the African coast to 30° West and further if necessary. Upshur advised him that slavers rarely exhibited signs that they were involved in illegal trade and often disguised themselves as legitimate traders. The slavers arrived on the coast, ran "into some river" and dropped off any slave-trade goods. They made deals with coastal slave dealers and sailed along the coast conducting legitimate trade until the time agreed to collect their human cargo.[5]

A small force compared to its British counterpart, the USN was meant to ensure a presence in key areas like the Mediterranean and the Pacific. The largest vessels were frigates, like the famous *Constitution,* armed with between thirty-six and fifty-four guns and typically used as flagships. The workhorses

---

[3]*Ibid.*, 97-101.

[4]United States, Congress, *U.S. Serial Set*, LXXIII, 35th Cong., 2nd sess., House of Representatives, Document No. 104, 3-5, Abel P. Upshur to Matthew Calbraith Perry, 30 March 1843. Hereafter, the *U.S. Serial Set* will be cited according to the recommended Library of Congress style, for example, *H.R. Doc*, No. 1, 35th Cong., 2nd sess.

[5]*Ibid.*

were schooners, brigs and sloops, armed with no more than twenty guns and with maximum crew complements of 200. The navy had some steamers, but they were rarely deployed for lack of foreign coaling stations. The African squadron reflected the wider composition of the USN, and the Webster-Ashburton Treaty meant that Washington had to keep a force equipped with at least eighty guns deployed along the African coast. When Matthew Perry first deployed to the coast in 1843, the navy gave him the brig *Porpoise* (ten guns), sloops *Saratoga* (twenty-two guns) and *Decatur* (sixteen guns) and frigate *Macedonian* (thirty-six guns guns). The squadron used Porto Praia in the Cape Verde Islands as its base and sailed as far north as Madeira and south to Cape Frio, but rarely ventured south of the Bight of Biafra. By the late 1850s, the squadron had no steamers, and most guns were concentrated on the impressive *Constitution*, "Old Ironsides."[6] In the end, the squadron's composition meant that it was more adept at cruising the coast to show the flag, helping nascent American colonies and collecting commercial intelligence.

Perry's orders to his officers generally reflected both the letter and the spirit of Upshur's instructions. He authorized them to use all necessary means to protect American-flagged ships from search by other nations. But he also reminded them to inform foreign warships if a suspected vessel had no right to American protection.[7] Schroeder concluded that Perry simply carried out his orders to focus on commerce protection: "[g]iven the horror of the slave trade, it is tempting to fault Perry, but that would place him in a historically inaccurate context."[8] Indeed, Perry's specific orders to several vessels show the American concentration on vessel protection, with few comments about the slave trade. *Decatur*, for example, was to collect as much intelligence on the legal and slave trade as possible, but was to keep "a special eye to the protection and advancement of American trade."[9]

Porpoise, under Lieutenant Commander Arthur Lewis, was already on station off the West African coast awaiting supplies. Perry's first order to Lewis was to check on American traders and settlements in the region "with a

---

[6]Donald L. Canney, *Africa Squadron: The U.S. Navy and the Slave Trade, 1842-1861* (Washington, 2006), 31, 36-37, 43, 49, 51 and 58.

[7]United States, National Archives (NA), Record Group (RG) 45, Letter Books of Commodore Matthew C. Perry, 10 March 1843-20 February 1845 (Perry Letter Books), Perry, General Order No. 1, 21 June 1843; General Order No. 2, 3 July 1843; Order, 1 August 1843; and General Order No. 10, 24 November 1843.

[8]Schroeder, *Matthew Calbraith Perry*, 260.

[9]NA, RG 45, Perry Letter Books, Perry to Joel Abbott, 22 December 1843; Perry to David Henshaw, 25 December 1843; and Perry to Abbot and Thomas T. Craven, 4 March 1844.

view to protection of the lawful commerce of the United States, and the suppression of the Slave Trade when prosecuted under the American Flag." In late 1843, Perry ordered *Porpoise*, then under Lieutenant Commander Thomas T. Craven, to sail along the coast to Gorée and then to the English settlement on the Gambia, where "you will take pains to inform the authorities and the principal head men that a sufficient number of American vessels of war is [sic] upon the coast to punish any interference with American lawful trade[.]"[10]

The reports of Commander Joel Abbot in *Decatur* and Commander Henry Bruce in *Truxton* are indicative of American activities and opinions during the squadron's early years. On 18 January 1844, *Decatur* arrived at King Cass Town, the site of an American missionary settlement. Officials hoped that the presence of a US warship near Gaboon would help US commerce and "the suppression of the slave trade." Abbott noted that traders carried out legitimate and slave-trade activities several degrees east and south of Perry's cruising limits. By late January 1845 *Truxton* had completed another cruise, after which Bruce reported that while slavers still carried on their activities from Gallinas, Americans were increasingly involved in legitimate trade.[11]

In contrast to the concern over commerce protection and promotion, the squadron reported little activity by slavers, and operations against them were minimal. Perry reported on 18 May 1844 that Commander Joseph Tattnall had captured two suspected slavers, *Uncas* and *Crawford*, although the courts later released them. Nevertheless, Perry told Secretary of the Navy David Henshaw that he had seen no indication of American involvement in the slave trade, although he was aware of the tactics and strategies used by slavers to avoid detection. He wrote that in the West Indies, if a US warship approached a slaver, "she displays Spanish colours and exhibits her Spanish papers[.]" Meanwhile, she displays "her American Flag and papers and fictitious log book" to prevent seizure by British warships. Given the disadvantages, Perry felt that it was impossible for the squadron to prevent "all these abuses" along the entire length of the West African coast.[12]

While Perry continued his operations, Washington settled on his replacement, Commodore Charles W. Skinner. Skinner was originally from Maine but considered himself a Virginian. When he took command of the four

---

[10]*Ibid.*, Perry to Arthur Lewis, 17 April 1843; and Perry to Craven, 12 October 1843.

[11]NA, RG 45, Squadron Letters, vol. 105, African Squadron, Extract of report from Joel Abbot, enclosure in Perry to Secretary of the Navy, 18 May 1844; and Henry Bruce to Perry, 25 January 1845.

[12]*Ibid.*, Perry Letter Books, Perry to Secretary of the Navy, 18 May 1844; Perry to Henshaw, 25 December 1843; and Perry to Secretary of the Navy, 18 May 1844.

warships in February 1845 he continued operations, and that spring a prize, the schooner *Spitfire*, arrived in Boston harbour for trial and was confiscated. But Secretary of the Navy George Bancroft told Skinner that because of budget constraints the Navy Department was unable to send reinforcements. He approved of Skinner's operations and hoped soon to be able to relieve him and a portion of his squadron.[13]

Skinner also emphasized commercial matters and offered few comments on the slave trade beyond the operational requirements of the squadron. Skinner believed that the USN should use as many vessels as possible to cover the entire coast and maintain a constant presence, but he believed that large armaments were unnecessary. He reported on West African commerce, yet admitted that his knowledge of the slave trade was "vague and unsatisfactory," although more time might provide greater detail. In the end, between April 1845 and March 1846 the squadron captured only six slavers. Indeed, between 1843 and 1850 the USN captured only seventeen vessels engaged in the slave trade.[14] As long as commerce protection and promotion were the squadron's primary objectives, officers, regardless of their personal opinions, offered very few comments on the slave trade.

Berriby and a Show of US Force

While the US was limited in its willingness and hence its ability to police the slave trade, the wider goal of protecting American interests allowed the USN to launch limited military strikes against lesser native powers in support of US strategy. The most important example of this was the attack on Berriby in 1843. This action on the Ivory Coast was in retaliation for an attack on the schooner *Mary Carver*. It is significant because it had long-term consequences for Americans on the coast and because the outcome reinforced the US belief that its West African strategy was correct, even if it made relations with the

---

[13]Canney, *Africa Squadron*, 67 and 71; Warren S. Howard, *American Slavers and the Federal Law* (Berkeley, 1963), appendix A, 214; NA, RG 45, Secretary of the Navy, Record of Confidential Letters (Secretary of the Navy Confidential Letters), 12 September 1843-28 February 1849, George Bancroft to Charles W. Skinner, 18 June 1845; and Secretary of the Navy, Letters Sent, 11 March-6 December 1845, Bancroft to Skinner, 7 November 1845.

[14]NA, RG 45, Squadron Letters, CVI, African Squadron, No. 8, Skinner to John Young Mason, 16 March 1846; No. 17, Skinner to Secretary of the Navy, 20 June 1845; No. 47, Skinner to Bancroft, 17 January 1836; and David Eltis, *et al.*, *The Trans-Atlantic Slave Trade: A Database on CD-ROM* (Cambridge, 1999). The total seventeen is technically for the period 1841-1850, but there were no US captures until 1843. While the database is useful, it is difficult to customize queries beyond those provided by the software.

natives tense. The British, for their part, concluded that the American use of sea power against Berriby made the natives more receptive to British policy.

The Secretary of the Navy reported to Congress in 1842 that natives had attacked the Salem merchant ship *Mary Carver*. On the coast, Perry's officers reported signs that Americans were in the midst of disputes. Thus, the US squadron was told to make its presence known to the locals, but Washington left the precise tactics to the commodore's discretion. Soon after Perry arrived on the coast he told the Governor of Cape Palmas that it was time for revenge. He also told Secretary Upshur that Governor Joseph Roberts of Liberia believed that force would "have a salutary influence in impressing upon the natives greater awe of the American flag." From this Perry concluded that "it is my purpose to communicate with all the various tribes along the Coast and to admonish them of the necessity of receiving and treating the American trading vessels in a friendly manner." Late in 1843, Perry attacked because he believed that slow reprisals only emboldened the natives against American traders. He expressed hope that his actions would restore a friendly relationship between legitimate traders and the Berriby people.[15]

By January 1844 Perry went so far as to advocate what today we would call "ethnic cleansing." He was knowledgeable about the native African economy and advocated an attack to secure American commercial interests. The Americans should destroy those villages where natives treated them poorly. He rationalized his plan with the understanding that the Cracow people were foreign to the coast and that the original inhabitants, who were friendly to US traders, would return if they felt secure. Lieutenant Craven in *Porpoise* provided some indication of the natives' reactions to Perry's action. The people of Little Berriby had moved inland and asked Perry's permission to rebuild the settlement along the coast. Craven thought that the natives now respected US power and would be friendly to Americans. Abbot also found that the natives were peaceful toward foreigners because of Perry's attack on Berriby.[16]

Where Britain used sea power to push African factors of production into legitimate commerce, the US used it to intimidate natives into trading with Americans while doing little against the slave trade. Nevertheless, the results were similar. When Commodore Skinner arrived on the coast, he had a different opinion of the attack on Berriby. When he passed Berriby in *Jamestown* the natives fled in horror; he observed similar cases of fear elsewhere on the coast and was aghast at what had occurred. But he too believed that the pacification

---

[15]NA, RG 45, Perry Letter Books, Perry to Governor or Person in Charge of the American Colony at Cape Palmas, Coast of Africa, 17 April 1843; Perry to Upshur, 3 August 1843; Perry to John B. Russwurm, 10 and 12 August 1843; and Perry to Henshaw, 21 December 1843.

[16]*Ibid.*, Perry to Henshaw, 15 January 1844; Squadron Letters, CV, African Squadron, Craven to Perry, 24 April 1844; and Abbot to Perry, 6 November 1844.

of Berriby added to American prestige. Thereafter, he reported that trade in hides, gold dust, palm oil, ivory and camwood in exchange for US products flourished. The benefits of American sea power had even reached into the African soul: "the lone missionary experiences and acknowledges the advantages arising from the protection of a flag at once feared and respected."[17]

The British also noted with pleasure the benefits of the US attack for its broader strategy. Indeed, the American presence fit perfectly with London's treaty-making goals. Murray noted that the region's character had changed significantly since the American naval action in December 1843. In 1848 the RN was able to sign a treaty with the Chiefs of Grand Berriby, who knew what would happen if they defied a naval power. While Murray noted that the Kroo and Fishmen tribes had never participated in the slave trade, the first three articles of the new treaty dealt with ending that trade and the fourth with free trade for the British.[18] Despite divergent strategies, US "peacetime" policy seemed to have had a positive impact on both American and British objectives.

The Mexican War and Curtailment of US West African Activities

Despite the seemingly positive results in West Africa, concern with potential trade growth remained subservient to affairs in America's home waters. Once the US acquired California, American attention was deflected into the Pacific. Consequently, commitments closer to home mitigated US naval effectiveness off West Africa and contributed to the British belief that American efforts were insincere. The strategic inflexibility that Smith Thompson feared in the 1820s was a reality by the time of the Mexican War, which led to the concentration of the small USN close to home and reduced the commitment to West Africa.

The US annexed Texas in 1845, and on 13 May 1846 war erupted with Mexico. That same day Congress authorized the arming of private merchantmen and the speedy completion of naval construction to aid the war effort. The US blockaded the Mexican coast and used Anton Lizardo, near Vera Cruz, as a coaling station for steam vessels. In October 1846 the USN seized Tampico, and in March 1847 land forces took Vera Cruz. Meanwhile, the Pa-

---

[17]*Ibid.*, Squadron Letters, CVI, African Squadron, No. 9, Skinner to Mason, 17 March 1845; No. 8, Skinner to Mason, 16 March 1846; and No. 17, Skinner to Secretary of the Navy, 20 June 1845.

[18]Great Britain, Parliament, *Parliamentary Papers* (*BPP*), 1849, LV, 266-267, Correspondence with British Commissioners and Representatives from British Vice-Admiralty Courts and Naval Officers on the Slave Trade (Class A), 1848-1849, enclosures in No. 187, Charles Hotham to Secretary of the Admiralty, 3 May 1848; enclosure 5 in No. 187, "Agreement with the Chiefs of Grand Bereby," 25 February 1848; and enclosure 6 in No. 187, Alexander Murray, "Observations of Commander Murray on the Agreement with the Chiefs of Grand Bereby," 26 February 1848.

cific squadron sailed north from Peru, blockaded Mexico's Pacific coast and took San Francisco Bay. On 4 July 1846, with the creation of the Republic of California, American territory had dramatically expanded to the west.[19]

The Americans duly informed the British of the war and the blockade, although US diplomats noted that many Britons eyed the conflict with unease. McLane found that it was unexpected in Britain, and American participation in the conflict was "unpopular." The British feared that the US would settle the boundary with Mexico before negotiating over Oregon, a concern McLane shared. But in this era of the emerging "New Rule," he warned that privateers and warships should be careful not to interfere with "the rights and commerce of neutrals" so that sea power would not harm Anglo-American relations.[20]

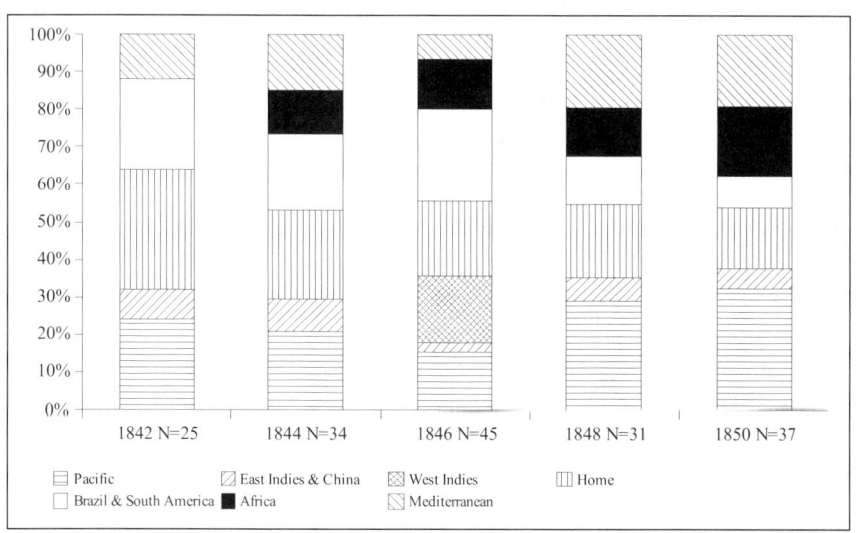

Figure 7.1:   US Naval Deployment, 1842-1850

Note: N = Number of warships

Source: Calculated from United States, *Annual Reports of the Secretary of the Navy* (Washington, DC, 1842-1850).

---

[19]Paolo E. Coletta, *The American Naval Heritage* (3rd ed., Lanham, MD, 1987), 117-118.

[20]NA, RG 59, Dispatches, Britain, No. 54, Louis McLane to James Buchanan, 3 June 1846.

Figure 7.1 shows the concentration of US sea power in home waters and in the West Indies during the Mexican crisis. At the same time, the African squadron was asked to take on more tasks without an increase in deployment. The West African squadron was meant to exercise a subtle presence along the coast rather than provide wartime support. Consequently, from 1846 until late 1849 the combined weight of problems pushed the USN to the sidelines in West Africa while the RN continued to negotiate free-trade treaties and to suppress the slave trade.

In October 1845 Commodore Skinner received information from newspapers that relations between the US and Mexico had deteriorated. Combined with the USN's budget restrictions, the newspapers should have provided Skinner with a reason for the lack of reinforcements. On 29 December 1845 Secretary Bancroft dispatched Commodore George C. Read to relieve Skinner. Because of the conflict with Mexico, however, Bancroft ordered Read to guard against "the depredations of privateers[.]" Bancroft also told Skinner to "exercise the utmost vigilance in protecting American commerce and interests" while sailing from West Africa to Boston and to pay particular attention to the possibility of Mexican privateers near Matanzas and Havana. During Read's outward voyage he encountered many ships but no Mexican privateers. After arriving on the coast he had an opportunity to assess the American squadron. He immediately saw the need for more vessels and concluded that the squadron would be unable to carry out all its assigned tasks.[21]

The squadron was under pressure to protect a wide area during the war. Consul William Carrol at St. Helena worried over newspaper reports that Mexicans were exacting reprisals on US merchantmen. He wanted protection from the West African squadron, but Read replied that St. Helena was too far away and that the best he could offer would be a fleet to convoy American merchant vessels. Read doubted that US merchant captains would accept the offer, however, because to wait for other vessels to form a convoy might deprive them of the advantage of being the first to arrive on the coast. The commodore concluded that "if the protection you suggest should become necessary," Carrol should ask the US Brazilian squadron for help. The African squadron was depleted, and Read told Secretary John Young Mason that "I

<hr />

[21]*Ibid.*, NA, RG 45, Squadron Letters, CVI, African Squadron, Nos. 34 and 38, Skinner to Bancroft, 12 and 20 October 1845; Secretary of the Navy Confidential Letters, 12 September 1843-28 February 1849, Bancroft to Read, 21 May 1846; and Bancroft to Skinner, 21 May 1846; Squadron Letters, LXXXII (pt.), African Squadron, Read to Bancroft, 26 June 1846; and *H.R. Doc.*, No. 104, 35th Cong., 2nd sess., 11-12, Bancroft to Read, 29 December 1845.

pray continually for a peace with Mexico to get these miserable sailing craft relieved."[22]

Other regions also requested protection by the African squadron. On 31 January 1847 the Secretary of the US legation at Madrid, Thomas Reynolds, wrote to "the officer in command of any armed vessel" of the US with his concerns about the war and the lack of any US naval protection for American interests abroad. On 31 May Read acknowledged Reynolds' letter. By then he had newspapers and correspondence from the US that supported Reynolds' request for assistance. In response, Read dispatched the warship *Marion* to Gibraltar. Read shared Reynolds' concern about the threat to American commerce from Mexican privateers if they succeeded in outfitting in England or Spain. But Read warned that *Marion*, after being on the West African coast for so long, was "by no means fit to cruise for privateers[,]" although it was the only vessel capable of carrying out such duties.[23]

In contrast, Read told Washington that he had met with the senior British and French naval officers on the coast. The RN, he reported, had a formidable force; its ships were numerous and large, which enabled them to stay off the slave-trading stations for longer periods than the smaller American warships. Read warned that even if the US deployed three times as many warships to the coast, it would still need two vessels off each suspected slaving station to stop and search every vessel. Meanwhile, the foreign commanders noted that they had not seen a US warship along the coast "for several months before" Read's arrival. Read felt that the situation was injuring naval morale because many sailors, he claimed, had arrived on the coast in hopes of suppressing the slave trade and supporting their nation's honour. He feared that US efforts would be futile unless Congress enacted tighter legislation against those involved in the slave trade. The squadron might be able to meet its obligations to protect legitimate US commerce, but "they are not likely to meet the expectations of those who desire the slave trade annihilated."[24]

During 1846 and 1847 the ongoing conflict with Mexico adversely affected both US naval operations along the African coast and Anglo-American naval cooperation. Palmerston pressed the Americans to increase their naval presence off Africa, and in particular to send vessels to the East African coast to suppress American involvement in the region's slave trade. But British Am-

---

[22]NA, RG 45, Squadron Letters, LXXXII 82 (pt.), African Squadron, Read to William Carrol, 12 March 1847, enclosure in Read to Mason, 26 March 1847.

[23]*Ibid.*, Reynolds to Officer in Command of Any Armed Vessel of the United States, 31 January 1847, enclosure in Read to Mason, 12 May 1847; and Read to Thomas C. Reynolds, 31 May 1847.

[24]*Ibid.*, Read to Bancroft, 16 September 1846.

bassador Richard Pakeham told Palmerston that he could not pressure the US further because "the whole of its available naval resources" were "required for the prosecution of the war with Mexico[.]"[25] Until the situation improved, American operations stalled, much to Britain's displeasure, but the British refrained from pushing the Americans too hard. Still, the 1847 *Parliamentary Papers* duly published Pakeham's comments for the Americans to see. But it was not just the war with Mexico that was leading the US to give West African affairs a low priority.

Legal Problems Curtail US Navy Efforts

For political and strategic reasons Washington left the US West African squadron on its own, stretched by too many tasks and focused more on commerce protection than slave-trade suppression. Legal problems also affected the deployment, for courts in the US handed the limited anti-slavery operations a serious setback in 1846-1847. The relevant cases, and Washington's reaction, are significant because they reveal how decisions by the judiciary tied the hands of the American squadron. But they also reveal Washington's insistence on uninterrupted trade, for slave-trade suppression played little role in the increase of American wealth.

When in 1846 the British warship *Actaeon* found *Malaga*, from Beverly, Massachusetts, loaded with goods thought used in the slave trade, the naval commander concluded that the vessel was guilty under US law of "aiding and abetting the slave trade." But New England Judge Charles L. Woodbury, and later another judge, Benjamin R. Curtis, ruled that such vessels violated no laws unless they had a direct stake in the slave trade. Thereafter, the authorities dropped the case against *Malaga*, and the owners sued.[26]

Secretary of the Navy Mason, a lawyer from Richmond, Virginia, told Read that several such cases had occurred. He understood the difficulty under which the US officers worked and "by no means desir[e]d to check or sensure [sic] the vigilance of American cruisers[,]" but the free flow of trade was more important. Mason wrote that to prevent "interruptions to lawful commerce" and to stop "complaints from innocent traders[,]" the USN had to be more careful when seizing suspect ships. The result was the further prioritizing of trade protection and an increasing fear among officers along the West African coast of the legal and career ramifications of stopping any vessel. The result for slave-trade suppression was ominous: Read told Washington that

---

[25]*BPP*, 1847, LXVI, 579-580, Correspondence with Foreign Powers Not Parties to Treaties or Conventions Giving Mutual Right of Search of Vessels Suspected of the Slave Trade (Class D), 1846, No. 95, Richard Pakeham to Palmerston, 13 December 1846.

[26]Howard, *American Slavers and the Federal Law*, 102-104.

reports had reached him that *Malaga* and *Casket* had returned to the African coast, loaded slaves and departed unmolested.[27]

Warren Howard has concluded that the result was a "mass shirking of assigned duties, carefully concealed from the American public[,]" that lasted for about two years until the damage suits were settled. But the fear of seizing suspected slavers was dictated by Washington's insistence that the USN focus on trade protection. The goal of using sea power to protect trade is significant because in the case of the US it failed to form a nexus with the suppression of the slave trade. The reality of US naval deployment therefore contradicts Judd Harmon's thesis that American naval deployment to protect commerce also resulted in the USN suppressing the slave trade.[28] Moreover, US policy had implications for Anglo-American relations as Britain again questioned the American commitment to slave-trade suppression.

The US Navy and Commercial Goals, 1847-1854

With legal and relief problems, the US West African squadron carried out its duties as best it could, but it focused increasingly on commercial protection. In the regions they patrolled, American officers, like their British counterparts, noted areas of increased commerce and avenues of potential advancement. In October 1846 the Americans believed that the RN's vigilance, and to some small extent that of the French navy, had suppressed the slave trade. Commodore Read was serious about his work and even declined Secretary Bancroft's personal request to stop at Madeira for wine.[29]

The cruise of the US warship *Marion* from October 1846 to April 1847 was typical of the work undertaken by the Americans during this period. During a visit to the Bight of Benin, Captain Simonds reported that commerce had declined and that he had seen no US ships. By 28 January he arrived off Cape Lopez and visited Cabinda, where the commander of the British warship *Larne*, the only vessel there, informed him that "no Americans had been there

---

[27]K. Jack Bauer, "John Young Mason," in Paolo E. Coletta (ed.), *American Secretaries of the Navy* (2 vols., Annapolis, 1980), I, 238; NA, RG 45, Secretary of the Navy Confidential Letters, 12 September 1843-28 February 1849, Mason to Read, 16 November 1846; Squadron Letters, LXXXIX (pt.), African Squadron, Read to Mason, 11 December 1846 and 10 and 31 March 1847.

[28]Howard, *American Slavers and the Federal Law*, 105; and Judd Scott Harmon, "Suppress and Protect: The United States Navy, the African Slave Trade, and Maritime Commerce, 1794-1862" (Unpublished PhD thesis, College of William and Mary, 1977), 1-3.

[29]NA, RG 45, Squadron Letters, LCCCII (pt.), African Squadron, L.E. Simonds to Read, 9 October 1846; and Read (Private) to Bancroft, 5 October 1846.

for months." Commodore Benjamin Cooper's 1849 cruising orders to Captain A.G. Gordon of the USS *Porpoise* are also indicative of the American patrol pattern near the end of this period. In July Cooper ordered *Porpoise* to sail south from Porto Praia and to pay particular attention to the Bight of Benin. *Porpoise* was to visit Monrovia, Bassa Cove, Sinon, Cape Palmas, the Bight of Benin and then Whydah, and it could sail farther along the coast at the captain's discretion.[30]

The Americans still captured slavers, but the results were disappointing because of court decisions. On 2 August 1846 *Marion* captured *Casket*, also from Beverly, near the Congo River and sent it to Boston for trial. But as with *Malaga*, the court dismissed the case. In 1847 *Chancellor* escaped from the British. Read had reports that *Chancellor* was involved in the slave trade and sent the warship *Dolphin* to find it. But Read also feared the British might fire on a legitimate US trader as they had on *Chancellor*. By April *Dolphin* had apprehended *Chancellor* and sent it to New York for trial; once again, the court also dismissed the case. Through all this there was little comment from Washington about the squadron's operations; Secretary Mason simply approved its actions and acknowledged the receipt of its dispatches.[31]

By 1849 the lacklustre American performance had increased concern among their British counterparts. In the autumn of 1849, for example, Commodore Fanshawe told US Commodore Francis H. Gregory that American merchant vessels were involved in the slave trade in Benguela, Angola and the Congo. Fanshawe was disappointed that the British had not encountered a single US warship south of the equator. Irritated, he concluded that the use of the American flag hurt British goals but that the RN could do nothing about it legally.[32] But that autumn the courts ruled in favour of the American officers

---

[30]*Ibid.*, Simonds to Read, 20 April 1847; and CVII, Cooper to A.G. Gordon, 10 May and 29 July 1849.

[31]NA, RG 45, Squadron Letters, CVI, African Squadron, No. 48 with enclosures A through H, Skinner to Bancroft, 27 January 1846 (and postscript dated 31 January 1846); Howard, *American Slavers and the Federal Law*, appendix A, 214-233; NA, RG 45, Squadron Letters, LXXXII (pt.), African Squadron, John Pope to Read, 5 March 1847; Read to Mason, 12 May, 15 July and 6 August 1847; Secretary of the Navy, Letters Sent, 12 June 1848-16 April 1849, Mason to W.C. Bolton, 31 August 1848; and *H.R. Doc.*, No. 104, 35th Cong., 2nd sess., 13-14, Mason to Cooper, 10 November 1848.

[32]*H.R. Doc.*, No. 104, 35th Cong., 2nd sess., 13-14, William Ballard Preston to Francis H. Gregory, 17 August 1849; and *BPP*, 1850, LV, 421, Correspondence with British Commissioners and Representatives from British Vice-Admiralty Courts and Naval Officers on the Slave Trade (Class A), 1849-1850, No. 208, Arthur Fanshawe to Secretary of the Admiralty, 1 January 1850; and enclosure 1 in No. 208, Fanshawe to Gregory, 26 December 1849.

sued by vessel owners, and the US began greater deployment farther south, thus allowing for greater cooperation with the British. Regardless, the squadron continued to implement US policy by supporting American colonies and commercial activities. Yet somewhat ironically, the new importance of California increased the significance of West Africa.

On 12 February 1850 Gregory provided an indication of his squadron's focus. He reported that a number of US merchant ships had arrived at Porto Praia bound for California and that the USN had provided assistance to those in need. He thought that American economic and strategic interests along the West African coast were increasing. John Marston, commander of the US warship *Yorktown*, also believed that the region's economy was strong, with exports of palm oil, camwood, ivory and coffee, among other items. Marston even called on the ACS to send more settlers. In early 1854 Commodore Isaac Mayo told Washington that he would, as ordered, send a vessel to the aid of Charles Hoffman, from Salem, who had difficulty with merchants who operated between Sierra Leone and Cape Roxo. Only after this task was completed would *Dale* sail to the southern coast to relieve *Perry*.[33]

Mayo knew the first commodore of the US West African Squadron, Matthew Perry. They had sat together on examining boards which assessed midshipmen in the 1840s. Further, Mayo had always been keen on the development of the nation's naval and maritime resources. He had a home in Annapolis and had recommended that town as the home of centralized naval education in 1845.[34] Like his gentlemanly British counterparts, Mayo believed that the appointment of consuls in West Africa would increase US commerce, take some pressure off the USN and help to suppress the slave trade. He felt, for example, that American commerce with Loanda, "the centre of trade and the chief sea port on the South Coast of Africa," needed the "presence of an American consul[.]" Mayo must have also surmised that such an appointment would provide an American presence on land that would take some pressure off his small squadron. He told Washington that a permanent consul could inspect ship's papers and cargo. He also noted that "too many of them, I fear, have of late employed our flag, while in the prosecution of the slave trade." Mayo even appointed several consuls during his tenure, including to Sierra

---

[33]NA, RG 45, Squadron Letters, CVIII, African Squadron, Gregory to Preston, 12 February 1850; John Marston to Gregory, 8 April 1850; and CX, Isaac Mayo to J.C. Dobbin, 25 January 1854.

[34]Park Benjamin, *The United States Naval Academy, Being the Yarn of the American Midshipman* (New York, 1900), 144-145.

Leone, the English settlement of Bathurst and the Angola region.[35] But such proactive US naval officers were in the minority.

The USN and the Slave Trade, 1850-1857

While the British solidified their West African policy, the USN maintained support for American commerce in West Africa, separate from the contentious issue of slavery and slave-trade suppression that divided the nation. Nevertheless, its post-1849 deployment against slavers became less complicated after favourable court decisions in the US. Freed from some of its legal restraints, the USN increased efforts against the slavers while still protecting legitimate commerce. But economics and slave-trade suppression remained separate.

One of the court decisions involved the infamous *Malaga*. In 1849 Judge John K. Kane of the Eastern Pennsylvania District concluded that *Malaga* had indeed operated under suspicious circumstances. He eased legal restrictions and found that the evidence that the vessel was chartered to a known slaver and carrying known slaving goods was sufficient for an arrest. As a result, US patrols resumed south of the equator in 1850, and "really suspicious vessels were arrested."[36]

Still, because the use of sea power to suppress the slave trade was of secondary importance, such efforts were subject to the whims of individual officers. Those who disliked the African coast, or who felt that the squadron was too small, curtailed deployment. Those who supported slave-trade suppression, on the other hand, believed that the squadron's base needed to be shifted southward to be effective against the illegal activity. By the late 1850s, like their British counterparts, US officers found that the slave trade was increasing and becoming better organized; they also concluded that much of it originated from New York. But the American deployment to the south lagged behind the British because of the earlier legal and re-enforcement problems. The British had a base at St. Helena, making their logistics easier, while distance forced the US to operate a long supply line from Porto Praia. This, combined with US suspicion of the British, set the stage for renewed conflict along the West African coast.

---

[35]NA, RG 45, Squadron Letters, CX, African Squadron, Mayo to Dobbin, 17 November 1853 and 3 April 1854, and enclosure, William C. Whittle to Mayo, 11 February 1854.

[36]Howard, *American Slavers and the Federal Law*, 106-108.

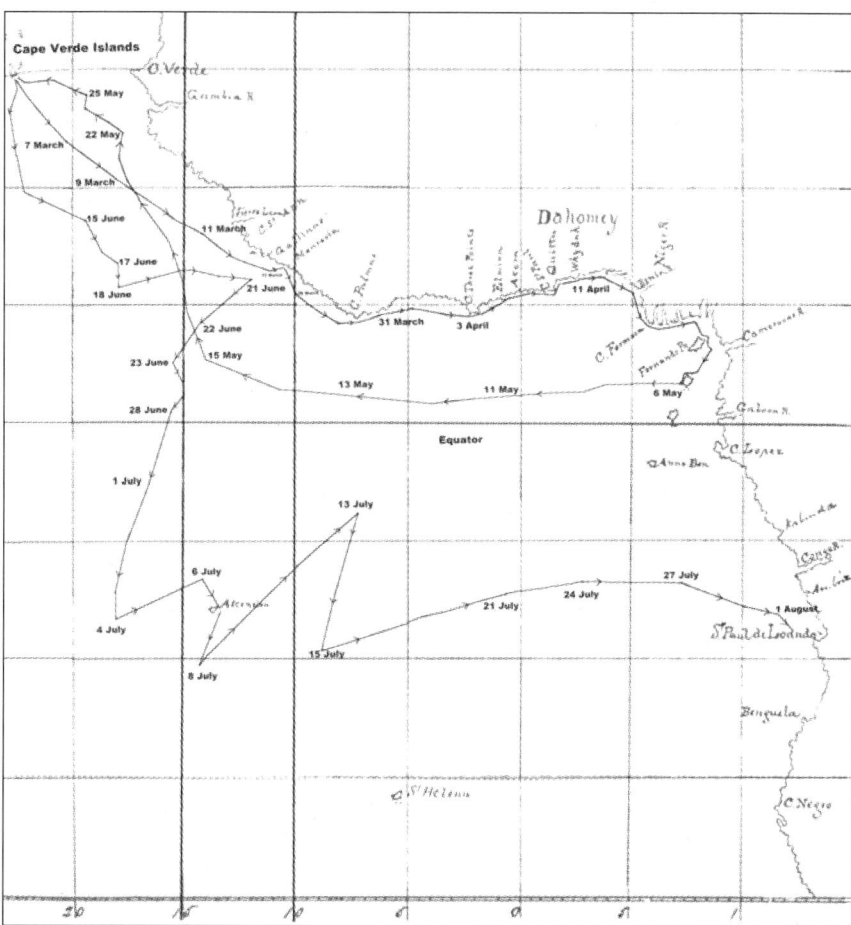

Figure 7.2: Commodore Gregory's Spring and Summer Cruises, 1850

Note: Although digitally enhanced, map is virtually identical to the original.

Source: United States, National Archives (NA), Record Group (RG) 45, Squadron
          Letters, CVIII, African Squadron, Francis H. Gregory to William Ballard
          Preston, 3 September 1850.

          In the wake of favourable court decisions, several US officers on the
West African coast showed a new initiative toward suppressing the slave trade.
Nevertheless, the British outpaced these efforts, leading to fear by the Ameri-
cans that the RN would drive them from the coast. Commodore Francis H.
Gregory in the sloop *Portsmouth* took command of a force of five vessels in
1850. While *Perry* was on patrol under the command of Andrew Hull Foote,

Gregory deployed the squadron farther south and concentrated efforts along the Bights of Benin and Biafra to disrupt US slave traders who supplied the Brazilian market. But the remote nature of the American supply depot put the squadron at a disadvantage; with only a maximum of three months' provisions, ships would have to sail down the coast and back before resting at Madeira. Consequently, he recommended that the navy move the depot to St. Helena or dispatch supply ships. Gregory's cruise from March to May 1850 illustrates both the logistical problems and overall US strategy (see figure 7.2).[37]

Gregory's orders to Foote are indicative of the former's strategy. On 9 January 1850 Gregory ordered Foote to sail south of the equator to Cape St. Mary's at 13° South. Gregory told him that his goal was to protect lawful American commerce and stop slavers from using the US flag. Foote was to pay particular attention to known slaving ports, such as Gallinas, Benguela, Loanda and Ambriz because Gregory had information that Americans might be involved in the slave trade between Cape St. Mary's and Cape Lopez. On 27 April 1850, Foote reported that he had encountered no slavers and that the British captured only one during the period.[38] Nevertheless, Foote was committed to the cause.

This was also an age of moral reform in the US, and in the maritime community in particular, which spawned seamen's friends' societies and improvement organizations; such movements found many advocates in the USN. Andrew Foote was a man who believed, among other things, in temperance and regular church attendance. Foote's pious beliefs extended to the West African coast, where he hoped to help his fellow man. He supported the ACS and later exclaimed that Christianity would bring civilization to the Africans.[39] As a result, Foote made successful slaver seizures. On 6 June 1850, for example, he spotted a suspicious vessel windward off Ambriz and sent a boat to investigate. The vessel was *Martha* from New York, flying the US flag. Its captain later explained that he believed that *Perry* was a British vessel, as he had information that *Perry* was no longer on that part of the coast. Foote seized the ship at 6 PM, and the captain later testified if *Perry* had failed, he was ready to

---

[37]*H.R. Doc.*, No. 104, 35th Cong., 2nd sess., 13-14, Preston to Gregory, 17 August 1849; NA, RG 45, Squadron Letters, CVIII, African Squadron, Gregory to Preston, 26 March and 3 September 1850; and Gregory to Secretary of the Navy, 14 October 1850.

[38]NA, RG 45, Squadron Letters, CVIII, African Squadron, Gregory to Andrew H. Foote, 9 January 1850; and Foote to Gregory, 27 April 1850.

[39]Harold D. Langley, *Social Reform in the United States Navy, 1798-1862* (Urbana, IL, 1967), 44-66; and Spencer C. Tucker, *Andrew Foote: Civil War Admiral on Western Waters* (Annapolis, 2000), 55-60 and 68. For details on Foote's beliefs in temperance, see Tucker, 39-51.

load a cargo of slaves. Foote sent the vessel to New York for trial, where the US District Court condemned it and sentenced the mate to two years in prison, but the captain skipped bail. Nevertheless, the Secretary of the Navy, the Virginian William Ballard Preston, had little to say about Foote's actions and simply noted approval. Preston was a known advocate of Jefferson's philosophy of the gradual elimination of slavery rather than radical abolition.[40]

In July 1850 Millard Fillmore became President after the death of Zachary Taylor. Fillmore was from New York and supported the navy. His administration also supported limited naval expansion and exploration squadrons, such as Matthew Perry's mission to Asia. But the President wished to preserve the Union and respected states' rights. At the urging of Southerners, he selected William A. Graham of North Carolina as Secretary of the Navy. In May 1851 Graham ordered Eli A.F. Lavallette to relieve Gregory. Despite the lofty goals of some Americans, others, like Lavallette, believed that the slave trade was already suppressed north of Cape Palmas. He also felt that the British had enough steamers in the Bight of Biafra to suppress the remaining trade. Meanwhile, Lavallette exclaimed, there was never any slave trade carried on north of Liberia and little American commerce. The US needed to move its base to St. Helena because the squadron was deployed as far south as St. Paul de Loanda. It had protected commerce, American citizens and settlers, and Lavallette believed it helped suppress the slave trade.[41]

John P. Kennedy, from a wealthy Baltimore merchant family, replaced Graham when the latter decided to run for Vice President. Kennedy believed in the potential for African economic expansion and dispatched Commander William F. Lynch to survey the coast from Liberia to the Gaboon. Although he hoped that Congress would provide more money for the service, the lawmakers failed to do so because the survey mission was at the behest of the Pennsylvania branch of the ACS, and Congress increasingly feared the divisive issue of slavery, regardless of the survey's mission. Focused on com-

---

[40]NA, RG 45, Squadron Letters, CVIII, African Squadron, Foote to Gregory, 7 June 1850; Andrew H. Foote, *Africa and the American Flag* (New York, 1854), 287-293; NA, RG 45, Secretary of the Navy Confidential Letters, 1 March 1849-28 February 1853, No. 2, Preston to Gregory, 9 July 1850; and Harold D. Langley, "William Ballard Preston," in Coletta (ed.), *American Secretaries of the Navy*, I, 243.

[41]John H. Schroeder, *Shaping a Maritime Empire: The Commercial and Diplomatic Role of the American Navy, 1829-1861* (Westport, CT, 1985), 95-99; Harold D. Langley, "William Alexander Graham," in Coletta (ed.), *American Secretaries of the Navy*, I, 257; *H.R. Doc.*, No. 104, 35th Cong., 2nd sess., 14-16, William A. Graham to Eli A.F. Lavallette, May 1851; and NA, RG 45, Squadron Letters, CIX, African Squadron, Lavallette to Graham, 20 May and 13 November 1851.

merce promotion, Kennedy believed that if the government intended the squadron only for slave-trade suppression, perhaps it should be disbanded.[42]

On 9 December 1852 Kennedy ordered Commodore Isaac Mayo, who would be in command for about two years, to relieve Lavallette. Mayo's force was smaller than Lavallette's, yet Washington expected him to cover the same territory. By 1853 the US commitment had declined further. Although the new President, Franklin Pierce, advocated a strong foreign policy, he wished to avoid the contentious slavery issue and so re-focussed the squadron on commerce protection and development. In turn, Mayo expressed his concern that the squadron had only three or four vessels to patrol the coast. The warships passed "singly, from point to point in succession, and two of them rarely meet[;]" it was "a force very inadequate" for the task. But focused on trade, with little will in Washington or on station to suppress the slave trade, American officers were concerned that Britain was achieving dominance on the coast.[43] In turn, British exacerbation at increasing US involvement in the slave trade combined to generate tension between the two nations that increased the possibility of conflict.

British Dominance and American Decline

The Americans observed British actions both in support of their commercial policy and against American-flagged vessels suspected of involvement in the slave trade. By the 1850s, USN officers not only feared the impact of British warships on US trade but also that its merchants and newly established steam lines were agents of imperial control. The Americans found that US traders were scarce on many parts of the African coast, while the British had ample mercantile representation. The US believed that it was the presence of the RN and the regular use of steam technology in the private sector that gave the British an advantage. To suspicious American observers, the RN, colonial officials and merchants – the gentlemanly capitalists – were achieving their goals.

Early in the history of Anglo-American shipping competition, inexpensive American wooden ships threatened to outpace their British counterparts. But Britain took advantage of iron and steam to outstrip the US in carrying capacity and trade routes. The result was that Britain had a grasp on merchant shipping that was unmatched. In 1850 the British owned fifty-two percent of world steam tonnage, while the Americans had only twenty-two per-

---

[42]Harold D. Langley, "John Pendleton Kennedy," in Coletta (ed.), *American Secretaries of the Navy*, I, 269-271.

[43]*H.R. Doc.*, No. 104, 35th Cong., 2nd sess., John P. Kennedy to Mayo, 9 December 1852; Schroeder, *Shaping a Maritime Empire*, 117-128; and NA, RG 45, Squadron Letters, CX, African Squadron, Mayo to Dobbin, 29 September 1854.

cent.[44] Freer trade thus allowed Britain to acquire cheap resources, export to countries under lower tariffs and maintain dominance with its industrial and shipping capacity. All Britain had to worry about was protecting trade from predators and "subsidized" products like slave-produced goods.

Although the East India Company favoured the African coast because it could ship goods to and from India without transhipment through hostile territory, it took companies awhile to establish steam lines. Early steam engines were large, had low-pressure boilers and consumed large amounts of coal. While increasing speed, the technology posed logistical problems. Daniel Headrick concluded that "at sea they had to either bring along an enormous supply of coal or be supplied by sailing ships."[45] But Robert Kubicek has shown that British colonial officials clamoured for steamers, which they believed would increase commerce, particularly with inland regions, and enhance the prestige of the officials in African and European eyes. The establishment of regular steam transport also gave the British better control over supply and demand; it increased efficiency and allowed a broader spectrum of British merchants to operate.[46] The competitive advantage threatened to drive American traders from the region.

Table 7.1
Import Sources, Africa and Canada, 1844-1856 ('000 £)

Years	Africa	Canada
1844-1846	2,898,000	5,559,000
1854-1856	5,218,000	5,740,000

Source: Ralph Davis, *The Industrial Revolution and British Overseas Trade* (Leicester, 1979), 93.

As discussed in chapter two, African exports to Britain rose during this period, while political leaders like Palmerston adhered to a policy of informal empire and the gentlemanly ethic. African imports doubled from the

---

[44]S.G. Sturmey, *British Shipping and World Competition* (London, 1962), 1, 9 and 12-14; and Richard Harding, *Seapower and Naval Warfare 1650-1830* (London, 1999), 35-36 and 134.

[45]Daniel R. Headrick, *The Tools of Empire: Technology and European Imperialism in the Nineteenth Century* (New York, 1981), 131-133. For the economics of the shift from sail to steam, see Gerald S. Graham, "The Ascendancy of the Sailing Ship 1850-1885," *Economic History Review*, 2nd ser., IX, No. 1 (1956-1957), 74-88.

[46]Robert V. Kubicek, "The Colonial Steamer and the Occupation of West Africa by the Victorian State, 1840-1900," *Journal of Imperial and Commonwealth History*, XVIII, No. 1 (1990), 9, 12-13, 19 and 21.

period 1844-1846 to 1854-1856 so that in monetary value Africa now rivalled
Canada as a source of primary resources, the statistic that concerned the gentlemanly capitalists the most (see table 7.1). By contrast, Africa-America
trade, while still rising, was far less. Figure 7.3 shows that US exports to the
Gold Coast, for example, rarely exceeded £40,000 per year and were largely
comprised of rum. Figure 7.4 shows that exports from the region rarely exceeded £50,000 and were mainly palm oil and gold dust. They peaked during
1849-1854, but then declined, largely because of the fall in the value of gold
dust due to greater American production.

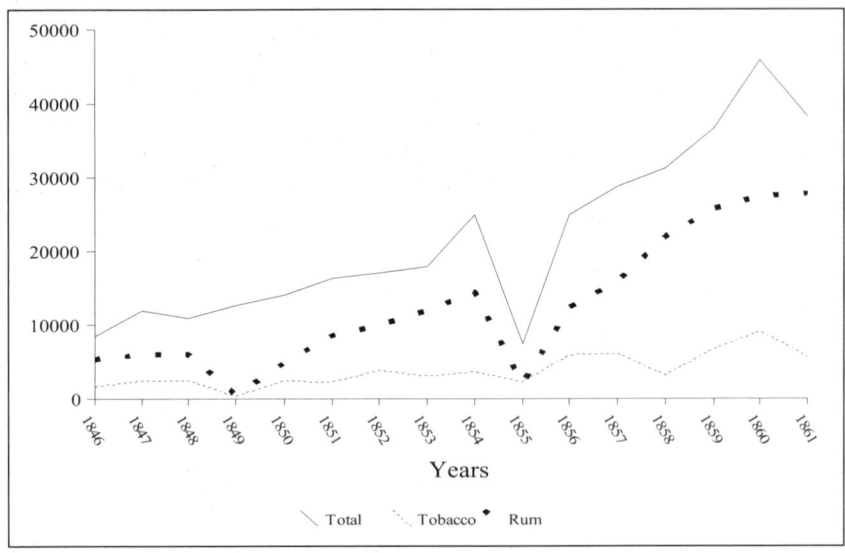

Figure 7.3: US Exports to the Gold Coast, 1846-1861 (£)

Note: Total US exports also included lumber and cotton goods from 1856, val-
               ued at only about £500 per annum. Flour exports ranged between £500
               and £2000 per annum. Because of the low values, these items have been
               omitted from this figure.

Source: Calculated from George E. Brooks, *Yankee Traders, Old Coasters and
               African Middlemen: A History of American Legitimate Trade with West
               Africa in the Nineteenth Century* (Boston, 1970), appendix G, 309.

Despite their caution, the British endeavours raised American concerns, especially when combined with the establishment of regular steam
communications between Britain and Africa in the 1850s. The Liverpool African Steamship Company, for example, started mail service in 1852 that went
as far south as Fernando Po. Another company, the Iron Steam Ship Com-

pany, also established a regular steam line to the African coast by 1853. Previously, Mayo observed, small transient US vessels of five to thirty tons had serviced the coast. But English merchants "now order them [supplies] from England; calculating almost to an hour, the time when they will be received; the returning steamers enables them to send back at a fixed period the produce of the country that has accumulated in their hands." Americans might be able to compete but would soon be driven from the region if they were unable to obtain a similar advantage. Mayo concluded that the British government "brought the great motive power of the age, to...drive all commercial rivals from the field[.]"[47]

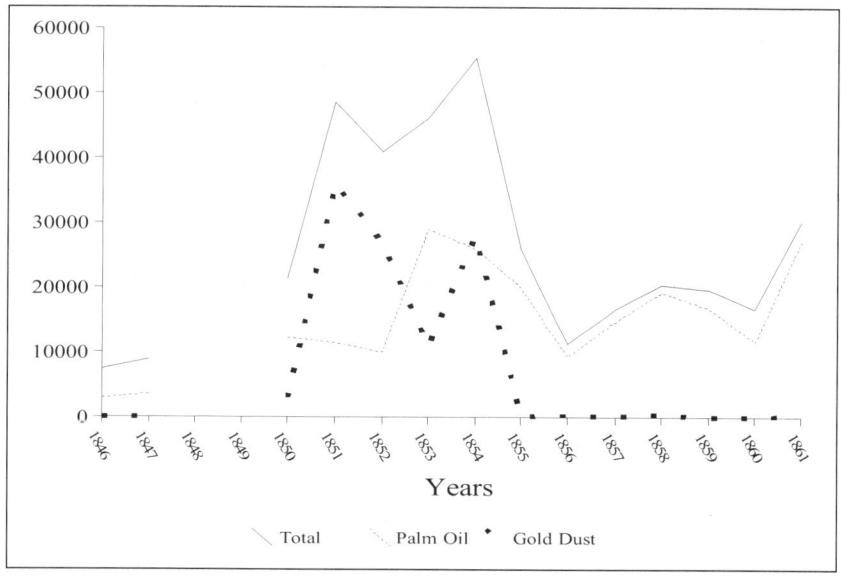

Figure 7.4: US Imports from the Gold Coast, 1846-1861 (£)

Note: Gaps represent missing. Import total also included ivory (highest from about £300 to £6000 per annum) and gum copal (highest from about £300 to £5000 per annum). Because of the low values and sporadic nature of these trades, they have been omitted from this figure.

Source: Calculated from Brooks, *Yankee Traders*, appendix H, 310.

---

[47]W.E.F. Ward, *The Royal Navy and the Slavers: The Suppression of the Atlantic Slave Trade* (London, 1969), 203; and NA, RG 45, Squadron Letters, CX, African Squadron, Mayo to Dobbin, 31 July 1854; and Mayo to [Secretary of the Navy], 22 August 1853. For details of the development of regular British shipping to the West African coast in this period, see Peter N. Davies, *The Trade Makers: Elder Dempster in West Africa, 1852-1972, 1973-1989* (London, 1973; reprint, St. John's, 2000), 7-15.

Americans warily perceived the benefits Britain achieved through its presence and the use of force against native powers. The US concluded trade agreements with the natives that contained pledges of equal access or "free trade," but they were less extensive than British pacts. Mayo had negotiated a trade treaty with the King of Lagos, for example, putting American commerce on an equal footing with that of other nations. But he also knew that Lagos was an important region and that Britain had used force to achieve its objectives when talks failed. Even so, after Britain suppressed the slave trade in a region, Mayo believed that it continued to use sea power to achieve its overall economic objectives. He correctly surmised the British strategy for the coast and knew that the British had integrated the USN into its strategic plan. Probably because of the growing crisis with Russia and the Crimean War, Mayo observed that the British had reduced their fleet along the coast and offered no objection to the Americans securing trade access because in their view the ultimate goal of commercial growth for all was more important.[48]

Mayo reported to Washington that "[t]he willingness with which the British Consul encouraged the King to take this step [the agreement with the Americans], probably sprung from" strategic considerations that resulted from their reduced naval commitment. But he warned that "[t]his [Lagos] is one of the most important commercial points on the West Coast of Africa & the English Government seem to be fully alive to the fact." Lagos was thriving; by 1854 it had a population of 18,000 "and must from its position become the centre of a very valuable trade." Mayo thus believed that the King's pledge to the Americans might prove useful if the French or British "should at any time attempt to obtain exclusive [trade] privileges."[49] But to American observers, it appeared that the British strategy to push African production factors into legitimate commerce had worked to the detriment of US traders.

While other factors undoubtedly contributed to the stagnation of African-American trade, Mayo's remarks also coincided with a period of sharp decline in American exports to Africa and African imports to America. In response to British advances, Mayo advocated a "line of steamers between Africa, and one of our Southern ports" to regain the trade that "in its infancy was fast falling into our hands when the foresight of the British...snatched it from us[.]" By 1855 Mayo's replacement, Thomas Crabbe, feared that the British might even drive the US out of its original colony at Liberia. He told Washington that the French and British treaties "are said to grant to the subjects of those countries equal rights in trade with the citizens of the Republic" of Liberia. Many in Liberia disliked those provisions, but "England, however, ap-

---

[48]NA, RG 45, Squadron Letters, CX, African Squadron, Mayo to Dobbin, 9 August 1854.

[49]*Ibid.*; and Richard L. Page to Mayo, 16 June 1854, enclosure in Mayo to Dobbin, 7 July 1854.

pears to be well established in the affections of Liberia, and will not patiently yield to any [treaty] alteration" adverse to its trade.[50]

The level of British interest and development in West Africa from 1850 to 1856 bred suspicions among American officers. While American officers were impressed with the British actions at Lagos, they also believed that the British only allowed the US along the coast as part of overall British strategy during the Crimean War. This period was critical in the establishment of the *Pax Britannica*; the British achieved regional economic dominance and with the end of the Crimean War had an unrivalled global naval force. Rather than trying to counter the British in West Africa, the Americans turned increasingly inward and toward the Pacific. In response to British sea power, Andrew Lambert concluded that after 1856 the US and other nations realized that competition was futile, and they "abandoned all pretence at deep water capacity in favour of coast defence, shore batteries and monitors[.]"[51]

As well, Anglo-American tension over slave-trade suppression remained. British suspicion about American motives increased as the slave trade continued, and American actions stagnated. On 24 October 1853, for example, the British warship *Crane* encountered the American-flagged *H.N. Gambrill* off Cabinda. The British were suspicious, inspected it on 28 October but released it. That evening, *Crane* came upon the US warship *Constitution* with Commodore Mayo on board and provided him with information about *H.N. Gambrill*. Rear Admiral Bruce told London that the information led Mayo to capture the vessel fifteen miles from the Congo. But Bruce felt that *H.N. Gambrill* had almost escaped because it raised the US flag. He told London that *Gambrill*'s master even had the "audacity" to raise the British flag when the American warship approached and claimed that he was a legitimate trader working for "Hatton and Cookson, Liverpool merchants trading at Ambriz."[52]

By late 1854 British and American warships observed the increased involvement in the slave trade by vessels based out of New York and Havana. On the way south the US warship *Marion* arrived at Loanda and fell in with the British warship *Philomel*. On 24 October, John M.D. Skene, commanding

---

[50]*Ibid.*, Mayo to [Secretary of the Navy], 22 August 1853; and CXI, Thomas Crabbe to Dobbin, 12 December 1855.

[51]Andrew D. Lambert, "The British Naval Strategic Revolution, 1815-1854," in Gordon Jackson and David M. Williams (eds.), *Shipping, Technology and Imperialism* (Aldershot, 1996), 156-160.

[52]Howard, *American Slavers and the Federal Law*, appendix A, 217; NA, RG 45, Squadron Letters, CX, African Squadron, Mayo to Dobbin, 10 November 1853; and *BPP*, 1854, LXXIII, 211, Correspondence with British Commissioners and Representatives from British Naval Forces on the Slave Trade (Class A), April 1853-March 1854, 211, No. 140, Bruce to Secretary of the Admiralty, 10 January 1854.

Philomel, reported to *Marion* the presence of two US-flagged ships in Loanda harbour. They were *Wild Pigeon* and *Oxford*, manned with foreign crews. The former, from New York, had arrived on 7 October with a consignment for a known slave trader, Francisco Antonio Flores, whom the British had asked locals to expel. *Oxford* was from New London; when one of Skene's officers boarded it off St. Helena, he found it "partly equipped for the slave trade[.]" Skene provided intelligence about the vessels to *Marion* so that its commander could take the necessary steps to stop the abuse of the American flag.[53]

Conditioned by a fear of increased British control over the region, the Americans eyed British actions with suspicion. Commander H.Y. Purviance told Mayo that he had met with Skene to discuss the matter and then sent one of his men to inspect the vessels, but he found no cause to detain them. Instead, Purviance remarked that "I am perfectly satisfied myself that both vessels were engaged in lawful trade." He took the word of *Oxford*'s master that the extra water casks were to transport palm oil and whiskey. The American officers concluded that the British must simply have concluded that *Oxford* was involved in the slave trade purely because it was an American ship.[54] Regardless of the outcome, it was clear that over this period the British believed that American involvement in the slave trade was increasing. The mutual scepticism kept Anglo-American relations cool.

Commodore Crabbe, who relieved Mayo in 1855, was the last US West African commodore before the next Anglo-American crisis developed. During his tenure, the squadron focused on commerce and colonial protection. But he was reluctant to undertake slave-trade suppression and quickly asked to be relieved of command. During a cruise down the African coast to Whydah and Princes Island from December 1855 to early January 1856, Crabbe observed no slavers, even in the notorious Whydah and Bight of Benin.[55] Nevertheless, he observed changes in British deployment, and by February 1857 he

---

[53]NA, RG 45, Squadron Letters, CX, African Squadron, H.Y. Purviance to Mayo, 30 November 1854; Mayo to Dobbin, 7 February 1855; and John M.D. Skene to Commander of United States Corvette *Marion*, 24 October 1854, enclosure in Mayo to Dobbin, 7 February 1855.

[54]*Ibid.*, Purviance to Mayo, 30 November 1854, enclosure in Mayo to Dobbin, 7 February 1855.

[55]*H.R. Doc.*, No. 104, 35th Cong., 2nd sess., 16-20, Dobbin to Crabbe, 17 April 1855; NA, RG 45, Secretary of the Navy Confidential Letters, 1 February 1853-17 October 1857, Dobbin to Crabbe (Confidential), 3 April 1855; Squadron Letters, CXI, African Squadron, Crabbe to Dobbin, 18 April, 8 June, 9 and 26 July, 7 August and 2 October (with Secretary's handwritten notation of 30 October) 1855 and 21 January and 25 February 1856.

made a startling discovery: the slave trade was continuing in a conspiracy centred on Havana and managed from New York.

During the investigation into the suspicious *Flying Eagle*, Crabbe discovered papers that seemed to show that there was indeed a conspiracy "carried on to some extent by an organised company" of New York and Havana residents. For example, the brig *P. Soule* delivered 479 slaves from the Benguela coast to Havana in February 1856. Crabbe concluded that American-flagged vessels involved in the slave trade were Portuguese owned, sailed from New York, manned largely by foreigners and covered by dubious American citizenship papers. Further, in mid-1856 Crabbe noted that within one week thirteen British warships had passed through the area "bound for the West Indies."[56] Unbeknownst to Crabbe, London had dispatched the British warships to the West Indies because of the activities of private citizens waging private wars in the Gulf and Central America. It was only a matter of time before more complaints arrived from US-flagged vessels of British "interference" in more sensitive American home waters.

Conclusion

The USN focused on commerce protection and promotion along the West African coast. Slave-trade suppression was a separate issue that rarely entered into the equation. The Mexican War, legal restraints and the squadron's primary duty curtailed slaver seizures. Instead, it collected commercial intelligence and retaliated against attacks on Americans. Because of the lack of support at home, only zealous officers, like Andrew Hull Foote, pursued slave-trade suppression with any vigour. But American officers also watched British advances, caused by the unified nature of British strategy, with suspicion. In turn, Britons looked upon American inaction with dismay. Consequently, the separate goals, strategy and tactics of the RN and USN threatened Anglo-American harmony as each questioned the other's sincerity. Yet rather than go to war, their shared belief that sea power could be used to further long-term objectives "peacefully" – at least with other nations – provided a mechanism through which they could relate. They maintained their commitments to their own interests, cooperated when goals overlapped and modified their use of sea power when they did not. In this way, sea power allowed the Anglo-American relationship to be dynamic even when their interests clashed.

---

[56]NA, RG 45, Squadron Letters, CXI, African Squadron, Crabbe to Dobbin, 21 January and 30 June 1856 (with enclosure, J.H. Ward, "Memorandum of English Man of War Steamers...," 26 June 1856) and 14 February 1857.

Chapter 8
Conflict Avoidance in the Equatorial Atlantic

Britain and America deployed naval forces to the West African coast, but divergent policies often generated tension. Britain combined slave-trade suppression with economic and strategic policies, while the US kept slave-trade suppression and commerce protection separate. The contrasting polices led to conflict as continued US involvement in the slave trade threatened British goals, and Americans feared that London meant to dominate African trade. But the role of sea power in furthering long-term goals peacefully provided a mechanism through which Britain and the US could prevent tensions from going too far. In short, sea power provided a safety valve that they adjusted to preserve relations, the balance of power and commercial endeavours.

Several interrelated cases in the equatorial Atlantic illustrate how Britain and America dissipated tension by controlling their use of sea power. To reduce the chances of conflict, they focused most of their slave-trade suppression on the West African coast, away from sensitive commercial traffic in the western equatorial Atlantic. They tried to cooperate by sharing intelligence rather than by undertaking questionable searches of vessels flying dubious flags. Moreover, when conflict arose, both remained calm and censured overzealous naval officers. Such sensitivity was particularly important in the western equatorial Atlantic, where US interests in connecting its east and west coasts through the Central American isthmus were paramount.

Close to home waters Americans saw little difference in the Royal Navy (RN) searching US-flagged ships for slavers or filibusters, private citizens waging an expansive war against Cuba and Central America. Rather than risk war, London acquiesced to American sensitivities and modified its naval policy accordingly. Rather than continue forceful actions against the slave trade that might drive places like Cuba into US hands, the RN patrolled for filibusters, while Britain reined in naval officers and disavowed the forceful actions of British representatives. The government would not let Northern abolitionists drag the country into war over slave-trade suppression close to American waters. London showed restraint, while for the sake of peaceful coexistence Washington eventually condemned filibuster activities and dispatched the United States Navy (USN) to stop them. By 1859, under continued British and domestic pressure, the US deployed a steamer force to patrol Cuba for filibusters and slavers and to protect its interests; another force would do the same off West Africa.

Britain, America and Patrols from the Western Atlantic

The United States established its squadron for South America, the Brazil Squadron, in 1826 after the southern independence crisis waned. Like most US squadrons, it showed the flag rather than effectively policing the seas against non-state actors like slavers. During the 1820s, the squadron often only consisted of two or three ships, and twenty years passed before the force intercepted any slavers. Even then, it only seized six between 1845 and 1849. In the end, the Mexican War drained resources, and Washington remained wary of becoming embroiled in South American disputes like that which had occupied Sir Charles Hotham. The Brazil squadron only peaked briefly in 1858 at approximately twenty ships. In 1855 Paraguay fired at the US warship *Water Witch* while it conducted scientific research. By 1858 the frustrated Americans dispatched a commissioner, 2500 sailors and warships to "settle" outstanding issues between the countries. Paraguay capitulated, apologized for the attack and signed a commerce and friendship treaty. Soon thereafter, the USN's deployment to the region returned to normal levels. Consequently, the RN remained the most consistent presence in the region. RN deployment to the southeast coast of America averaged about ten ships during the 1850s, although the nearby North American and West Indies stations averaged sixteen vessels. Even so, London wanted peace, and the £10 million in investments in South America was an important consideration. London warned captains to be careful of taking sides in disputes, or using too much force, to allay fears that Britain sought to use naval power for commercial leverage. Gunboat diplomacy was rare, with the exceptions of the occupation of the Falkland Islands (1832) and Malvinas (1833). Instead, Britain used sea power to uphold gentlemanly ideals and to ensure that the new republics treated British merchants fairly, with the knowledge that doing otherwise was unwise.[1] Britain proceeded with caution, aware that it operated close to American interests.

Off Brazil, the RN had some success against the slave trade, stopping eleven slavers between December 1835 and April 1839. Nevertheless, the First Lord of the Admiralty, Lord Minto, reported to Parliament in 1838 that further efforts were futile without greater naval force or better anti-slave trade treaties. Thus, in 1845 Parliament gave the government the power to act against Brazil, which had "never lifted a finger to enforce her own laws against the slave trade[.]" Meanwhile, in Greece Don Pacifico had his house destroyed in an anti-Semitic attack in 1847 and claimed British citizenship; the RN blockaded

---

[1]Frederick Moore Binder, *James Buchanan and the American Empire* (Selensgrove, PA, 1994), 259-261; United States, *Annual Reports of the Secretary of the Navy* (Washington, DC, various years); Donald L. Canney, *Africa Squadron: The U.S. Navy and the Slave Trade, 1842-1861* (Washington, DC, 2006), 111-114 and 234; and Barry M. Gough, "Sea Power and South America: The 'Brazils' or South American Station of the Royal Navy 1808-1837," *American Neptune*, L, No. 1 (1990), 29-31.

Piraeus in retaliation in January 1850. Palmerston accepted French mediation rather than go to war, and the public supported his proclamation that the government would protect its subjects anywhere. Moreover, the Brazilian slave trade became a target. In June 1850 the RN entered Brazilian ports to seize suspected slavers. On 4 September the Brazilians capitulated and passed a law deeming the slave trade as piracy.[2] With the traffic to Brazil dramatically curtailed, Anglo-American maritime interaction focused farther north as American expansionists eyed Central America, and the Cuban slave trade increased.

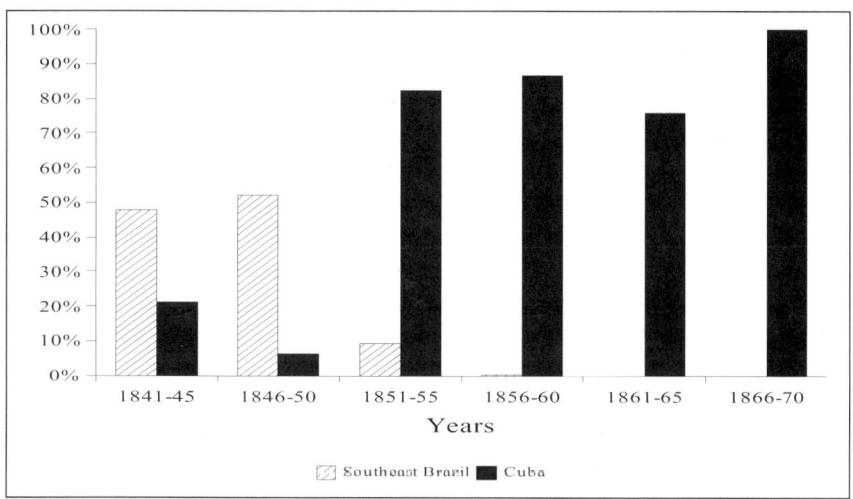

Figure 8.1: Relative Slave Destinations, Southeast Brazil and Cuba, 1841-1870

Note: Regions of little importance have been omitted

Source: Calculated from David Eltis, *et al.*, *The Trans-Atlantic Slave Trade: A Database on CD-ROM* (Cambridge, 1999).

---

[2]Leslie Bethell, *The Abolition of the Brazilian Slave Trade: Britain, Brazil and the Slave Trade Question 1807-1869* (Cambridge, 1970), 150, 242-266 and 327-363; Judd Scott Harmon, "Suppress and Protect: The United States Navy, The African Slave Trade, and Maritime Commerce, 1794-1862" (Unpublished PhD thesis, College of William and Mary, 1977), 145-155; W.E.F. Ward, *The Royal Navy and the Slavers: The Suppression of the Atlantic Slave Trade* (London, 1969), 165; Muriel E. Chamberlain, *Lord Palmerston* (Cardiff, 1987), 72-74; Herbert S. Klein, *The Atlantic Slave Trade* (Cambridge, 1999), 190; and Christopher Lloyd, *The Navy and the Slave Trade: The Suppression of the African Slave Trade in the Nineteenth Century* (London, 1949; reprint, London, 1968), 139-148.

After the abolition of West Indian slavery in the early 1830s, the region's economic importance began to decline. As Andrew Lambert noted, "the falling values of local produce were rapidly transforming it from an economic motor into a backwater." When Britain's reform of the sugar duties, West Indian bank failures and the abandoning of sugar plantations in the 1840s further weakened the region's economy, London "would do little to help, simply waiting for better times." But when Britain took a firm stand against Brazil, merchants feared the disruption of trade, and radicals like Cobden remained friendly with America. British free trade fuelled the demand for cheap Cuban sugar in the 1840s and increased the Cuban slave trade (see figure 8.1). But David Murray has shown that Britain was more cautious with its Cuban than its Brazilian strategy for fear that "British intervention in Cuba could lead to what no British government wanted – the American annexation of the island."[3]

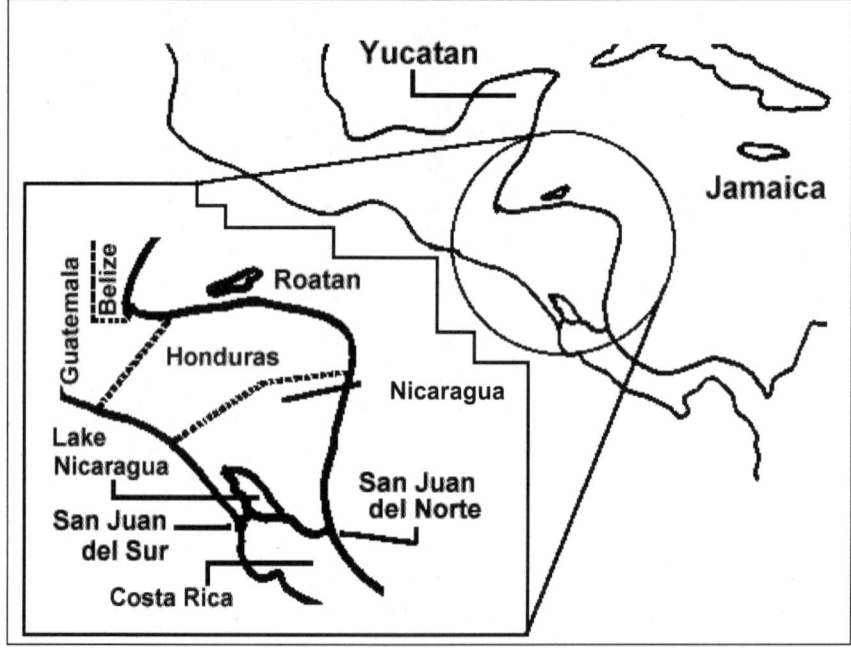

Figure 8.2:   Nicaraguan Isthmus

Note: Locations and boundaries are approximate

Source: Courtesy of the author.

---

[3]Andrew D. Lambert, *Trincomalee: The Last of Nelson's Frigates* (London, 2002), 48-49; and David R. Murray, *Odious Commerce: Britain, Spain and the Abolition of the Cuban Slave Trade* (Cambridge, 1980), 208.

The Monroe Doctrine proclaimed that the western Atlantic was American and that other states interfered at their peril. Regardless, after the 1820s piracy crisis, the Americans offered few objections to the presence of the RN or British settlements close to the US. As American strategic interests shifted to its west coast, interest in Central America grew as a potential transit point between the Atlantic and Pacific. This put the US in conflict with British holdings in the region. The British had several settlements in Central America, in particular the Mosquito Coast and Belize, both later significant because they commanded potential isthmian routes between the Atlantic and Pacific (see figure 8.2). Harry Allen concluded that many disputes were closer geographically to the US than to Britain and that from 1847 to 1861 Anglo-American tensions centred mainly on Central America and control of the isthmus.[4] But rather than go to war the two nations settled their differences in the Clayton-Bulwer Treaty (1850) whereby each party agreed not to colonize any transit zone; their navies patrolled the peace for those who might upset the deal.

London was concerned only if other nations threatened its sovereignty in the transit zone. In 1852, for example, Lord Granville, the Foreign Secretary, explained that the government wished to rid itself of its protectorate over Greytown on the Mosquito Coast. Moreover, he believed that "any new arrangement with respect to Greytown should be advantageous to the construction of the projected canal across Central America by way of Lake Nicaragua and the River S[an] Juan, favourable to the tranquility and prosperity of the countries adjacent" and agreeable to the desires of the US. Consequently, he explained that "[t]here is no reason why the two Gov[ernmen]ts...both being desirous to terminate a somewhat difficult affair in the best mode that offers, should not by their good understanding and efficient [cordial] cooperation, bring it to a prompt and satisfactory conclusion."[5]

In its relations with Central America, London took a pragmatic and liberal approach, hoping to secure unfettered access to any route from the Atlantic to Pacific. Therefore, Britain sought a negotiated settlement over the status of Belize, first with Spain, which had nominal sovereignty over the territory, and then with the new Central American states when they encroached on areas settled by Britons. When the US expressed concern because of the region's strategic importance, London proposed a peaceful resolution rather than going to war over a distant settlement. The US reciprocated; while it believed

---

[4]Mary Wilhelmine Williams, *Anglo-American Isthmian Diplomacy, 1815-1915* (Washington, DC, 1916; reprint, New York, 1965), 28-36; and Harry C. Allen, *Great Britain and the United States: A History of Anglo-American Relations (1783-1952)* (London, 1954), 49 and 422-436.

[5]Great Britain, National Archives (TNA/PRO) 30/29/20/11, 1st Earl Granville Papers – Mosquito Question (Granville Papers), Granville to Crompton, n.d. All the letters in this collection are from c. 1852.

that the area was important strategically, Washington also realized the commercial benefits of a peaceful resolution to disputes over access.

The main British settlement was Belize, originally settled by "freebooters" who preyed on Spanish trade. The nearby Mosquito Coast commanded the Atlantic side of the San Juan River that led inland to Lake Nicaragua. Britain gained control of Belize during European wars, but by the Treaty of Amiens (1802) it returned sovereignty to Spain; this was confirmed by the Treaty of Madrid (1814). But there were British settlers in Belize, and Spain failed to exercise governance, a weakness that increased after the Spanish-American revolutions. As a result, Britain exerted practical sovereignty, appointing superintendents accountable to the Governor of Jamaica, but it refrained from officially declaring it a colony. British loggers soon fanned out from the principal settlements into areas unpopulated but for natives.[6]

The *status quo* was satisfactory until Spain lost control of its colonies in the 1820s. The Central American states formed the short-lived United Provinces of Central America (1824), comprised of Costa Rica, El Salvador, Nicaragua, Honduras and Guatemala. The US soon settled its differences with Spain and recognized the new states. But Britain wavered and was unable to agree with Mexico about the status of Belize. Consequently, the 1826 Anglo-Mexican Treaty failed to define whether Spain, Britain or Mexico controlled the disputed region, and Britain continued its *de facto* administration.[7]

Britain on several occasions asked Spain to cede formal sovereignty over Belize. In 1835 the Spanish foreign minister, Martínez de la Rosa, agreed verbally to this proposal, but with continued political instability in Spain, talks stalled. Meanwhile, British settlers and business enterprises, such as the Eastern Coast of Central America Commercial and Agricultural Company based in London, received land grants from the Guatemalan government in the disputed border region. Nevertheless, the status of British Honduras – Belize – was left unresolved as the Central American nations continued to evolve.[8]

In 1841, Archibald Macdonald, the British Superintendent in Belize, went to the mouth of the San Juan River, raised the Mosquito flag and declared the Mosquito Coast a British protectorate with initial support from London. Macdonald knew the region's strategic importance. If another country possessed the Bay Islands, for example, it "would be a death blow to [the] Commerce of British Honduras" in the event of war. Meanwhile, the population grew from 10,000 in 1835 to 13,000 by the end of the decade. But in London Palmerston concluded that "the best thing to do was 'to let the Spaniards forget

---

[6]R.A. Humphreys, *The Diplomatic History of British Honduras, 1638-1901* (London, 1961), 10-17.

[7]*Ibid.*, 18-27.

[8]*Ibid.*, 38-46.

it.'" His successor, Aberdeen, took the same stand "out of respect for Spain."[9] It was a quiet policy as long as British interests were safe.

During the Crimean War, Washington expelled the British ambassador for recruiting in the US. Some of the British public called for retaliation, but Cabinet continued a conciliatory approach and the US envoy, George M. Dallas, stayed in London. Palmerston told Parliament in 1856 that adopting a bellicose attitude toward the US was no way to "persuade the American people to cultivate the most friendly relations with England[.]" Cabinet even ordered "the naval commander in Central American waters...to avoid anything that might be construed as provocation." Palmerston continued this policy despite some concerns about the US: slavery still offended him, and even in 1855 he speculated that Britain could defeat the US. But E.D. Steele has argued that the realization that there was little support in Britain for war with America countered Palmerston's bravado. As a result, Britain adopted a realistic policy that led to "acquiescence in the American demand that Britain should retire from her Central American territories with the exception of British Honduras."[10]

After the Crimean War, Britain was wary of another conflict, newspapers urged peace and Palmerston felt that Britain and the US had "too many interests in common" to go to war. He felt safe complaining to France and the US about differing interests because strong commercial ties would help prevent conflict. He "insisted that Britain should practice an assertive diplomacy while reflecting that for good reasons it would not lead to war with her main rivals." Palmerston wanted to protect British interests in the West Indies, but issues removed from sensitive holdings were less important to the public. For example, when another dispute loomed over islands off the coast of British Columbia in the Pacific Northwest, the Duke of Argyll told Russell in December 1859 that the public would not support the government in a conflict over "a matter which concerns them so remotely." Therefore, Britain decided to withdraw from its Central American possessions away from the disputed isthmus, although Colonial Secretary Newcastle protested on behalf of the British inhabitants.[11]

---

[9]Williams, *Isthmian Diplomacy*, 2-25 and 37-42; TNA/PRO, Admiralty (ADM) 128/34, 169-170 and 283-291, George Grey to John Barrow, 6 August 1835; John Russell, 3 April 1841, Archibald MacDonald to Russell, January 1841; and Humphreys, *British Honduras*, 43-46.

[10]Palmerston, quoted in Evelyn Ashley, *The Life and Correspondence of Henry John Temple Viscount Palmerston* (2 vols., London, 1879), II, 336-337; and E.D. Steele, *Palmerston and Liberalism, 1855-1865* (Cambridge, 1991), 56-57.

[11]Williams, *Isthmian Diplomacy*, 212-223 and 227-266; Steele, *Palmerston and Liberalism*, 246; and TNA/PRO 30/22/25, Russell Papers (RP), Argyll to Russell, 19 and 21 December 1859, as quoted in Steele, *Palmerston and Liberalism*, 294.

In contrast, while the era began with American maritime interests focused on foreign trade, coastal trade was growing in importance. With the close of the Mexican War, American shipping, naval interests and sensitivity to Central America increased. The 1850s were marked by a significant shift in America's strategic outlook. Southern expansionists believed that the Gulf of Mexico and Central America offered new lands where the slave South could expand. The Senate Committee on Foreign Relations advocated American annexation of the Yucatan, and Ambassador James Buchanan called for the US to possess Cuba to counter British commercial influence. Finally, the thought of a lucrative transportation route to the newly acquired Pacific coast attracted US investors and shipping magnates like Cornelius Vanderbilt to the isthmus.[12]

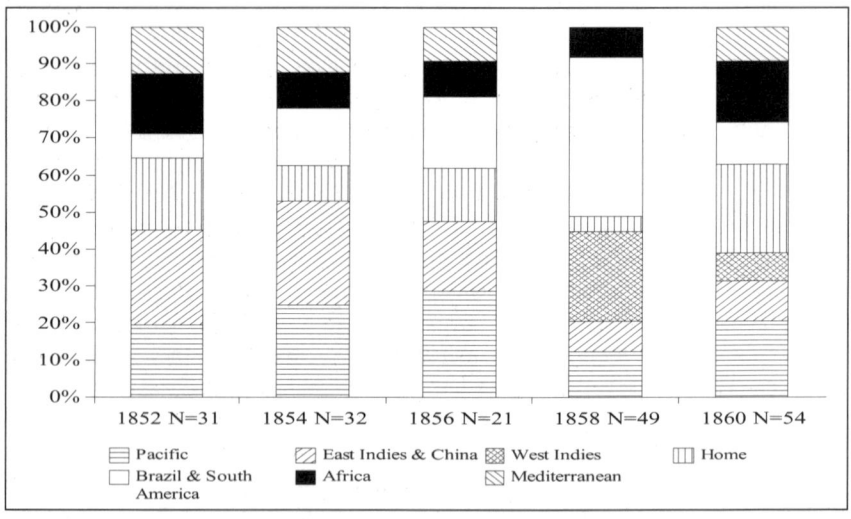

Figure 8.3:   US Navy Vessel Deployment, 1852-1860

Note: N = Number of Warships.

Source: Calculated from United States, *Annual Reports of the Secretary of the Navy* (Washington, DC, 1842-1860).

US naval deployment reflected this shift in American maritime focus. Figure 8.3 reveals that during the 1850s the western equatorial Atlantic and the Pacific were the sites of between seventy and ninety percent of total American naval deployment. In contrast with the African coast, Congress supported this strategic shift and authorized the USN and the postal service to contract private

---

[12]Charles H. Brown, *Agents of Manifest Destiny: The Lives and Times of the Filibusters* (Chapel Hill, NC, 1980), 5-6, 16-18 and 29-39.

companies to service Oregon. The rise in traffic between the east and west coasts of America epitomized shifting US interest. Gold shipments from the Pacific to the east coast, for example, rose from $4,140,200 in 1849 to a staggering $40,233,915 by 1852, dwarfing the value of American trade with Africa.[13] US interests in the region were growing, while London wished to avoid frivolous conflicts over distant holdings. Consequently, the nations resolved their disputes rather than go to war and modified their use of sea power to relieve the tensions that had accumulated between them.

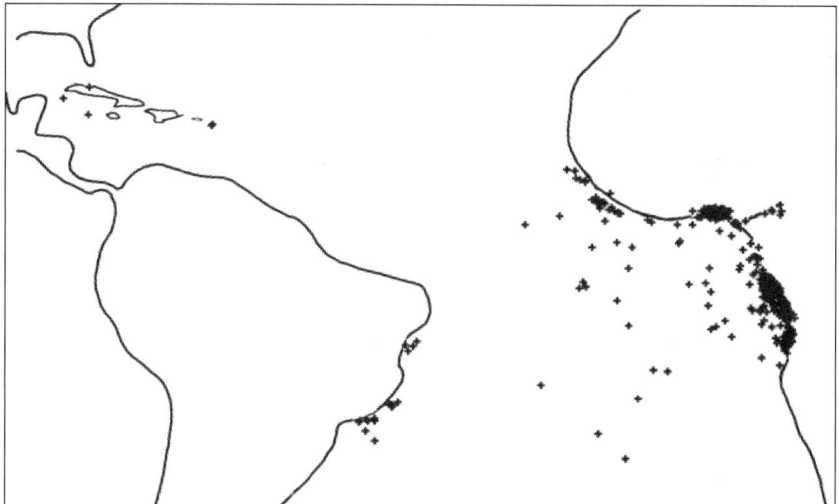

Figure 8.4:   Royal Navy Slaver Seizures, 1840-1848 and 1855-1864

Note: + denotes approximate location of seizures for which head money was awarded; only those for which location was given (481 of 794) included.

Source: Calculated from Great Britain, Parliament, *Parliamentary Papers* (*BPP*), 1850, LV, 89-108, Slave Vessels Captured and Number of Slaves Taken; 1861, LXIV, 359-361, Return of Slave Vessels Captured by H.M. Ships of War, 1855-1859; and 1865, LVI, 537-530, Return of Slave Vessels Captured by H.M. Ships of War, 1860-1864.

Britain and America believed in the freedom of commerce in the western equatorial Atlantic and focused most of their use of sea power along the West African coast during the dispute over slave-trade suppression. In 1850 the Admiralty asked its officers for their opinions on the best strategy to end the slave trade. Charles Hotham, for example, articulately phrased the reason for general British strategy to Sir Francis Thornhill Baring, First Lord

---

[13]*Ibid.*, 224.

of the Admiralty and nominal head of the Baring family. Hotham argued that on the Brazilian side, for instance, it would be difficult to stop a "slaver amongst a herd of [merchant] vessels[.]" Moreover, with the Americans protesting against strong British actions, the RN was afraid of sparking a diplomatic incident close to American interests. Historians like Christopher Lloyd have agreed that the British focused mainly on West Africa using Denman's strategy of close blockade. And David Eltis found the navy was successful in stopping eighty-five percent of slavers off the African coast.[14] Meanwhile, a plot of RN seizures of slavers provides further evidence of this focus (see figure 8.4).

Facing similar problems, the USN reached the same conclusion. The threat to business was clear if sea power was applied too forcefully. Andrew Hull Foote, for instance, told the American Colonization Society (ACS) that if patrols were carried out only on the American side of the Atlantic, slavers would scatter after departing from Africa and be hard to find. The US also had difficulty differentiating slavers and legitimate traders on its side of the Atlantic. For example, in November 1858 Judge Alexander G. Magrath declared that in such cases he was unable to differentiate legal and illegal cargo.[15] Deployment in the western Atlantic would hurt trade, prolong the suffering of the slaves and jeopardize international relations. Furthermore, as the region close to home became more important strategically for the US, Washington became more sensitive to British activities in Central America.

The US meant the deployment of a larger USN force in the late 1850s to maintain the uneasy Anglo-American peace over the isthmus and slave-trade suppression. The American force was divided into two theatres: the western Atlantic, covering the Gulf of Mexico and the Central American coast, and the West African coast. It was to protect American commerce from undue harassment by the RN and to intercept American filibusters which London believed were a prelude to wider American territorial expansion. Still, Americans saw no difference between stopping US-flagged ships or filibusters, but for the sake of good relations London accepted the US position on Central America. From 1857 London realized that the US was sensitive about the region and that it

---

[14]Philip Ziegler, *The Sixth Great Power: A History of One of the Greatest of All Banking Families, the House of Barings, 1762-1929* (New York, 1988), 158-159; TNA/PRO, ADM 123/173, "Reports from Various Officers as to the Best Means to be Adopted for the Abolition of the African Slave Trade, 1850;" Charles Hotham to Sir Francis Baring, March 1850; Lloyd, *Navy and the Slave Trade*, 165; and David Eltis, *Economic Growth and the Ending of the Transatlantic Slave Trade* (New York, 1987), 100-101.

[15]Andrew H. Foote, *The African Squadron: Ashburton Treaty, Consular Sea Letters* (Philadelphia, 1855), 13; and Warren S. Howard, *American Slavers and the Federal Law* (Berkeley, 1963), 95-100.

interfered at its peril. Naval deployment in West Africa thus suited the goals of both countries. Policing from the African side concentrated the RN and prevented interference with legitimate Atlantic trade that could spark conflict with the US. Focused largely on the West African coast, Washington and London sought to defuse potential conflicts. Both governments preferred squadron commodores who took a calm approach and reprimanded officers who threatened Anglo-American relations.

British Conflict-Resolution Strategy

Off West Africa, Britain sought to avoid conflict with the USN to preserve Anglo-American relations and prevent an Atlantic-wide war. This objective was clear soon after the US established its permanent West African squadron. On 12 December 1843 the Admiralty wrote its squadron about the 1842 treaty and provided guidelines. The squadrons were to share intelligence and join each other when they stopped vessels of any flag. But if a suspicious vessel flew the American flag, even if it carried slaves, the Admiralty only allowed the RN to act in conjunction with the USN. If a ship was American, the squadron was to report the incident to London immediately.[16] The goal of the treaty was to preserve Anglo-American relations through protocols that governed the use of sea power.

The maturation of Britain's conflict-avoidance strategy, as applied to naval relations, was illustrated best during the command of Sir Charles Hotham between 1846 and 1849. Selected because of his diplomatic reputation, Hotham told Lord Auckland that "an angry shot or a blow here may in spite of both governments [French and British] bring us into war." Therefore, he would not provoke the French "consciously" but would "do my duty, giving praise where it is due, & throwing blame on the shoulders of those [British officers] who merit it." Hotham also hoped to placate other countries to reduce tension and told his officers that if any nation objected to British searches, they were to deny any deliberate interference in trade.[17]

---

[16]United States, Congress, *U.S. Serial Set*. LXXIII, 35th Cong., 2nd sess., House of Representatives, Document 104, 22-24, G. Cockburn and W.H. Gage to John Foote, 12 December 1843. Hereafter, the *U.S. Serial Set* will be cited according to the recommended Library of Congress style, for example, *H.R. Doc.*, No. 104, 35th Cong., 2nd sess.

[17]University of Hull (UH), Brymor Jones Library (BJL), Archives and Special Collections (A&SC), DDHO 10/8, Sir Charles Hotham, Letter Books (Hotham Letter Books), Hotham to Auckland, 25 September 1847; and DDHO 10/11, Sir Charles Hotham (Hotham Secret Letter Book), Hotham to Commander Moneypenney, 26 August 1848.

Auckland confirmed that Hotham was "right in repressing your officers in the instances in which they have committed acts of haste and indiscre-
tion[.]" The RN was to carry out its duties but reprimand officers who threatened diplomatic relations. Hotham confided to Commander Dunlop that the
goal was to remain at peace with all its "allies" while the RN carried out its
tasks. Hotham warned that "[i]f they [any country] have violated any treaty
then it becomes an affair between the two govt & with which we as naval officers have no concern." The British applied this concept to Anglo-American
relations on both sides of the Atlantic, and the Americans reciprocated. The
upheavals of 1848 in Europe, for example, led Lord Dundas to fear a general
war. He warned that "we may keep out of it," but "when ever [sic] a shot is
fired – we ought to be well prepared – on both sides of the Atlantic[.]"[18]

Anglo-American Cooperation off West Africa, 1840s and 1850s

Britain defined its strategy, applied it to Anglo-American relations and hoped
for cooperation from the US. Both nations believed that sea power could further long-term goals but used their navies differently, which limited cooperative efforts. The USN protected American interests off West Africa, while the
RN combined slave-trade suppression and commercial objectives with actions
to counter the French. The effect of the difference was clear to Perry, who
told RN Commodore John Foote on 20 May 1844 that because his squadron
was small, had other duties and was responsible for a wide area, joint cruising
would be "less effective than might be desired[.]"[19]

Four of the Perry brothers had fought in the War of 1812, and Matthew Perry still eyed the British with suspicion. He expressed his suspicions in
a private memorandum to the Secretary of the Navy in May 1844. Perry was
wary of Britain's continued desire for a mutual right of search and believed
that the British hid their true motives under claims about slave-trade suppression. Still, he lived up to his reputation for thoughtfulness and told the Secretary that since he might have misjudged the British, his comments should re-

---

[18]*Ibid.*, DDHO 10/2, Sir Charles Hotham, Letters from Lord Auckland,
Auckland to Hotham, 20 December 1847; DDHO 10/11, Hotham Secret Letter Book,
Hotham to Dunlop, 28 May 1848; and DDHO 10/3, Sir Charles Hotham, Letters from
Lord Dundas, Dundas to Hotham, 31 October 1848.

[19]United States, National Archives (NA), Record Group (RG) 45, Squadron
Letters, CV, African Squadron, Matthew C. Perry to Foote, 20 May 1844; and *H.R.
Doc.*, No. 104, 35th Cong., 2nd sess., 21, Perry to Secretary of the Navy, 21 May
1844.

main confidential.[20] Despite allegations of unwarranted British interference with US shipping, he developed a working relationship with his British counterparts. Nevertheless, British and American vessels rarely cruised together, and "cooperation" was mostly restricted to sharing intelligence.

The rules for the use of sea power were most successful when American and British vessels cruised in tandem. The joint patrols south of the equator in 1850, for example, were the first since the Tucker-Paine agreement. *Perry* cruised with *Cyclops* off Ambriz in April and May 1850, with little tactical result. Later, *John Adams*, cruising with *Cyclops*, captured the American slaver *Excellent*. Arthur Fanshawe called this the "first fruit of our renewed co-operation[.]"[21] But in the absence of joint cruising, the treaty provided an incentive for the British to find a US warship to handle a suspect vessel rather than board it and sour diplomatic relations.

In a speech to the ACS, Andrew Hull Foote concluded that without the Webster-Ashburton Treaty, "British officers would not have gone in search of an American cruiser to report" suspected slavers. In August 1844, for example, when John Foote told Perry that he suspected that the American vessel *Imogene* was a slaver, the American thought it prudent to investigate.[22] It is clear that the most important dynamic of the Anglo-American relationship along the West African coast was conflict and its resolution. Up and down the "chain of command," at the naval and political levels, Britons and Americans worked to mitigate their disputes over the application of sea power rather than further threaten Anglo-American relations.

Anglo-American Conflict in West Africa, 1840s and 1850s

Historians like Robert L. Robinson have concluded that by the end of Perry's tenure the British were little threat to the US. But Perry's successor, Charles Skinner, believed that on the West African coast "we most frequently come in contact with our great commercial rival; here, under the pretext of ascertaining nationality, our vessels are liable to be boarded[.]"Americans became increas-

---

[20]John H. Schroeder, *Matthew Calbraith Perry: Antebellum Sailor and Diplomat* (Annapolis, 2001), 116; and NA, RG 45, Perry Letter Books, Perry to Secretary of the Navy, 21 May 1844.

[21]Andrew H. Foote, *Africa and the American Flag* (New York, 1854), 273-278 and 311-318; and NA, RG 45, Squadron Letters, CVIII, African Squadron, Arthur Fanshawe to Francis H. Gregory, 17 May 1850.

[22]Foote, *African Squadron*, 5-6; Foote, *Africa and the American Flag*, 301-323; NA, RG 45, Squadron Letters, CVIII, African Squadron, Foote to Gregory, 14 September 1850; CV, African Squadron, Perry to John Young Mason, 28 November 1844, with enclosures A and B.

ingly wary of British dominance on the coast. British treaty-making efforts, ostensibly to establish free trade, suppress the slave trade and counter French moves, drew American attention. The US believed that other powers, especially Britain, sought to carve up the African coast for their exclusive domain. Perry, for instance, believed that only with diligence would the local people accept American goods, like cotton cloth. He worried that the British enjoyed a monopoly under the RN's protection and that the Americans "enjoy but a share of what is left[.]" Perry, as Hotham later concluded, also believed that the French were attempting to establish outposts along the coast to annoy "the numerous American and English Merchant vessels that are constantly traversing the Northern and Southern Atlantic" in the event of war.[23] But the British counter-plan to French actions raised equal concern in American eyes.

Americans eyed the treaty-making commander Alexander Murray with suspicion when in 1847 he and Governor Joseph Roberts of Liberia discussed British recognition of the colony's independence. The Americans were also suspicious when Murray arrived at Cape Palmas, near another American settlement, and "engaged in making treaties with the native chiefs who owned the territory contiguous to the settlements in Liberia."[24] A protectionist outlook coloured American naval reaction to the British, and the US did not take the time to comprehend their true intentions. British actions in stopping American-flagged vessels and its economic policy contributed to the tension. Within this dynamic, however, several incidents showed that the nations, and their naval officers, sought to prevent relations from degenerating.

In early 1844, for example, the British stopped the American-flagged *Roderick Dhu* on suspicion of slaving. Perry exclaimed that HMS *Spy* had passed *Roderick Dhu* at a "cable's length" and must have seen that it was a legitimate trader. He told John Foote that it was unjust for the British to stop US-flagged vessels in international waters. He also reminded Foote that Britons were involved in the slave trade and that British goods found their way into the slave-trade cycle. Regardless, his biographer, John H. Schroeder, concluded that Perry "refused to let these exchanges escalate," passed reports of problems with the British to Washington and "let the matter stand." Perry

---

[23]Robert L. Robinson, "Commodore Matthew C. Perry and the Protection of American Rights in West Africa, 1843-1845," *Southern Quarterly*, V, No. 1 (1966), 63; NA, RG 45, Squadron Letters, CVI, African Squadron, No. 44, Charles W. Skinner to George Bancroft, 15 December 1845; Perry Letter Books, Perry to David Henshaw, 29 January 1844; and Perry, "Memorandum 'AA' to accompany communication No. 76 to Navy Department," 18 November 1844.

[24]*Ibid.*, Squadron Letters, LXXXII (pt.), African Squadron, George C. Read to Mason, 11 December 1846; Alexander Murray to Joseph Roberts, 8 December 1846; Roberts to Murray, 10 December 1846, enclosures in Read to Mason, 11 December 1846; and Read to Mason, 12 May 1847.

moderated his views and confessed that Americans often sold ships into the slave trade and admitted that convicting them was difficult.[25]

Foote also tempered his squadron's use of sea power and told Perry that rather than board several suspected US-flagged slavers, like the barque *Eleanor*, he reported them to the Americans. Perry and Foote seemed to respond to each other's desire for a cordial relationship. Perry told Foote that he believed that both governments were sincere in their goals. He trusted that the officers of both nations would behave as their governments had instructed while "being careful not to interfere with the duties of each other." Perry thanked Foote for the polite manner in which the RN officer had supplied information and wished him the best on his return to England.[26]

At the political level, both nations used their officers as "scapegoats" to calm diplomatic relations. From the British perspective, if the Americans made serious objections, London investigated and punished. Washington also reprimanded officers whom they believed threatened Anglo-American relations. Captain P.C. Dumas of the merchant ship *Cyrus*, for example, told the Secretary of the Navy that during a voyage to Cabinda in June 1844 HMS *Alert* treated his vessel like a pirate ship. A crew boarded without uniform under British officer C.J. Bosanquet, took the ship's papers and refused to return them. Perry concluded that if someone had sold *Cyrus* into the slave trade, Bosanquet's actions were justified. While Aberdeen supported the officer, he told McLane that Bosanquet was overzealous and disciplined him. Aberdeen hoped that the Americans would pursue the complaint no further.[27]

The decade closed along the West African coast with continued American objections to overzealous British officers. In late 1858 London again reprimanded officers for the sake of Anglo-American relations. In September, for instance, the Admiralty ordered *Alecto* home after it seized the American-flagged vessel *Caroline*, although London defended the actions of its officers against what they believed to be a slaver. In 1859 the Americans accused the RN of telling US vessels that if they kept flying the American flag, the RN

---

[25]Schroeder, *Matthew Calbraith Perry*, 118-119; and NA, RG 45, Perry Letter Books, Perry to Foote, 4 March 1844.

[26]NA, RG 45, Perry Letter Books, Perry to Foote, 4 March 1844.

[27]*Ibid.*, Perry to William Jones, 6 January 1845; Great Britain, Parliament, *Parliamentary Papers (BPP)*, 1846, L, Correspondence with British Commissioners and Representatives from British Vice-Admiralty Courts and Naval Officers on the Slave Trade (Class A), 1845, 129-130, enclosure 209 in No. 9, P.C. Dumas to Secretary of the Navy, 15 August 1845 [misdated, actually 15 August 1844] and 140-141, enclosure 233 in No. 9, C.J. Bosanquet to Jones, 12 May 1845; and NA, RG 59, Dispatches, Britain, No. 5, Aberdeen to Louis McLane, 15 September 1845, enclosure in McLane to James Buchanan, 18 September 1845.

would send them to the US where authorities would try them as pirates and execute them. London doubted the claim, but to appease the Americans the Under-Secretary of State for Foreign Affairs, Seymore Fitzgerald, told the Admiralty about them. The Admiralty warned its officers to make no such threats against US vessels or destroy evidence. It instructed Rear Admiral Frederick William Grey to "warn the officers under your command to guard against any just cause of complaint being given to the Government of the United States[.]"[28]

The US exerted similar restraint over its officers. In early 1846, for example, British officers accused the Americans of not patrolling certain regions, like Cabinda. Lord Aberdeen thus asked the British Ambassador to Washington, Richard Pakenham, to communicate the details to the US government. Late in 1845 Commodore Skinner, upset at criticisms from British officers, declared that *Yorktown* had recently sailed for the region, "is probably there now," and had come "to protect the American flag from violation." Aghast at what he felt was British intransigence, such as the continued forcefulness of Commander Bosanquet, Skinner warned that any foreign warship that visited American-flagged vessels did so at its peril. In response, Commodore Jones of the RN replied that he was following orders, but "lament[ed] the disagreement[s] which exist between us." Still, he assured Skinner that the British tried to operate with restraint. He offered "a final assurance, that among the orders which I have received from my Superiors, none have been more stringent and imperative than those in relation to the rights of those Foreign Vessels which sail under the Flags of Powers which have not conceded to us the right of mutual search." Furthermore, Jones pledged that "my attention has been very especially directed to the Vessels of the United States of America." Nevertheless, he felt that Skinner's remarks were unjustified. In turn, Pakenham duly communicated Skinner's comments and Jones' response to Washington, where Secretary of the Navy Mason also wanted good Anglo-American relations maintained. He confided to Commodore Read, Skinner's replacement, that the British Ambassador to Washington and Lord Palmerston were concerned about Skinner's belligerent comment that further British action "may interrupt the harmony which happily exists between our respective Governments." Mason impressed on Read that "care must be taken to give no just cause for" complaint by London.[29]

---

[28]TNA/PRO, ADM 123/164, Frederick W. Grey to Secretary of the Admiralty, 13 November 1858; Seymore Fitzgerald to Secretary of the Admiralty, 30 April 1859; and Admiralty to Grey, 4 May 1859.

[29]*BPP*, 1847, LXVI, Correspondence with Foreign Powers Not Parties to Treaties or Conventions Giving Mutual Right of Search of Vessels Suspected of the Slave Trade (Class D), 1846, 555-556, No. 77, Aberdeen to Richard Pakenham, 3 April 1846; NA, RG 59, Notes from the British Legation in the US to the Department

On the West African coast Britain and the US shared intelligence and sometimes cooperated. For the sake of Anglo-American relations they worked to contain potential conflicts and reduce tensions so that each nation's objectives could be met. Officers with reputations for calm and reasoned decision-making were called upon, while those who threatened the peace were reprimanded. The use of sea power was a safety valve through which Anglo-American disputes could be contained. On the western side of the Atlantic, where the consequences of conflict had broader ramifications because of the closeness of sensitive American home waters, naval relations also provided a release mechanism to reduce tensions when Anglo-American interests clashed.

Anglo-American Relations and Central America

Despite British influence over Belize and Superintendent Macdonald's activities, Washington remained unconcerned until Britain pursued Texas in its war against the slave trade and when tensions between Mexico and the US degenerated into war. On 18 October 1840 Palmerston told General Hamilton of Texas that Britain would recognize its independence if it entered into an agreement with the British for slave-trade suppression. But Palmerston's efforts proved futile, and the US "annexed" Texas in 1845. In December 1845 President James K. Polk warned European powers that an attempt at a "balance of power" strategy within North America was unacceptable. Fearing British influence in the region, New Granada (Colombia) and the US signed a treaty in 1846 giving the Americans the non-exclusive right to the Panama isthmus for lawful commerce.[30] The region was in turmoil in the wake of the collapse of the United Provinces. Soon, private American citizens, known as filibusters, intervened in the wars. With new American interest in the region, London realized that it had to settle outstanding issues with the US.

Palmerston, again in the Foreign Office, saw in 1846 the ramifications of the American acquisition of California. In response, he extended the

---

of State, 1791-1906, XXIII, 30 April 1845-16 December 1846, Pakenham to Buchanan, 25 April 1846, with enclosures Skinner to Jones, 4 November 1845 and Jones to Skinner, 25 December 1845; and RG 45, Secretary of the Navy Confidential Letters, 12 September 1843-28 February 1849, Mason to Read, 16 November 1846.

[30]*BPP*, 1841, XXX, sess. 1, Correspondence with Foreign Powers Not Parties to Conventions Giving Mutual Right of Search of Vessels Suspected of the Slave Trade (Class D), 1840, 802-803, No. 82, Palmerston to General Hamilton, 18 October 1840; Humphreys, *British Honduras*, 52; United States, *Congressional Globe*, 29th Cong., 1st sess., appendix, 1-8, James K. Polk, "Message of the President of the United States," 2 December 1845; Williams, *Isthmian Diplomacy*, 45-46 and 53-54; and Samuel Flagg Bemis, *A Diplomatic History of the United States* (New York, 1936; 5th ed., New York, 1965), 244-246.

boundaries of British territory in Central America to control the San Juan River and the potential transit route. The British, using a force of Mosquitans, took control of San Juan del Norte in 1848 and renamed it Greytown. The Americans failed to do anything overt to stop this but signed a treaty with Nicaragua giving the US the exclusive right to build a canal through its territory. The British responded by signing a similar pact with Costa Rica for the potential Greytown Atlantic terminus. But when the British negotiator convinced an RN officer to seize Tigre Island on the Pacific Coast and run up the British flag, Palmerston disavowed the action.[31] Central America was becoming part of a diplomatic chess game that threatened Anglo-American relations.

Palmerston told US envoy George Bancroft, former Secretary of the Navy, that Britain had no desire to exploit its Central American possessions; it had enough colonies, and Britain and the US had common interests in the region. Bancroft remained wary, and Palmerston was suspicious of American talk of Manifest Destiny. He agreed to the seizure of San Juan simply to keep the Americans from securing a monopoly on a transit route. But *The Times* advised a peaceful settlement between all parties. Kenneth Bourne has surmised that Palmerston knew he had to modify British strategy toward America because of the nation's growth from the Atlantic to the Pacific. Bourne concluded that "the best Britain could now do was very cautiously to contain the expansion of the United States into Central America and the Caribbean." The resulting compromise to allow the US into the region was the Clayton-Bulwer Treaty (1850). London sent Sir Henry Bulwer, a "friend and protégé of Palmerston's[,]" to Washington to negotiate the agreement.[32]

The free-and-open access philosophy to any isthmian transit route was similar to, and consistent with, Britain's West African policy. Rather than precipitate war, Britain sought equal access under the protection of naval power. The Clayton-Bulwer Treaty stated that neither nation would control, fortify or establish colonies on the isthmus. Secretary of State John M. Clayton and Sir Henry negotiated in a tense atmosphere because the Americans were still concerned about Britain's Central American possessions. After both nations signed the treaty, London's problem was how to implement it while private American expansionists still roamed the isthmus. If the US continued actively to pursue control over Central America in violation of the new treaty, it was difficult for Britain to abandon its settlements. This led to a slow series of negotiations with

---

[31]Williams, *Isthmian Diplomacy*, 51; and Bemis, *Diplomatic History of the United States*, 247-250.

[32]Williams, *Isthmian Diplomacy*, 68-74 and 80-109; and Kenneth Bourne, *The Foreign Policy of Victorian England, 1830-1902* (Oxford, 1970), 56-60.

Central American states to protect British rights while London transferred locations like the Mosquito Coast and Bay Islands to local sovereignty.[33]

The Filibusters

During the late 1840s American commercial, territorial and strategic interests focused on the North American continent, making the US more sensitive to events close to home. Many Americans coveted Cuba as a potential slave state, while the new Central and South American nations were weak and susceptible to industrialists and filibusters who advocated the "Manifest Destiny" of American hegemony. Filibusters were Spanish-American nationalists and American expansionists who led private military expeditions against other nations, usually in Central and South America, using the US as a base.[34] America's interests in Central America are significant because they reveal the strategic importance that Americans placed on the region.

Such interests put them in direct opposition to historical British concerns. Consequently, London feared that the filibuster expeditions were preludes to American annexation of strategically important islands, like Cuba, while the slave trade that continued from the island thwarted wider British economic goals. Nevertheless, the British believed that forceful action would simply drive Cuba into American hands. Regions farther south in Central America were far from the public's interest, so London was wary of provoking a conflict over them and sought to pacify the US. Eventually, the Americans reciprocated, and the USN and RN, while maintaining a careful watch on each other, patrolled for filibusters. Anglo-American tension escalated during the filibuster crisis, but rather than go to war, both nations exercised restraint.

Filibuster raids from American territory into Cuba and Central America had been a problem since the 1840s. Expansionist Southerners called for the annexation of Cuba to create a new slave state. At the same time, some Cuban whites were upset with the arbitrary rule of the Spanish Captain-General. The nexus of interests brewed conditions whereby Cuban nationalist filibusters, like Narciso López, although officially condemned by President Taylor, launched raids from the US against Cuba. Southerners like Jefferson Davis, John C. Calhoun and citizens around New Orleans supported them.

---

[33]Bemis, *Diplomatic History of the United States*, 249-250; Williams, *Isthmian Diplomacy*, 73-74 and 80-109; and Humphreys, *British Honduras*, 55-58.

[34]Janice E. Thomson, *Mercenaries, Pirates, and Sovereigns: State-Building and Extraterritorial Violence in Early Modern Europe* (Princeton, 1994), 78 and 118-119; and Brown, *Agents of Manifest Destiny*, 17-18.

López's endeavours ended in August 1851, however, when Spanish authorities captured and executed him in Cuba.[35]

The filibusters also raised concerns in France and Britain that the Americans, fresh from their territorial gains in Mexico, wanted Cuba. During the López expeditions, the Governor of the Bahamas, John Gregory, remarked that if the US seized Cuba, it would be as significant as British possession of Gibraltar, for it would give the Americans the power to lock up the trade of the Gulf. Palmerston agreed, but slavers continued to operate from Cuba, undermining British efforts to support Spain. Palmerston felt able to take stronger actions with Brazil, but he also realized that because the Cuban upper class prospered from slavery, such a policy applied to Cuba might push it into American arms. Instead, the Admiralty diverted vessels, such as *Trincomalee*, to Havana to protect British interests "and warn off American invasions, official or unofficial." When López's operations continued, Britain and France united to preserve the *status quo*. The Admiralty ordered its West Indian forces to "give Spain any assistance she required to defeat any future American filibustering expeditions against Cuba[;]" by January 1852 the orders were rescinded when the threat diminished.[36]

Rather than push the Americans further, France and Britain suggested, as others had during the piracy crisis, an agreement to protect Cuba's "independence." The British believed that even if rejected, the offer would eliminate the US expansionist cry that Cuba was about to fall into British hands. Although President Fillmore and Secretary of State Webster wanted to agree to the terms, it was an election year. In the end, Fillmore lost the election, and Webster died. Edward Everett, interim Secretary in the lame-duck administration, noted the British and French assurances and reiterated that the US had no desire to acquire Cuba. Nevertheless, he cautioned the other powers that it was a strategically important island. As Samuel Flagg Bemis has shown, over time Britain and America "let the matter drop."[37]

While tensions remained high between the two nations, they never went to war. In Central America, while America and Britain settled their differences, American industrialists, like Cornelius Vanderbilt, continued their activities. In 1853 Vanderbilt's Accessory Transit Company and Greytown officials disagreed over the placement of coaling facilities. When the latter destroyed some company buildings, the Navy Department dispatched the warship *Cyane*, but Washington backed down when it was revealed that the company had violated agreements with Greytown. In 1854, after a company cap-

---

[35]Bemis, *Diplomatic History of the United States*, 314-316.

[36]Murray, *Odious Commerce*, 224-225 and 227; and Lambert, *Trincomalee*, 56-57.

[37]Bemis, *Diplomatic History of the United States*, 317-319.

tain killed an African citizen, Greytown residents pillaged company property, and Washington sent *Cyane* again. Its captain asked the commander of HMS *Bermuda* to intervene, but the latter simply protested "the contemplated bombardment" of the town. Getting no response, *Cyane* bombarded the town on 13 July as *Bermuda* observed the action.[38]

Palmerston was deeply concerned about the Greytown affair and thought that it "seems to require a serious determined course." The American naval commander had attacked a town that Palmerston believed "all the world" knew was under British protection. Moreover, the Americans had entered and burned the British consulate. Palmerston concluded that US motives were clear: it was done "at the Instigation of a private company of adventurers, & to protect a man who had in open day committed a wanton & barbarous murder." Consequently, Palmerston believed that Britain had to counter the American actions immediately. His reaction is significant because, while he realized it was an affront to British interests, he also knew that caution was required to prevent Anglo-American tension from harming wider strategic interests.[39]

Palmerston thought it naïve to believe that the American commander had acted without Washington's permission. He postulated that under the circumstances, the US government would "not of its own accord give us any satisfaction or apology" and that the only question that remained was how long he should give the US to apologize. Nevertheless, he knew that a "quarrel with the United States is at all times undesirable" and that under the circumstances Britain had to avoid war with America "when we are engaged in War with another power." Embroiled in war with Russia, Britain could ill afford another conflict. While Palmerston believed that Britain had crippled Russian naval power, he calculated that "what is of great importance [is that] we are sure at present of not having France against us as an Ally of the United States." Still, he was wary of not responding to US actions in Central America because that nation was "always trying [to see] how far they can continue to go."[40]

Palmerston believed that the calculus favoured Britain rather than the US since it was winning its conflict with Russia and still had loyal colonies in North America. He also believed that the American public sided with Britain because they were "dissatisfied with" what occurred in Greytown and that the government was "itself ashamed of what it has done & not doing to avow this

---

[38]Williams, *Isthmian Diplomacy*, 171-174; and United States, *Senate Journal*, 33rd Cong., 2nd sess., 28 July and 4 December 1854.

[39]University of Southampton (US), Hartley Library (HL), Archives and Special Collections (A&SC), Broadlands Archive (BA), Palmerston Papers (PP), United States (US)/1-18, Palmerston, "Memorandum on a Draft from Lord Clarendon to Mr. Crompton about American Destruction of Grey Town," 10 September 1854.

[40]*Ibid.*

act." In sum, Palmerston advocated a firm stand and felt that the Americans would eventually capitulate, but he knew that London had more important matters at hand than a needless conflict with the US. It did not hurt that he also knew that the US "have no navy of which we need be afraid."[41]

In America, as Palmerston predicted, Congress demanded answers. President Pierce reported that the government had ordered *Cyane* to show restraint, that it had paused between salvos and that "there was no destruction of life." The people of Greytown, "blacks and persons of mixed blood," were no better than pirates. The protests from London were more about "harshness than of justice." Moreover, Pierce implied, the British had bombarded communities less offensive than Greytown "with much greater severity, and where not cities only have been laid in ruins, but human life has been recklessly sacrificed, and the blood of the innocent made profusely to mingle with that of the guilty." While upset, London avoided military confrontation over the incident. The British were still embroiled in the Crimean War, and the London *Globe* declared that aboriginal rights were too insignificant for war with America.[42]

Because the conflict-avoidance and resolution strategy had prevented war, the British continued it. As early as 1852 Captain Henry Foote, for example, believed that a settlement with the US over territorial issues in Central American was impossible because the Americans demanded too many concessions. Still, he concluded that the two countries should try to purchase a strip of land from the Mosquito King that would be enough to accommodate a canal zone. As off West Africa, Britain recalled any officers it felt might upset Anglo-American relations. In one case in 1852, Granville explained to the American legation in London that Sir George Seymour "disapproved of Captain Ford's conduct at Grey Town and has recalled him from that Station."[43]

But while the British could select which officers to dispatch to the various stations, the presence of filibusters and commercial adventurers had hurt Anglo-American talks over implementing the Clayton-Bulwer Treaty. Central American filibusters became embroiled in the commercial rivalries, working with rival parties for control of the San Juan River and Lake Nicaragua.[44] Pierce had prosecuted British agents who had recruited in the US for the

---

[41]*Ibid.*

[42]United States, *Senate Journal*, 33rd Cong., 2nd sess., 4 December 1854; and Williams, *Isthmian Diplomacy*, 174-186.

[43]TNA/PRO 30/29/20/11, Granville Papers, Henry Grant Foote to Granville, 7 January 1852; and Granville to Abbott Lawrence, 9 January 1852.

[44]Vanderbilt wanted a fast steamer, *Prometheus*, to run from New York to San Juan del Norte, while the 1000-ton steamer *Pacific* would operate from San Juan del Sur to San Francisco; other vessels would ply the San Juan River and Lake Nicara-

Crimean War, and he had to act against US citizens engaged in similar activities or face renewed criticism from London. Although he could do little about the commercial rivalries, he did dispatch the USN to stop filibusters who harmed Anglo-American relations. Meanwhile, the RN stood watch, ready to protect British citizens.[45] Each side sent naval forces to monitor its opponent's activities. Nevertheless, neither side confused maintaining their interests with a needlessly apocalyptic confrontation.

Pierce warned American citizens against filibustering and disavowed the local US representative's premature recognition of the new Nicaraguan government, headed by filibuster William Walker. In the midst of the Kansas-Nebraska controversy over the extension of slavery, Northerners hardly wanted Southern expansion into Central America.[46] Therefore, Pierce distanced himself from *Cyane*'s actions at Greytown and issued proclamations against filibustering, although the British remained wary, fearing that Washington secretly supported Walker as a means to control the Central American isthmus. In response, in July 1856 London dispatched ten warships to Greytown "as a reminder to Walker (and to the United States) [parentheses in original] of British Power until his collapse." Yet Walker was president of Nicaragua by June, and led by Costa Rica, the Central American states went to war with Nicaragua to oust him.[47]

President Pierce again publicly condemned filibuster activities in 1856, but he also warned that the isthmus was as important to Washington as the Suez was to "the maritime Powers of Europe[.]" He claimed he wanted free and open access for all nations and was disappointed when Britain seized San Juan del Norte and renamed it Greytown. Still, once Walker was ousted

---

gua. He created the American Atlantic and Pacific Ship Canal Company and then spun off its Nicaraguan operations into the Accessory Transit Company. For details of how Vanderbilt and his rivals, Charles Morgan, Cornelius K. Garrison, Edmund Randolph and Alexander P. Crittenden, used the conflict to vie for control over isthmus shipping, see Brown, *Agents of Manifest Destiny*, 240-243, 320-321, 352-355 and 378-380.

[45]The Neutrality Act of 1794, and subsequent laws consolidated in the Neutrality Act of 1818, forbade US citizens from serving in foreign navies or outfitting armed vessels within the US for the use of a "foreign belligerent" or against anyone with whom the US was at peace; Thomson, *Mercenaries, Pirates, and Sovereigns*, 78 and 118-119.

[46]The Kansas-Nebraska Act was passed in 1854 and allowed the citizens of Kansas and Nebraska to decide if they wanted slavery in their states. Nebraska bordered on Iowa, a stronghold of Northern antislavery activists.

[47]Thomson, *Mercenaries, Pirates, and Sovereigns*, 127-128; Williams, *Isthmian Diplomacy*, 189-191, 194-197, 200-201 and 211; and Francis X. Holbrook, "The Navy's Cross – William Walker," *Military Affairs*, XXXIX, No. 4 (1975).

the naval strategy was to patrol for any renewed filibuster activity rather than try to gain territory. For instance, USS *St. Mary's*, under the command of Charles Henry Davis, was sent to San Juan del Sur on the Pacific coast to prevent Walker and his forces from interfering with US interests. Walker launched several expeditions and tried to evade detection, but Americans increasingly saw him as a fanatic, and few objected when Honduras captured and executed him.[48]

The Democrat James Buchanan, the next President, also condemned filibustering, wanted good relations with Britain and supported peaceful American expansion. He told Congress that filibusters interfered with Washington's desire for free access to the isthmus. He declared that "[w]e desire, as the leading Power on this continent, to open, and...protect every transit route across the isthmus, not only for our own benefit, but that of the world[.]" To maintain the route's neutrality, Washington encouraged the Central American states to settle with Britain, and the British signed treaties with Honduras on 28 November 1859 and with Nicaragua on 28 January 1860. Both pacts respected British settlement rights on the Bay Islands, while Britain agreed to release its protectorate into Nicaraguan sovereignty.[49] Washington worked to calm rivalries while British and American naval officers agreed to leave disputes to the diplomats. The two nations maintained an uneasy peace, while naval forces patrolled for those who might upset it. War would have disrupted the wider interests of both nations.

Accommodation and Naval Policing in the Equatorial Atlantic

With the renewed strategic sensitivity of the western Atlantic and the Gulf of Mexico for American shipping between the Atlantic and Pacific, RN seizures of American-flagged slavers also heightened tensions. The British handled the crisis as they had the Central American issue; London saw no point in war with the US over the slave trade. The Gulf of Mexico was different than West Africa, and Britain modified its naval policy to reduce Anglo-American tension. In 1858 the Law Officers solidified British naval strategy: it was best to police the slave trade along the African coast, away from the legitimate trade

---

[48]Great Britain, *Foreign and State Papers* (*BFSP*), XLVII, 1856-1857, Franklin Pierce to Senate and House of Representatives, 15 May 1856; Holbrook, "Navy's Cross," 119-201; and Brown, *Agents of Manifest Destiny*, 418 and 451-457.

[49]Bemis, *Diplomatic History of the United States*, 327-330; John Bassett More (ed.), *The Works of James Buchanan: Comprising His Speeches, State Papers, and Private Correspondence* (12 vols., New York, 1960), X, 103, Buchanan to Lord Clarendon, 23 February 1857; Binder, *James Buchanan*, 221-225; *Congressional Globe*, 35th Cong., 2nd sess., 216-217, Buchanan to Senate, 7 January 1858; and Williams, *Isthmian Diplomacy*, 212-223 and 227-266.

of commercial rivals. Because of RN seizures, the US agreed in 1859 to dispatch a stronger naval force to the Gulf of Mexico and to West Africa, ostensibly to patrol for slavers. Many Americans believed that Britain had no right to stop US-flagged ships near US waters, but they also admitted fault for failing to suppress the slave trade. Each nation modified its sea power policies to accommodate the other and reduce diplomatic tensions.

Some scholars have claimed that there was a deliberate British naval "build-up" to pressure the US into action against the slave trade, but there is little evidence to support this.[50] With the increased slave trade by 1857, the British dispatched four additional gunboats to Cuban waters to assist Spanish authorities to police this commerce. But at the urging of its Law Officers, the Admiralty ordered them to stop only slavers without papers or flags. In the spring of 1858 the RN captured two slavers, later condemned in Vice-Admiralty courts, but in the process they also stopped sixty-one American vessels. Nevertheless, London reined in the RN when it threatened to drag Britain into an unwanted war with the US. After American protests, the Foreign Secretary, Lord Malmesbury, admitted that the dispatch of the gunboats was poor judgment and that the British focus should have remained on Africa.[51]

The American press, diplomats and politicians condemned Britain's right of search, which was of particular concern because of incidents on the US side of the Atlantic. After the British stopped several American ships near US coastal waters in 1858, the *New York Times* demanded that the government stop the slave trade to placate the British. But it also believed that Washington needed to act against "the British fleet," whose actions seemed part of "some preconcerted [British] schemes which require further explanation[.]"In London, Dallas provided the British with several examples which showed that RN activities had interfered with American trade. He noted, for example, that in March the warship *Styx* reportedly stopped an American vessel carrying wood from Jamaica to New York. As well, at least three American vessels were boarded at Sapra La Grande by a British warship, probably *Buzzard*. The Americans also reported numerous other incidents, particularly in the Gulf of Mexico. Dallas believed the US should abrogate the 1842 treaty, but President Buchanan thought otherwise. In May 1858 the President asked Congress for

---

[50]For some examples, see Harmon, "Suppress and Protect," 136-138; and Earl E. McNeilly, "The United States Navy and the Suppression of the West African Slave Trade, 1819-1862" (Unpublished PhD thesis, Case Western Reserve University, 1973), 209-210.

[51]Murray, *Odious Commerce*, 262-264.

more power to increase the strength of the US squadron in the Gulf of Mexico "and confront the British when they halt American ships at sea."[52]

Many in Congress brought up British interference with American coastal trade. Democratic Senator Robert Toombs of Georgia reminded colleagues that the Constitution protected Americans from such searches in their own homes. Yet Britain, "without any forms of law," claimed a similar right "in the Gulf of Mexico at our own doors." Others echoed the *New York Times* that the US should stop the slave trade. Hugh Soulsby has noted that Senator Stephen Douglas, Democrat from Illinois, "followed the traditional Western attitude of extreme hostility" toward the British. But in reality he appreciated American culpability and demanded that Washington address London's concerns and send better warships to the West African and Cuban coasts to suppress the slave trade. Nevertheless, Douglas declared that the government must first focus on commerce protection in the Gulf of Mexico.[53]

Despite British claims that they issued orders to their ships to stop harassing American-flagged vessels, the acts continued and stirred political and public outrage in the US. As a result, Congress gave the President the power to act. While he dispatched a force into the Caribbean headed by Flag Officer Edward McCluney, he showed less willingness to use the USN to protect the coastal trades. On 31 May 1858 Dallas told Lord Malmesbury that British actions around Cuba, the Gulf of Mexico and off the West African coast were "sudden and seemingly systematised assaults" on American commerce. Dallas reported that Malmesbury seemed impressed by this urgent briefing. The issue was reported in *The Times*, which declared that Britain would be equally upset if the USN had committed such acts against British-flagged vessels.[54]

Britain again seemed willing to settle the dispute rather than risk war with the US. Dallas reported that "I have the assurance of the leading men among the [free trade] Radicals that they are averse to this system of meddling

---

[52]*New York Times*, 20 April and 13 May 1858; TNA/PRO, ADM 1/5699, George M. Dallas to Earl of Malmesbury, 7 July 1858; and *Congressional Globe*, 35th Cong., 1st sess., 2495-2496, Senate, 29 May 1858.

[53]*Congressional Globe*, 35th Cong., 1st sess., 2495-2498, Senate, 29 May 1858; Hugh Graham Soulsby, *The Right of Search and the Slave Trade in Anglo-American Relations, 1814-1862* (Baltimore, 1933), 159-160; and Binder, *James Buchanan*, 261-262.

[54]Soulsby, *Right of Search*, 165; *Congressional Globe*, 35th Cong., 1st sess., 2496-2498, Senate, 29 May 1858; Binder, *James Buchanan*, 261-262; McNeilly, "United States Navy," 210-211; Harmon, "Suppress and Protect," 136-138; W.E. Burghardt Du Bois, *The Suppression of the African Slave-Trade to the United States of America, 1683-1870* (New York, 1896; reprint, New York, 1965), 161; Howard, *American Slavers and the Federal Law*, 148, 152 and 154; and NA, RG 59, Dispatches, Britain, No. 104, Dallas to Lewis Cass, 1 June 1858.

with the rights and business of others[.]" Further, on 2 June 1858 the British Ambassador, Lord Napier, told Secretary of State Lewis Cass that London would not "sanction or support any system of supervision over the traders of the US in the narrow seas almost within sight of their own shores." The reason, Napier confided to Malmesbury, was that London would not let Northern crusaders push London into war. In July, Hutt tried to capitalize on the diplomatic dispute and again called for the African squadron to be disbanded. But "Tories and Whigs combined" to defeat his motion, 223 to twenty-four. The government, however, reined in its warships and hoped that the powers could develop ways to identify and search suspect vessels.[55]

At the same time, Crown Law Officers clarified RN procedures to avoid conflict and restrict naval activity on the African coast. They advised that naval actions in the "Bights of Benin or Biafra, will be subject to very different [strategic] considerations [than] if attempted in the Florida Gulf Stream" where there was heavy legitimate commercial traffic. As a result, in the summer of 1858 British Commodore Kellett reported that he had ordered a stop to searches and the withdrawal of his forces from Cuban waters. Farther south, Captain W. Cornwallis Aldham told US Commodore McIntosh that the British had the right to search vessels at Greytown, which was a British protectorate. On 11 November the British received reports of filibusters in the area and questioned vessels for information. McIntosh protested that he saw no difference in searching American ships for "'Filibusters' or Africans." But it was not worth a confrontation, and, as off West Africa, the parties concluded that diplomats, rather than broadsides, should settle the dispute.[56]

As the incidents continued, in June 1859 Washington sent warships to the Gulf of Mexico and the West African coast (see table 8.1).[57] The squadron in the Americas was to protect "trade and commerce, and to resist the unlawful search or seizure of American vessels[.]" But the force was also "to arrest and prevent all unlawful expeditions from the United States" to Central Amer-

---

[55]NA, RG 59, Dispatches, Britain, No. 106, Dallas to Cass, 4 June 1858; TNA/PRO, ADM 1/5699, Napier to Malmesbury, 7 June 1858; Murray, *Odious Commerce*, 266; and Soulsby, *Right of Search*, 163.

[56]TNA/PRO, ADM 123/167, J.D. Harding, Fitzroy Kelly and H.M. Cairns [illegible] to Malmesbury, 16 June 1858; NA, RG 45, Squadron Letters, CII, Home Squadron, James McIntosh to C.H.A.H. Kennedy, 18 June 1858; McIntosh to Isaac Toucey, 12 July and 3 December 1858; W. Cornwallis Aldham to McIntosh, 28 and 30 November 1858; and McIntosh to Aldham, 26 and 29 November 1858.

[57]Binder, *James Buchanan*, 259-261.

ica that threatened regional stability.[58] To placate the British, Cass assured Lord Lyons that the Cuban force would intercept those slavers that "may escape the vigilance" off Africa. As off West Africa, the RN would no longer interfere with American rights. Rather than go to war, both sides settled the dispute by modifying the use of their navies. Although further talks stalled, and Cass refused to attend an international conference in London on the right of search, Secretary of the Navy Isaac Toucey told William Inman that joint cruising with the British was "highly desirable" and that the US was "sincerely desirous" to end the slave trade and prevent interference with American-flagged ships.[59]

Table 8.1
US Navy Deployment to West Africa and the Gulf of Mexico, 1859

Station	Name	Propulsion	Guns
Africa	*San Jacinto*	Steam Propeller	17
	Mohican	Steam Propeller	7
	Sumter	Steam Propeller	6
	Mystic	Steam Propeller	6
	4 vessels total		36 guns total
Gulf of Mexico			
	Fulton	Side Wheel Steamer	4
	Crusader	Steam Propeller	6
	Wyandotte	Steam Propeller	6
	Mohawk	Steam Propeller	6
	Water Witch	Side Wheel Steamer	3
	5 vessels total		25 guns total

Source: Great Britain, National Archives (TNA/PRO), Admiralty (ADM) 123/164, enclosure in Lyons to Russell, 21 July 1859.

---

[58]*Congressional Globe*, 36th Cong., 1st sess., appendix, 15, Toucey, "Report of the Secretary of the Navy," 2 December 1859; and Howard, *American Slavers and the Federal Law*, 59. McNeilly, "United States Navy," 204-230, termed the West African deployment of some of these vessels the "Buchanan Offensive." But his chronology was blurred, and he failed to note that the USN's 1858 deployment was for filibuster patrols.

[59]TNA/PRO, ADM 123/164, Cass to Lord Lyons, 7 June 1859; and Lyons to Russell, 21 July 1859; *Congressional Globe*, 36th Cong., 1st sess., appendix, 13, Toucey, "Report of the Secretary of the Navy," 2 December 1859; Soulsby, *Right of Search*, 173; and TNA/PRO, ADM 123/164, Toucey to William Inman, 6 July 1859, enclosure in [Admiralty] to [Grey], 5 August 1859.

Conclusion

By 1860 the task of British and American naval commanders was clear: when Anglo-American economic interests were threatened, they were to cooperate. In February 1860, for example, traders asked the British and American navies for protection. The USN's *Marion* with men from the RN's *Falcon* repulsed attacks on two British factories. The Americans concluded that "our force and that of the English...co-operated in concert & harmony."[60] But as Anglo-American tensions eased, the outbreak of the Civil War caused complications. With slavery as a key issue, Washington believed that the RN's policing of the slave trade would help the blockade against the Confederates.[61] Nevertheless, Britain remained wary and again avoided becoming embroiled in conflict.

---

[60]NA, RG 45, Squadron Letters, CXIV, Thomas W. Brent to Inman, 6 March 1860, enclosure in Inman to Toucey, 28 July 1860.

[61]Lincoln blockaded the South's coast, an action that received recognition from Britain. But the USN had to reorganize its force, purchase idle merchant vessels and construct new ships to make the blockade effective. See William M. Fowler, Jr., *Under Two Flags: The American Navy in the Civil War* (New York, 1990), 39-59.

Chapter 9
The Civil War and Conflict Resolution in the Equatorial Atlantic

The British did not see the coming of the US Civil War because they judged it more likely that the Americans would continue to emphasize expansion rather than becoming embroiled in an internal conflict. Palmerston tolerated the US and believed that its expansion to the south would provide regional stability and a people with a "gentlemanly" ethos with whom Britain could deal. Moreover, if the US did this it would reduce the possibility that it would plot to annex British North America. Edward Steele concluded that "the second Palmerston government, like the preceding Tory administration, carried appeasement of the United States to lengths scarcely imaginable[.]"[1] But with the storm clouds gathering, the new Confederate States of America (CSA) caused a problem. The Foreign Office warned the Admiralty to act with caution, an approach that best suited British interests.[2]

Similarly, the US reconciled its maritime difficulties with Britain so it could focus on the war effort. Washington granted London the right to search suspected US slavers, but the British remained cautious lest it be dragged into the Civil War. To avoid any future conflict over the application of sea power, both nations agreed on passports for vessels involved in the legitimate transport of Africans. Across the equatorial Atlantic, the role of sea power was modified during this tense era. Anglo-American naval operations in the equatorial Atlantic were flexible because neither side wanted to expand the war.

As the US came fragmented, Britain sought to remain neutral while protecting its maritime interests. The election of Abraham Lincoln made Brit-

---

[1]E.D. Steele, *Palmerston and Liberalism, 1855-1865* (Cambridge, 1991), 292-293.

[2]While the intricacies of the historiographic debate over British attitudes are beyond the scope of this work, they have been covered admirably in Duncan Andrew Campbell, *English Public Opinion and the American Civil War* (Woodbridge, 2003), 2-13. Campbell notes, for example, the differences between the "traditionalist" and "revisionist" interpretations. The former believed that "the British aristocracy, the upper-middle class and political conservatives were solidly pro-South while radicals, the lower-middle and working classes were firmly pro-North." (p. 2). Nevertheless, Campbell concluded that British intervention in the Civil War was "unpopular in England" and that "Palmerston, it seems, read the public mood well" (p. 240). The present study therefore is closer to the revisionist than to the traditional interpretation.

ish financial circles uneasy, and the "gentlemanly capitalists" were deeply concerned that the divisions between North and South would injure their economic interests. They wanted peace maintained and urged the British government to try to broker a settlement between Washington and Richmond, the capital of the new CSA.

Thomas Baring, former Lord of the Admiralty and Liberal MP, reflected these concerns, for the Barings were worried that any long-term conflict would affect their bottom line. On 21 December 1860 Lord Russell, then Prime Minister Palmerston's Foreign Secretary, explained to Baring that "Lord Palmerston & I think it would be very unsafe for us to mediate in American affairs, unless we were called upon by both parties to do so – & even then we should be unwilling." After alluding to Baring's request, Russell explained to Palmerston that "I am inclined to think we ought not to meddle between two very angry parties – They probably would not thank us & we might displease both sides of this vehement confederacy."[3] Wanting peace maintained, the slave trade ended and links with both North and South maintained, London had to reassess its American policy as the US disintegrated.

Although concerned about becoming involved in the Civil War after the outbreak of hostilities in the spring of 1861, Russell proposed that Britain call for a ceasefire. Others, like Home Secretary George Lewis, believed that such a plan was improbable because it was unlikely that either North or South would consider a ceasefire as long as it believed it could win the internal conflict. Moreover, if Britain became involved as a peacemaker, it might be forced to help settle the North-South border and mediate the question of whether slavery should continue in an independent South. There were no clear solutions to these problems, and London could be damned either way. Lewis concluded that while every "person who sympathizes with the distress of the Lancashire [cotton] operatives must wish that the ordinary trade with the Gulf States should be re-established[,]" the uncertainties outweighed the benefits to Britain. He believed that "looking to the probable consequences of this philanthropic proposition, we may doubt whether the chances of evil do not preponderate over the chances of good." It was, he opined, "[b]etter to endure the ills we have, [t]han fly to others which we know not of."[4] As of 1862 the British government surmised that neither North nor South had a decisive advantage and that it was best for Britain to remain neutral.

---

[3]Great Britain, National Archives (TNA/PRO), 30/22/97, Russell Papers, John Russell to Thomas Baring, 21 December 1860; Russell to Palmerston, 29 December 1860.

[4]University of Southampton (US), Hartley Library (HL), Archives and Special Collections (A&SC), Broadlands Archive (BA), Palmerston Papers (PP), Cabinet Papers (CAB) 178-82, George C. Lewis, "Memorandum on the American Question," Confidential, 17 October 1862.

During the first two years of the Civil War Britain maintained its previous maritime strategy of conflict avoidance. In May 1861 the Law Officers, who had earlier expressed serious reservations about any naval involvement in the western equatorial Atlantic, were adamant that any involvement in the seizure of Southern-flagged ships or in delivering intelligence to the US Navy (USN) might violate British neutrality laws. Since the Admiralty feared doing anything that might draw Britain into the conflict, it modified its strategy accordingly. London declared neutrality, and the Royal Navy (RN) ceased sharing intelligence with the USN.[5]

As the Northern blockade of the South tightened, Palmerston declared that "[w]e ought to do all we can consistently with our Honor [sic] and our Rights, to avoid war with the United States, but we should only invite aggression by tamely submitting to obvious wrong." Consequently, he instructed Lord Lyons, the British ambassador to Washington, to ask the US government about the conditions of the blockade and to ascertain if it planned to follow the "law of nations."[6] By August 1861 Palmerston prepared for the worst and planned reinforcements for British North America, noting that "our relations with Washington are in a ticklish condition. No reliance can be placed on Seward and Lincoln from week to week." Although hoping to avoid war, he felt that "if we are known to be ready and prepared we shall not be attacked."[7]

The situation stood on the precipice in November 1861 when the US warship *San Jacinto*, recently withdrawn from Africa, boarded the British mail steamer *Trent* and took two Confederate representatives bound for Britain into custody (see figure 9.1). The *Trent* affair epitomized Anglo-American maritime relations during the post 1812 era. Charles Francis Adams, the US envoy in London, concluded that for "centuries" British policy toward the sea was "dictatorial, and especially towards the United States[.]"[8] Yet now the Americans had boarded a British ship in the belief that the British openly helped the Confederates. London readied for war and ordered Lyons to prepare to come home from Washington with "the archives of his office." In West Africa the

---

[5]TNA/PRO, Admiralty (ADM) 123/166, Wodehouse to Admiralty, 28 February 1861; ADM 123/167, J.D. Harding, Richard Bethell and [illegible] to Earl Russell and E. Hammond to Secretary of the Admiralty, 16 and 17 May 1861; and Romaine to Baldwin Walker, 18 May 1861.

[6]*Ibid.*, 30/22/27, Russell Papers (RP), Palmerston, 3 August 1861.

[7]US, HL, A&SC, BA, PP, CAB/LE/230, Palmerston to Lewis, 26 August 1861.

[8]United States, National Archives (NA), Record Group (RG) 59, Dispatches, Britain, No. 67, Charles Francis Adams to Russell, 6 November 1861, enclosure in Adams to William H. Seward, 8 November 1861.

Admiralty ordered Rear Admiral Baldwin Walker to prepare to protect commerce and destroy enemy trade. By 15 January 1862, Walker dispatched the warship *Penguin* with orders to attack Americans on the coast immediately upon a declaration of war.[9] Fortunately, diplomatic events overtook Walker.

Figure 9.1:   USS *San Jacinto*

Source: United States, Library of Congress, Prints and Photographs Division, Detroit Publishing Company Collection, USS *San Jacinto*, LC-D4-20104.

Palmerston believed that anti-British sentiment in America left Lincoln and Secretary of State Seward with little room to manoeuvre. Ernest N. Paolino has concluded that Seward, an advocate of American expansion, believed in cooperation with other powers and the use of force only as a last resort to further US interests. With American naval resources devoted to the Civil War and the virtual abandonment of the West African coast, Seward gave way to pragmatism and agreed to grant London the mutual right of search it had long desired so that British sea power might increase the effectiveness of the blockade on the South. Moreover, Britain's unease about Canada, its trade with the North, Washington's fear of having to fight a two-front war and French support for Britain combined to help settle the affair.[10]

---

[9]TNA/PRO, ADM 123/166, Romaine to Walker, 4 December 1861; Paget to Walker or Senior Officer at Sierra Leone, 18 December 1861; and Walker to Alan Gardner, 15 January 1862.

[10]Steele, *Palmerston and Liberalism*, 297; Ernest N. Paolino, *The Foundations of the American Empire: William Henry Seward and U.S. Foreign Policy* (Ithaca,

Rather than war, on 13 November 1861 Lyons and Seward signed an informal memorandum of understanding to clarify their maritime relations. It permitted British and American cruisers to stop, search and detain each other's ships within thirty leagues of the West African coast. Hugh Soulsby argued that this agreement was a "war-time measure" to gain European support for the North while freeing the USN for use against the South. The parties ratified the agreement on 20 May 1862 as the Anglo-American Treaty (1862), which was virtually identical to the Quintuple Treaty that the Americans had earlier rejected. Although Americans had long objected to British actions, Seward now hoped that "foreign" fleets in the Gulf would "employ not only additional influence, but also additional force in suppressing the slave trade."[11]

The agreement would also allow the British government to placate its critics by showing that it was doing something about the slave trade. In the autumn of 1862 William E. Gladstone, the great British Liberal, suggested that the choice that Britain faced was "between inaction on the one hand, and an interference limited to moral means on the other." Gladstone knew that London had important domestic considerations. Lancashire had "borne with heroic patience" the disruption in trade, but "who can be certain that the positive suffering, the actual hunger which we have every reason to fear is endured there, may not at some time, at some place, perhaps from some apparently trivial incident, give rise to an outbreak [of violence]?" Moreover, he believed that the government had to act before British public opinion bonded too closely with the Southern cause, even though it was "tainted by its connection with slavery." Gladstone was convinced that if the war dragged on, the South would ultimately win, and Britain would be unable to convince Richmond to abolish or even modify slavery.[12]

London had experience with operations in such a volatile region. In February 1862, for example, Russell was concerned about the "complications that might" ensue if the British attempted to "[v]erify the character of vessels"

NY, 1973), 32 and 145; and Arthur Power Dudden, *The American Pacific: From the Old China Trade to the Present* (New York, 1992), 60-61.

[11]NA, RG 59, Dispatches, Britain, No. 82, Adams to Seward, 3 December 1861; No. 95, Adams to Seward, 27 December 1861; No. 97, Adams to Seward, 2 January 1862; No. 163, Adams to Seward, 22 May 1862; and Diplomatic Instructions of the Department of State, 1801-1906, Great Britain, No. 169, Seward to Adams, 24 January 1862; TNA/PRO, ADM 123/166, Lyons to Russell, 13 November 1861; Lyons and Seward, "Informal Memorandum," 13 November 1861; Paget to A.H. Layard, 16 January 1862; Lyons to Russell, 11 February 1862; Admiralty to Walker, 5 June 1862; and Hugh Graham Soulsby, *The Right of Search and the Slave Trade in Anglo-American Relations, 1814-1862* (Baltimore, 1933), 174.

[12]US, HL, A&SC, BA, PP, CAB/178-82, W.E.G, "The War in America," Secret, 24 October 1862.

around Cuba even if authorized to do so by Washington. Accordingly, Britain stayed clear of the conflict and re-focused its efforts on the West African coast. To prevent a potential future crisis, London and Washington in late 1862 entered into one final agreement over the application of sea power. To prevent unintended seizures, the British planned to issue passports, signed by a government minister, to vessels involved in legitimate voyages, such as the transport of free Africans. Washington agreed to do the same, and by September the British and American Mixed Commission courts at the Cape of Good Hope, Sierra Leone and New York were prepared to receive captured vessels.[13] Both the US and especially Britain modified their maritime policies to try to reduce Anglo-American tensions.

Palmerston's problem during these years was his belief that Britain had to walk a fine line between capitulating to Washington's demands and maintaining its own honour and interests. The Confederates, for instance, had bought vessels from British shipyards and armed and employed them as commerce raiders; the most famous was *Alabama*. While this aggravated the North, Palmerston believed that he had to maintain British national honour even in the face of Washington's protests. He explained to Russell that "we are intitled [sic] to execute our own municipal law within the United Kingdom and to prevent if we can any equipment of a ship of war destined to act hostilely against a friendly power." Nevertheless, he added that "we have no right to inquire as to a Ship of War belonging to a State which we acknowledge as a belligerent where that ship was built[,] what country it crew are nations of, where it was armed not having been armed in the United Kingdom." Still, Britain faced a quandary over vessels like *Alabama*. Palmerston noted that "she sails from a British port unarmed and essentially not a ship of war."[14]

The British government wanted to maintain its honour, but in the end it capitulated to its wider interest of placating the US government. When the Confederates continued to purchase British-built ships after the *Alabama* controversy, London bought those that were under construction on the Mersey rather than face more protests from Washington. Meanwhile, although Palmerston wanted an independent South for economic and strategic interests, he reconciled this with his desire to end the slave trade. He realized that the British public would never sanction an end to the Civil War that allowed slavery to

---

[13]NA, RG 59, Dispatches, Britain, No. 116, Adams to Seward, 18 February 1862; and No. 191, Russell to Adams, [17] July 1862, enclosed in Adams to Seward, 18 July 1862; and TNA/PRO, ADM 123/166, E. Hammond to Secretary of the Admiralty, 18 September 1861; ADM 123/167, Adams to Russell, 22 August 1862; Romaine to Walker, 27 August 1862; S. Walcott to Frederic Rogers, 2 September 1862; Robert Phillemore to Russell, 25 September 1862; and Hammond to Secretary of the Admiralty, 4 October 1862.

[14]TNA/PRO, 30/22/27, RP, Palmerston, 23 August 1863.

continue.[15] Palmerston therefore took a cautious approach when dealing with the US during the Civil War even if this confounded outside observers.

The observations of US Secretary of the Navy Gideon Welles about the dynamics of British policy show that liberals on both sides of the Atlantic hoped to contain their maritime disputes during the conflict. In April 1863 he wrote in his diary his concern that Britain and the US would go to war over the conflict with the South. Still, he remained cautiously optimistic because such a war would be a "calamity to us, but scarcely less serious to her" because their trade and mutual interests in the Atlantic bound them together. America had a navy, could disrupt British communications with its North American colonies and could licence privateers. He hoped that "the policy and tone of England might be modified."[16]

Welles found hope for peace in the attitudes of some of his British colleagues. On 13 May 1863, for example, he noted that Russell's speeches on American affairs "are less offensive than some things we have had, and manifest a dawning realization of what must follow if England persists in her unfriendly policy." Welles was pleased that the British often referred touchy matters, such as vessel searches, mail openings and naval deployment, to the Law Officers of the Crown for sober consideration. He confided to his diary that it might be a hint "to Seward to be more prudent and considerate" in return. For his part, Welles remained calm and refused to send a squadron to the British coast to intercept Confederate raiders outfitting there, noting that such an action would "be likely to embroil us with that power." But he also knew that the British government sought to meet American concerns: "the Secretary of State assures me in confidence that the armoured [Confederate] vessels building in England will not be allowed to leave."[17] While London and Washington differed, they both held to the philosophy that their wider interests would be harmed if they directly confronted each other during the Civil War.

In the end, the British worked to further their objectives and avoided war with the US. After a meeting with Secretary of State Seward on 18 September 1863, Welles wrote in his diary that the US was prepared to act if the British let Confederate raiders go to sea. But Seward assured him that "[t]he English Ministry are our friends with the exception of the chief [Palmerston]." There was evidence of divisions in the British Cabinet as they weighed their options in dealing with the Americans. Welles recalled that on 4 November 1862, for instance, the British told Seward they had no control over the Con-

---

[15]Steele, *Palmerston and Liberalism*, 298-301. For more details on the formation of British public opinion and the Civil War see Campbell, *English Public Opinion*.

[16]Howard K. Beale (ed.), *Diary of Gideon Welles: Secretary of the Navy under Lincoln and Johnson* (3 vols., New York, 1960), I, 2 April 1863.

[17]*Ibid.*, I, 13 May and 29 August 1863.

federate ships, but that the next day "they gave us assurance they should not come out."[18] Welles had detected the surface bubbles that showed how Palmerston and his Cabinet formulated their responses to the American crisis.

At the close of the Civil War, Russell wrote Charles Francis Adams, the American envoy to London and son of John Quincy Adams, to express the British government's desire to open a new, amicable and cooperative chapter in Anglo-American relations. Russell told Adams that London was pleased with the American intention to maintain good relations. Furthermore, he assured Adams that Britain "has steadily endeavoured to discountenance, and in a measure to check, the injurious operations of many of Her Majesty's subjects." Ultimately, Russell believed that "public writers and speakers" had tried to generate "ill-will and hatred between the two nations" but was pleased that Adams "share[d] in none of those suspicions and endorse none of those charges of an unfriendly and unfair disposition on the part of Her Majesty's Government." Still, the Civil War had left outstanding issues between Britain and the US resulting from the *Alabama* claims and American accusations that Britons were less than neutral during the conflict.[19]

Russell believed that Britain had acted properly during the war. When American courts ruled that a state of war existed between North and South, Britain had upheld its neutrality laws. Moreover, he felt that it was hypocritical of Washington to claim that London was not entitled to recognize belligerent rights and declare its neutrality when the Americans had exercised similar rights during the South American rebellions against Spain and Portugal. At that time John Quincy Adams had declared that the European nations could have used American courts to seek redress against US-built vessels which had attacked their interests. The older Adams noted that they were unable to do so because the American government had no jurisdiction to stop the activities of men on the high seas.[20] Therefore, Russell concluded, Britain was free to refuse to grant compensation to the US for the activities of commerce raiders like *Alabama*. London, Russell declared, had acted with due diligence to ensure that no Briton violated the nation's neutrality, but offering an olive branch, he expressed the government's pleasure that the North had won the war and abolished slavery. Despite disagreement with the US, he hoped that they could settle their differences amicably. The end of the Civil War, Russell hoped, ushered in a new age in North Atlantic relations. He asked that

> our two nations, therefore, instead of captious discussions, respect the honour and believe in the friendly intentions of

---

[18]*Ibid.*, 18 September 1863.

[19]US, HL, A&SC, BA, PP, US/1-18, Russell to Adams, 30 August 1865.

[20]*Ibid.*

each other. In this manner we may preserve unbroken the ties of peace, and exercise a beneficial influence on the future destinies of the nations of the world.[21]

Within weeks, Palmerston was dead, and Russell was once more Prime Minister.

In the equatorial Atlantic the US and Britain worked to reduce tensions, maintain the balance of power and prevent future conflicts. They modified their use of sea power and set conditions on its application so they could pursue their separate objectives while avoiding war. Undoubtedly, more cautious members of the British Cabinet, like Russell, convinced Palmerston to adopt a liberal approach toward the Americans. Still, as Duncan Campbell has concluded, "Britain had neither permanent friends nor permanent enemies – only permanent interests. The Confederacy was not one of these."[22]

Conclusion: Seapower and the Equatorial Atlantic, 1819-1865

From 1819 to 1865 Britain and the US used sea power in the equatorial Atlantic tactically and strategically. Tactically, they hunted pirates and slavers depending upon their level of political commitment. Strategically, both deployed their navies to protect and promote commerce and check the activities of other nations. The British had clear objectives, backed by unified support from the government and commercial class. In contrast, American policy could only focus on commercial affairs until the Civil War dealt a death blow to domestic slavery. When their separate uses of sea power conflicted with other goals, tension resulted. But because Britain and the US wished to pursue their objectives and avoid war, this common philosophy allowed sea power to be used to smooth their relationship. To accommodate each other, they modified its use.

British gentlemanly capitalism, humanitarianism and liberalism formed a nexus with emerging American commercial goals and allowed the peaceful use of sea power. Through this device, Britain and America related, furthered their clashing interests and avoided military conflicts. They tried to cooperate over divisive issues, like slave-trade suppression, reined in naval officers who threatened Anglo-American relations and deployed those who were more diplomatic than confrontational. Anglo-American naval relations in the equatorial Atlantic reveal that the nations were neither friends nor enemies. Instead, their relationship was dynamic as each avoided conflict that would disrupt their wider interests. This study therefore clarifies the nature of that

---

[21]*Ibid.*

[22]Campbell, *English Public Opinion*, 240-245.

relationship in the early nineteenth century and contributes to the history of Anglo-American relations.

Kenneth Bourne concluded in his study of Anglo-American relations on the North American continent that each nation had suspicions about the other.[23] These percolated into their diplomatic and naval relations over piracy and slave-trade suppression. American suspicion of Britain was greatest over the latter because of the contentious nature of slavery in the US and fears that British naval efforts interfered with American commercial endeavours. Meanwhile, British unease over the USN's deployment to fight pirates and filibusters illustrated London's fear of American motives in the Gulf of Mexico and Central America. Anglo-American mistrust often clouded their naval relations in the equatorial Atlantic. Rebecca Berens Matzke concluded that the use of the RN was a warning to America to contain its passions.[24] But those in power in both nations wished to avoid war. Sea power allowed "peaceful" communication of their policies and objections and gave each the opportunity to modify the behaviour that the other disliked.

Andrew Lambert has described the RN, particularly between the Crimean and First World wars, as "the world's most powerful political instrument[.]"[25] But Herbert Richmond concluded that rivalries harmed the effectiveness of sea power. Athens, for example, reached the height of power but then fell for "want of a wise policy of mutual support and mutual sacrifice in the maintenance of her sea power."[26] An opposite dynamic occurred in the early nineteenth century. This study has shown that London believed that it was better to further objectives peacefully than to face the prospects of war with other nations. Britain found that rather than driving the US from the sea, it needed American cooperation to eradicate piracy and suppress the slave trade in the equatorial Atlantic.

The British gentlemanly capitalist ideal, free trade mentality and liberalism combined during this period with traditional strategic objectives – countering French moves and protecting West Indian interests – to mould British naval policy and relations with the US. Cain and Hopkins' "gentlemanly capitalist" thesis has been criticized for coming too close to seeing "'Great Britain,' 'the USA' or the whole of 'the City of London' as if these were or-

---

[23]Kenneth Bourne, *Britain and the Balance of Power in North America, 1815-1908* (London, 1967), 3-10.

[24]Rebecca Berens Matzke, "Britain Gets Its Way: Power and Peace in Anglo-American Relations, 1838-1846," *War in History*, VIII, No. 1 (2001), 19.

[25]Andrew D. Lambert, *The Foundations of Naval History: John Knox Laughton, the Royal Navy and the Historical Profession* (London, 1998), 12.

[26]Herbert Richmond, *Sea Power in the Modern World* (London, 1934), 20-21.

ganic entities making a decision or advocating a particular line of action."[27] But this analysis has revealed that throughout the British system, from White-hall, the Admiralty and its officers and representatives in the regions, Britons worked to further overall national goals in the equatorial Atlantic while they avoided provoking interference by other nations.

Canning, for example, worked to secure British interests with the re-bel Spanish-American states, but only when the time was "ripe." In turn, the government deployed the RN due to pressure at home to protect British com-mercial interests. Meanwhile, the humanitarian goal of slave-trade suppression combined with the desire to further economic growth to shape British naval policy along the West African coast. The British sought to move African pro-duction factors into expanding legitimate commerce and maintaining peace with other nations. Although the Cain and Hopkins model is controversial for the era of imperial decline, it holds for the period under consideration here. [28] It helps provide an explanation for one component of the dynamic of Anglo-American relations in the early nineteenth century. For the gentlemanly capi-talists and their allies, war would undermine the peaceful development of over-seas trade. Consequently, sea power had its limits.

The combined political objectives and philosophies limited the extent to which Britain would use sea power against other nations, like the US, to compel them to do its bidding. For the nineteenth century, Eric Hobsbawm concluded that "the British government rarely lost its cool...Diplomacy, the 'great game' between secret agents, even the occasional war, were not con-fused with the apocalypse."[29] This was also true in its naval relations with the US. British policymakers avoided all-out war that was in no one's interests, as when disputes arose over the right of search, especially close to American shores in the 1850s.

The US developed its naval policy from a different perspective, but the result was the same: a desire to avoid conflict. During the piracy crisis the Monroe administration deployed forces to the Gulf of Mexico to protect trade. Others in the administration, like Thompson, were concerned about strategic "over-stretch" if it also deployed forces to the West African coast to meet Britain's demands for slave-trade suppression. Nevertheless, they tried to ap-pease the British and convince them that the US was acting against the slave trade. Similarly, during the 1840s, as the potential for American economic expansion overseas grew, leaders like Upshur and Webster agreed that sea

---

[27]Raymond E. Dumett, "Exploring the Cain/Hopkins Paradigm: Issues for Debate, Critique and Topics for New Research," in Dumett (ed.), *Gentlemanly Capital-ism and British Imperialism: The New Debate on Empire* (London, 1999), 11.

[28]*Ibid.*, 25-37.

[29]Eric Hobsbawm, *On History* (New York, 1997), 259.

power was important to nurture those interests. But they also realized that co-operation with Britain was important to keep the RN from interfering with American shipping. As Buchanan, Cass, and Seward learned, such "appease-ment" was critical to solve access disputes over the Central American isthmus and to keep Britain out of the Civil War.

This study therefore advances the study of the history of Anglo-American relations that has operated along a continuum of extremes. At one pole, the British and Americans were enemies with a gradually formed friend-ship. At the opposite, they were friends whose disputes were anomalies as each learned to relate to the other. Instead, the comparative approach reveals that underlying political policies shaped British and American naval relations and kept the lines of communication open. The two nations managed disputes through modifications to naval policies to address, as least temporarily, the concerns of the other party. In this way, the wider commercial and strategic objectives of both nations could continue. Most previous studies have sought to explain how similar or different historical Anglo-American relations were to today's special friendship.[30] Few have endeavoured to explain the relationship beyond this paradigm.

Martin Crawford, however, has shown how various "conduits" com-municated each nation's views of the other. His study of *The Times* and its close connection with the political elite revealed that misunderstandings accu-mulated when communications flowed only in one direction. During the Civil War, Britain relied more on newspaper accounts from the North than the South. But the South became upset when Britain failed to support its cause on economic grounds, such as the supply of cotton. Conversely, the North be-came disillusioned when Britain declared neutrality despite its opposition to slavery. In turn, *The Times*' editorials objected to Lincoln's emancipation plans and continued to attack the North, yet were subdued in covering the *Trent* af-fair. Crawford concluded that while the British were ideologically close to the South, they increasingly identified more with the "rapidly industrializing, bourgeois North[.]"[31]

Certainly, an additional conduit in the Anglo-American relationship was required to aid this identity connection and release accumulated tension. The sea provided one such interface between Britain and America. Both na-tions worked to maintain two-way "communications" along this conduit to solve their diplomatic disputes. Therefore, as this study shows, Britain and America were not friends, but they kept their relationship from spiralling into

---

[30]See chapter one above.

[31]Martin Crawford, *The Anglo-American Crisis of the Mid-Nineteenth Cen-tury: The Times and America, 1850-1862* (Athens, GA, 1987), 3-5, 13-14 and 135-138.

war. Nevertheless, in this period they intended their philosophy to further their separate interests rather to forge an altruistic "special" relationship.

Through the conduit of the sea, the "dialectical process" that Lionel Gelber described conditioned Anglo-American relations. He concluded that "the English-speaking peoples diverge and then, on a new plane, reconcile clashing interests for the sake of a still higher common interest."[32] In this case, their "common interest" was furthering their own separate objectives. Both used sea power for trade protection but also realized that it could support long-term commercial expansion; reconciling their differences was to their mutual advantage. Interest groups – merchants like Hoffman, the gentlemanly capitalists and the Lords and anti-slave traders like Wilberforce, Buxton and the American Colonization Society – demanded that their governments use sea power to support long-term policy. Liberalism and the rise of free trade in Britain, and leaders like Palmerston, Peel, Upshur and Webster, then facilitated the use of sea power to further these long-term goals and avoid war.

In this context, this study also opens several avenues for further research. Scholars might expand the analysis spatially to assess Anglo-American relations in the Pacific during this period. Arthur Dudden, for example, recognized British, French and American rivalries in that region, particularly over Hawaii. In December 1842 President Tyler warned the other powers against annexing Hawaii. The next year HMS *Carysfort*, commanded by Lord George Paulet, declared the Sandwich Islands a British protectorate. But London, as in the regions examined in this study, "repudiated Paulet's brash act" for the sake of diplomatic relations.[33] During the 1850s, London also feared US filibuster raids against Hawaii, and *Trincomalee* was often at the islands as deterrence.[34] During the Crimean War, Barry Gough showed that Britain again feared a coalition of its enemies, this time Russia aided by American privateers outfitted in California. Consequently, Rear Admiral David Price dispatched *Artemise* and *Amphitrite* to California to defend British interests.[35]

Further work might also increase our understanding by expanding into the post-Civil War period and the controversial era of British imperial decline. Donald Yerxa concluded that in 1898 the German threat forced Britain to

---

[32]Lionel M. Gelber, *America in Britain's Place: The Leadership of the West and Anglo-American Unity* (New York, 1961), 14.

[33]Arthur Power Dudden, *The American Pacific: From the Old China Trade to the Present* (New York, 1992), 58-59.

[34]Andrew D. Lambert, *Trincomalee: The Last of Nelson's Frigates* (London, 2002), 94-95.

[35]Barry M. Gough, *The Royal Navy and the Northwest Coast of North America, 1810-1914: A Study of British Maritime Ascendancy* (Vancouver, 1971), 114.

withdraw from the Caribbean to concentrate its forces closer to home.[36] After the Civil War, the US turned inward to concentrate on internal development. In the eastern equatorial Atlantic, the scramble for Africa began. In Europe, Bismarck used the military to establish the German Empire; Albert Imlah concluded that he renewed "the notion that war could be a useful and profitable instrument of national policy." Consequently, nations retrenched under the shields of protectionism and growing conscript armies. London remained the world's financial centre, although Berlin was a competitor.[37] But what occurred in Anglo-American naval relations between 1865 and Yerxa's era?

Because of the socio-economic changes during the nineteenth century, historians can also advance the social history of naval officers. For example, Michael Lewis analyzed the British naval officer class and concluded that it had to be created. Most believed that Britain needed those of the "higher classes" for naval leadership; simple seamen were inadequate. His assessment of their social and geographic origins revealed that they remained connected to the aristocratic class.[38] Cain and Hopkins, and others, surmised a "nexus" between the gentlemanly capitalists directing the "economics and politics of the empire" and the "command hierarchies of both the army and navy[.]"[39] This study strengthens this theory. Officers like Rowley, the son of a naval officer, were wary that he would stretch the West Indies squadron too far if he met all the mercantile demands. In contrast, the ruling elite selected officers like Hotham, with his aristocratic Yorkshire connections, for their ability to use diplomacy to further British strategic and commercial goals.

---

[36]Donald A. Yerxa, *Admirals and Empire: The United States Navy and the Caribbean, 1898-1945* (Columbia, SC, 1991), 5-6. For their relations in the Pacific, see Hugh B. Hammett, "The Cleveland Administration and Anglo-American Naval Friction in Hawaii, 1893-1894," *Military Affairs*, XL, No. 1 (1976), 27-32.

[37]Albert H. Imlah, *Economic Elements in Pax Britannica: Studies in British Foreign Trade in the Nineteenth Century* (Cambridge, MA, 1958), 17-19.

[38]Michael Lewis, *England's Sea-Officers: The Story of the Naval Profession* (London, 1939; reprint, London, 1948), 34-41; Lewis, *The Navy in Transition, 1814-1864: A Social History* (London, 1965), 19-44; Lewis, *A Social History of the Navy, 1793-1815* (London, 1960); Christopher Lloyd, *The British Seamen, 1200-1860: A Social Survey* (London, 1968); and N.A.M. Rodger, *The Wooden World: An Anatomy of the Georgian Navy* (London, 1986). More recent studies include Brian Vale, "Appointment, Promotion and 'Interest' in the British South America Squadron, 1821-3," *Mariner's Mirror*, LXXXVIII, No. 1 (2002), 61-68; and Gregory C. Kennedy, "Britain's Policy-Making Elite, The Naval Disarmament Puzzle, and Public Opinion, 1927-1932," *Albion*, XXVI, No. 4 (1994), 623-643.

[39]Dumett, "Exploring the Cain/Hopkins Paradigm," 40 and fn. 66.

Meanwhile, my previous work revealed that the background of US naval officers evolved between 1845 and 1861 to include more from the commercial class.[40] Yet Peter Karsten showed that US officers, like Naval Academy Superintendent Louis Goldsborough and Alfred Thayer Mahan, son of the army's Professor Mahan, despised merchants. Goldsborough believed that they were greedy, while Mahan, the prophet of US naval expansion, held "the Academy disdain for those who 'attach to the making and having [of] money' a value in excess of what Mahan thought proper."[41] These views were contrary to those held by the British gentlemanly capitalists, some American politicians and some fellow officers. Yet despite personal opinions on slavery, the USN supported commercial endeavours, and officers like Mayo offered opinions on economic development. Clearly, the attitude of US officers reflected the changing American society. An important aspect of comparative analysis would be to assess what impact class connections and education had on professional beliefs over the nineteenth century as nations rose and economies changed. A "paired study" of Britain and America, with different dominant or rising classes, would highlight any trends.[42]

---

[40]Mark C. Hunter, "'...With the Propriety and Decorum which Characterize the Society of Gentlemen:' The United States Naval Academy and its Youth, 1845-1861" (Unpublished MA thesis, Memorial University of Newfoundland, 1999), chapters 3 and 4. See also Hunter, "Youth, Law, and Discipline at the US Naval Academy, 1845-1861," *The Northern Mariner/Le Marin du nord*, X, No. 2 (2000), 23-39.

[41]Peter Karsten, *The Naval Aristocracy: The Golden Age of Annapolis and the Emergence of Modern American Navalism* (New York, 1972), 186-189. For a similar study, see Christopher McKee, *A Gentlemanly and Honorable Profession: The Creation of the U.S. Naval Officer Corps, 1794-1815* (Annapolis, 1991). McKee used "gentlemanly" as a descriptor for the officers. He concluded that the USN developed a good officer corps because it selected the proper men from the beginning and moulded them to the navy's requirements. Most midshipmen in the pre-1815 navy were from maritime regions and had family maritime traditions; although they were from the "middle class," they were financially insecure. Most obtained appointments through political and naval connections.

[42]Although dealing with the twentieth century, such a study is Dirk Bönker, "Naval Professionalism and the State in Turn-of-the-Century Germany and America," in William M. McBride and Eric P. Reed (eds.), *New Interpretations in Naval History: Selected Papers from the Thirteenth Naval History Symposium* (Annapolis, 1998), 111-138. Bönker, 111, concluded that German and American officers "pursued comparable domestic agendas predicated on the creation of an autonomous politico-institutional space beyond any serious civilian control." Robert L. Davison, "In Defence of Corporate Competence: The Royal Navy Executive Officer Corps, 1880-1919" (Unpublished PhD thesis, Memorial University of Newfoundland, 2005) has discovered a conservative RN officer class confronting the decline of empire, technological change and the ramifications for the officer class and its political connections.

National goals shaped the differences behind the application of sea power in the equatorial Atlantic. These differences fomented Anglo-American conflict when opposing views of the "interest aggregations" clashed. But both nations believed that they could use sea power to further their economic objectives peacefully. The US strategy to use its navy to nurture and protect trade and Britain's pragmatic liberalism allowed sea power to be a mechanism of accommodation. Because of their grander objectives, London and Washington were able to maintain peace between their nations. When tensions mounted, they modified their use of sea power to reach an accommodation.

Both nations tried to keep their relations in a state of equilibrium. To those ends, Anglo-American naval relations acted as a pathway to clear, even if only temporarily, any disequilibrium in Anglo-American understanding. Once cleared, each side moved forward with its policies until a new diplomatic disequilibrium formed that again was cleared using the safety valve of rearranging naval forces or recalling or substituting naval officers. To buttress this dynamic, ambassadors communicated the policy between capitals at the diplomatic level; naval officers did the same in their own realm. Furthermore, in Britain the policies and actions were duly recorded and published in *Parliamentary Papers* for all to read. Such actions satisfied each side that the other was sincere enough to leave disagreement to the diplomats. In the Anglo-American relationship, both nations were realists, pragmatists and possibly opportunists rather than friends.

Select Bibliography

Unpublished Sources

National Archives, Kew (TNA/PRO)

Admiralty (ADM)

1/273-275. Correspondence and Papers. Jamaica, 1713-1839, Nos. 1-445, 1823.

1/1572. Letters from Captains, Surnames B, 1825.

1/1675. Letters from Captains, Surnames C, 1821.

1/2188. Letters from Captains, Surnames M, 1822.

1/5574. Africa, 1847.

1/5596. From Admirals, Captains and Lieutenants, 1849.

1/5699. Correspondence and Papers. In-Letters, From Foreign Office, 1858.

2/1585-1589. Out-Letters. Military Branch: Foreign Stations, November 1824-May 1829.

7/712. Miscellanea. Reports, etc. about the Navy of the USA, 1826-1852.

50/136. Admiral's Journals. Sir C. Rowley, 24 August 1820-6 June 1823.

123/164. Africa Station: Correspondence. Foreign Powers. American Activities, 1857-1860.

123/166. Africa Station. Correspondence. Foreign Powers. American and Portuguese Activities.

123/167. Africa Station: Correspondence. Foreign Powers. French and American Activities, 1860-1863.

123/173. Africa Station: Correspondence. Slave Trade. Reports Setting Out the Best Means for the Abolition of the Slave Trade, 1850.

123/177. Africa Station: Correspondence. Slave Trade. Dahomey, Lagos, etc., Southern Division, Brazil, Cuba and Native Chiefs, 1857-1860.

128/34. North American and West Indies Station: Correspondence, Reports and Memoranda. Jamaica Division. General, 1818; 1822; and 31 December 1827-30 October 1843.

Navy List, 1820-1830 and 1843-1861.

Foreign Office (FO)

2/4. General Correspondence before 1906. Africa: Consuls Fraser, Beecroft. Consular Domestic, 1850.

84/775. General Correspondence before 1906. Africa (West Coast): Consular, Mr. Duncan, Mr. Beecroft, 1849.

84/1031. General Correspondence before 1906. Bight of Benin (Lagos): Consul Campbell, 1857.

5C. Political and Administrative Correspondence, September 1846.

5D. Political and Administrative Correspondence, October 1847.

6H. Political and Administrative Correspondence, December 1847.

7C. Political and Administrative Correspondence, May-August 1848.

27. Opinions of Cabinet Members, 28 June 1859-29 May 1865.

97. Legation in Washington, January 1863-October 1865; and July 1859-October 1865.

1st Earl Granville Papers (TNA/PRO 30/29)

20/11. Mosquito Question.

Lord John Russell: Papers, c. 1800-1913 (TNA/PRO 30/22).

University of Hull, Brynmor Jones Library, Archives and Special Collections

Hotham Family Papers (DDHO)

10/1. Sir Charles Hotham. General Correspondence, May 1846-July 1856.

10/2. Sir Charles Hotham. Letters from Lord Auckland at the Admiralty, Relating to...Command of the Squadron on the Coast of Africa..., August 1846-December 1848.

10/3. Sir Charles Hotham. Letters from Lord Dundas...Relating to...Command on the Coast of Africa, October 1846-February 1849.

10/8. Sir Charles Hotham. Letter Book, Coast of Africa, August 1846-September 1848.

10/11. Sir Charles Hotham. Secret Letter Book, August 1847-April 1849.

10/47. Sir Charles Hotham. Notebook Containing Biographical Details of [by his sister Mrs. Anne Barlow], and Newspaper Cuttings Relating to..., 1846-1852.

University of Southampton, Hartley Library, Archives and Special Collections

MS 62. Broadlands Archive. Palmerston Papers.

GC/AU/45-68. General Correspondence. Lord Auckland.

PP/CAB/178-182 and LE/230. Cabinet Papers.

PP/MM/US/1-18. United States.

PP/SLT. Slave Trade.

National Archives (NA), Washington, DC.

Naval Records Collection of the Office of Naval Records and Library (RG 45)

Correspondence of the Secretary of the Navy Relating to African Colonization, 1819-1844.
Letter Books of Commodore Matthew C. Perry, March 10, 1843-February 20, 1845.
Letters Received by the Secretary of the Navy from Commanding Officers of Squadrons ("Squadron Letters"), 1841-1886. Vols. 89 (pt.), 102, 105, 106, 107, 108, 109, 110, 111 and 112.
Secretary of the Navy, Letters Sent.
Secretary of the Navy, Record of Confidential Letters.

General Records of the Department of State (RG 59)

Dispatches from United States Ministers to Great Britain, 1791-1906.
Diplomatic Instructions of the Department of State, 1801-1906.
Great Britain.
Notes from the British Legation in the US to the Department of State, 1791-1906.
Annual Reports of the Secretary of the Navy, 1820-1860.

Published Sources

Adams, Charles Francis (ed.). *Memoirs of John Quincy Adams: Comprising Portions of His Diary from 1795 to 1848.* 12 vols. Philadelphia, 1874; reprint, Freeport, NY, 1969.
Allen, Harry C. *Great Britain and the United States: A History of Anglo-American Relations (1783-1952).* London, 1954; reprint, Hamden, CT, 1969.
American Commercial and Daily Advertiser (ACDA). Various years.
Anderson, John L. "Piracy and World History: An Economic Perspective on Maritime Predation." *Journal of World History,* VI, No. 2 (1995), 175-199. Reprinted in Pennell, C.R. (ed.). *Bandits at Sea: A Pirates Reader.* New York, 2001, 82-106.
Ashley, Evelyn. *The Life and Correspondence of Henry John Temple Viscount Palmerston.* 2 vols. London, 1879.
Bartlett, C.J. *Great Britain and Sea Power.* Oxford, 1963.
Bartlett, Irving H. *John C. Calhoun: A Biography.* New York, 1993.

Bauer, K. Jack. "The Golden Age." In Kilmarx, Robert A. (ed.). *America's Maritime Legacy: A History of the U.S. Merchant Marine and Shipbuilding Industry since Colonial Times*. Boulder, CO, 1979, 27-63.

_____. "John Young Mason." In Coletta, Paolo E. (ed.). *American Secretaries of the Navy*. 2 vols. Annapolis, 1980, I, 231-240.

_____. *A Maritime History of the United States: The Role of America's Seas and Waterways*. Columbia, SC, 1988.

Baugh, Daniel A. "Admiral Sir Herbert Richmond and the Objects of Sea Power." In Goldrick, James and Hattendorf, John B. (eds.). *Mahan Is Not Enough: The Proceedings of a Conference on the Works of Sir Julian Corbett and Admiral Sir Herbert Richmond*. Newport, RI, 1993, 13-38.

Beale, Howard K. (ed.). *Diary of Gideon Welles: Secretary of the Navy under Lincoln and Johnson*. 3 vols. New York, 1960.

Bemis, Samuel Flagg. *A Diplomatic History of the United States*. New York, 1936; 5th ed., New York, 1965.

_____. *John Quincy Adams and the Union*. New York, 1956.

Benjamin, Park. *The United States Naval Academy, Being the Yarn of the American Midshipman*. New York, 1900.

Bertram, Marshall. *The Birth of Anglo-American Friendship: The Prime Facet of the Venezuelan Boundary Dispute – A Study of the Inter-reaction of Diplomacy and Public Opinion*. Lanham, MD, 1992.

Bess, H. David and Farris, Martin T. *U.S. Maritime Policy: History and Prospects*. New York, 1981.

Bethell, Leslie. *The Abolition of the Brazilian Slave Trade: Britain, Brazil and the Slave Trade Question 1807-1869*. Cambridge, 1970.

Beyan, Amos J. *The American Colonization Society and the Creation of the Liberian State: A Historical Perspective, 1822-1900*. Lanham, MD, 1991.

Binder, Frederick Moore. *James Buchanan and the American Empire*. Selensgrove, PA: Susquehanna University Press, 1994.

Bönker, Dirk. "Naval Professionalism and the State in Turn-of-the-Century Germany and America." In McBride, William M. and Reed, Eric P. (eds.). *New Interpretations in Naval History: Selected Papers from the Thirteenth Naval History Symposium*. Annapolis, 1998, 111-138.

Bourne, Kenneth. *Britain and the Balance of Power in North America, 1815-1908*. London, 1967.

_____. *The Foreign Policy of Victorian England, 1830-1902*. Oxford, 1970.

_____. *Palmerston: The Early Years, 1784-1841*. New York, 1982.

Brooke, George M., Jr. "The Role of the United States Navy in the Suppression of the African Slave Trade." *American Neptune*, XXI, No. 1 (1961), 28-41.

Brooks, George E. *Yankee Traders, Old Coasters and African Middlemen: A History of American Legitimate Trade with West Africa in the Nineteenth Century*. Boston, 1970.

Brown, Charles. *Agents of Manifest Destiny: The Lives and Times of the Filibusters*. Chapel Hill, NC, 1980.

Brown, David. *Palmerston and the Politics of Foreign Policy, 1846-55*. Manchester, 2002.

Bruchey, Stuart W. *Enterprise: The Dynamic Economy of a Free People*. Cambridge, MA, 1990.

Burton, David H. *British-American Diplomacy 1895-1917: Early Years of the Special Relationship*. Malabar, FL, 1999.

Cain, P.J. and Hopkins, A.G. *British Imperialism, 1688-2000*. 2nd ed. London, 2001. [This is a one-volume edition of Cain and Hopkins' original *British Imperialism*].

Campbell, Charles S. *Anglo-American Understanding, 1898-1903*. Baltimore, 1957.

———. *From Revolution to Rapprochement: The United States and Great Britain, 1783-1900*. New York, 1974.

Campbell, Duncan Andrew. *English Public Opinion and the American Civil War*. Woodbridge, 2003.

Canney, Donald L. *Africa Squadron: The U.S. Navy and the Slave Trade, 1842-1861*. Washington, DC, 2006.

Chamberlain, Muriel E. "Reading History: New Light on British Foreign Policy." *History Today*, XXXV (1985), 43-48.

———. *Lord Palmerston*. Cardiff, 1987.

Coletta, Paolo E. *The American Naval Heritage*. Washington, DC, 1978; 4th ed. Lanham, MD, 1987.

——— (ed.). *American Secretaries of the Navy*. 2 vols. Annapolis, 1980.

Colledge, J.J. *Ships of the Royal Navy*. 2 vols. New York, 1969-1970.

Corbett, Julian S. *Some Principles of Maritime Strategy*. New York, 1911; reprint, New York, 1972.

Crawford, Martin. *The Anglo-American Crisis of the Mid-Nineteenth Century: The Times and America, 1850-1862*. Athens, GA, 1987.

Cunningham, Noble E., Jr. *The Presidency of James Monroe*. Lawrence, KS, 1996.

Current, Richard N. "Daniel Webster: The Politician." In Shewmaker, Kenneth E. (ed.). *Daniel Webster "The Completest Man."* Hanover, NH, 1990, 1-18.

Curtin, Philip D. *The Image of Africa: British Ideas and Action, 1780-1850*. Madison, WI, 1964.

Daunton, Martin J. "'Gentlemanly Capitalism' and British Industry, 1820-1914." *Past and Present*, No. 122 (1989), 119-158.

Davies, Peter N. "Shipping and Imperialism: The Case of British West Africa." In Jackson, Gordon and Williams, David M. (eds.). *Shipping, Technology and Imperialism*. Aldershot, 1996, 46-62.

_____. *The Trade Makers: Elder Dempster in West Africa, 1852-1972, 1973-1989*. London, 1973; reprint, St. John's, 2000.

Davis, David Brion. "The Uncertain Antislavery Commitment of Thomas Jefferson." In Goodheart, Lawrence B., Brown, Richard D. and Rabe, Stephen G. (eds.). *Slavery in American Society*. 3rd ed. Lexington, MA, 1976, 83-95.

Davis, Ralph. *The Industrial Revolution and British Overseas Trade*. Leicester, 1979.

Davison, Robert L. "In Defence of Corporate Competence: The Royal Navy Executive Officer Corps, 1880-1919." Unpublished PhD thesis, Memorial University of Newfoundland, 2005.

Drescher, Seymour. "Whose Abolition? Popular Pressure and the Ending of the British Slave Trade." *Past and Present*, No. 143 (1994), 136-166.

_____. *Capitalism and Antislavery: British Mobilization in Comparative Perspective*. New York, 1987.

Du Bois, W.E. Burghardt. *The Suppression of the African Slave-Trade to the United States of America, 1683-1870*. New York, 1896; reprint, New York, 1965.

Dudden, Arthur Power. *The American Pacific: From the Old China Trade to the Present*. New York, 1992.

Dumett, Raymond E. (ed.). *Gentlemanly Capitalism and British Imperialism: The New Debate on Empire*. London, 1999.

_____. "Exploring the Cain/Hopkins Paradigm: Issues for Debate, Critique and Topics for New Research." In Dumett, Raymond E. (ed.). *Gentlemanly Capitalism and British Imperialism: The New Debate on Empire*. London, 1999, 1-43.

Eltis, David. *Economic Growth and the Ending of the Transatlantic Slave Trade*. New York, 1987.

_____, et al. *The Trans-Atlantic Slave Trade: A Database on CD-ROM*. Cambridge, 1999.

Fieldhouse, D.K. *Economics and Empire, 1830-1914*. London, 1973; reprint, Ithaca, NY, 1984.

Fischer, Lewis R. (ed.) *The Market for Seamen in the Age of Sail*. St. John's, 1994.

Foote, Andrew H. *The African Squadron: Ashburton Treaty: Consular Sea Letters*. Philadelphia, 1855.

_____. *Africa and the American Flag*. New York, 1854.

Fontenoy, Paul E. "Ginseng, Otter Skins, and Sandalwood: The Conundrum of the China Trade." *The Northern Mariner/Le Marin du nord*, VII, No. 1 (1997), 1-16.

Fowler, William M., Jr. *Under Two Flags: The American Navy in the Civil War*. New York, 1990.

Gallagher, J. "Fowell Buxton and the New African Policy, 1838-1842." *Cambridge Historical Journal*, X, No. 1 (1950), 36-58.

Gash, Norman. *Aristocracy and the People: Britain, 1815-1865*. London, 1979.

_____. *Sir Robert Peel: The Life of Sir Robert Peel after 1830*. London, 1972; revised ed., London, 1986.

Gelber, Lionel M. *America in Britain's Place: The Leadership of the West and Anglo-American Unity*. New York, 1961.

_____. *The Rise of Anglo-American Friendship: A Study in World Politics, 1898-1906*. London, 1938.

Glete, Jan. *Navies and Nations: Warships, Navies and State Building in Europe and America, 1500-1860*. 2 vols. Stockholm, 1993.

Goldrick, James and Hattendorf, John B. (eds.). *Mahan Is Not Enough: The Proceedings of a Conference on the Works of Sir Julian Corbett and Admiral Sir Herbert Richmond*. Newport, RI, 1993.

Goldstein, Jonathan. "For Gold, Glory and Knowledge: The Andrew Jackson Administration and the Orient, 1829-1837." *International Journal of Maritime History*, XIII, No. 2 (2001), 137-163.

Goodheart, Lawrence B., Brown, Richard D. and Rabe, Stephen G. (eds.). *Slavery in American Society*. 3rd ed. Lexington, MA, 1976.

Gough, Barry M. "Profit and Power: Informal Empire, the Navy and Latin America." In Dumett, Raymond E. (ed.). *Gentlemanly Capitalism and British Imperialism: The New Debate on Empire*. London, 1999, 68-81.

_____. "The Royal Navy and the British Empire." In Winks, Robin W. (ed.). *The Oxford History of the British Empire. Vol. 5: Historiography*. Oxford, 1999, 327-341.

_____. *The Royal Navy and the Northwest Coast of North America, 1810-1914: A Study of British Maritime Ascendancy*. Vancouver, 1971.

_____. "Sea Power and South America: The 'Brazils' or South American Station of the Royal Navy, 1808-1837." *American Neptune*, L, No. 1 (1990), 26-34.

Grampp, William D. "How Britain Turned to Free Trade." *Business History Review*, LXI, No. 1 (1987), 86-112.

Graham, Gerald S. "The Ascendancy of the Sailing Ship, 1850-85." *Economic History Review*, 2nd ser., IX, No. 1 (1956-1957), 74-88.

_____. *Empire of the North Atlantic: The Maritime Struggle for North America*. London, 1958.

_____. *The China Station: War and Diplomacy, 1830-1860*. New York, 1978.

_____ and Humphreys, R.A. (eds.). *The Navy and South America 1807-1823: Correspondence of the Commanders-in-Chief on the South American Station.* London, 1962.

Great Britain. *Foreign and State Papers (BFSP).* XI (1823-1824), XII (1824-1825), XXX (1841-1842) and XLVII (1856-1857).

_____. Parliament. *Parliamentary Papers (BPP).* 1822 (XXII), 1823 (XVIII), 1826 (XXVI), 1835 (LI), 1840 (XLVII), 1841 (Session 1, XXX), 1842 (XLIV), 1843 (LIX), 1846 (L), 1847 (LXVI), 1847-1848 (LXIV), 1849 (LV), 1850 (IX, LV), 1852 (LIV), 1854 (LXXIII), 1857-1858 (LXI), 1861 (LXIV) and 1865 (LVI).

Greenhill, Basil and Giffard, Ann. *The British Assault on Finland 1854-1855: A Forgotten Naval War.* Annapolis, 1988.

_____ and _____. *Steam, Politics and Patronage: The Transformation of the Royal Navy, 1815-54.* London, 1994.

Grove, Eric. *Maritime Strategy and European Security.* London, 1990.

Halpern, Paul G. "Comparative Naval History." In Hattendorf, John B. (ed.). *Doing Naval History: Essays toward Improvement.* Newport, RI, 1995, 75-92.

Hamilton, C.I. *Anglo-French Naval Rivalry 1840-1870.* Oxford, 1993.

Hammett, Hugh B. "The Cleveland Administration and Anglo-American Naval Friction in Hawaii, 1893-1894." *Military Affairs*, XL, No. 1 (1976), 27-32.

Harding, Richard. *Seapower and Naval Warfare 1650-1830.* London, 1999.

Harmon, Judd Scott. "Marriage of Convenience: The United States Navy in Africa, 1820-1843." *American Neptune*, XXXII, No. 4 (1972), 264-276.

_____. "Suppress and Protect: The United States Navy, The African Slave Trade, and Maritime Commerce, 1794-1862." Unpublished PhD thesis, College of William and Mary, 1977.

Hattendorf, John B. (ed.). *Doing Naval History: Essays toward Improvement.* Newport, RI, 1995.

_____. "Mahan Is Not Enough: Conference Themes and Issues." In Goldrick, James and Hattendorf, John B. (eds.). *Mahan Is Not Enough: The Proceedings of a Conference on the Works of Sir Julian Corbett and Admiral Sir Herbert Richmond.* Newport, RI, 1993, 7-12.

Headrick, Daniel R. *The Tools of Empire: Technology and European Imperialism in the Nineteenth Century.* New York, 1981.

Hemphill, W. Edwin (ed.). *The Papers of John C. Calhoun.* 24 vols. Columbia, SC, 1971.

Hickey, Donald R. *The War of 1812: A Forgotten Conflict.* Urbana, IL, 1989.

Hidy, Ralph W. *The House of Baring in American Trade and Finance: English Merchant Bankers at Work, 1763-1861.* New York, 1949; reprint, New York, 1970.

_____. "The Organization and Functions of Anglo-American Merchant Bankers, 1815-1860." *Journal of Economic History*, I, supplement (1941), 54-66.

Hobsbawm, Eric. *On History*. New York, 1997.

Hobson, J.A. *Imperialism: A Study*. London,1902; reprint, London, 1988.

Holdbrook, Francis X. "The Navy's Cross – William Walker." *Military Affairs*, XXXIX, No. 4 (1975), 197-202.

Howard, Warren S. *American Slavers and the Federal Law*. Berkeley, 1963.

Humphreys, R.A. *The Diplomatic History of British Honduras, 1638-1901*. London, 1961.

Hunter, Mark C. "Piraten im Golf von Mexiko im frühen 19. Jahrhundert." In Roder, Hartmut (ed.). *Piraten – Abenteuer oder Bedrohung?* Bremen, 2002, 52-65.

_____. "'…With the Propriety and Decorum which Characterize the Society of Gentlemen:' The United States Naval Academy and its Youth, 1845-1861." Unpublished MA thesis, Memorial University of Newfoundland, 1999.

_____. "Youth, Law, and Discipline at the US Naval Academy, 1845-1861." *The Northern Mariner/Le Marin du nord*, X, No. 2 (2000), 23-39.

Hutton, Frankie. "Economic Considerations in the American Colonization Society's Early Efforts to Emigrate Free Blacks to Liberia, 1816-36." *Journal of Negro History*, LXVIII, No. 4 (1983), 376-389.

Imlah, Albert H. *Economic Elements in Pax Britannica: Studies in British Foreign Trade in the Nineteenth Century*. Cambridge, MA, 1958.

Jackson, Gordon and Williams, David M. (eds.). *Shipping, Technology and Imperialism*. Aldershot, 1996.

Jackson, Scott Thomas. "Impressment and Anglo-American Discord, 1787-1818." Unpublished PhD thesis, University of Michigan, 1976.

Jervis, Robert. "Navies, Politics, and Political Science." In Hattendorf, John B. (ed.). *Doing Naval History: Essays toward Improvement*. Newport, RI, 1995, 41-49.

Jones, Howard. *Crucible of Power: A History of American Foreign Relations to 1913*. Wilmington, DE, 2002.

Jones, Howard. "Daniel Webster: The Diplomatist." In Shewmaker, Kenneth E. (ed.). *Daniel Webster: "The Completest Man."* Hanover, NH, 1990, 203-229.

_____. *To the Webster-Ashburton Treaty: A Study in Anglo-American Relations, 1783-1843*. Chapel Hill, NC, 1977.

Karsten, Peter. *The Naval Aristocracy: The Golden Age of Annapolis and the Emergence of Modern American Navalism*. New York, 1972.

Kaufmann, William W. *British Policy and the Independence of Latin America, 1803-1828*. New Haven, 1951; reprint, New York, 1967.

Kennedy, Gregory C. "Britain's Policy-Making Elite, the Naval Disarmament Puzzle, and Public Opinion, 1927-1932." *Albion*, XXVI, No. 4 (1994), 623-643.

Kennedy, Paul. "The Influence and the Limitations of Sea Power." *International History Review*, X, No. 1 (1988), 2-17.

_____. *The Rise and Fall of British Naval Mastery*. London, 1976.

_____. *The Rise and Fall of the Great Powers: Economic Change and Military Conflict from 1500 to 2000*. London, 1988.

Kielstra, Paul. *The Politics of Slave Trade Suppression in Britain and France, 1814-48: Diplomacy, Morality and Economics*. New York, 2000.

Kilmarx, Robert A. (ed.). *America's Maritime Legacy: A History of the U.S. Merchant Marine and Shipbuilding Industry Since Colonial Times*. Boulder, CO, 1979.

Kinsbruner, Jay. *Independence in Spanish America: Civil Wars, Revolutions, and Underdevelopment*. Albuquerque, NM, 1994.

Klein, Herbert S. *The Atlantic Slave Trade*. Cambridge, 1999.

Kubicek, Robert V. "The Colonial Steamer and the Occupation of West Africa by the Victorian State, 1840-1900." *Journal of Imperial and Commonwealth History*, XVIII, No. 1 (1990), 9-32.

Lambert, Andrew D. *Battleships in Transition: The Creation of the Steam Battlefleet 1815-1860*. Oxford, 1984.

_____. "The British Naval Strategic Revolution, 1815-1854." In Jackson, Gordon and Williams, David M. (eds.). *Shipping, Technology and Imperialism*. Aldershot, 1996, 145-161.

_____. *The Crimean War: British Grand Strategy, 1853-56*. Manchester, 1990.

_____. *The Foundations of Naval History: John Knox Laughton, the Royal Navy and the Historical Profession*. London, 1998.

_____. *The Last Sailing Battlefleet: Maintaining Naval Mastery, 1815-1850*. London, 1991.

_____. "Politics, Technology and Policy-Making, 1859-1865: Palmerston, Gladstone and the Management of the Ironclad Naval Race." *The Northern Mariner/Le Marin du nord*, VIII, No. 3 (1998), 9-38.

_____. *Trincomalee: The Last of Nelson's Frigates*. London, 2002.

_____. *War at Sea in the Age of Sail 1650-1850*. London, 2000.

Langley, Harold D. "John Pendleton Kennedy." In Coletta, Paolo E. (ed.). *American Secretaries of the Navy*. 2 vols. Annapolis, 1980, I, 269-277.

_____. "William Alexander Graham." In Coletta, Paolo E. (ed.). *American Secretaries of the Navy*. 2 vols. Annapolis, 1980, I, 257-276.

_____. "William Ballard Preston." In Coletta, Paolo E. (ed.). *American Secretaries of the Navy*. 2 vols. Annapolis, 1980, I, 242-255.

_____. *Social Reform in the United States Navy, 1798-1862*. Urbana, IL, 1967.

Lewis, Michael. *England's Sea-Officers: The Story of the Naval Profession*. London, 1939: reprint, London, 1948.

_____. *The Navy in Transition, 1814-1864: A Social History*. London, 1965.

_____. *A Social History of the Navy, 1793-1815*. London, 1960.

Lloyd, Christopher. *The Navy and the Slave Trade: The Suppression of the African Slave Trade in the Nineteenth Century*. London, 1949; reprint, London, 1968.

_____. *The British Seaman, 1200-1860: A Social Survey*. London, 1968.

Long, David F. *Nothing Too Daring: A Biography of Commodore David Porter, 1780-1843*. Annapolis, 1970.

Louis, William Roger (ed.). *The Robinson and Gallagher Controversy*. New York, 1976.

Lynn, Martin. "Consul and Kings: British Policy, 'the Man on the Spot,' and the Seizure of Lagos, 1851." *Journal of Imperial and Commonwealth History*, X, No. 2 (1982), 150-167.

_____. "The 'Imperialism of Free Trade' and the Case of West Africa, c. 1830-c. 1870." *Journal of Imperial and Commonwealth History*, XV, No. 1 (1986), 22-40.

Mahan, Alfred Thayer. *The Influence of Sea Power upon History, 1660-1805*. Englewood Cliffs, NJ, 1980.

_____. *The Life of Nelson: The Embodiment of Sea Power of Great Britain*. Boston, 1899; reprint, Annapolis, 2001.

_____. *The Influence of Sea Power upon the French Revolution and Empire, 1793-1812*, 2 vols. Boston, 1892; reprint, New York, 1980.

_____. "Subordination in Historical Treatment." *Annual Report of the American Historical Association for the Year 1902*. Washington, DC, 1903, 49-63.

Marx, Jennifer. *Pirates and Privateers of the Caribbean*. Malabar, FL, 1992.

Mathias, Peter. *The First Industrial Nation: An Economic History of Britain, 1700-1914*. London, 1969; 2nd ed., London, 1983.

Matzke, Rebecca Berens. "Britain Gets Its Way: Power and Peace in Anglo-American Relations, 1838-1846." *War in History*, VIII, No. 1 (2001), 19-47.

McBride, William M. and Reed, Eric P. (eds.). *New Interpretations in Naval History: Selected Papers from the Thirteenth Naval History Symposium*. Annapolis, 1998.

McKee, Christopher. *A Gentlemanly and Honorable Profession: The Creation of the U.S. Naval Officer Corps, 1794-1815*. Annapolis, 1991.

McNeilly, Earl E. "The United States Navy and the Suppression of the West African Slave Trade, 1819-1862." Unpublished PhD thesis, Case Western Reserve University, 1973.

Miller, Joseph C. *Way of Death: Merchant Capitalism and the Angolan Slave Trade, 1730-1830*. Madison, WI, 1988.

Mitchell, B.R. (ed.). *British Historical Statistics*. Cambridge, 1988.

Modelski, George and Thompson, William R. *Seapower in Global Politics, 1494-1993*. Seattle, 1988.

More, John Bassett (ed.). *The Works of James Buchanan: Comprising His Speeches, State Papers, and Private Correspondence*. 12 vols. New York, 1960.

Morison, Samuel Eliot. *The Maritime History of Massachusetts, 1783-1860*. Boston, 1921; reprint, Boston, 1979.

Mottram, R.H. *Buxton the Liberator*. London, 1946.

Murray, David R. *Odious Commerce: Britain, Spain and the Abolition of the Cuban Slave Trade*. Cambridge, 1980.

The New York Times. Various years.

Newton, Wesley P. "Origins of United States-Latin American Relations." In Shurbutt, T. Ray (ed.). *United States-Latin American Relations, 1800-1850: The Formative Generations*. Tuscaloosa, AL, 1991, 1-24.

Nicholas, H.G. *Britain and the United States*. London, 1963.

_____. *The United States and Britain*. Urbana, IL, 1975.

North, Douglass C. *The Economic Growth of the United States, 1790 to 1860*. Englewood Cliffs, NJ, 1961.

Palmer, Sarah. *Politics, Shipping and the Repeal of the Navigation Laws*. Manchester, 1990.

Paolino, Ernest N. *The Foundations of the American Empire: William Henry Seward and U.S. Foreign Policy*. Ithaca, NY, 1973.

Pardue, Jeffrey David. "Agent of Imperial Change: James MacQueen and the British Empire, 1778-1870." Unpublished PhD thesis, University of Waterloo, 1997.

Payne, Kevin A. "Naval Impressment in Hull, 1793-1815." Unpublished MA thesis, University of Hull, 1998.

Pennell, Richard. "State Power in a Chronically Weak State: Spanish Coast-guards as Pirates, 1814-50." *European History Quarterly*, XXV, No. 3 (1995), 353-379.

Perkins, Dexter. *The Monroe Doctrine, 1823-1826*. Cambridge, MA, 1932; reprint, Gloucester, MA, 1965.

Petrie, Donald A. *The Prize Game: Lawful Looting on the High Seas in the Days of Fighting Sail*. Annapolis, 1999.

Platt, D.C.M. *Finance, Trade, and Politics in British Foreign Policy 1815-1914*. Oxford, 1968.

_____. *Foreign Finance in Continental Europe and the United States, 1815-1870: Quantities, Origins, Functions and Distribution*. London, 1984.

_____. *Latin America and British Trade 1806-1914*. London, 1972.

Pollock, Thomas R. "The Historical Elements of Mahanian Doctrine." *Naval War College Review*, XXXV, No. 4 (1982), 44-49.

Popham, Hugh. *A Damned Cunning Fellow: The Eventful Life of Rear-Admiral Sir Home Popham, KCB, KCH, KM, FRS, 1762-1820.* Tywardreath, 1991.

Porter, Andrew (ed.). *Oxford History of the British Empire. Vol. 3.* Oxford, 1999.

_____. "Introduction: Britain and the Empire in the Nineteenth Century." In Porter, Andrew (ed.). *Oxford History of the British Empire. Vol. 3.* Oxford, 1999, 1-28.

Pratt, Julius W. *A History of United States Foreign Policy.* New York, 1955; 4th ed., Englewood Cliffs, NJ, 1980.

_____. *Expansionists of 1812.* New York, 1925; reprint, Gloucester, MA, 1957.

Rediker, Marcus. *Between the Devil and the Deep Blue Sea: Merchant Seamen, Pirates, and the Anglo-American Maritime World, 1700-1750.* Cambridge, 1987.

Rehnquist, William H. "Foreword: Daniel Webster and the Oratorical Tradition." In Shewmaker, Kenneth E. (ed.). *Daniel Webster: "The Completest Man."* Hanover, NH, 1990, xi-xviii.

Reynolds, Clark G. *Command of the Sea: The History and Strategy of Maritime Empires.* London, 1976.

Richmond, Herbert. *Sea Power in the Modern World.* London, 1934.

Ritchie, Robert C. *Captain Kidd and the War against the Pirates.* Cambridge, MA, 1986.

_____. "Government Measures against Piracy and Privateering in the Atlantic Area, 1750-1850." In Starkey, David J., van Eyck van Heslinga, E.S. and de Moor, J.A. (eds.). *Pirates and Privateers: New Perspectives on the War on Trade in the Eighteenth and Nineteenth Centuries.* Exeter, 1997, 10-28.

Roberts, Shirley. *Charles Hotham: A Biography.* Carlton, Vic, 1985.

Robinson, Robert L. "Commodore Matthew C. Perry and the Protection of American Rights in West Africa, 1843-45." *Southern Quarterly*, V, No. 1 (1966), 47-63.

Robinson, Ronald and Gallagher, John. *Africa and the Victorians: The Official Mind of Imperialism.* London, 1961; 2nd ed., London, 1981.

Roder, Hartmut (ed.). *Piraten – Abenteuer oder Bedrohung?* Bremen, 2002.

Rodger, N.A.M. *The Wooden World: An Anatomy of the Georgian Navy.* London: Collins, 1986.

Schroeder, John H. *Matthew Calbraith Perry: Antebellum Sailor and Diplomat.* Annapolis, 2001.

_____. *Shaping a Maritime Empire: The Commercial and Diplomatic Role of the American Navy, 1829-1861.* Westport, CT, 1985.

Schurman, Donald M. "Julian Corbett's Influence on the Royal Navy's Perception of its Maritime Function." In Goldrick, James and Hattendorf, John B. (eds.). *Mahan Is Not Enough: The Proceedings of a Conference on the Works of Sir Julian Corbett and Admiral Sir Herbert Richmond*. Newport, RI, 1993, 51-63.

Semmel, Bernard. *Liberalism and Naval Strategy: Ideology, Interests and Sea Power during the Pax Britannica*. Boston, 1986.

_____. *The Rise of Free Trade Imperialism: Classical Political Economy, the Empire of Free Trade, and Imperialism, 1750-1850*. Cambridge, 1970.

Shewmaker, Kenneth E. (ed.). *Daniel Webster: "The Completest Man."* Hanover, NH, 1990.

Showalter, Dennis E. "Toward a 'New' Naval History." In Hattendorf, John B. (ed.). *Doing Naval History: Essays toward Improvement*. Newport, RI, 1995, 129-139.

Shurbutt, T. Ray (ed.). *United States-Latin American Relations, 1800-1850: The Formative Generations*. Tuscaloosa, AL, 1991.

Soulsby, Hugh Graham. *The Right of Search and the Slave Trade in Anglo-American Relations, 1814-1862*. Baltimore, 1933.

Sprout, Harold and Sprout, Margaret. *The Rise of American Naval Power, 1776-1918*. Princeton, 1939; reprint, Annapolis, 1970.

Starkey, David J. "Pirates and Markets." In Fischer, Lewis R. (ed.). *The Market for Seamen in the Age of Sail*. St. John's, 1994, 59-80. Reprinted in Pennell, C.R. (ed.). *Bandits at Sea: A Pirates Reader*. New York, 2001, 107-124.

_____, van Eyck van Heslinga, E.S. and de Moor, J.A. (eds.). *Pirates and Privateers: New Perspectives on the War on Trade in the Eighteenth and Nineteenth Centuries*. Exeter, 1997.

Staudenraus, P.J. *The African Colonization Movement 1816-1865*. New York, 1961.

Steele, E.D. *Palmerston and Liberalism, 1855-1865*. Cambridge, 1991.

Strauss, W. Patrick. "James Kirke Paulding." In Coletta, Paolo E. (ed.). *American Secretaries of the Navy*. 2 vols. Annapolis, 1980, I, 165-175.

Streifford, David M. "The American Colonization Society: An Application of Republican Ideology to Early Antebellum Reform." *Journal of Southern History*, XLV, No. 2 (1979), 201-220.

Sturmey, S.G. *British Shipping and World Competition*. London, 1962.

Symonds, Craig L. *Navalists and Antinavalists: The Naval Policy Debate in the United States, 1785-1827*. Newark, DE, 1980.

Temperley, Harold. *The Foreign Policy of Canning, 1822-1827: England, the Neo-Holy Alliance and the New World*. London, 1925; 2nd ed., London, 1966.

Thistlethwaite, Frank. *The Anglo-American Connection in the Early Nineteenth Century*. Philadelphia, 1959.

Thomas, Hugh. *The Slave Trade: The Story of the Atlantic Slave Trade, 1440-1870*. New York, 1997.

Thompson, William R. "Some Mild and Radical Observations on Desiderata in Comparative Naval History." In Hattendorf, John B. (ed.). *Doing Naval History: Essays toward Improvement*. Newport, RI, 1995, 93-114.

Thomson, Janice E. *Mercenaries, Pirates, and Sovereigns: State-Building and Extraterritorial Violence in Early Modern Europe*. Princeton, 1994.

The Times (London). Various years.

Tucker, Spencer C. *Andrew Foote: Civil War Admiral on Western Waters*. Annapolis, 2000.

_____. *The Jefferson Gunboat Navy*. Columbia, SC, 1993.

United States. Congress. *Annals of Congress*. 14th Cong., 2nd sess; 15th Cong., 1st sess; 15th Cong., 2nd sess.; 17th Cong., 1st sess.; and 17th Cong., 2nd sess.

_____. _____. *Congressional Globe*. 27th Cong., 2nd sess.; 29th Cong., 1st sess.; 35th Cong., 1st sess.; 35th Cong., 2nd sess.; and 36th Cong., 1st sess.

_____. _____. *Register of Debates*. 18th Cong., 2nd sess.; 19th Cong., 2nd sess.; 20th Cong., 1st sess.; 21st Cong., 2nd sess.; and 22nd Cong., 1st sess.

_____. _____. *Senate Journal*. 33rd Cong., 2nd sess.

_____. _____. *US Serial Set* (*S. Doc.* and *H.R. Doc.*). LXXXIII, 18th Cong., 1st sess.; LXXXIX, 18th Cong., 2nd sess.; CXXV, 19th Cong., 1st sess.; XXLIV, 19th Cong., 2nd sess.; CLXIII, 20th Cong., 1st sess.; and 35th Cong., 2nd sess.

_____. _____. *US Statutes at Large*, III and IV.

Vale, Brian. "Appointment, Promotion and 'Interest' in the British South America Squadron, 1821-3." *Mariner's Mirror*, LXXXVIII, No. 1 (2002), 61-68.

Ward, W.E.F. *The Royal Navy and the Slavers: The Suppression of the Atlantic Slave Trade*. London, 1969.

Wattenberg, Ben J. (ed.). *The Statistical History of the United States from Colonial Times to the Present*. New York, 1976.

Watt, D. Cameron. *Succeeding John Bull: America in Britain's Place*. Cambridge, 1984.

Webster, Charles K. *The Foreign Policy of Palmerston 1830-1841: Britain, the Liberal Movement and the Eastern Question*. 2 vols. London, 1951.

_____. (ed.). *Britain and the Independence of Latin America, 1812-1830: Select Documents from the Foreign Office Archives*. 2 vols. London, 1938; reprint, New York, 1970.

Williams, Mary Wilhelmine. *Anglo-American Isthmian Diplomacy, 1815-1915*. Washington, DC, 1916; reprint, New York, 1965.

Wiltse, Charles M. and Moser, Harold D. (eds.). *The Papers of Daniel Webster*. 14 vols. Hanover, NH, 1974-1989.

Winks, Robin W. (ed.). *The Oxford History of the British Empire. Vol. 5: Historiography*. Oxford, 1999.

Wood, Robert S. "Domestic Factors, Regime Characteristics, and Naval Forces." In Hattendorf, John B. (ed.). *Doing Naval History: Essays toward Improvement*. Newport, RI, 1995, 67-71.

Yerxa, Donald A. *Admirals and Empire: The United States Navy and the Caribbean, 1898-1945*. Columbia, SC, 1991.

Ziegler, Philip. *The Sixth Great Power: A History of One of the Greatest of All Banking Families, the House of Barings, 1762-1929*. New York, 1988.